1985

SA.

4/5'

Terry O'Shea.
43 Church Hill
Klein & Ockerse St.
Hillbrow
2000
South Africa

SOUTH AFRICA

AND THE

CONSOCIATIONAL OPTION

A Constitutional Analysis

SOUTH AFRICA
AND THE
CONSOCIATIONAL OPTION

A Constitutional Analysis

by

L J BOULLE

BA (Natal) LLB (Stell) LLM (Lond) PhD (Natal)

Associate Professor in the Department of Public Law,
University of Natal, Durban, South Africa
Visiting Research Fellow in the University of Michigan Law School, Ann Arbor 1983/4

Juta & Co, Ltd

CAPE TOWN   WETTON   JOHANNESBURG

First Published 1984

© Juta & Co, Ltd 1984

PO Box 123, Kenwyn 7790
Republic of South Africa

ISBN 0 7021 1434 0

SET, PRINTED AND BOUND IN THE REPUBLIC OF SOUTH AFRICA
BY THE RUSTICA PRESS (PTY.) LTD., WYNBERG, CAPE

D 428

Preface

The aim of this work is to provide a situated focus on the recent constitutional developments in South Africa. These developments are dealt with against an historical background, are analysed comparatively in relation to established notions of western constitutionalism, and are related to the theory of consociational democracy.

Commentators from several ideological perspectives have alluded to the period of crisis through which the South African state system has been passing.[1] The crisis tendencies are observable in the economic, social and political spheres of society and have resulted in several changes and adaptations in these areas in the late 1970s and early 1980s. However, the constitutional activities during this period comprise to a large extent a response to the legitimacy crisis affecting the political system. Legitimacy manifests itself at the level of 'symbolic interaction' at which the authority, as distinct from the power, of a regime is maintained.[2] A crisis of legitimation involves the incapacity of a system to sustain a widespread belief that its political institutions are the most appropriate and legitimacy problems of varying degrees are discernible in many modern states. Most forms of power strive for legitimation, which contemporarily assumes a rational-legal form[3] and is closely related to notions of legality and constitutionalism.[4] Regardless of how unrealistic they might be, in the sense of non-descriptive of how power is actually exercised in society,[5] constitutional arrangements are a significant factor in a system's claim for recognition. However, while legitimacy presupposes the impersonality and objectivity of legality, legality alone does not imply legitimacy.

In South Africa the legitimacy crisis has become acute because the constitutional order has continued to exclude from the main political process those with increasing political demands. Since 1976 an extensive constitutional debate has dominated South Africa's domestic political agenda, culminating in the 1983 constitution for whites, coloureds and Indians.[6] Also since 1976 the government's constitutional policy for blacks has been more vigorously pursued, and there have been numerous subsidiary constitutional activities as well. These developments reflect a quest for some kind of rational-legal legitimacy for the system. However, while government according to the positive law will be legal it will not be legitimate unless the constitutional order satisfies minimal requirements in respect of its democratic qualities and method of composition and enactment.[7] South Africa's past constitutional forms have been unilaterally imposed by the dominant group and have never had the democratic legitimacy of the orthodox models of constitutional government. It was thus necessary to advance alternative justificatory theories for them: for blacks the separate development principle and concepts of international law, and for coloureds and Indians the principle of self-determination. In neither case did these theories greatly enhance the credibility of the political institutions in question.

This work investigates the extent to which consociational democracy, and its ancillary principles, has been used to justify the emergent constitutional arrangements for non-blacks. It also assesses the extent to which consociational-type institutions have come to form part of the control process in the inclusive political system. It constitutes a monograph on South Africa's political constitution in the light of consociational theory. The topic is dealt with descriptively from a predominantly legal-institutional perspective and emphasis is given more to the structural than to the civil rights aspects of the constitutional system and apartheid. Where the work is analytical it does not purport to be anormative.

The publication is based on a dissertation submitted to the University of Natal, Durban, in February 1982. The original chapters 1 to 6 have been retained in modified and abridged form, but the last four chapters have been omitted; the new chapters 7, 8 and 9 take account of events up to 2 November 1983. One of the risks of commenting on a fast-changing field is instant obsolescence. At the date of publication the 1983 constitution has been enacted but its predecessor is still in force. The descriptions of the previous constitution in chapters 4 and 6 are therefore in the present tense. The new system is due to be implemented in late 1984 but it is conceivable that this will occur on a piecemeal basis and that some existing arrangements will be effective beyond that date.

Apart from the numerous acknowledgements made in the thesis the author is indebted to his examiners for several helpful suggestions. My wife Alison's encouragement and share of the labours, and the assistance of Mr Richard Cooke of the publishers, has greatly facilitated the task of completing the work under difficult logistical conditions.

L J BOULLE
Ann Arbor, Michigan
December 1983

NOTES AND REFERENCES

[1] e g H Adam & H Giliomee *The Rise and Crisis of Afrikaner Power* (1979) 7–15; R de Kadt *The South African State System in Crisis* (University of Natal, 1981) 1–6; J Saul & S Gelb *The Crisis in South Africa* (1981); L J Boulle 'The likely direction of constitutional change in South Africa over the next five years' in W H B Dean & D van Zyl Smit (eds) *Constitutional Change in South Africa* (1983) 57.

[2] Cf S M Lipset *Political Man* (1963) 77ff; C J Friedrich *Limited Government— A Comparison* (1974) 111; J Habermas 'Legitimation Problems in the Modern State' in *Communication and the Evolution of Society* (1979) 178; J H Schaar *Legitimacy in the Modern State* (1981) 15–52.

[3] Cf M Weber's categories of legitimacy—*The Theory of Social and Economic Organisation* (T Parsons (ed) 1947) 130ff.

[4] See P Rosen 'Legitimacy, Domination and Ego Displacement' in A Vidich & M Glassman (eds) *Conflict and Control—Challenge to Legitimacy of Modern Governments* (1979) 75; A P D d'Entreves *The Notion of the State* (1967) 141–50; Friedrich op cit 110–18.

[5] C J Friedrich *Constitutional Government and Democracy* (4 ed, 1968) 583.

[6] In this work use is made of the statutory categories of race and ethnicity in terms of which constitutional development occurs.

[7] K C Wheare *Modern Constitutions* (2 ed, 1966) 62–6; B O Nwabueze *Constitutionalism in the Emergent States* (1973) 24–8.

Contents

Table of Principal Statutes

Table of Cases

1   Modern Western Constitutionalism

1. INTRODUCTION

The story of modern Western constitutionalism has been depicted as a great debate between British and American constitutional principles which, it is traditionally asserted, have been responsible for the two historic versions of stable democracy, the British parliamentary and the American presidential systems.[1]* Despite the historical and institutional differences between these two systems they are both based on the assumption that the essence of democracy is majority rule. Arend Lijphart has suggested that within a typology of democratic political systems the British and American versions can, on the basis of this common feature, be contrasted with the system of consociational democracy, which challenges the notion that democracy should be equated with majority rule.[2] The political competition that takes place in an adversarial context and according to predominantly majoritarian rules in the traditional liberal democracies is replaced in a consociational system by élite co-operation and consensual decision-making according to what may loosely be called the 'power-sharing' principle. The distinction between majoritarian rule in an adversarial context and power-sharing in a co-operative context is a central theme of this work.

Although the identification of democracy with majority rule is widespread within the contemporary liberal democracies there was an earlier principle in many political systems according to which decisions had to be reached unanimously.[3] The majority principle came to be recognised gradually throughout Western Europe but was, and continues to be, justified in widely differing terms. Thus it has been said, in different times and contexts, to be based on the superior force of the majority,[4] on various theories of natural law,[5] on the theory of the social contract,[6] on a variety of legal fictions,[7] on its utilitarian function,[8] and on its 'certain naturalness'.[9] Its contemporary justification tends towards a pragmatic basis. If it is not possible to achieve a unanimity of political opinion, the optimal situation, then convenience and practical necessity require that the will of the majority should prevail, if only as a last resort. The normative principle that modern government rests on the consent of all the governed must be balanced against the need in practice for effective government—and in certain cases this means quick and decisive decision-making, provided it carries the minimum support of a bare majority. The only alternative to majority rule, it is argued, is 'minority rule', for which there can be no theoretical or practical justification.

But the liberal-democratic tradition has always experienced a tension between the principles of majoritarian democracy, based on the rights of popular majorities, and constitutionalism, founded on the fear of an abuse of power. Thus it was asked: if majority rule is the essence of democracy does this entail unlimited power for a bare majority? And conversely, if

1

constitutionalism involves limitations on the exercise of power can it also limit the popular will? The constitutionalists tended to answer the latter question in the affirmative and were able to draw on a long, if somewhat diverse, intellectual tradition in support of the view that popular majorities should be constitutionally restrained. Locke's belief in rule by the majority accommodated a concern for minority rights, and he regarded rulers as liable to be replaced if they acted tyrannically.[10] Rousseau, who espoused a more radical majoritarian viewpoint, differentiated between the majorities necessary for 'grave and important' matters (near unanimity) and matters requiring 'an instant decision' (a majority of one vote).[11] Madison had a constitutional rather than a populist notion of democracy,[12] Burke regarded majority rule as 'a most violent fiction of law',[13] and both De Tocqueville and Mill regarded the 'tyranny of the majority' as an evil against which a political system should be on its guard.[14] In the twentieth century writers from Hayek to Finer to Rawls have perceived the need to restrict majority rule through various constitutional devices in order, respectively, to limit the scope of governments' activities, to allow minorities the means to become a majority, and to acquire a more just body of legislation.[15] Dahl sought to resolve the contradiction between populist and constitutionalist democracy by developing the hybrid notion of polyarchy democracy.[16]

Friedrich's views on constitutionalism and democracy can be regarded as representative of modern liberal constitutionalists.[17] By constitutionalism Friedrich understands a system of government in which authority is constitutionally divided among various bodies and its exercise is subject to legal restraints and controls. He points out that constitutionalism was at the outset not democratic, but rather aristocratic.[18] Democracy spread gradually through the nineteenth and twentieth centuries with the extension of the franchise and the elimination of public discrimination, until popular majorities came to be recognised as the only basis of legitimate government.[19] But for Friedrich it is unrealistic, and contrary to fact, to assert that a 'bare majority' should have unlimited power in a democracy. There is a need for flexibility in determining what should constitute a majority for different purposes, and a good constitution should demarcate clearly what are grave and more important decisions, and require qualified majorities in these cases. Provided the constitutional limits are accepted by the popular majority there need be no conflict between democracy and constitutionalism. Should the limitations on popular majorities entrench the position of minorities then, according to Friedrich following Locke, the majority in the community retains a residuary power to change the constitutional order by revolutionary means. For Friedrich majority rule remains the quintessence of democracy, provided it is not taken to mean 'majority-of-one'. Among the constitutional devices traditionally adopted to restrain majorities have been bicameralism, the separation of powers, the federal division of competence, proportional electoral systems, qualified majorities in deliberative bodies, checks and balances, constitutional rigidity, bills of rights, and judicial review. These devices are designed to limit the scope of majority rule, the kind of matters on which majorities have final authority, and the speed with which the objectives of majorities can be put into effect.[20]

The conventional theories of constitutionalism have been extensively criticised from the behaviouralist and marxist perspectives, inter alia for their misleading view of where power actually lies in a political system. They are said to be overly formalistic in the treatment of the distribution of political authority and the legal restraints thereon, and to be concerned with the question of whose views should prevail in a democratic system rather than with whose views actually do prevail. There is much substance in these views, but as this work is concerned mainly with the constitutional allocation of authority in political systems it is unnecessary to develop this critique of liberal-constitutionalism. What is relevant for present purposes are the factors in a constitutional system which determine whether the will of the majority can prevail on matters requiring authoritative decisions or whether it is institutionally restrained. These include:

(i) The electoral system—whether this operates on the plurality principle in single-member constituencies to the advantage of the major parties, or on a proportional basis in multi-member constituencies so as to ensure the representation of minority parties;

(ii) The law-making process—whether this allows bare legislative majorities to enact their policies, or whether enactments require qualified majorities, or approval by a review chamber or the electorate;

(iii) The executive—whether it comprises exclusively members of the majority parliamentary party or whether it is a multi-party parliamentary executive, or has a separate popular mandate;

(iv) The allocation of competence—whether competence is allocated exclusively to a few authorities or is widely dispersed among many on a functional and territorial basis;

(v) The constitutional amending procedure—whether this is rigid or flexible;

(vi) The sites of political competition—whether there is only one decisive site, as in a unitary parliamentary system, or numerous sites established by a separation and division of powers;

(vii) A bill of rights—whether or not this is constitutionally entrenched and enforceable by the judiciary;

(viii) Referenda—whether a referendum is constitutionally prescribed for certain decisions, and whether there is a right of popular initiative.

The above factors determine the extent to which a constitutional system is potentially responsive to politically organised majorities, although the extent to which practical effect can be given to their collective claims depends on a range of additional extra-constitutional factors. Conversely, but subject to the same qualification, they determine the extent to which the rights of political minorities are constitutionally safeguarded and they are enabled to work towards creating a new majority. In the following sections specific attention is given to these factors in an investigation of the relationship between majoritarianism and constitutionalism in the two historic liberal-democratic constitutional systems.

The term 'majority', however, is in need of brief elucidation. While definitionally the term denotes the greater number in or part of a certain group,[21] the term is a multi-faceted one, as can be illustrated by reference to the electoral system. Thus by 'overall majority' is understood at least fifty per cent plus one of those voting in an election, a total which may not be attained where there are more than two candidates; 'absolute majority' has the same meaning, save that the percentage is usually calculated in terms of those entitled to vote, as opposed to those actually voting. These two terms can be distinguished from 'relative majority', which denotes a plurality of votes; where there are more than two candidates a relative majority could constitute an overall minority. A further distinction can be drawn between a 'simple majority', namely fifty per cent plus one, and a 'qualified majority', for example a two-thirds or three-quarters majority; the latter could also involve concurrent majorities within specified subgroups, or even unanimity. Thus while majority rule is usually understood in terms of simple or overall majorities, many of the constitutional features of the liberal democracies involve one or more forms of qualified majoritarianism, and the electoral system frequently operates according to the relative majority principle.

2. THE BRITISH PARLIAMENTARY SYSTEM

(a) General constitutional principles

The term 'Westminster system' has no precise constitutional or political meaning, and has been particularly misused in the South African context. In its wider sense it denotes all the main features of the British political system, which are a product of a largely evolutionary development originating in medieval times.[22] Even in its modern form the system remains predominantly uncodified and regulated more by the norms of political conduct, or constitutional conventions, than by legal rules. Its main institutions are a constitutional monarchy, a bicameral legislature, a parliamentary executive, an independent judiciary and a politically neutral civil service. While there do exist subnational institutions the constitution is unequivocally unitary and the system of government relatively centralised. The most important rule of the constitutional system is the supremacy of parliament, which finds its justification in that institution's representative composition. The House of Commons is elected on the basis of a universal franchise through an electoral process that gives rise to a predominantly two-party system and an adversarial style of politics. Although there are no constitutional guarantees of human rights or judicial safeguards against an abuse of power the Rule of Law serves to qualify the supremacy of Parliament and provide some protection for the individual.

The term 'Westminster system' is also used in a narrower sense to refer to only certain features of the British constitution. In this sense it denotes

'A constitutional system in which the head of state is not the effective head of government; in which the effective head of government is a Prime Minister presiding over a Cabinet composed of Ministers over whose appointment and removal he has at least a substantial measure of control; in which the effective branch of government is parliamentary inasmuch as ministers must be members of the legislature; and in which ministers are collectively and individually responsible to a freely elected and representative legislature'.[23]

In this definition attention is focused on the executive branch of government and its institutional relationship with the legislature which gives rise to the particular British form of parliamentary government, although there are other species of parliamentarism. The main feature of this system evolved out of two distinct historical processes: the differentiation of the functions of government which led to the limitation of the Crown's powers, and the subsequent requirement that the Crown's ministers should have the confidence and support of the majority in the Commons.[24] The close institutional relationship between the legislature and executive is traditionally regarded as the essence of the Westminster system and its most distinctive feature. Bagehot described it as the 'efficient secret' of the constitution, involving 'the close union, the nearly complete fusion, of the executive and legislative powers'.[25] Bagehot's objective was to expose the 'fallacies' of Montesquieu and Blackstone who ascribed the stability of the English system to the separation of powers doctrine,[26] but subsequent critics have pointed out that the close relationship between the executive and legislature does not exclude the importance of the constitutional distinction between the two: English constitutionalism has always recognised the need for a partial separation of government functions and a partial separation of personnel.[27] Bagehot's concept of fusion also obscured the notion of balance between cabinet and parliament which was central to the classical theory of British parliamentary government and was effected through the mechanisms of dissolution and ministerial responsibility.[28] However, the notion of balance has in turn been rendered outdated with the rise of the party system and the contemporary domination of parliament by the cabinet, and dissolution and ministerial responsibility no longer play the role attributed to them during the classical period of parliamentary government.

Although constitutional theorists still disagree on the exact nature of the relationship between the cabinet and parliament and the implication of the weak separation of powers that it involves, it is this feature which distinguishes the Westminster system from both the presidential system with its non-parliamentary executive, and other systems of parliamentary government.[29] Cabinet ministers in the Westminster system must be members of parliament on appointment, or become so within a certain period of grace.[30] Executive authority vests predominantly in the cabinet, where members are collectively and individually responsible to parliament for its exercise. The theoretical diffusion of executive authority results in residual powers remaining with the head of state, but these tend to be of a ceremonial or nominal nature and are exercised on the advice of the cabinet. The most important function of the head of state is the appointment of the Prime Minister who, by convention, must be the leader of the majority party in the elective house; the Prime Minister effectively appoints and dismisses other members of the cabinet, but they remain nominally servants of the Crown. Although the cabinet depends for its tenure on the support of parliament, the two-party system tends to ensure its stability for the full term of a parliament's life. Ultimate political control remains in the hands of the electorate and is exercised in periodic elections. While this traditional constitutionalist view of the Westminster system provides only a very limited insight into the actual operation of the British political process, it does allow an investigation of the majoritarian aspects of the system.

(b) Majoritarian features

As far as its institutional arrangements and constitutional allocation of competence are concerned, the Westminster system can be described as thoroughly majoritarian in the following respects:[31]

(i) The electoral system operates according to the plurality principle in single-member constituencies. This entails the election in each constituency of the candidate with a relative majority of votes, which in contests between more than two candidates could constitute an overall minority. The system favours dominant parties because votes cast for losing candidates have no post-electoral effect, and smaller parties are unable to translate their electoral support into parliamentary seats unless it is strategically concentrated in certain constituencies. This can result in inadequate representation for minorities, to the point of their being effectively disfranchised. The system has tended to produce two major parties with broad national support and of almost equal strength, but since there is no direct arithmetical relationship between the number of seats won by a party and its overall electoral support the party with minority popular support could secure a legislative majority. Hence Wade's remark that it is a 'crude majority system'.[32] Further distortions arise through the delimitation process. Although the principle of equality in the voter strengths of constituencies has been accepted for some time it is still not practised,[33] and is further aggravated by the fact that Scotland and Wales are more generously represented in Parliament than England.[34] The majoritarian electoral system is said to have the advantages of presenting a clear choice to the electorate and of fulfilling clearly the competing rolls of government and opposition; it produces both a legislature and a government, and the government–opposition dichotomy in the Commons establishes clear lines of responsibility. By virtue of its parliamentary majority and the convention of joint responsibility the government is able to provide strong and effective leadership and to give effect to its policies. But many contemporary commentators have called for electoral reform so as to give rise to fairer electoral outcomes; these calls usually advocate a more porportional electoral system which would produce a less arbitrary apportionment of seats.[35]

(ii) The Westminster parliament in its legislative capacity functions on a majoritarian basis that enables the government, acting through the dominant party, to enact legislation even against the objections of a large minority. Because legislation requires only a simple parliamentary majority, and that majority may reflect only a small electoral majority, or even minority, a statute may rest on a very narrow basis of popular consent. The same procedure is followed for all legislation, even constitutional amendments being subject to no suspensory or absolute veto exercisable by a sizeable minority. Nor does the system of standing legislative committees modify this process in any significant way, as is the case in other countries.[36] The majority party dominance also extends to parliament's elective, control, financial and legitimising functions.[37]

(iii) The cabinet usually comprises solely members of the majority party, and there need be no representation of legislative or electoral minorities. As the executive is the main instrument of modern systems of government, majoritarianism at this level, which is intrinsic to the Westminster system,[38] has far-reaching consequences. The single-party cabinet can utilise its parliamentary majority to ensure its continuance in office,[39] and to secure the enactment of its legislative proposals.[40]

(iv) The majority party not only forms a single-party cabinet but it captures the 'spoils' of government on a winner-takes-all basis. As far as the allocation of resources, the provision of public services, the extraction of means from various sources, and the making of public and quasi-public appointments are concerned, the cabinet is in a pre-eminent position and is subject to few constitutional restraints; and through its control of the bureaucracy it has the advantage of access to information, an important political resource. At the apex of the system is the Prime Minister with extensive powers of patronage in relation to members of his cabinet, caucus and party, and this has led to the suggestion that cabinet government has been replaced recently with a system of prime ministerial government.[41]

(v) The principle of legislative supremacy entails that there are no geographical or functional areas from which parliamentary authority is barred and therefore within which the parliamentary majority is precluded from intervening. As contemporary constitutional reformers point out, fundamental human rights, the status of minorities, the long-standing principles of the constitutional system, all are theoretically at the mercy of a sovereign parliament in the setting of a flexible constitution. While subnational law-making authorities do exist their continued tenure depends on parliament's pleasure. The corollary of legislative supremacy is the fact that the courts have no testing right over legislation, properly enacted, and no supervisory constitutional role.

(vi) The centralisation of authority in the Westminster system is a majoritarian feature that emanates from two other constitutional principles. The first is the supremacy of parliament which renders the constitution unitary and entails no legislative rivals to this central institution. The second is the doctrine of ministerial responsibility which, despite its political inefficacy, has, with the rise of the administrative state, resulted in more and more powers being granted to ministers as the only persons who can be identified as responsible within the parliamentary structure of government.[42] The Westminster constitutional system tends to concentrate political power and not to divide it between different institutions and levels of government, and in a highly centralised system of government there are relatively few important sites of political competition and therefore few opportunities for the majority party's dominance to be contested.

As far as its institutional arrangements and constitutional allocation of competence are concerned, the Westminster system is consistently majoritarian and involves a winner-takes-all competition at one decisive site, namely the constituency elections.[43] The development of competitive two-party politics makes success in this highly centralised site of political competition of crucial importance. The party that gains a simple overall majority in the election controls parliament, thereby gaining exclusive access to executive power and control of various ancillary institutions. The principle of parliamentary supremacy limits the independent status of the judiciary; when a conflict of interests arises its subordinacy becomes apparent.[44] This has led to descriptions of the system of government as an 'elective dictatorship'.[45] But while there is a growing clamour for the modification of many of these constitutional features so as to impose more effective curbs on the power of government, the majoritarianism in the British constitutional system has in reality always been mitigated by a number of factors.

(c) **Limits on majoritarianism**

The paradox of the Westminster constitutional model is that despite its many nominally majoritarian features the British system of government is not highly majoritarian in practice. Constitutional lawyers have always asserted that the British system is characterised by a strong sense of constitutionalism, or limited government—that British democracy is 'qualified democracy' because of the formal and informal restraints on the majority's power.[46] The same may not be true as far as the Westminster export models are concerned because most of the factors mitigating majoritarianism in Britain derive from its peculiar constitutional history and political culture, factors which are clearly not for export. Among these constitutional and political features are the following:

(i) The first restraint derives from the certainty of a general election every five years, and often more frequently. This tends to result in a regular alternation in office between the two major parties—Laski remarked that the success of the system lies in the opposition's 'proximity to office'.[47] The alternation in office derives from the dual balance of power between two relatively even-sized parties which require only small fluctuations in voter allegiance to turn the opposition into the major party, and vice versa;[48] despite the pre-eminence of the dominant parties this phenomenon gives considerable leverage to the minority 'floating vote'. Lijphart goes so far as to say that alternation in government is the 'vital condition' of democracy,[49] for without it the primary rule of democracy (that citizens are entitled to participate in decision-making) is violated by the secondary rule (that the will of the majority should prevail), in that the minority is effectively excluded from power for an extended period.[50] Alternation in power prevents majority rule from becoming indefinite and unqualified rule by one group. The real prospect that the government will soon be in opposition acts as a restraint on the theoretically extensive powers and prevents real hardships for the current opposition. Likewise the alternation phenomenon encourages minorities to accept their temporary status, as well as the general rules of the game.[51] Thus winners do not in fact take all, nor losers lose all.

(ii)   The Rule of Law plays a significant normative role in the Westminster system in that the constitution has grown up out of a recognition of it.[52] In the first place it qualifies the principle of legislative supremacy in practice, in that the legal values inherent in the Rule act as a restraint on the otherwise unlimited scope of parliament's powers, thereby fulfilling a similar function to a justiciable bill of rights.[53] The restraint that the doctrine imposes on parliament is both political and moral[54] and it provides a partial substitute for legal safeguards. This clearly implies an understanding of the rule in terms of the preservation of basic procedural and substantive liberties and not simply as the principle of legality, in which form it is more easily reconcileable with, and does not effectively qualify, parliamentary supremacy.[55] The Rule of Law affects the exercise of executive power in two ways:[56] it requires the executive's powers to be authorised by statute and the common law and therefore subject to some control by the judiciary, and it implies that these powers should not be so extensive as to permit inroads on basic rights except in cases of emergency. The judicial control over legislation can be directly or indirectly curtailed by statute, and extensive discretionary powers can be granted in wide enabling legislation, but the Rule of Law does provide some check on legislative and executive power, thereby mitigating the majoritarianism of the Westminster system.

(iii)   'Checks and balances' are not a prominent feature of the Westminster constitutional system, but deserve some attention. The weak separation of powers has given rise to two main reciprocal controls between parliament and cabinet, dissolution and ministerial responsibility, but these controls have only a limited contemporary significance. Legislative power is distributed among the component parts of the 'Queen-in-Parliament', each of which must function in order to give rise to a valid enactment. The House of Lords retains a suspensory veto which has in the past, albeit very seldomly, been used to restrain the legislative activities of the Commons. By convention the royal veto constitutes an even more remote restraint, but reinforces the fact that the principle of legislative supremacy cannot be applied by a single institution.[57] The diffusion of executive power between the Crown and cabinet leaves the former with residual prerogative powers which could be used in exceptional circumstances.[58] The judiciary has some control over the executive's powers and the way it exercises them, but generally the checks and balances in the Westminster system provide only a limited qualification on majoritarian rule.

(iv)   While single-party cabinets based on clear parliamentary majorities are regarded as the normal pattern of Westminster government the reality is somewhat different: as Butler points out coalitions or quasi-coalitions have been in power in Britain for about one third of the twentieth century.[59] This phenomenon is attributed to the weakening of the

forces which have traditionally given the country single-party governments[60]—there has been a breakdown in the national homogeneity and
voter discipline which fitted the nation into the stable two-party mould,
and the electoral system is now producing indeterminate results which
make coalitions necessary and a more permanent feature of political
life.[61] In the British context this process is seen to have the disadvantage of blurring lines of responsibility and obscuring the clear-cut
choices which a two-party system provides,[62] but it has the advantage,
in the context of this analysis of majoritarianism, of reducing the costs
of adversary politics. A genuine coalition is a limited form of power-
sharing.

(v) During the 1970s the devolution movement in Britain gathered
momentum and had potential implications for the majoritarian features
of the constitution. Notwithstanding the absence of legislative rivals to
parliament Britain has always had a degree of non-centralised government effected through local authorities. There has also been a system
of administrative decentralisation to Wales and Scotland through the
Welsh and Scottish offices respectively. But whereas decentralisation
refers to the exercise of central powers by officials of the central
government in various regions,[63] devolution denotes the exercise of
delegated powers by regional political institutions not directly answer-
able to the central government, but without the latter relinquishing its
overall control.[64] The recent devolution initiatives were not altogether
innovative in that Northern Ireland had a devolved parliament and
executive from 1922, until London resumed direct control in 1972. The
two devolution bills considered in 1978 made provision for locally-
elected assemblies in Scotland and Wales, the former to have legislative and executive authority on devolved matters, and the latter to
administer certain laws of Westminster in Wales. Neither assembly
would have independent sources of finance and through this and other
features overall political and constitutional control would be retained
by the central government. The bills received the royal assent but failed
to attract sufficient support in separate Scottish and Welsh referenda to
be brought into operation. The prospects for devolution are at present
uncertain, but it is clear that if federalism is understood as the process
of federalising a political community and transforming a unitary state
into a federally organised whole,[65] then devolution would be an important part of the federal process which would have a significant effect on
the majoritarianism of the British constitutional system.[66]

(vi) Finally commentators from Bagehot to Friedrich to Finer have emphasised that parties in Britain do not push their principles to their logical
conclusion and that the British political traditions ensure that the
majority does not impose its will continually on the minority.[67] This is
not only a consequence of the alternation-in-power phenomenon but
also of the nature of the political culture that results in the two dominant parties being broad coalitions of interest groups. The recognition
of the opposition is a long-standing political and parliamentary practice
and on important issues the leader of the opposition is consulted by the

government. The government's sensitivity to public opinion was apparent on the contentious issue of Britain joining the European Economic
Community where the government resorted to a form of 'direct democracy' by holding a referendum; it clearly felt that such a major policy
decision required more than the approval of the bare majority in both
houses of parliament and sought wider support. Britain is regarded as a
prime example of a liberal-democracy and in a liberal-democracy government is, by definition, qualified, and majority rule is in practice
qualified majority rule.

Thus despite the 'thorough majoritarianism' evident in Westminster constitutional theory constitutional democracy tends to prevail over populist
democracy in Britain. Further distortions of the theory have been caused by
two phenomena of modern industrial societies, namely bureaucratic power
and corporatism. Of the former Sedgemore has said, 'One cannot under-
stand how power is exercised in Britain unless one can appreciate the
interaction of Prime Ministerial power and civil service power'.[68] And
corporatism has been said to threaten parliamentary democracy directly by
by-passing ministers, by-passing parliament and by-passing the people.[69]
But while these, and the other factors mentioned above, severely qualify
the majoritarian and competitive aspects of the original Westminster model
they do not necessarily operate when it is applied in an alien setting.

3. THE AMERICAN PRESIDENTIAL SYSTEM

(a) General constitutional principles

If the essential feature of the Westminster system is its parliamentary
government the corresponding feature of presidentialism is the fixed-term
non-parliamentary executive that derives from the separation of powers
principle. These ingredients are found most clearly in the constitutional
system of the United States, and American presidentialism has in turn
served as a model for other presidential regimes. As is the case with the
Westminster system the constitutional allocation of public power in the
United States provides a limited, and at times deceptive, picture of the
American political system. There has been a greater legalism associated
with the United States' constitution because of its codified nature and the
authoritative function of the Supreme Court, and a resulting emphasis on
'constitutional law' and not the constitution. However, as this work is
concerned primarily with the constitutional framework of government attention is given mainly to the formal institutions in the United States, and
particularly to those at the national level of government. In this context it is
usually asserted that there are three outstanding features of the constitutional system: the separation of powers, the checks and balances, and the
federal division of competence.

The separation of powers has traditionally been regarded as the fundamental principle of the American constitution.[70] In so far as there is an
almost complete separation of the personnel of the legislative and executive
branches it differs from the weak or partial separation of powers of the
British parliamentary system. The prominence of this principle was appar-

ent in the original format of the 1787 constitution. Provision was made first, and by implication foremost, for the legislative power, which was vested in a Congress comprising the popularly elected House of Representatives and a Senate formally designed to reflect state interests.[71] Executive power was vested in the President,[72] to be elected for a four-year period, thus giving him a different constituency and mandate to the legislature. It is to the old theory of the separation of powers that the democratic value of the non-parliamentary executive is traceable—a president popularly elected to perform executive functions should not be limited in that capacity by a body elected for another purpose.[73] The President could appoint cabinet ministers who would remain accountable to him, and not to the legislature from whose deliberations they were excluded; he was also empowered to appoint and remove public office-holders, thus making him the administrative head of government as well.[74] The judicial power was vested in the Supreme Court and other inferior courts that Congress might establish;[75] members of the Supreme Court would be appointed by the President[76] and it would have both original and appellate jurisdiction. This basic structure has remained fundamentally unaltered since its inception,[77] although from the constitution's inception all three organs of government came to exercise powers beyond these allocated to them, in contravention of any strict notion of separation of powers.

The separation of powers was qualified by the second prominent feature of the United States constitution, the checks and balances, which were designed to subject each branch of government to some influence and control from the others.[78] The most important of the internal checks and balances is the bicameral structure of the national legislature; the Senate and House of Representatives have virtually identical legislative and financial powers, neither being able to override the other.[79] Of more significance are those that operate externally to each branch of government, so that none can act without the approval and support of another, notwithstanding that the legislature and executive each have a direct popular mandate.[80] Acting as restraints on Congress's legislative capacity are the President's powers to initiate and veto legislation,[81] although the veto can be overridden by a two-thirds majority in Congress[82] and does not exist in relation to constitutional amendments. A further check on Congress is the courts' power, not expressly provided but asserted early in the history of the constitution,[83] to review the constitutionality of legislation. As far as the President and other members of the political executive are concerned, they are subject to removal by Congress through the impeachment process and their actions can be invalidated by the court in its capacity as arbiter between government and nation, and between the branches of government. The President also requires senatorial approval for appointments to the Supreme Court and other key positions, and ratification by the Senate of treaties negotiated by him,[84] and although he can appoint federal officials, the power to create public offices vests in Congress. Members of the Supreme Court are appointed by the President (with senatorial approval) and are subject to impeachment by Congress. The Court's structure and jurisdiction is subject to the authority of Congress, and judges are dependent on the administration to give effect to their decisions. Thus while the separation of powers in the United States' constitution ensures that the main exercise of each power is entrusted to one person or institution, the checks and balances introduce a minor participation for other persons and institutions.[85] Congress acquires a quasi-judicial function in relation to impeachments,[86] the Senate an executive function in relation to the treaty-making and appointment processes, and the President a role in the law-making process;[87] the Court, through its review powers, can act as a 'council of revision' or 'superlegislature' and final policy-maker for the nation. While the extent of these modifications to the separation of powers was not always precisely envisaged by the founding fathers, they are integral features of the contemporary constitutional system in the United States.

The third salient feature of the United States' constitution is the federal division of power between the national and state authorities, with each set of institutions having a direct impact on citizens within its jurisdiction. It was sought to safeguard the distribution of competence and the status of each level of government through the supremacy of the constitution and the rigid amending procedure, and the authority of the judiciary came to be used to enforce the constitution's supremacy and to resolve conflicts between the levels of government. Partly because of the rigid amending procedure most changes relating to the federal aspects of the constitution were made through judicial interpretation, and over time the original federal principles were significantly modified. The general trend has been for the federal jurisdiction to be enlarged at the expense of the states' jurisdiction, and the constitutional division of competence has not prevented the national authorities from exercising power on most important areas of government. 'Co-ordinate' federalism has given way to 'co-operative' and 'organic' federalism, and resulted in a system which is decidedly less federal.[88] But the federal principle is still regarded as a reality in the United States, particularly in relation to political parties and the electoral system,[89] and there has been evidence of a greater concern from the Burger Court for the rights of states in the federal system.[90]

(b) The United States' constitution and majoritarianism

The American system of government has always been regarded as a constitutional democracy, based on a distrust in government and faith in the division, diffusion, limitation and sharing of authority.[91] Each of the constitution's three main features can be regarded as a qualification of the system's fundamental premise of majority rule. The basic elements of federalism—the territorial distribution of competence, the supremacy of the constitution and the authority of the federal judiciary—have a counter-majoritarian effect at the national level; furthermore, the territorial distribution of competence allocates to the individual states, each of which is a minority in the national context, authority on matters of state (or minority) interest.[92] The division of competence, together with the functional separation of powers, serves to prevent a concentration of power in a single institution, thereby excluding the possibility of any 'sovereign' authority.[93] The checks and balances involve a further qualification of majoritarianism in that the interdependence of the various authorities necessitates the co-operation of more than one for a given power to be exercised. Bicameralism serves as a restraint on the popular majority in the House of Representatives, and the Senate has a *liberum veto* in respect of presidential appointments;[94] the President, through his legislative veto power, can require laws to achieve a two-thirds rather than a simple majority in Congress. The courts have a 'counter-majoritarian' effect in relation to their two main constitutional functions—upholding the supremacy of the constitution and enforcing the Bill of Rights. Finally 'super majorities' are required to effect formal amendments to the constitution, a factor not unrelated to the few amendments since its inception. It cannot be said of American presidentialism, as it can of the Westminster system, that authority is constitutionally allocated on the basis of a 'winner-takes-all' competition at a single decisive site. There is rather a multiplicity of sites, both functional and territorial, and from a comparative point of view one would expect the system to operate more slowly than its British counterpart in giving effect to majority views.[95] An examination of specific aspects of the three main institutions provides further insight into the question of majoritarianism in the United States' constitutional system. It becomes evident that the principle of majority rule underlies both Congress and the presidency, whereas the Supreme Court's powers are partly premised on the need for minority protection.

As far as Congress is concerned both the electoral system and the legislative process are formally majoritarian. Elections for the House of Representatives are held in single-member constituencies according to the plurality principle, with the same consequences as in the Westminster model. The system produces two broadly aggregative parties which dominate the House and there is no assured representation for minority parties. The arithmetical discrepancies between votes polled and seats won by these parties, are not, however, as great as in Britain, for two principal reasons: the apportionment decisions of the 1960s which introduced the doctrine of 'quantitative majoritarianism'[96] in terms of which electoral constituencies came to be equally delimited to ensure that all votes would be of approximately equal weight;[97] and the existence of solid blocks of constituencies which, until recently, did not change their party representation.[98] Senators are elected on a majoritarian basis in district or state-wide elections with the same political consequences for minority parties; however, in the Senate all states have equal representation, which entails over-representation for the smaller states and has an anti-majoritarian effect on the overall composition of Congress. The legislative process is also majoritarian in that enactments require simple majority votes in each House, with the exception of constitutional amendments or the reversal of the presidential veto, which both require qualified majorities. In the latter case a congressional minority,[99] and in the former a minority of states as well,[100] can obstruct the congressional majority. Two other factors involve significant variations on the Westminster legislative process—the relative absence of party discipline in the US Congress,[101] and the highly developed committee system through which most legislative decisions are taken.[102] These factors give rise to norms of bargaining and compromise which differ from the adversarial pattern of Westminster decision-making. Although majoritarianism is the general rule underlying the composition and functioning of Congress it is variously qualified in practice.

In the executive branch of government majoritarian elements are also prevalent, and are aggravated by the periodic accumulation of powers in the presidency. The presidential electoral system is predominantly majoritarian and leans strongly in favour of the dominant parties and against minor parties. Although an absolute, and not a relative, majority of electoral college votes is required for a candidate's election, non-major parties have little access to the college because of the 'unit rule' which earmarks all the electoral college votes of a particular state to the candidate with a relative majority of popular support therein. Votes cast for losing candidates in each state have no further effect on the electoral result.[103] The electoral college system is no more than a mode of electing the president by majorities in the states rather than a direct popular majority.[104] Numerous proposals have been made for the reform of this system, although little consensus has been achieved on an alternative. Where a constitution makes provision for a single functionary to hold office for a fixed period it is difficult to build proportionality into the electoral system, although other forms of minority safeguard are possible. In fact the frequent alternation in the presidential office required by the US constitution mitigates to some extent the effects of the presidential electoral system, which is a crucial site of competition in the political system. The loose nature of American political parties also makes this less of a zero-sum competition than might otherwise be the case.

Although the constitutional position of the President has always been pre-eminent the accretion of power to the presidency is a relatively modern phenomenon. Executive authority vests initially in the President who has a wide discretion in cabinet appointments; the cabinet is not a collective body and tends to have less influence over him than has a parliamentary cabinet over a Prime Minister. The President has extensive patronage in the form of appointments and other spoils of government, and a new incumbent can make substantial changes of administrative personnel outside the competitive ranks of the bureaucracy, unlike an incoming British Prime Minister. The President has been referred to as the 'chief legislator',[105] and various incumbents have accumulated extensive powers in crucial areas such as foreign and military affairs. They have been assisted in the process by their powers of patronage and ability to appeal to the electorate for direct support, and have not always been impeded by the constitutional checks and balances. The inefficacy of the checks and balances is exemplified by the past inability of Congress to scrutinise and control the executive,[106] in particular the President and his white house staff, a development which led to the 'imperial presidency'[107] in the 1970s. The crisis of Watergate has been described as the product of a long build-up in the concentration of presidential power and the failure to adhere to the limitations on authority explicitly and implicitly contained in the constitution.[108] The scope and extent of presidential influence have diminished appreciably since the Watergate era[109] and have given way to a more stable balance of power between the

legislature and executive,[110] although the bureaucracy continues to intervene in all fields of government, undermining the separation of powers
doctrine and the notion of checks and balances. Majoritarianism and the
concentration of power are therefore important features of the executive
branch with implications for the constitutional system as a whole.

The 'counter-majoritarian' role of the Supreme Court in its review capacity is the subject of very extensive analysis and dispute and can only be
briefly referred to here.[111] Hamilton was of the view that the Court would
be the 'least dangerous' branch of government because it would have
'neither force nor will, but merely judgement'.[112] When it first asserted its
power of judicial review it purported to restrict itself to legal issues so that it
could not be accused of usurping the majoritarian powers of Congress and
the President. It has been suggested that this led to the development of a
constitutional myth to reconcile the conflicting demands for majoritarianism
and the preservation of minority rights: according to the myth Congress and
the President were to decide 'political' issues by majority rule, while the
Supreme Court would protect the 'legal rights of minorities as set out in the
constitution'.[113] But the myth could not account for an increasing number
of judgments, particularly during the era of the Warren Court,[114] in which
the Court gave decisions on clearly political issues. It became a more active
political organ of government and moved from a constructionist position to
one where it began balancing competing societal interests.

Judicial activism evoked the response that the Court was intervening in
areas over which it had no jurisdiction, and on matters which should have
been dealt with by the legislative and executive organs. Hence the accusa-
tions of judicial 'usurpations',[115] and terms such as 'super-legislator'[116] and
'imperial judiciary'[117] came to be used in relation to the Supreme Court.
From early charges that the Court was counter-majoritarian,[118] and was
thereby frustrating the wishes of popular majorities, developed the notion
of 'minority rule by nine old men'[119] and it was suggested that judicial
behaviour involved the subjection of the majority to the 'tyranny of the
minority'.[120] An important element of these criticisms was the fact that
Supreme Court justices are not elected, constitute a relatively isolated élite,
and, apart from a remote threat of impeachment, enjoy tenure for life. The
fact that the ultimate power of constitutional amendment rests with the
political organs is not seen as being of great significance, since this procedure requires the support of a 'super-majority'.[121]

In response to these criticisms it has been suggested that the notion of
government by judiciary is a gross overstatement of the case.[122] The Supreme Court has always had a 'political' role, and has a self-imposed body of
rules aimed at encouraging restraint and avoiding controversial issues.[123] It
is pointed out that the judiciary is no less representative than other institutions such as the presidency and bureaucracy,[124] that the judicial majority
usually reflects the majority in the wider political system,[125] and that the
court can be overridden through constitutional amendment.[126] Recently
attempts have been made to reconcile judicial review and democratic
theory. Ely proffers a 'representation-reinforcing' theory of review in terms
of which the courts would be actively concerned with ensuring representa-

tive and effective participation in the political process and preventing discrimination against certain minorities, without deciding on the substantive merits of political choices.[127] While there has been some change in the extent of judicial activism in the Burger Court,[128] the whole question of the proper role for the judiciary within the American constitutional system remains a controversial one.[129]

Thus only a complex overall picture can be provided of majoritarianism in the United States' constitution. This can be attributed partly to the long-standing dualism in American political thought: a desire for limited government on the one hand, and for democratically responsible government on the other.[130] The separation of powers, checks and balances, federal division of competence, constitutional rigidity and judicial review are associated with the former, and the populist and majoritarian aspects with the latter. The result is 'an imperfectly anti-democratic judicial process and an imperfectly democratic political process'.[131] For the purposes of this work, however, it can be concluded that whereas the Westminster parliamentary system is designed to give quick effect to majority wishes the American presidential system is designed to restrain popular pressures and protect vested groups and interests.[132]

4. CONCLUSION

In this chapter a description has been given of the constitutional frameworks of the two historic versions of liberal-democracy, British parliamentarism and American presidentialism. The description and comparison have been made at a fairly high level of constitutional abstraction, providing a conventional and idealised version of the two systems. It overlooks the fact that there is a large degree of ideological agreement among political leaders from different parties in each system, particularly in relation to the economic base of the system;[133] this clearly has implications for the political choices facing the electorate and the significance of political competition. The conventional constitutionalist view also makes unwarranted assumptions as to the neutrality of the various state institutions, which are assumed to be impartial instruments of the legislative and political executive. Nevertheless this level of analysis seems most appropriate for the present stage of the constitutional debate in South Africa. It has revealed that both systems are premised on the principle of majority rule and an adversarial political context, but various constitutional and political factors combine to prevent majority rule from becoming unrestrained and indefinite rule by a bare majority. They are both constitutional democracies in the traditional sense of that term. South Africa's constitutional system has never conformed to either of these two models, and at its best could be regarded as an attenuated version of Westminster parliamentarism.[134] In its opposition to this system the liberal tradition in South Africa has frequently drawn comparatively on the British and American precedents in prescribing a process of constitutional reform for the country.[135] There have been suggestions that South Africa's attenuated Westminster system should be adopted through a serious of gradual reforms involving, inter alia, the extension of the franchise (possibly in terms of educational or property qualifications) the restoration of the Rule of Law, the removal of references to race and ethnicity in the constitution (and statute book generally), and the reformation of institutions such as the now defunct Senate. Other suggestions have been made with reference to American constitutionalism, involving a separation of legislative, executive and judicial powers, a territorial-federal devolution of competence, a justiciable bill of rights, and other checks and balances designed to fragment power and preserve liberty. These proposals have not been uncritical of the majoritarian aspects of liberal-democratic constitutionalism and have suggested that they require modification to accommodate the 'multi-racial' conditions of South African society, but the constitutional recommendations have generally been based on the principle of majority rule in an adversarial political system.

One of the criticisms of the liberal tradition has been that its constitutional proposals are based on an individualistic model of politics and society,[136] and that it tends to emphasise constitutional measures without considering the social and political preconditions for their operation.[137] Moreover its majoritarian assumptions are said to be ill-suited to a divided plural society such as South Africa in which there are likely to be permanent political majorities and permanent minorities, with the latter being unable to convert to majority status and being excluded indefinitely from power. This is to violate the 'primary rule' of democracy, that those affected by political decisions should have a chance of participating directly or indirectly in their making, and to replace it with the 'secondary rule', that the will of the majority should prevail.[138]

Consociationalism challenges the notion that democracy should be equated with majority rule and attempts to replace it with the proportionality principle at every level of government. This principle allows all groups to be represented in decision-making processes and to influence decisions according to their proportional strength. Although consociationalism does not provide an analytical constitutional model it has a deep sense of constitutionalism and its principles have a close affinity with the constitutional features of the liberal-democracies which are designed to qualify majoritarianism and safeguard minority interests, although its successful operation requires other institutional and extra-constitutional preconditions. It provides an alternative to the British and American systems of government which, it is argued, is better suited to a divided plural society. For the South African government it implied the prospect of a new legitimising theory for its rejection of majority rule and liberal constitutionalism.

NOTES AND REFERENCES

[1] C J Friedrich *The Impact of American Constitutionalism Abroad* (1967) 12; cf G Almond & G Powell *Comparative Politics* (1966) 5.

[2] Arend Lijphart 'Consociational Democracy' 1968–9 *World Politics* 267; 'Majority Rule Versus Democracy in Deeply Divided Societies' 1977 *Politikon* 113.

[3] See D V Cowen *The Foundations of Freedom* (1961) 104ff.

[4] Cf Sir James Stephen's well-known comment, 'We count heads instead of breaking them' (quoted in Cowen op cit 105).

[5] Grotius *De Jure Belli ac Pacis* 2.5.17; see Huber *Heedendaagse Rechtsgeleertheyt* 4.3.1–20 and cf Puffendorf *Droit de la Nature et des Gens* 7.2.15.

[6] John Locke *Two Treaties of Government* Bk II ch 8 (Everyman's Library ed, 1977, 165–6); J J Rousseau *The Social Contract* Bk IV ch 2 (Everyman's Library ed, 1913, 88).

[7] Cowen op cit 106.

[8] A de Tocqueville *Democracy in America* (1835) ch 14 (World's Classics ed, 1946, 183). For De Tocqueville, 'The very essence of democratic government consists in the absolute sovereignty of the majority'.

[9] John Rawls *A Theory of Justice* (1972) 356.

[10] Locke op cit 224ff.

[11] Rousseau op cit 251.

[12] J Madison *The Federalist Papers* (1788) No 10 (Mentor Books ed, 1961, 77–83).

[13] E Burke *An Appeal from the New to the Old Whigs* in B W Hill (ed) *Burke on Government, Politics and Society* (Fontana ed, 1975) 373.

[14] A de Tocqueville op cit 182–98; J S Mill *On Liberty* (1859) ch 1 (Dent & Sons ed, 1972, 68f).

[15] F A Hayek *The Constitution of Liberty* (1960) 103–17; S E Finer *Comparative Government* (1970) 62–6; Rawls op cit 129.

[16] R A Dahl *A Preface to Democratic Theory* (1956) ch 3; see also Dahl's *Polyarchy: Participation and Opposition* (1971).

[17] C J Friedrich *Limited Government: A Comparison* (1974) 34–49; see also the articles on Friedrich in J Pennock & J Chapman (eds) *Constitutionalism* (1979).

[18] Cf Walter Bagehot's aversion to the 'ultra-democratic' theory—*The English Constitution* (2 ed, 1872) (World's Classics ed, 1974, 129ff). Dicey's notion of parliamentary sovereignty assumed an unrestricted franchise although he did not canvass this issue; he did, however, accept the majority rule viewpoint. A V Dicey *An Introduction to the Study of the Law of the Constitution* (10 ed, 1959) 83. See also C B Macpherson *The Real World of Democracy* (1965) 1–11.

[19] Cf Finer op cit 35.

[20] See Rawls op cit 224. For Rawls there is an inverse relationship between the degree to which a constitution is majoritarian and the extent of 'equal political liberty'. See also S A de Smith *The New Commonwealth and its Constitutions* (1964) 107–9.

[21] Vol VI *Oxford English Dictionary* 59.

[22] See e g S A de Smith *Constitutional and Administrative Law* (4 ed, 1981) 27ff; E C S Wade & G Phillips *Constitutional and Administrative Law* (9 ed by A W Bradley, 1979) 32ff; O Hood Phillips & P Jackson *Constitutional and Administrative Law* (6 ed, 1978) 19ff.

[23] De Smith *The New Commonwealth and its Constitutions* 77–8.

[24] See G Carter & J Herz *Government and Politics in the Twentieth Century* (3 ed, 1973) 35–6; the second process overtook the first and made it superfluous.

[25] Bagehot op cit 9. By the 'efficient' part of the constitution Bagehot understood those parts by which in fact it worked, and he contrasted these with the 'dignified' parts which brought it into force and attracted its motive power. J A G Griffith aptly describes Bagehot's oft-cited work as 'unhappily misleading' ('The Political Constitution' 1979 *Modern LR* 1 at 2).

[26] Cf C F Strong *Modern Political Constitutions* (8 ed by M G Clarke, 1972) 211f—this is one of the many works which eulogises Bagehot's contributions.

[27] See Wade & Phillips op cit 48; M C Vile *Constitutionalism and the Separation of Powers* (1967) 226f; C J Friedrich *Limited Government* 18f. In recent English decisions the separation of powers doctrine has been invoked to prevent the judiciary from intruding in the legislative field (*Hinds v The Queen* [1977] AC 195; *Duport Steels Ltd v Sirs* [1980] 1 WLR 142) although there is evidence of the doctrine's continued vitality in other areas: C Munro 'The Separation of Powers: Not Such a Myth' 1981 *Public Law* 19–24.

[28] Vile (op cit 126ff) convincingly exposes Bagehot's limited insight into English constitutional history, during which the two theories of mixed government and separation of powers had been combined into the single theory of the balanced constitution which was based not on the fusion of all power in one set of hands but a partial separation of powers. Bagehot did no more than 'expose' the long since discredited, extreme theory of separation of powers which he assumed to underlie the English constitution; he overlooked the more subtle division of power between, and interdependence of, the executive and legislature.

[29] The parliamentary systems of Western Europe are also characterised by the inter-locking of the executive and legislature but differ from the Westminster system in various ways which place the executive in a weaker position: in some cases the executive has no power of dissolution, in others the President is vested with real executive powers, and in others the multi-party system leads to frequent votes of no-confidence and cabinet resigna-

tions. As parliamentary government generally depends for its stability on the two-party system these governments tend to be unstable.

[30] This arrangement is followed faithfully in the Westminster export models. The older Commonwealth countries (New Zealand, Australia, Canada, South Africa) developed from representative to responsible government, at which stage the responsibility of the executive to the locally-elected legislature was ensured by law or convention; the relationship between the executive and legislature in these countries still conforms to the Westminster model, with local variations in style and practice. In many of the other Commonwealth countries the executive branch of government is also parliamentary, either through force of statute or through the incorporation by reference of relevant British conventions. De Smith *The New Commonwealth and its Constitutions* 82ff; Carter & Herz op cit 37ff.

[31] See A Lijphart 'Majority Rule versus democracy in deeply divided societies' 1977 *Politikon* 113 at 115; M Wiechers 'Possible Structural Divisions of Power in South Africa' in J Benyon (ed) *Constitutional Change in South Africa* (1978) 107 at 111.

[32] H W R Wade *Constitutional Fundamentals* (1980) 9.

[33] After the last delimitation the average size of the English constituencies was 64 134 electors, but this ranged from 25 023 to 96 830, an extraordinary maldistribution (see A H Birch *The British System of Government* (4 ed, 1980) 69–71). The standard constitutional law texts mention, but tend to gloss over, this phenomenon.

[34] For a tabulation of these distortions, which includes the 1979 general election, see H M Drucker (ed) *Multi-Party Britain* (1979) 13; see also E Lakeman *How Democracies Vote* (1970) 39ff.

[35] Wade op cit 20. See also S E Finer (ed) *Adversary Politics and Electoral Reform* (1975); N Johnson *In Search of the Constitution* (1977) 217–19; Lord Hailsham *The Dilemma of Democracy* (1978) 183–9.

[36] See S A Walkland 'Committees in the British House of Commons' in J Lees & M Shaw *Committees in Legislatures—A Comparative Analysis* (1979) 242 at 249; but select committees 'compensate in limited fields for the deficiencies of the party confrontation in the Commons' (262).

[37] See P Norton *The Commons in Perspective* (1981) 47–79.

[38] Dissolution in the means whereby a deadlock deriving from a legislative majority hostile to the executive can be broken. A fresh appeal is made to the electorate so that the legislative majority and the executive will once again be of the same mind—this is the only basis on which parliamentary government can operate. See S E Finer *Five Constitutions* (1979) 55f.

[39] The system requires relatively centralised and disciplined political parties to ensure the majority parliamentary support on which the cabinet continuously depends.

[40] As numerous commentators have pointed out the Commons has become no more than an extension of the executive and is not a 'legislature' in the true sense of the word; e g Norton op cit 73.

[41] R Crossman (ed) *Walter Bagehot: The English Constitution* (Fontana, 1963) 54; but cf J P Mackintosh *The British Cabinet* (3 ed, 1977) 428–58, 628–31; S E Finer *Comparative Government* (1970) 169–74.

[42] See the perceptive analysis of N Johnson *In Search of the Constitution* (1977) 81ff.

[43] Cf A du Toit *Federalism and Political Change in South Africa* (1974) 21.

[44] See Johnson op cit 85.

[45] By Lord Hailsham. See *The Dilemma of Democracy* (1978) 126–32.

[46] e g S A de Smith *Constitutional and Administrative Law* (4 ed, 1981) 29; C J Friedrich *Limited Government* (1974) 46; Wade & Phillips *Constitutional and Administrative Law* (9 ed, 1977) 30; Hood Phillips & Jackson *Constitutional and Administrative Law* (6 ed, 1978) 27.

[47] H Laski *Parliamentary Government in England* (1938) 176; Bagehot's observation was, 'Two can play at that fun' (op cit 206).

[48] See the classic account of the two-party system in Britain in I Jennings *The British Constitution* (4 ed, 1952) 63f ('. . . opposing the Cabinet will be another party accepting the principle of majority rule, but expecting sooner or later to replace the party in office and form a Cabinet in turn . . .').

[49] A Lijphart 'Majority Rule Versus Democracy in Divided Societies' 1977 *Politikon* 113 at 115.

[50] Cf W A Lewis *Politics in Africa* (1965) 64ff.

[51] In a sense this begs the question since a basic underlying consensus is a *sine qua non* for the functioning of this system.

[52] Cf C F Strong *Modern Political Constitutions* (8 ed, 1972) 251.

[53] Hood Phillips & Jackson (op cit 39) describe the doctrine as involving 'the existence in the English Constitution of certain principles almost amounting to fundamental laws'.

[54] C J R Dugard *Human Rights and the South African Legal Order* (1978) 30; Dicey, the 'father' of the Rule of Law, recognised the implications of the concept for his notion of parliamentary sovereignty (op cit 406–14).

[55] On its meanings see A S Mathews 'The Rule of Law—A Reassessment' in E Kahn (ed) *Fiat Iustitia* (1983) 294–311.

[56] A S Mathews *Law, Order and Liberty* (1971) 26; cf I Jennings *The Law and the Constitution* (5 ed, 1959) 46ff.

[57] Cf Vile op cit 305.

[58] In English constitutional law the Crown's prerogative can never be completely replaced by conventions.

[59] D Butler (ed) *Coalitions in British Politics* (1978). The clear coalition governments were the two war-time coalitions and the national government of 1931, but there have been six other periods of 'minority rule', where the government has depended on the votes or abstention of at least one opposition party.

[60] Butler op cit 113.

[61] Cf H M Drucker (ed) *Multi-Party Britain* (1979): 'Britain no longer has a simple two-party political system. The old concept must be replaced' (at 1). Since Drucker's book appeared the Social Democratic Party has been formed from among former members of both major parties; in an electoral alliance with the Liberals it scored several by-election successes in 1981–2, but the 1983 election showed it incapable of breaking the Labour–Conservative domination of Parliament. Some constitutional commentators (e g Wade & Phillips op cit 31) have suggested that the constitutional structure of Britain does not necessarily rest on the two-party system, but it seems clear that any permanent departure from this pattern would bring significant changes to the political process. See also N Johnson op cit 63ff.

[62] Butler op cit 118; see also Johnson op cit 68. Other traditional arguments against coalitions are that they do not render the electorate sovereign, they make for unresponsive government, and they involve weak government.

[63] Hood Phillips & Jackson op cit 714–15.

[64] The definition provided in the *Report of the Royal Commission on the Constitution* (Kilbrandon) Cmnd 5460 (1973) para 543. The report distinguished further between administrative, executive and legislative devolution. See Wade & Phillips op cit 372–8. Also V Bogdanor *Devolution* (1979), and for a comparative view H Calvert (ed) *Devolution* (1975).

[65] See C J Friedrich *Constitutional Government and Democracy* (4 ed, 1968) 193f.

[66] The federal process would clearly require other institutional changes, such as the reform of the House of Lords and a federal role for the judiciary. See V Bogdanor 'Devolution and the Constitution' 1978 *Parliamentary Affairs* 252.

[67] Bagehot op cit 130; C J Friedrich *Limited Government* (1974) 46; S E Finer *Comparative Government* (1970) 183ff.

[68] B Sedgemore *The Secret Constitution* (1980) 33.

[69] Sedgemore op cit 36. Commentators have been reluctant to define corporatism and to stipulate the extent to which Britain has moved from pluralism to corporatism. Schmitter has characterised it as 'a system of interest representation in which the constituent units are organised into a limited number of singular, compulsory, non-competitive, hierarchically ordered and functionally differentiated categories, recognised or licensed (if not created) by the state and granted a deliberate representational monopoly within their respective categories in exchange for observing certain controls on their selection of leaders and articulation of demands and supports'. P Schmitter *Corporatism and Public Policy in Authoritarian Portugal* (1975) 9. See also J K Galbraith *The New Industrial State* (2 ed, 1972) 297ff; K Middlemas *Politics in Industrial Society* (1979) 371–88; J Richardson & A Jordan *Governing Under Pressure* (1979) 161–3; J Harrison *Pluralism and Corporatism* (1980). On corporatism and consociationalism see below, 54.

[70] See G Caney 'The Separation of Powers' in G Graham & S Graham *Founding Principles of American Government* (1977) 98.

[71] Art I.

[72] Art II.

[73] Strong op cit 232.

[74] B Schwartz *Constitutional Law* (1972) 143.

[75] Art III.

[76] Art I s 2.2.

[77] The main formal changes to this structure have been the XII and XXIII amendments (dealing with the election of the President and Vice-President) and the XXIV amendment (providing for the popular election of senators).

[78] As Vile (op cit 18) observes, the amalgam of the doctrine of separation of powers with the theory of checks and balances formed the basis of the United States constitution; this single, essentially American, doctrine replaced the pure doctrine of separation of powers which had been espoused in revolutionary America.

[79] See Finer op cit 224.

[80] Cf J Lees *The Political System in the United States* (1969) 36.

[81] A more remote check is the Vice-President's role as president of the Senate, in which he has a casting vote in the event of an equality in deliberative votes.

[82] The so-called 'pocket veto' prevents Congress from overriding a presidential veto of measures passed at the end of a congressional session.

[83] *Marbury v Madison* (1803) 1 *Cranch* 137. Some support for the court's review powers is to be found in Arts III and IV of the constitution, but it is also an inevitable consequence of constitutionalism. Cf Lees op cit 43; E L Barrett *Constitutional Law* (5 ed, 1977) 17–39; R Mc Closkey *The American Supreme Court* (1960) 3–53.

[84] Appointments require the Senate's 'advice and consent' and by convention this check has been considerably expanded; treaties require approval by a two-thirds majority in the Senate but presidents have bypassed this requirement through the device of 'executive agreements'.

[85] Friedrich *Constitutional Government and Democracy* 184.

[86] The House acts as 'prosecutor' and the Senate as a 'court'. Cf C H Pritchett *The American Constitution* (2 ed, 1968) 203–5.

[87] The President has been referred to as the 'chief legislator'—R G Tugwell *The Emerging Constitution* (1974) 398.

[88] G Sawer *Modern Federalism* (1976) 98–108.

[89] Lees op cit 66; Finer op cit 215ff; Tugwell op cit 536–41.

[90] See L H Tribe 'Unravelling National League of Cities: The New Federalism and Affirmative Rights to Essential Government Services' 1977 *Harvard LR* 1065; R Y Funston *Constitutional Counter-Revolution? The Warren Court and the Burger Court* (1977) 345ff; and the collection of articles on this theme in 1977 *Yale LJ* 1018–296.

[91] See Friedrich *Limited Government* 34–49.

[92] This assumes a form of 'dual federalism' which no longer exists, but the point still has a qualified relevance.

[93] Although the constitution divides sovereignty one could say in a legalistic sense that the United States has a sovereign power equivalent to the Queen-in-Parliament, namely two-thirds of both Houses of Congress together with three-quarters of all the states, but the difficulty of mobilising the constituent parts makes the comparison unrealistic. See Vile op cit 205.

[94] Cf Friedrich op cit 57.

[95] Cf G Carter & J Herz *Government and Politics in the Twentieth Century* (3 ed, 1973) 53.

[96] M Uhlmann 'The Supreme Court and Political Representation' in L Theberge (ed) *The Judiciary in a Democratic Society* (1979) 91 at 92; and see L H Tribe *American Constitutional Law* (1977) 737ff.

[97] This occurred through judicial interpretation of the 'equal protection' clause of the Fourteenth Amendment as requiring equality of access for citizens to the political process through equal representation in legislative bodies, but can also be seen as a logical outcome of the majoritarian principle. In *Baker v Carr* 369 US 186 (1962) the rule that apportionment laws were beyond judicial cognisance (*Colegrove v Green* 328 US 549) (1946) was rejected, and the court in *Reynolds v Sims* 377 US 533 (1964) gave constitutional effect to the principle that all votes should be of equal weight. However, the reapportionment decisions of the Warren Court have been greatly criticised; see e g R Berger *Government by Judiciary* (1977) 69–98; Uhlmann op cit 91–109.

[98] See E Lakeman *How Democracies Vote* (3 ed, 1970) 34. The reapportionment of electoral districts served to provide some measure of proportional representation to blacks.

[99] That is one-third of the members of either house.

[100] That is one-quarter of the states.

[101] Cf J Sundquist 'The Crisis of Competence in our National Government' 1980–1 *Political Science Quarterly* 183. Both the federal nature of the political process and the absence of a parliamentary executive have caused the national parties in the US to be relatively weak and enjoy less internal discipline than in Britain. The plethora of special interest groups and developed lobby system also detract from the adversarial norm.

[102] See J Lees 'Committees in the United States Congress' in Lees & Shaw (eds) *Committees in Legislatures* (1979) 11–60.

[103] C H Pritchett *The American Constitution* (2 ed, 1968) 313. In 1966 the state of Delaware unsuccessfully challenged the rule on this basis, and because it favoured the large states, and created the possibility of minority presidents: *Delaware v New York* 385 US 895 (1966).

[104] C J Friedrich *Constitutional Government and Democracy* (4 ed, 1968) 399. This arrangement also means that a candidate could be elected with only minority overall support, but this has happened only on one occasion.

[105] See R G Tugwell *The Emerging Constitution* (1974) 398.

[106] See P B Kurland *Watergate and the Constitution* (1978) 28.

[107] See A Schlesinger's work *The Imperial Presidency* (1973). Schlesinger suggests that Nixon concluded that the separation of powers had so frustrated government on behalf of the majority that the constitutional system had become intolerable (252); one of his attempted solutions was to transform the presidency of the constitution into a plebiscitory presidency (377).

[108] Kurland op cit 4. Kurland (at 172) attributes the executive's dominance to judicial constructions of the constitution which allowed it to exercise the national power over foreign affairs, to occupy the entire field of government and regulation, and to acquire extensive powers through delegation. The separation of powers doctrine became ineffective in restraining the exercise of these powers and was further blurred by party allegiance.

[109] See T E Cronen 'A Resurgent Congress and the Imperial Presidency' 1980 *Political Science Quarterly* 209-37.

[110] J Sundquist (*The Decline and Resurgence of Congress* (1981)) shows how Congress reasserted itself in financial, foreign and military affairs, and tightened its control over the bureaucracy.

[111] For an extensive bibliography see G Schubert *Judicial Policy Making* (rev ed, 1976).

[112] A Hamilton *The Federalist* No 78 (Mentor Books ed, 1961, 465); cf A Bickel's well-known work *The Least Dangerous Branch: The Supreme Court at the Bar of Politics* (1963).

[113] See C Abernathy 'America's Supreme Court and the Balance of Justice' (Byliner series, Oct 1979).

[114] 1954-69. The Court's most notable decisions were in the fields of legislative reapportionment, race relations and criminal accused's rights. In fact there has been a long tradition in the US of presenting social and political problems as questions of law to be resolved by the courts and the doctrine of 'substantive due process' had developed in the early part of the twentieth century. See L J Theberge (ed) *The Judiciary in a Democratic Society* (1979) xi.

[115] e g A Bickel *The Supreme Court and the Idea of Progress* (1970) 3.

[116] Berger op cit 2-3.

[117] P Kurland in Theberge op cit 21-2.

[118] See A Bickel *The Least Dangerous Branch* (1962) 16-23.

[119] See C J Friedrich *Limited Government* (1974) 46.

[120] P Kurland in Theberge op cit 23.

[121] See J Grano 'Judicial Review and a Written Constitution in a Democratic Society' 1981 *Wayne LR* 1-75.

[122] R Funston *Constitutional Counter-Revolution? The Warren Court and the Burger Court* (1977) 12.

[123] Funston op cit 23.

[124] D Horowitz *The Courts and Social Policy* (1977) 18.

[125] Schubert op cit 209. Other writers, however, suggest that to speak of 'counter-majoritarianism' is to misconstrue the true basis of majority rule.

[126] On four occasions the amendment procedure has been used to overule Supreme Court decisions: the tenth, fourteenth, sixteenth and twenty-sixth amendments. See L H Tribe *American Constitutional Law* (1977) 50-1; A P Grimes *Democracy and the Amendments to the Constitution* (1978).

[127] J H Ely *Democracy and Distrust—A Theory of Judicial Review* (1980) 181ff. In recent times the Court has moved from the protection of individuals to the protection of groups in relation to such matters as affirmative action and class actions.

[128] Funston op cit 327-73.

[129] See Tribe op cit 47-52.

[130] See Funston op cit 11-12.

[131] Tribe op cit 51.

[132] Carter & Herz op cit 53, and 145; as M Vile (*Constitutionalism and the Separation of Powers* (1967) 335) observes, the emphasis in the former system is on coordination and in the latter on control.

[133] For this level of analysis see R Milliband *The State System in Capitalist Society* (1969) 63ff.

[134] See chapter 4 below.

[135] See e g D Molteno *The Molteno Report for the Progressive Party* (1960), K Heard *Political Systems in Multi-Racial Societies* (1961), D V Cowen *Constitution-Making for a Democracy* (1960) and *The Foundations of Freedom* (1961). For a critique of liberal-constitutionalism with specific reference to South Africa see the Sprocas report *South Africa's Political Alternatives* (1973) 128ff.

[136] See C B Macpherson *The Real World of Democracy* (1966) 1–11.

[137] See the Sprocas report 127ff.

[138] W A Lewis *Politics in West Africa* (1965) 64ff; A Lijphart 'Majority Rule Versus Democracy in Deeply Divided Societies' 1977 *Politikon* 113 at 115.

2 Pluralism and the Plural Society

1. INTRODUCTION

Consociational democracy has been presented as an alternative to the majoritarian-based parliamentary and presidential systems described in the previous chapter. The consociational writers challenge not only the identification of democracy with majority rule, but also the notion that stable democracy is not viable in divided plural societies. They advance consociationalism as an explanatory theory for the viability and stability of certain liberal democracies with plural societies, and as a normative system for other plural societies. Consociationalism is therefore intimately related to theories of pluralism.

Concepts of pluralism have been used extensively in the study of comparative politics and nearly all countries have at times been described as pluralistic. However pluralism is not capable of precise definition and is used in different senses by different intellectual traditions although they are all concerned with the same basic issue, namely the relationship between unity and diversity in society.[1]* In order to provide some clarity to the concept reference will be made to the three principal senses in which it has been used by social and political theorists:[2] first by the English political pluralists, secondly by their American counterparts, and thirdly by the anthropologists and sociologists in relation to the theory of the plural society. It is with the third of these usages that consociationalism is most closely related.

One of the objects of this chapter is therefore to provide some definitional coherence to the terms 'pluralism' and 'plural society' which are used with increasing laxity by political actors in the South African constitutional debate.[3] A further object is to situate the theory of consociationalism by relating it to the different traditions in political theory and political sociology. Finally by identifying the type of pluralist theory used by the government as a legitimising ideology it is possible to indicate the government's likely constitutional strategies for the future.

2. POLITICAL PLURALISM

The sense in which pluralism is used in political thought has only a tenuous connection with its meaning in the theory of the plural society.[4] The former focuses on the distribution of political power in society, and the latter on the relationship between social conditions and political behaviour and stability. The two distinct traditions of political pluralism are dealt with in chronological order.

(a) English political pluralism

English political pluralism emerged in the early decades of the present century and was promoted by writers such as J N Figgis, Harold Laski, and

25

G D Cole,[5] most of whom had strong socialist leanings. The theory rested on three basic principles:

(i) The first was that liberty is the most important political value and is best preserved by the dispersal of power in society. The fear of concentrated power was a pervasive feature of pluralist thought.[6]

(ii) The second principle was that groups should not be depicted merely as collections of individuals but as having a real personality. The English pluralists argued that groups could not adequately be understood simply in terms of the lives of their individual members, and that both political and legal theory should take more seriously their substantive personality and consequent rights.[7] Maitland was one of the first pluralist writers to assert that groups were real entities in society, and he drew on the work of Otto van Gierke who, although writing on German nationalism and not himself a pluralist thinker, emphasised the significance of groups and their claim to legally recognised rights and privileges.[8]

(iii) The third principle involved a denial of the theory that in every state there must be a sovereign. As far as legal sovereignty was concerned pluralism took issue with the view that law is simply the will of the sovereign irrespective of its content or character. This involved a rejection of Bentham's sovereign legislator and Austin's positive law, as well as the model of the state as a legal order in which a determinate authority acts as the ultimate source of power.[9] The pluralists also criticised the notion of political sovereignty, which held that in every society there is an ultimate authority which can resolve disputes and demand obedience, as being of doubtful factual correctness and having dangerous moral consequences.[10]

In developing their doctrine the English pluralists were reacting against nineteenth century liberalism and utilitarianism, which had placed the individual in a social vacuum and focused exclusively on the relationship between the individual citizen and the sovereign state. By drawing on the evidence of man's interest in, and loyalty to, a plurality of groups, they emphasised the group nature of politics.[11] The view that the individual's relationship with the state was mediated by groups and associations was averse to the classical liberal tradition, which was based on an individualistic or atomistic model of politics and society and viewed politics in terms of a basic opposition between the individual and the state.[12] In the pluralist view the groups and associations in society were characterised by voluntary (and hence at times overlapping) memberships, were equal in status with one another, and possessed autonomy in deciding on their own rules of behaviour.

The function of the state, according to this tradition, was to provide and maintain the framework within which groups interacted and pursued their substantive purposes, and to guarantee the continued existence of the groups.[13] The state's authority was limited by other powers in society, exercised by different non-state organisations, with whose autonomy it ought not to interfere. Political action was perceived not as the exercise of sovereign power, but as the interplay of a variety of plural associations resulting at times in a conflict of wills arising from the complex network of group relationships. Freedom was formulated not negatively, in terms of the limitations on governmental powers, but positively, as the equal opportunity for self-realisation by individuals in their groups or social structures. By spreading power according to the diversity of functions it had to perform the state could maximise the opportunities for freedom and development. In this view of politics the participatory role of the citizen became crucial—he had a duty to become involved both in the state and in the society as a whole, and participated through his membership in a plurality of groups. Moreover, as the state created areas of freedom in which groups could operate, the groups and their members shared responsibility for the society's conditions—pluralism of responsibility became a feature of the pluralist model.[14] Finally, in so far as the citizen was faced with a choice between conflicting loyalties, to the state and organisations in competition to it, he might at times be compelled to give his loyalty to a non-state group and resort to civil disobedience.

The English pluralist view implied more complex institutional arrangements than the direct democracy of Rousseau, or the simple representative mechanisms described by Locke.[15] Nicholls refers to various institutional embodiments of pluralism, such as the guilds envisaged by the guild socialists, as well as to various forms of corporativism and functionalism which it advocated.[16] The pluralist model could be described as essentially 'federal' in so far as it implied a functional division of power among corporate groups.[17] Laski observed that for a proper understanding of any society it should be regarded as essentially 'federal' in nature.[18] By this he meant that general activities which interested all members of society belonged to the state, while activities which were primarily specific in their incidence should be administered by those most directly affected by them; the latter activities interested the state only in so far as they affected the rest of the community, in which event it might ultimately exercise its reserve power. The criterion for the functional devolution of power was social utility. However, although functional federalism was an essential doctrine of English pluralism its constitutional principles remained largely undefined.

The influence of English political pluralism had begun to wane before the emergence of its American counterpart. It had tended to be more normative than empirical, and it was criticised because it ignored the complex reality of group life and the possibility of the groups becoming oligarchical and unscrupulous, it incorrectly presupposed the individual's interest and rationality in politics, and it tended to overlook the dangers of deadlock and stalemate in the political system.[19] Even its proponents began to perceive the need for something beyond a vigorous group life, such as national leadership and a more purposeful role for the state. The tradition's opposition to state absolutism, and its emphasis on the dispersal of power and the group nature of politics, constituted its main contributions to political theory.

(b) American political pluralism

Pluralism has been the dominant tradition within American political sociology for several decades.[20] It has purported to be an explanation of, and justification for, the United States' political system, although, as the critics observe, the system has been viewed at times in a rather romantic light. The tradition may be traced back to De Tocqueville, with his reflections on self-governing 'intermediate bodies' capable of countervailing both an atomistic society and a totalitarian state, and Arthur Bentley, who portrayed the political arena as comprising a large number of groups each attempting to promote a particular interest.[21] These themes were developed by subsequent American theorists who came to associate democracy with pluralism; far from viewing differences in social and political positions as being incompatible with democratic ideals the pluralists saw in their balanced adjustment the essential conditions for democracy. In pluralist theory policy outcomes were perceived as the result of group processes, and not individual rational choices as envisaged by classical democratic theory.[22]

In the 1950s American pluralist theory began to take on the role of an ideology and to be applied in a descriptive and prescriptive manner.[23] A free society was said to be characterised by a multiplicity of semi-autonomous groups whose leaders compete for political power. The groups are characterised by cross-cutting cleavages, and the multiple affiliations[24] of individuals prevent the emergence of exclusive loyalties which would exacerbate conflict.[25] The existence of multiple affiliations, together with a commitment to common values and a competitive balance of power, leads to the integration and stability of such a society.[26] The political structure is also plural, in that equal political rights are exercised by its citizens in a constitutional system embodying a separation of legislative, executive and judicial powers, a justiciable bill of rights, and a federal or quasi-federal division of competence.[27] Not only is political power fragmented among the branches of government, but it is shared between the state and a number of private groups and individuals.[28] As far as the relationship between the groups and state is concerned Wolff[29] distinguishes between two different theories in the pluralist tradition: the 'vector-sum' version in which the different groups are seen to exert pressures on government agencies which formulate a compromise, and the 'referee' version, in which the state is perceived as a passive co-ordinating authority which upholds the rules for competition and conflict resolution. In the latter theory groups achieve their goals directly, and in the former indirectly through organising as pressure groups. Both theories emphasise the value of a plurality of interest groups in society and a decentralisation of public power.[30]

In opposition to the pluralist writers of the fifties other theorists began to emphasise the élitist nature of the American polity,[31] and while this criticism was to stimulate a vigorous defence of the orthodox pluralist position it led ultimately to a redefinition of the concept—whereas historically pluralism had implied active citizen participation in group and public affairs (and a reasonable equality of bargaining power among interest groups), it began to mean competition among élites and organised groups, irrespective of whether decision-making within the groups was dominated by the few.[32] American pluralism's emphasis on group behaviour led to the decline of individualism and to élitist theories of democracy.[33]

It is beyond the scope of this work to provide a detailed critique of the pluralist political model. One of the most persistent criticisms is that, while purporting to be empirical, it ignores the realities of the American political process which has been blatantly undemocratic vis-à-vis groups which have shown the greatest degree of cultural or social pluralism. This can be expatiated in terms of Wolff's three-point criticism. The first is that existing groups are in practice always favoured over groups in the process of formation, thereby inhibiting social change.[34] The second is that in the case of intergroup conflicts the system consistently favours the stronger over the weaker party, and legitimate interests which are unorganised find their disadvantaged position perpetuated.[35] These two criticisms are based on the empirical evidence of the American system. The third is based on an alternative philosophy of society which rejects the pluralist notion that there is no such thing as the public interest or the common good in the modern state. While the pluralist emphasis on public competition among groups might be appropriate for solving some problems of distributive justice it is inadequate for solving problems relating to the common good or for reorganising society on a large scale. This requires the broader vision of 'community' which Wolff attempts to formulate as an alternative to the pluralist model.[36] From the class perspective Szymanski advances two primary criticisms of pluralism.[37] The first concerns its assumption that American society is composed of a diversity of equally powerful groups reflecting the interests of most people, when in fact only half the population belongs to voluntary associations, most of which have only a peripheral interest in politics. The second concerns the function of the state, which in the pluralist model is that of reconciling the various group influences and converting them into state policies; this approach fails to recognise the limited number of policies which the state can follow without causing socio-economic disruption of the society, and the fact the state's main purpose might be to defend the predominance of a particular class.[38] Despite these criticisms the pluralist view of society continues to predominate in the United States, and in western countries generally.

3. THEORIES OF THE PLURAL SOCIETY

The most recent tradition of pluralism finds expression in the theory of the plural society. Whereas pluralism for the American political pluralists is a condition of democracy, for the plural society theorists it is a threat to the democratic viability of societies. In this context a 'plural society' is understood as one which contains two or more communities based on distinct factors of culture, race, caste, class, language or religion. The lines of differentiation, or 'cleavages', tend to be deep and mutually reinforcing, and there is a relative absence of cross-cutting cleavages and multiple group affiliations.[39] Political divisions follow closely the lines of social cleavage, leading to sharp conflicts between the politically-organised groups, or 'segments'—hence the notion of 'conflict pluralism' in contradistinction to 'equilibrium pluralism'.[40] The relationships between the different segments are invariably characterised by inequality, and the prevalence of political dissensus and conflict deriving from cultural and social diversity frequently results in the non-democratic regulation of the plural society and minority political domination.

This model of the plural society was first developed by Furnivall, and was based on his study of tropical colonies in which he was concerned with the impact of western capitalism on Asian pre-capitalist societies.[41] He defined a plural society as one 'comprising two or more elements or social orders which live side by side, yet without mingling, in one political unit'.[42] Each section of the community lived separately and held by its own language, religion and culture, meeting only with members of other groups in the market-place in buying and selling. The plural society was created largely by economic forces, and was the distinctive character of tropical economy with its division of labour along racial lines and differential incorporation of ethnic groups, which created distinct 'economic castes'.[43] This type of society was characterised by the absence of a 'social will', which made democracy impossible.[44] The society was held together by the colonial power and a common economic system, and its basic political problem was one of integration. Furnivall advocated federalism as a method of reintegrating such societies, and likened the plural society in its political aspect to a confederation of states which united for certain common ends but otherwise remained separate. The plural society, however, lacked the traditional confederal features of a voluntary union, territorially segregated sections, and the possibility of secession. It should be emphasised that in Furnivall's theory the conflict in a plural society did not emanate from racial or cultural divisions per se, but because economic boundaries and exploitation co-incided with these differences.[45]

In developments since Furnivall the conflict theory of pluralism has been extended beyond the tropical scene to all heterogeneous, that is culturally and socially stratified, societies. Smith, its main proponent, reacts against this extended usage.[46] He distinguishes between heterogeneous societies, which may exhibit varying degrees of pluralism, and plural societies proper. The former are characterised by a common system of basic institutions shared by the majority of their members, who are differentiated at the secondary level of institutional and organisational specialisation, while the latter are characterised by incompatible institutions (the sole institutional framework that incorporates the aggregate is government), and dominated by one of the cultural groups, usually a minority. For Smith, then, political domination by a cultural minority is part of the definition of the plural society. His other contribution concerns the mode of incorporation of the various groups into the public domain, which determines their access to political power. In the plural society the groups are differentially incorporated, resulting in unequal access to government and minority domination, whereas if incorporation occurred on a consociational basis there would be equal access to government. Federation can be seen as a constitutional equivalent of the latter mode of incorporation.[47] The maintenance of the plural society, for Smith, is a function of its common economic system, and non-democratic regulation and coercion by the dominant minority which subordinates the political institutions of other groups. The heterogeneous society, on the other hand, has social cohesion as the basis of its stability and does not develop a rigid and hierarchical ordering of relations between the different sections. Smith's contribution extends Furnivall's perceptions within a general theoretical framework.

Van den Berghe broadens the scope of the pluralist approach in his attempt to explain the development of the majority of multi-national societies in terms other than those of consensus functionalism or marxism.[48] Unlike Furnivall or Smith, he conceives pluralism as a variable, rather than an all-or-none phenomenon; plural societies are not regarded as *sui generis*.[49] A society is pluralistic, for Van den Berghe, to the extent that it is structurally segmented and culturally diverse and exhibits a relative lack of value consensus, relative rigidity and clarity of group definition, and a relative presence of conflict and lack of integration. Pluralism is a matter of degree, and societies may range from the relatively homogeneous to the extremely pluralistic. A distinction is drawn between cultural and social pluralism in society: the former denotes the existence of ethnic groups themselves, and hence cultural diversity, while the latter denotes distinct social sections, each with analogous, and hence duplicated, sets of institutions.[50] While cultural pluralism in a society inevitably involves a degree of social pluralism, the converse is not necessarily true, and groups which share the same culture may nevertheless be relegated to inferior positions on the basis of race, class or caste membership. Van den Berghe refers to this feature as secondary pluralism.

Van den Berghe is also concerned with the question of how stability may be maintained in multi-national societies in such a way that structural inequalities based on ethnicity are minimised.[51] These societies are held together by relations of power and relations of production, but the crucial variable in multi-national states is the 'degree of symmetry'[52] in the relationship between ethnic groups, that is, the extent to which the groups are in a hierarchy and there is political domination and economic exploitation. Most multi-national societies begin with a dominant group, whose policy towards subordinate groups can range from genocide, to enslavement, to indirect rule through the co-option of subordinate élites, to democratic pluralism. The last configuration is the most infrequent and its constitutional arrangements are consociational in nature:[53] proportional ethnic representation, entrenchment of minority rights, and local autonomy. The persistence of such a state as an entity depends on neither coercion nor consensus, but on the realisation that economic and political interests are best advanced by staying together in a sensibly arranged political union. For Van den Berghe minority government is not directly relevant to the question of social and cultural pluralism, although it is associated with the first three types of multi-national state.

In his contribution to the theory of the plural society Schlemmer[54] attempts to explain the variation in the degree of conflict among different plural societies. He builds on the earlier theorists in identifying the constituent dimensions of pluralism—inter alia, cultural distinctiveness, power disparities, socio-economic differentials, 'consciousness' of class, group or culture, and perceptions of relative deprivation. For Schlemmer the essential basis of conflict in plural societies is not cultural incompatibility, but the nature of the 'social formation'. The distribution of power and privilege in a plural society is regulated within social institutions which are associated with corporate group organisations. The corporate groups are formed through the élite mobilisation of people, which is inherent in the nature of a plural society, but they also involve a degree of popular involvement in the system—that is popular insistence on the satisfaction of needs and interests articulated through the group. For Schlemmer the degree of mass popular participation in the interaction between corporate groups is the essential feature of plural societies, because this creates various forces and needs in the political economy—the defence of popular material and status interests, the fervour of mass ideologies (eg 'nationalism'), and the maintenance of group integrity. Schlemmer refers to this basic dynamic of plural societies as 'popular social communalism', a process in which class, identity and power are combined and articulated to serve the interests of the corporate groups, and which determines the degree of conflict.

It is apparent from this survey that there is a divergence of views among the conflict pluralists as to the defining characteristics of a plural society, and its essential sources of conflict. While all societies exhibit pluralism, in the sense of a diversity of groups which sustain social relationships with one another,[55] only societies with certain kinds of pluralism qualify as 'plural societies'. 'The extreme case of a plural society is a society of total identities, of self-contained cultural systems or exclusive racial groups',[56] but such a society will be infrequently identified; for Mitchell it would be 'a contradiction in terms'.[57] For the discussion of pluralism in South Africa Bekker's definition of a plural society is the most appropriate:

> '. . . a political unit which maintains cultural differences, structural units with boundaries coinciding with the differences, and a model of differential incorporation.'[58]

As a sociological theory conflict pluralism has been criticised from the consensus functionalist and marxian perspectives, particularly the latter.[59] It is said that it denies the fundamental importance of the economic base and the class structure of social conflict, it reifies cultural differences as if they were immutable,[60] it disregards the existence of 'third column' institutions which are generated by the interaction between groups,[61] some of its proponents emphasise political domination to the exclusion of economic interdependence,[62] and it fails to explain the origins, development and directions of change in plural societies.[63] Other critics of the theory assert that there must be something other than force and economic interest that holds plural societies together—something in the way of a common set of values.[64] In this work, however, it is not proposed to evaluate the explanatory capacity of pluralist theory vis-à-vis structural functionalism or historical materialism. It is relevant that this theory of pluralism, albeit in a distorted version, is used as a legitimising ideology by the South African government, and it is also this tradition which is associated with consociationalism. The theory provides some insight into the thinking behind the government's constitutional strategies and the attraction of consociationalism as a legitimising theory.

4. SYNTHESIS

While the three pluralist traditions are all concerned with the relationship between unity and diversity in society, each provides a different emphasis:[66] the British tradition of political pluralism emphasises the importance of individual liberty and group life and the need to limit the activity of the state, American political pluralism emphasises the value of a plurality of groups with cross-cutting memberships and the sharing of power between these groups and government agencies, and the plural society tradition focuses on the cultural diversity in society and its negative implications for the political process and the stability of the system. Because of the basic antithesis between the two latter approaches, it is convenient to draw the following distinction:

(i) The term 'plural society' denotes highly segmented and conflict-prone societies;

(ii) The term 'pluralistic society' denotes societies in which there are many politically significant groups with cross-cutting memberships and interests.

The political form of the plural society is sectional domination, and of the pluralistic society liberal democracy.[68] As Kuper points out, the transition from a divided plural society to an open pluralistic society is likely to be extremely difficult because of the difference in their social structure.[69]

It is difficult to incorporate the various trends in the pluralist perspectives into a single system, in particular the 'equilibrium' model of American political pluralism and the 'conflict' model of the plural society, which imply two basic types of society. Nevertheless Degenaar attempts to frame a pluralist model in which insights from all three traditions are incorporated.[70] This model displays the following characteristics, inter alia, of the state and society:

1. The state loses its assumed character of sovereignty and can therefore not claim any absolute nature;

2. The state is viewed as only one of the groups through which a society operates;

3. Society is seen as the co-existence and interrelatedness of individuals and groups within a geographic unit acting according to systems of rules;

4. Each group is seen as a group of individuals acting within the same system of rules and cultivating common values through continual contact with one another;

5. The relation between citizen and state is not only direct and immediate, but also indirect and mediated; the citizen belongs to a variety of groups which the state must take into account in its dealings with individuals;

6. By means of spreading power over the whole of society, in such a way that a continual structuring and restructuring of power takes place, the concentration of power in the state can be effectively opposed;

7. It is possible for a plurality of loyalties to co-exist in society, and the state must compete with this plurality of claims to the loyalty of the citizen;

8. The autonomy of groups, residing in the fact that groups decide themselves on the rules that govern their behaviour, should not be viewed in an encapsulating way, but rather as a voluntary basis for being open to one another as regards contact, tension, criticism, influence and co-responsibility.

The emphasis in this model is on organisational pluralism and, as Degenaar shows, a number of its characteristics are not evident in the South African system. Degenaar proceeds to introduce the dimension of cultural diversity, which allows him to frame three further analytical models which are relevant to the subject of this work.[71] The first is the conflict pluralist model, which emphasises the fact that cultural and ethnic diversity inevitably leads to the undemocratic domination by one group over others; this leads back to Smith's version of the plural society outlined above. The second is the consensus or open pluralist model, in which the effects of cultural diversity are mitigated by cross-cutting group affiliations which tend to diminish the probability of conflict by building up mutual trust and an integrated society; this leads back to the American tradition of democratic pluralism. The third is the consociational pluralist model, which recognises cultural diversity as a decisive factor, but maintains stability and avoids conflict through negotiation and co-operation at the élite level, despite the absence of voluntary associations and cross-cutting affiliations. The consociational model is dealt with in the following chapter. It is first necessary to outline the case which, from the consociational perspective, is made against a majoritarian-based constitutional order in a divided plural society, and to relate the various theories of pluralism to South Africa.

5. THE PLURAL SOCIETY AND MAJORITARIAN DEMOCRACY

The case against majority rule for plural societies can be summarised as follows:[72] Although majoritarianism is a basic principle of liberal-democratic constitutionalism its effect is mitigated in practice by various constitutional and political factors. One such factor is the homogeneous political culture of the British and American systems, a product of their pluralistic societies which comprise numerous interest-groups with cross-cutting memberships.[73] The political culture of the Anglo-Saxon democracies can be contrasted with the fragmented political culture of the continental European systems. This is a product of their divided plural societies, which display predominantly reinforcing, and not cross-cutting, politically relevant cleavages. The fragmented political culture in these societies gives rise to political conflicts between clearly defined segments, making viable and stable democratic government difficult. This accounts for the widespread belief in comparative politics[74] that a movement away from a fragmented towards a homogeneous political culture could reduce the likelihood of instability and conflict, and improve the prospects of stable democracy. Without such a transition, it is said, its prospects are not good, even in the established First World countries. The 'democratic pessimism'[75] extends to the Third World countries which also tend to lack the cross-cutting, politically relevant, affiliations which give rise to a homegeneous political culture, and for some pluralist writers such as Smith the undemocratic regulation of conflict is a defining feature of the plural society in these countries. Moreover, there has in recent times been an accentuation of ethnic and linguistic conflict arising from a reassertion of communal attachments in plural societies.[76] This phenomenon has challenged the assumptions of the 'political modernisation' theorists that the political significance of cultural, ethnic and religious ties would diminish with economic development, and that the process of national integration would lead to the eradication of communal attachments and their replacement with a national loyalty. Smock & Smock suggest that[77]

> 'The politicisation of plural subgroups and the significance of its political implications have caught many social scientists unprepared . . . communal attachments do not quietly wither away with exposure to modernizing influences. Quite the contrary, modernization often creates the very conditions necessary for the incubation of strong communal identities and sets the stage for communal competition.'

In the light of this evidence it is argued that it is possible neither to depluralise such societies through a process of modernisation and nation-building, nor to manage and regulate their conflicting forces democratically.[78] It is pointed out that the majoritarian features of the British and American constitutional systems, and the resulting government-versus-opposition dichotomy, are unsuited to plural societies because they assume flexible voting patterns and changes in voter allegiance. Because political preferences consistently coincide with lines of cleavage in plural societies the majoritarian principle produces permanent political majorities and permanent minorities. The 'logic of the situation' precludes rotation in office and an alternating monopoly of power, upon which both the Westminster and presidential systems depend for their democratic functioning.[79] With no alternation the government-versus-opposition dichotomy could have drastic consequences for those excluded indefinitely from office; furthermore they would have no incentive to abide by the rules of the game. This pattern involves a violation of what Lewis calls the primary rule of democracy, namely that all citizens should have the opportunity to participate in decision-making, if only through elected representatives.[80] Rabushka & Shepsle suggest that 'majoritarianism is the cause of the dominant community',[81] and their paradigm of politics in plural societies involves the sectional domination of decision processes, a decline in democratic competition, electoral machinations, and political violence, resulting in the destabilising of the whole polity.

While the consociational school is not over-sanguine about the prospects of democracy in divided plural societies, its members can be regarded as the 'democratic optimists'.[82] Operating on the assumption that it is not possible to depluralise a plural society through assimilation or partition, they assert that its conflict can be democratically regulated, provided it is not done on the basis of majoritarian rule. The principles of consociationalism require alternative constitutional devices to the majoritarian features of the traditional liberal-democratic constitutional systems.

6. SOUTH AFRICA AND PLURALISM

(a) The plural society

The theory of the plural society has been applied to South Africa by several writers, a result partly of the difficulty of explaining the existence and maintenance of South African society in terms of consensus functionalism.[83] Emphasis is placed on the extensive cultural heterogeneity of South Africa which derives from the cultures of three continents.[84] Western European culture was English and Dutch, and through a process of acculturation achieved dominance. The imported Indian and indigenous black cultures survived this process in varying degrees. The lines of cultural division do not, however, coincide with 'racial' divisions, as the term 'race' is used in the South African context.[85] Thus although coloureds share the dominant culture[86] they are relegated to an inferior position because of their 'racial' classification, a feature which Van den Berghe describes as secondary pluralism. The classification system[87] has resulted in the existence of identities imposed by the dominant group and not voluntarily assumed on the basis of perceived common interests, and this has complicated the pattern of social stratification and segmentation. Membership of the statutorily defined groups is ascribed at birth, and intergroup mobility is difficult. The single criterion of 'race' entails important political, social and economic consequences for an individual in terms of the existing legal order. Internally each 'racial' group is further subdivided according to different criteria and with differing degrees of rigidity: the white group on the basis of language, religion and class, the coloured group on the basis of class and physical traits, Indians on the basis of religion, language, class and caste, and blacks on the basis of ethnicity, tribal loyalty, class and degree of urbanisation. Thus the stratifications in South Africa are based on race, language, religion, culture, class, colour, tribalism and urbanisation, and are maintained partly by custom and partly by law. The fundamental cleavages are not generally muted by cross-cutting memberships in associations, which for legal and traditional reasons have tended to be 'homogeneous' in composition. The main exceptions emanate from religious affiliation, the process of acculturation, and the continuing industrialisation of the country.[88]

If pluralism is a matter of degree then South Africa can be regarded as highly pluralist with a large convergence in the lines of cleavage. It also features the sectional domination associated with plural societies in that the white group is at the apex of a hierarchical system controlling political and economic power and enjoying the consequential privileges, and beneath whites are coloureds, Indians, and blacks.[89] The statutory groups are differentially incorporated into the society on each of the political, economic and status axes.[90] Van den Berghe[91] has described South Africa as an example par excellence of a plural society, in the sense in which he uses the term. He perceives a proliferation of separate societies with different institutions and facilities, different goals and opportunities, and differing values and points of view. In the absence of value consensus, coercive measures are required to ensure stability and enforce laws, and the inherent conflict could lead to the breakdown of the system. Bekker's definition of a plural society could also be applied to South Africa in all its essential elements.[92] And Degenaar suggests that,

'the present situation can be described in terms of conflict pluralism with a possible development in the direction of consociational pluralism which could be the stage of transition towards a fully-fledged consensus pluralism . . .'.[93]

Degenaar further suggests that consociational democracy should take priority over majoritarian democracy as being better suited to the nature of South Africa's divided plural society, a view shared by others who apply the theory of the plural society to this country.

The main critique of pluralist theory in its application to South Africa comes from the class perspective, which holds that racial and cultural pluralism are not in themselves relevant, or have only peripheral relevance, to the fundamental class conflict in society.[94] In reality conflict is attributable to the cleavages between classes having opposed economic interests, and the concepts of ethnicity, language and religion used by the pluralists serve only to conceal the real nature of this conflict. The 'racial' conflict is a consequence of class divisions, and ethnic mobilisation is attributable to 'false consciousness' on behalf of the working class.[95] It is also argued from this perspective that the political and economic systems in South Africa are not operating in opposition to each other, and that racial domination flows from the needs of the capitalist mode of production. From this follows the view that economic development will not necessarily lead to political liberalisation, and that there is no possibility of fundamental political change under the present economic system.[96] Since there has been no basic antagonism between the state's past political strategies and the imperatives of the economy, present constitutional developments should not be seen as the inevitable breaking down of irrational and ideological racial factors by economic imperatives, as espoused by the liberal tradition. The marxist and neo-marxist analyses of conflict in South Africa have been criticised in turn for their tendency to overlook subjective reality and their preoccupation with economic factors. It is said that racial discrimination in South Africa cannot be explained solely as a product of the system of production, and that racial prejudice and discrimination cannot be discounted in terms of false consciousness. While this is a very perfunctory treatment of class theory it is beyond the scope of this work to enter the race–class polemic.

The pluralist writers, however, do not generally elevate pluralism to a general theory of society, but regard it as a useful variant theory. Van den Berghe, for example, does not emphasise cultural factors to the exclusion of economic factors. In their study Slabbert & Welsh[97] define the nature of the conflict in South Africa as 'structural inequality of wealth, status and power'. Because the inequalities are institutionalised on the basis of statutorily defined concepts of 'race' and 'ethnicity', these concepts acquire a political salience and the conflict tends to be articulated in racial–ethnic terms. While they do not deny the importance of the class conflict (and the authors concede the large degree of overlap between colour and class), they argue that in the political arena the conflict is seldom articulated in economic terms, or in terms of the interests of a particular economic class; and they suggest that where class and ethnic solidarities compete, ethnicity will invariably prevail. There have also been attempts to combine some aspects of pluralist theory with class theory. Leftwich[98] advances an alternative conceptualisation of the structure of class, culture and colour to that of Van den Berghe:

> '*class categories*, defined by their relationship to the means of production, are consti-
> tuted by a variety of corporate groups, based on colour and culture and "nationality"
> which sometimes overlap.'

This view emphasises the class basis to the structure of relations, but also the way in which classes are divided by factors of colour and culture. In his article on black labour in South Africa John Rex concludes that the analysis justifies neither wholly pluralist nor wholly marxist conclusions:

> '. . . What is evident is certainly not the pluralism of cultural segments which either
> Furnivall's analysis . . . or Smith's . . . suggests. If there is division, the divisions can be
> seen to be functionally inter-related within an overall pattern of political conflict
> generated by the capitalist development . . . a specific kind of class struggle there
> undoubtedly is, namely one in which the classes are groups of varying histories and
> ethnic origins who enter the modern society with varying rights and degrees of right-
> lessness . . . all the groups and segments in this society are held locked together, albeit
> in a bitter conflict, not solely by the institution of government, but by a rapidly
> expanding economy. . . .'[99]

Despite the complexity of this unresolved debate, as well as the elusive nature of the pluralist concept, notions of pluralism are used fast and free in the South African constitutional debate.[100] The government projects an image of a society which is socially plural 'in the *horizontal* sense of being "multi-national"'[101] with reference to the statutory concepts of race and ethnicity; no recognition is given to the class features of the society, nor to the fact that within a common economic system the society is 'vertically and hierarchically structured in terms of the differential access to political power, economic welfare and social esteem, by groups and categories defined variously in class, colour and cultural terms'.[101] The theory of the plural society has an important legitimising function in the government's projection of cultural diversity as the main source of social instability and political conflict. It is also used to legitimise its constitutional policies of separate development for blacks and parallel development for whites, col-oureds and Indians, in the absence of a legitimising ideology of minority domination.[102] Constitutional reform is articulated in terms of the need to accommodate the various population groups in such a way that none can dominate the others. This reform eschews majoritarian democracy and has at times has been identified with consociationalism, with its close associa-tion to theories of pluralism. Other internal groups, such as the official parliamentary opposition, employ a looser notion of pluralism and empha-sise its negotiational aspects.

Even assuming no major discrepancy between legitimising rhetoric and constitutional reform, the political significance of these constitutional devel-opments will be affected, inter alia, by the extent to which pluralist theory correctly identifies the sources of conflict in South African society. The perception of government policy as a manipulation of race and ethnicity in pursuit of a divide-and-rule strategy has led to an extensive discrediting of pluralist theory, irrespective of its intrinsic validity.

(b) Political pluralism

The South African polity lacks all the main ingredients of the traditions of political pluralism. The pluralist aversion to a concentration of power is not apparent in the South African political system, which has shown a tendency to concentrate power in the central authorities, more particularly the cabinet and bureaucracy. This tendency may be partially attributed to specific constitutional features, such as the unitary nature of the constitution which has facilitated the growth of the central legislature's powers at the expense of provincial and local authorities. The flexibility of the constitution and the doctrine of sovereignty, in both its legal and political forms, have also been conducive to a concentration of power, and, in combination with the system of parliamentary government, have enabled the white executive to dominate all other branches of government and thereby control the political system. The absence of a bill of rights and a judicial testing right has added further strength to the arm of the central government. While separate development can be said to have given rise to a 'plural' devolution of power along territorial and functional lines, this has not threatened the sovereignty of the central legislature, nor has it proved a substantial check on the process of centralisation. The system of government is highly authoritarian, without any plural division of power 'based on a division of functions according to social utility'.[103]

As far as group formation and activity in South Africa are concerned, there is also little resemblance to the pluralist model. The most severe deviations have been caused by state intervention, in the form of direct and indirect statutory restrictions on the composition and membership of groups and associations. Even the membership of political parties is circumscribed by law,[104] which has led to a disjunction between 'official' and 'actual' groups in South Africa.[105] The absence of voluntary group identities and cross-cutting group memberships has affected the groups' other functions in society: they tend not to be open to one another, and their sporadic contacts are inclined to be inhibited and unsuccessful.[106]

Besides playing a crucial role in defining group boundaries, and in creating divisions within such groups, the South African state also polices intergroup boundaries and unilaterally confers legitimacy on, or withdraws it from, existing or emerging groups. The government tends to restrict the activities of non-state groups such as universities, schools, churches and trade unions. Degenaar cites specific instances of the government's acting in a non-pluralist manner, such as when it warns these organisations not to interfere in politics.[107] While the state's role in pluralist theory is to ensure the co-existence of groups so that the greatest freedom is granted to them and individuals, the tendency in South Africa is for the state to deny political participation on a pluralist basis to groups other than itself. When the state assumes its character of sovereignty, groups tend to become subordinated and absorbed by it.[108] Thus while the 'white' political system may comprise a number of competing interest groups, the pattern does not spread through society as a whole. The inequalities in power and resources of non-white groups preclude any notion of an overall competitive balance of power. The system has more affinity with the conflict than the equilibrium pluralist model.

7. CONCLUSION

This chapter has sought to explicate the concepts of pluralism and the plural society, to relate them to South Africa, and to reveal some of the legitimising theories accompanying the government's constitutional strategies. The dependence of these strategies on statutory concepts of race and ethnicity has inevitably led to the invocation of the theory of the plural society in justification thereof, regardless of the real relevance of pluralist theory or the government's form of statutory pluralism to the conflicts in South African society. This factor will have a major significance for the long-term efficacy and legitimacy of the government's constitutional reforms.

Nevertheless because political formation must legally occur in the context of statutory group definitions it is inevitable that at the present stage of the constitutional debate the conflict over political rights is expressed in terms of these definitions. Historically the conflict has resulted from the differential incorporation of whites, blacks, coloureds and Indians into the political system. By virtue of their exclusive ability to elect and be elected to the main institutions of government the dominant white group has been able to regulate conflict unilaterally. Recently the government has sought to extend political rights more widely without jeopardising its structural dominance through a system of majority rule. The principles of consociationalism indicated alternative institutional methods of achieving this objective.

NOTES AND REFERENCES

[1] The concept of pluralism originated in the eighteenth century as a philosophical doctrine with monism as its antonym and was extended to fields such as theology, sociology and politics. In its literal sense it is an abstract principle referring to 'many' or 'several'. See R Breitling 'The concept of pluralism' in S Ehrlich & G Wootton *Three Faces of Pluralism* (1980) 1 at 15.

[2] See D Nicholls *Three Varieties of Pluralism* (1974) 38ff.

[3] A high point in terminological abuse was the former designation 'Department of Plural Relations' for the Department of Co-operation and Development. Cf W Thomas *Plural Democracy* (1977).

[4] L Kuper ('Plural Societies: Perspectives and Problems' in L Kuper & M Smith (eds) *Pluralism in Africa* (1971) 7) refers to the 'quite antithetical' traditions which may be discerned in regard to the nature of societies characterised by pluralism. He is referring to the 'equilibrium model' of pluralism of the American school of political pluralists which associates democracy with pluralism, and the 'conflict model' of pluralism of the 'plural society' theories. See also A Lijphart *The Politics of Accommodation* (2 ed, 1975) 2.

[5] Nicholls op cit 5–12.

[6] R Presthus ('The Pluralist Framework' in H S Kariel (ed) *Frontiers of Democratic Theory* (1970) 274 at 282–5) suggests that the origins of the pluralist rationale lie far back in history—the ancient fear of impersonal and arbitrary government and the realisation that 'power corrupts in geometric proportion as it grows'. See also K D McRae 'The Plural Society and Western Political Thought' 1979 *Canadian Journal of Political Science* 675ff.

[7] This approach had important implications in the field of law and challenged legal practice to replace the fiction theory of group personality, as advanced by Von Savigny and applying to corporate persons, with the recognition that behind legal personality was a real social entity which could develop and change its original purpose. See Nicholls op cit 8–9.

[8] H S Kariel 'Pluralism' in *International Encyclopaedia of Social Sciences* 164–8.

[9] H Laski *A Grammar of Politics* (1925) 50f.

[10] Ibid 44. According to Laski the monistic notion of the state as a 'hierarchical structure in which power is, for ultimate purposes, collected at a single centre' was both 'administratively incomplete and ethically inadequate'. The remedy lay, *inter alia*, in decentralisation and corporate representation: Laski 'The Pluralistic State' in *The Foundations of Sovereignty* (1921) 24, 66. As Kariel (op cit 167) expresses it, 'They [the pluralist thinkers] found sovereignty divisible and allegiance to the state contingent and qualified. They argued what American statesmanship—insisting on bills of rights, on a separation of powers, and on the institution of federalism—had concluded more than a century before.'

[11] Acknowledgement here to J Degenaar 'Pluralism and the Plural Society' in A de Crespigny & R Schrire (eds) *The Government and Politics of South Africa* (1978) 223–44; and his essay ' 'n Model van Pluralisme' in Degenaar *Moraliteit en Politiek* (1976) 92–110.

[12] See the Sprocas report *South Africa's Political Alternatives* (1973) 127–30, and references cited there. The report observes that despite its departure from the methodological individualism of the liberal tradition, political pluralism may itself be derived from that tradition, or more particularly its constitutional features. American pluralism, on the other hand, tends to be justified more in terms of a social-psychological insight into the group basis of personality and society.

[13] For Laski the state was just one of many groups in society, but Figgis regarded it as a group composed of groups: Nicholls op cit 12–14.

[14] Degenaar 'Pluralism and the Plural Society' 232.

[15] See R P Wolff 'Tolerance' in *The Poverty of Liberalism* (1968) 122 at 125.

[16] Nicholls op cit 54–6.

[17] It necessitated a framework of legal institutions to resolve intergroup conflicts, including such constitutional features as judicial review and a bill of rights.

[18] Laski op cit 59.

[19] See Kariel 'Pluralism' 166–7; Degenaar 'Pluralism and the Plural Society' 240–1.

[20] See Nicholls op cit 28ff.

[21] A de Tocqueville *Democracy in America* (OUP ed, 1946) 126–33; A R Bentley *The Process of Government: A Study of Social Pressures* (1908). Bentley has been described as the 'father' of American pluralism, De Tocqueville as the 'spiritual father'.

[22] The notion of a 'classical theory of democracy' is, however, less precise than is often assumed—see C Pateman *Participation and Democratic Theory* (1970) 1–44.

[23] e g D Truman *The Governmental Process* (1951). Wolff (op cit 126ff) cites three specifically American factors which contributed to the theory of pluralism—the federal structure, the penchant for dealing with problems by means of voluntary associations, and the role of 'ethnic politics'.

[24] On the importance of multiple affiliations see W Kornhauser *The Politics of Mass Society* (1960) 81f; cf S M Lipset *Political Man* (1959) 87–90.

[25] As Kuper (Kuper & Smith op cit 9) points out, this extends the concept of pluralism to the level of individual pluralism.

[26] E A Shils *The Torment of Secrecy* (1956) 155f; Kornhauser (op cit 104) does not postulate the inevitability of common values in the equilibrium model of pluralism, and refers to its fluidity and diversity of value-standards.

[27] On the 'constitutional basis' of political pluralism see H S Kariel *The Decline of American Pluralism* (1961) 7–13. Another feature of this system would be the legitimacy of its constitutional and political structures.

[28] Cf Presthus op cit 280–1.

[29] Wolff op cit 129; see also Nicholls op cit 23.

[30] On the decentralisation of the United States' system see the contribution of R Dahl *A Preface to Democratic Theory* (1956). This aspect highlights the antithesis of pluralism to monism, by which is meant the acceptance of the state as the highest sovereign power to which all other associations are legally subordinate. See Presthus op cit 280. See also Madison's anticipation of the pluralist standpoint in *The Federalist Papers*, No 10.

[31] Nicholls op cit 26f. This approach is exemplified by C Wright Mills *The Power Elite* (1959).

[32] Presthus op cit 301; and cf R Dahl *Who Governs? Democracy and Power in an American City* (1961). The first formulation of this model is attributed to Joseph Schumpeter *Capitalism, Socialism and Democracy* (1942). See also P Bachrach *The Theory of Democratic Elitism* (1967); Pateman op cit 3–21.

[33] See C B MacPherson *The Life and Times of Liberal Democracy* (1977) 77–91 and references cited there. MacPherson suggests use of the term 'pluralist elitist equilibrium model'. Cf R Presthus 'Toward a post-pluralist theory of democracy' in Ehrlich & Wootton op cit 65–79.

[34] Op cit 150. This criticism relates to the vector-sum theory of pluralism which requires state recognition of emergent groups, while the following criticism relates to the 'referee version' in which the state plays a more passive role.

[35] A criticism first articulated by Kariel *The Decline of American Pluralism* 240. On the bias of pluralism see S Lukes *Power—A Radical View* (1974): Lukes suggests that pluralism provides a 'one dimensional view' of power.

[36] In his essay 'Community' in Wolff op cit 162–95. Nicholls (op cit 31) describes the suggestions of Wolff as a statement of the 'new Rousseauism'.

[37] A Szymanski *The Capitalist State and the Politics of Class* (1978) 4–6.

[38] Cf R Milliband *The State in Capitalist Society* (1969) 4f. Marxism provides the most important alternative to the pluralist view. A notable attempt to integrate marxist ideas into a pluralist framework was by S M Lipset *Political Man* (1959); see Szymanski op cit 16–18 and the references cited there. See also S Ehrlich 'Pluralism and Marxism' in Wootton & Ehrlich op cit 34–45.

[39] This is to paraphrase H Eckstein's definition of pluralism (*Division and Cohesion in Democracy* (1966) 34) which was adopted by the leading consociational theorist, A Lijphart *Democracy in Plural Societies* (1977) 3–4.

[40] See L Kuper 'Plural Societies: Perspectives and Problems' in L Kuper & M Smith (eds) *Pluralism in Africa* (1971) 7; Kuper & Smith's work remains the most authoritative statement on the theory of the plural society. See also M Fortes *The Plural Society in Africa* (SAIRR, 1970).

[41] J S Furnivall *Netherlands India—A Study of Plural Economy* (1944) and *Colonial Policy and Practice—A Comparative Study of Burma and Netherlands India* (1948). J H Boeke *Economics and Economic Policies of Dual Societies* (1953) also contributed to the early formulation of the theory.

[42] Furnivall *Netherlands India* 446. 'Society' is thus understood in political and administrative, and not sociological, terms. While Furnivall initially included South Africa, Canada and the United States as plural societies, he later limited his definition and described these as societies with plural features, and distinguished them from the tropical plural societies.

[43] Furnivall gave close attention to the question of how far the principles of orthodox economics were applicable to a plural society.

[44] In this sense it provided a diametrically opposed perspective to consensus functionalism.

[45] See e g M Cross 'On Conflict, Race Relations and the Theory of the Plural Society' 1971 *Race* 479.

[46] M G Smith began employing the concept in his studies of the Caribbean: *The Plural Society in the British West Indies* (1965); see also 'Social and Cultural Pluralism' 1960 *Annals of the New York Academy of Sciences* 763–85; 'Institutional and Political Conditions of Pluralism' in Kuper & Smith op cit 27–61.

[47] Cf S Bekker 'The Pluralist Approach of Pierre van den Berghe' 1975 *Social Dynamics* 12.

[48] See P van den Berghe *South Africa, A Study in Conflict* (1965); 'Pluralism and the Polity: A Theoretical Exploration' in Kuper & Smith op cit 68–90; *Race and Ethnicity* (1970); 'Integration and Conflict in Multi-National States' 1975 *Social Dynamics* 3–10.

[49] See Bekker op cit 13.

[50] See Bekker op cit 13ff; Nicholls op cit 48f.

[51] See Bekker op cit 14.

[52] Van den Berghe 'Integration and Conflict in Multi-National States' 6.

[53] Switzerland provides the most clear-cut case and is classified as a consociational democracy.

[54] L Schlemmer 'Theories of the Plural Society and Change in South Africa' 1977 *Social Dynamics* 3–16.

[55] L Kuper 'Ethnic and Racial Pluralism: Some Aspects of Polarization and Depluralization' in Kuper & Smith (op cit 459–87) 465.

[56] A A Mazrui 'Pluralism and National Integration' in Kuper & Smith (op cit 333) 347.

[57] J C Mitchell *Tribalism and the Plural Society* (1960) 25f: 'The term "plural society" itself is a contradiction since the idea of "society" in terms of usual sociological definition implies "unity"—the antithesis of plurality. The problem of plural societies, then, lies in this contradiction—in what way can these societies be both "plural" and "societies". . . .'

[58] Bekker op cit 12.

[59] See M G Smith 'Some Developments in the Analytic Framework of Pluralism' in Kuper & Smith (op cit 415) 421 for a summary of the four most general objections to the

theory; cf D McK Irvine 'Plural Societies and Constitution-making' in J A Benyon (ed) *Constitutional Change in South Africa* (1978) 94.

[60] Cf H Adam in Adam & Giliomee *The Rise and Crisis of Afrikaner Power* (1979) 45.

[61] J Rex *Race Relations in Sociological Theory* (1970) 11.

[62] Cf H Lever *South African Society* (1978) 99.

[63] Bekker op cit 11; as S Greenberg (*Race and State in Capitalist Development* (1980) 18) observes, the theory does not explain why a cultural minority whose position has been built on 'differential incorporation' begins 'incorporating' other groups.

[64] D Nicholls *Three Varieties of Pluralism* (1974) 45.

[65] Adam op cit 45.

[66] Cf J Degenaar 'Pluralism and the Plural Society' in De Crespigny & Schrire (eds) *The Government and Politics of South Africa* (1978) 223.

[67] Cf L Kuper 'Plural Societies: Perspectives and Problems' in Kuper & Smith (op cit 7) 22.

[68] Op cit 14.

[69] Kuper op cit 16–22; Kuper concedes, however, that a theoretical synthesis of the two models might be possible. See also the Sprocas report *South Africa's Political Alternatives* (1973) 84.

[70] Degenaar op cit 230–33. For this purpose he defines pluralism as 'a political philosophy in which man is described as acting in society not as an isolated and sovereign individual but within a plurality of groups'.

[71] Degenaar op cit 238–9.

[72] See the recent discussion of this topic in T Hanf, H Weiland & G Vierdag *South Africa—The Prospects of Peaceful Change* (1981) 3–10 and the references cited therein.

[73] The argument has been criticised for greatly overstressing the homogeneity of Western societies, particularly in relation to the economic base of the political system.

[74] See Nicholls op cit 56; A Lijphart *The Politics of Accommodation* (2 ed, 1975) 3.

[75] The term is Lijphart's: *Democracy in Plural Societies* (1977) 2–3; cf Hanf *et al* op cit 4–6.

[76] On this theme see S P Huntington in the foreword to E Nordlinger *Conflict Regulation in Divided Societies* (1972); N Glazer 'The Universalisation of Ethnicity' 1975 *Encounter* 8; A Rabushka & K Shepsle *Politics in Plural Societies* (1972); D & A Smock *The Politics of Pluralism* (1975); N Kasfir *The Shrinking Political Arena* (1976); M Essman 'The Management of Communal Conflict' 1973 *Public Policy* 49; Crawford Young *The Politics of Cultural Pluralism* (1976); A Lijphart 'Religious vs Linguistic vs Class Voting: The "Crucial Experiment" of comparing Belgium, Canada, South Africa and Switzerland' 1979 *The American Political Science Review* 442.

[77] Op cit 3–4 and references cited there; for these writers communalism involves 'the overriding attachment to groups sharing inherited bonds based on religion, ethnic descent, language, race or regional origin'.

[78] See in particular Rabushka & Shepsle op cit 212ff; but cf Crawford Young op cit 125.

[79] See H Adam 'The Failure of Political Liberalism' in Adam & Giliomee op cit 258 at 273; cf Smock & Smock op cit 331: 'The winner-takes-all ethos that characterises the Westminster model does not suit many plural societies because it almost assuredly means that some communal groups will be in power at the expense of others.'

[80] W A Lewis *Politics in West Africa* (1965) 64–6. And see above, 18.

[81] Op cit 90; 'white' politics in South Africa shows some affinity to their paradigm. See also Nordlinger op cit 36.

[82] Cf Hanf *et al* op cit 7–8.

[83] e g P van den Berghe *South Africa—A Study in Conflict* (1965); J Rex 'The Plural Society: The South African Case' 1971 *Race* 401; L Kuper *Race, Class and Power* (1974); L Schlemmer 'Theories of the Plural Society and Change in South Africa' 1977 *Social Dynamics* 3. For surveys of the literature see Adam & Giliomee op cit 42–50; Hanf *et al* op cit 10–15; V V Razis *Swords or Ploughshares?* (1980) 91–129.

[84] See Van den Berghe op cit 38–72; H Lever *South African Society* (1978) 1–36.

[85] As Lever (op cit 5) points out, racial differentiation in South Africa has a social rather than a scientific basis.

[86] Coloured persons share two identifying characteristics, language and religion, with the Afrikaans subculture.

[87] The system is regulated mainly by the Population Registration Act 30 of 1950 and the National States Citizenship Act 26 of 1970, but many statutes incorporate their own classification. It is clear from the former act (s 1) that 'coloureds' form a residual category. Endogamy is enforced by the Prohibition of Mixed Marriages Act 55 of 1949.

[88] L Kuper 'Political Change in White Settler Societies' in Kuper & Smith op cit 180; Sprocas *South Africa's Political Alternatives* (1973) 84–5.

[89] See Lever op cit 7.

[90] See A Leftwich 'The Constitution and Continuity of South African Inequality: Some Conceptual Questions' in Leftwich (ed) *South Africa: Economic Growth and Political Change* (1974) 127 at 133.

[91] P van den Berghe *Race and Racism* (1967) 64.

[92] See above, 32.

[93] Degenaar op cit 238.

[94] See L Kuper *Race, Class and Power* (1974); M Legassick 'South Africa: Capital Accumulation and Violence' 1974 *Economy and Society* 253; F A Johnstone *Race, Class and Gold: a Study of Class Relations and Racial Discrimination in South Africa* (1976), and the references in Adam & Giliomee op cit 46–50, Razis op cit 91–111, Hanf *et al* op cit 10.

[95] Cf S Greenberg *Race and State in Capitalist Development* (1980) 406.

[96] See M Legassick 'Legislation, Ideology and Economy in Post-1948 South Africa' 1974 *Journal of Southern African Studies* 5–35.

[97] F van Zyl Slabbert & D Welsh *South Africa's Options—Strategies for Sharing Power* (1978) 28.

[98] Leftwich op cit 158.

[99] 'The Plural Society: The South African Case' 1971 *Race* 401 at 412.

[100] H Adam & H Giliomee *The Rise and Crisis of Afrikaner Power* (1979) 42–3; and see Schlemmer op cit; W V Vosloo 'Pluralisme as teoretiese perspektief vir veelvolkige naasbestaan in Suid-Afrika' 1977 *Politikon* 4–14; W H Thomas *Plural Democracy* (1977).

[101] Leftwich op cit 158.

[102] Adam & Giliomee op cit 45.

[103] Degenaar op cit 228.

[104] Mainly by the Prohibition of Political Interference Act 51 of 1968.

[105] Slabbert & Welsh op cit 11.

[106] See M Savage's analysis of group and personal interaction in 'Major Patterns of Group Interaction in South African Society' in L Thompson & J Butler (eds) *Change in Contemporary South Africa* (1975) 280–302; see also Peter Harris 'Interest Groups in the South African Political Process' in D Worrall (ed) *South Africa: Government and Politics* (2 ed, 1975) 253–84.

[107] Degenaar op cit 233; see also J van der Vyver 'The Function of Legislation as an Instrument for Social Reform' (1976) 93 *SALJ* 56–67.

[108] Ibid. See also M Wiechers *Staatsreg* (3 ed, 1981) 189.

3 The Consociational Alternative

1. INTRODUCTION

The consociational school[1]* of writers takes issue with the pluralist prop-osition that stable democracy is not viable in divided plural societies be-cause they lack the 'essential' cross-cutting cleavages and multiple group affiliations that ensure its viability in open pluralistic societies. It also challenges the tendency to equate democracy with majority rule, as that principle is applied in both the Westminster and presidential systems of government, and it prescribes alternative norms of decision-making better suited for plural societies. Consociational democracy thus implies the need to modify both pluralist theory and conventional notions of democratic government. In the literature consociationalism is approached from three different, though related, perspectives.[2] These are: first, as a pattern of social structure which emphasises the degree of religious, ideological, cultu-ral or linguistic segmentation in a society;[3] secondly, as a pattern of élite behaviour, emphasising the process of decision-making and conflict regula-tion;[4] and thirdly, and more elusively, as an underlying characteristic of the political culture arising from historical circumstances.[5] In this chapter the second approach is pursued, though its close relationship with the third becomes apparent.

In the second approach consociationalism is a function of the political system in a divided plural society in which there is close co-operation between the leadership élites of all significant groups, who make a conscious effort to transcend the cultural and social fragmentation at the mass level. Overarching élite accommodation is a substitute for cross-cutting cleavages and multiple group affiliations; here 'accommodation' denotes the process of settling divisive issues and conflicts despite a minimal political consensus. The immobilising and destabilising effects of cultural fragmentation are counteracted by the deliberate political efforts of pragmatic and prudent leaders. The corollary of élite accommodation is relative self-containment and mutual isolation for the different subcultural segments; consociational-ism not only expressly recognises these segments but makes provision for their cultural and political autonomy. For empirical examples of conso-ciationalism its proponents point to relevant periods in the history of Aus-tria, Switzerland, Belgium and the Netherlands, and to less striking exam-ples outside Europe. Whereas traditional typologies of political systems had not accounted for these smaller European democracies, which tended to be stable despite lacking a homogeneous political culture, the consociational writers argue that they fit into pluralist theory as modified in terms of the consociational phenomenon of élite accommodation. They also suggest that consociationalism can serve as a normative model for other plural societies.

While consociational democracy relies substantially on prudent leader-ship and élite co-operation it also implies different forms of decision-making

45

* The Notes and References to this chapter commence on page 66.

to those associated with the Anglo-American constitutional tradition. It rejects the majoritarian bias of this tradition and avoids majoritarianism in the representative, decision-making and distributive areas of government. It replaces the adversarial aspects of the Westminster and presidential systems with joint consensual rule, and the government-versus-opposition dichotomy and alternation-in-power phenomenon with permanent power-sharing among all significant groups. Consociationalism stands in particularly sharp contrast to the Westminster system, with its tendency to concentrate political power in the hands of the electoral majority, and it has received attention in the South African constitutional debate as a possible alternative to that system.

Consociationalism does not, however, provide an analytical constitutional model, and may be encountered in a variety of institutional arrangements. Its essential elements are as much a product of political convention as the institutional need to co-operate. Nevertheless, some constitutional features are more conducive to consociational politics than others, and in the present context these can be referred to as consociational institutions or devices—for example, an electoral system based on proportional representation. Conversely a plurality electoral system would be regarded as a counter-consociational institution. This makes it possible not only to identify consociational elements in non-consociational systems, since most political systems combine co-operative consociational features with competitive majoritarian features, but also to describe the optimal constitutional framework for consociational government (see below).

2. GENERAL CHARACTERISTICS OF CONSOCIATIONALISM

The most significant figure within the consociational school is Arend Lijphart. In his early writings[6] he attempted to account for the 'paradoxical' nature of the Dutch political system—a stable democracy despite the country's divided social structure. He identified four closed social groups (or 'pillars') in the Netherlands, namely the Catholics, Calvinists, Liberals and Socialists, each having its own organisations and political parties,[7] with relatively few overlapping memberships among them. He attributed the Dutch secret to the *pacificatie* of 1917, when, faced with serious intersegmental conflict on several issues, the respective leaders agreed to co-operate politically at the élite level. The accommodation became institutionalised over time, and was supported by a basic sense of nationalism in the Netherlands, a significant cross-cutting of the religious and class cleavages, and the deferential character of the Dutch electorate. In terms of his understanding of the Dutch experience Lijphart suggested a refinement of pluralist theory: there could be stable democracy in a divided plural society if there was over-arching co-operation at the élite level. The mutual isolation of segments could even be conducive to stable democracy provided the leadership was of the right quality.

Although the Dutch experience of consociationalism endured only until the late 1960s Lijphart, in his later writings,[8] developed a general model of consociational democracy which he applied prescriptively to other plural societies. Élite co-operation was the main distinguishing feature of this model.[9] Institutionally he defined consociational democracy in terms of four characteristics which serve as the basis of the following analysis, although there are some differences of opinion in the consociational school on these defining elements. Each characteristic can be compared and contrasted with a corresponding (usually majoritarian) feature of the Westminster and presidential systems and cumulatively they serve to share, diffuse, separate, decentralise and limit power.[10] In overall terms they give rise to a system of power-sharing at the national level of government, and group autonomy at the subnational level.[11]

(a) Grand coalition[12]

The most important feature of a consociational system is the grand coalition in which the leaders of all significant groups in the society are represented.[13] It is in this institution that leadership élites are able to transcend the subcultural cleavages at the mass level and lend stability to the political system. The grand coalition is the 'summit diplomacy' forum where bargains are struck by group leaders without requiring direct popular ratification. It is a cartel of pragmatic élites.

In both its composition and functioning the grand coalition deviates from the assumptions of majority rule and the government-versus-opposition pattern in which an elected majority enjoys extensive power for the duration of its majority status. The competitive majoritarian model embodies a principle of exclusion in relation to the composition of the cabinet and its decision-making processes, which denies minorities access to power for the duration of their minority status.[14] The principle becomes less exclusive if the minority can achieve majority status and there is an alternation in office, but becomes highly exclusive where minority status is of indefinite duration, as is the tendency in divided plural societies. The basis of the grand coalition's composition, by contrast, is the principle of inclusion, which entails proportional participation for all minorities in the coalition regardless of whether their status is permanent or not,[15] and this reduces the need for an alternation in office. Their presence and participation in the grand coalition are made meaningful by the other consociational devices, which allow minorities to induce a consensual type of decision-making that is not institutionally required in the case of single-party Westminster or presidential cabinets.[16] Consensus and a coalescent style of leadership in the grand coalition become the characteristics of a consociational political system.

Grand coalitions are found in various institutional forms but the prototype is the coalition cabinet, as exemplified by the Swiss national executive, the federal council. This body consists of seven members chosen by the main political parties in proportion to their electoral strength, and the presidency rotates among the members on an annual basis.[17] Many of the Swiss cantons also have power-sharing executives which are composed and function along similar lines. During Austria's consociational experience the coalition principle was applied within the national cabinet and an extra-constitutional coalition committee, in both of which the two major political parties were equally represented. Another variety of grand coalition is found in the case of economic or cultural councils which might have only informal and advisory powers, but nevertheless play a significant role in the political process.[18] There are also occasions where cabinets are formed not on the grand coalition basis but with a broader political base than is required by a majoritarian system. This tendency is discernible even in Britain, with its thoroughly majoritarian parliamentary system, when exceptional circumstances have required the promotion of national policies.[19] A distinction should be made, however, between coalitions formed prior to elections with the avowed aim of conflict regulation, and common government coalitions which merely represent post-electoral marriages of political convenience.[20] In the latter case if one or more major conflict group is not included in the coalition the arrangement will not have a consociational outcome, and could even lead to the divisive 'outbidding' phenomenon from those who are omitted.[21]

The grand coalition is the focal institution of a consociational system but its efficacy is largely dependent on the other consociational characteristics.

(b) Mutual veto[22]

While the grand coalition enables all groups to participate in the decision-making process, the availability of the mutual veto ensures that the participating groups, including minorities, are able to influence that process materially. The veto can be viewed from two closely related perspectives—as a device to ensure that there is unanimity among those present on all decisions, or as a device to enable minorities to prevent the taking of decisions which might adversely affect their essential interests. There is a tendency for the second aspect to be accentuated since a minority veto, with its connotation of negative minority rule, is perceived as a contentious deviation from the majoritarian principle which gives minorities disproportionate power and leverage.[23] In consociational theory, however, it is seen as necessary to afford minorities both voices and vetoes, primarily within the grand coalition, but also in other branches of government such as the legislature and even the judiciary. The concept recalls Calhoun's doctrine of the 'concurrent majority', which required that each interest or combination of interests in society should consent to the making and execution of laws in order to safeguard minorities against the will of 'democratic majorities'.[24] Calhoun found manifestations of his doctrine in the separation of powers, checks and balances, and amending process of the United States constitution, and most codified constitutions embody the principle in a rigid amending procedure.

Numerous variations are possible in relation to the availability and effect of the veto power. It could operate in respect of all decisions, or only those which affect certain vital interests, and it might be exercisable by groups of differing minimum sizes. It could operate at the national or subnational levels of government, in different branches of government, and its effect could be suspensive or absolute. Different combinations of these variations are found in practice. Differences are also found in the veto's constitutional status—whether it is a constitutional right, is formally agreed upon by the respective parties but lacks constitutional force, or is informally practised and based on usage and convention. In the Netherlands and Switzerland the veto principle has been applied informally, in Austria it was the product of a formal agreement, in Belgium the former informal understanding was incorporated into the constitution in 1970 and now requires a concurrent majority on cultural and linguistic matters, and during Lebanon's consociational period the Christians and Muslims had a legislative veto as a constitutional right. There are advantages in the formal availability of the mutual veto in a system which has no tradition of political compromise and consensus, whereas a legacy of élite co-operation renders this less necessary.

In the light of the earlier discussion on majoritarianism it is clear that the mutual veto involves a radical departure from majority rule, and even from the less extreme forms of qualified majoritarianism. While its purpose is to effect a form of joint consensual rule, or power-sharing, the manifest danger of the veto is the immobilisation of government, or at least a radical deceleration of the governing process.[25] If political choices do not have outcomes the resultant inaction or delay inevitably favours the status quo and vested interests.[26] Whatever the normative appeal of consensual decision-making a non-consensual path appears necessary for at least some outcomes.[27] The consociational writers attempt to relativise these disadvantages by emphasising the mutuality (or double edge) of the veto, the security it affords minorities who might otherwise favour a violent alternative, and the institutional necessity it creates for compromise where governmental action is essential. In the long term, they argue, and with the growth of mutual trust and the benefit of experience, it can be a feasible principle of government. Of all the consociational characteristics, however, it is the most potentially disruptive and requires a great sense of responsibility from leadership élites.

(c) Proportionality[28]

The proportionality concept is usually used in relation to electoral systems which do not operate on a majoritarian or plurality basis, but in consociational theory it is extended to the decision-making process as a whole.[29] The function of proportionality is to ensure that all groups influence decisions and actions in proportion to their numerical strength, in contrast to the 'winner-takes-all' outcomes in majoritarian systems. The principle applies primarily in the proportionately composed grand coalition, where it is an essential complement to the coalition and veto principles, but it also operates at other levels in the normative consociational model.

First, at the electoral level the proportionality principle ensures representation for all parties in joint legislative authorities in direct proportion to their electoral support. Proportional representation implies proportional influence in decision-making if the mutual veto is also available in these authorities. Indirect elections, such as those for a coalition cabinet, can also be conducted on a proportional basis. A second area of operation is the appointment level, where the principle ensures that all non-elective government positions are proportionately allocated among the various groups.

This pertains particularly to the bureaucracy, but the principle could be extended to public corporations, advisory boards and administrative tribunals. A third area is the allocation level, where the principle ensures an equitable distribution of public funds and other 'spoils' of government. At these various levels the principle is designed to minimise conflict by reducing the degree of competition for governmental power, administrative positions, and scarce resources.[30] Two variations of proportionality are the over-representation of minorities, and parity of representation for all groups;[31] these arrangements result in exaggerated influence for minorities, in contradistinction to the majorities who are favoured in non-consociational systems.

The proportionality principle is not alien to modern constitutionalism and is encountered in different forms in numerous constitutional systems. It is applied in federal systems in such matters as equal unit representation in the federal chamber,[32] and proportionality as a basis of representation, public service appointments, or resource allocation is found in the constitutional provisions and practices of numerous non-consociational systems. But in many cases it is applied eclectically and inconsistently, and has a limited impact on the majoritarian bias of the constitutional system as a whole. In the normative consociational model, on the other hand, proportionality has more extensive and consistent application, and it precludes the possibility of majoritarian rule. It 'abolishes the sharp distinction between winners and losers; both majorities and minorities can be "winners" . . .'.[33] Although the proportionality principle is never encountered in its pure form in practice, it has been widely employed in the Netherlands, Switzerland, Austria and Belgium, where it has had an important accommodationist role.[34]

While the problems relating to the mutual veto are partly normative, those relating to the proportionality principle are predominantly practical. Policy decisions are difficult to take along proportional lines,[35] as are decisions of a dichotomous nature which require clear-cut resolution. The consociationalists suggest that these problems can be partially mitigated over time through the practice of reciprocal concessions and package deals, so that a group disadvantaged on one occasion will be preferred on another.[36] Difficulties also pertain to the filling of a single prominent position. Here it is necessary to provide for the frequent rotation of office (that is proportionality in the temporal dimension)[37] as occurs with the Swiss presidency. Where more than one position has to be filled the proportionality principle tends to emphasise the quantitative, rather than the qualitative, dimension, and fails to take account of the fact that some offices may be considerably more important than others, a factor that hampers effective proportional patronage in public office. Finally, as a basis for making public appointments proportionality tends to prefer the equal treatment of groups to the respective merits of individual appointees, which can incur costs in terms of ability and efficiency; here it introduces some of the problems encountered in 'affirmative action' programmes, with which it shares a common function. These problems, however, are an inevitable consequence of the consociational approach and, it is argued, should be compared with the manifest problems of majoritarianism in a divided plural society. They have, however, led to attempts to refine consociational theory. Steiner[38] suggests a form of decision-making by 'interpretation' that takes account not only of the numerical strength of various groups but also their political status. While this approach raises problems of its own, it does allow intensities of preference to be considered in the process of interpreting the sense of a meeting or hearing.

(d) Segmental autonomy[39]

The function of the first three consociational features is to establish a system of joint decision-making by leadership élites on matters of national concern, and thereby effect at the highest level of government a power-sharing arrangement among the various segments in a plural society. The fourth feature completes the overall picture by requiring the delegation of as much authority as possible to the respective segments, with the object of allowing autonomous rule-making and rule-application by each segment without interference from the others, or the joint authorities.[40] Application of the segmental autonomy principle has led, in practice, to the creation of exclusive segmental organisations which have a form of 'personal jurisdiction' over members of an individual segment on matters such as education, the media and industrial relations, and a diarchical constitutional order. Segmental autonomy involves not only a recognition of segmental cleavages in society but also a reinforcement of them through this type of organisational pluralism. It also involves a significant deviation from majoritarianism in that areas of decision-making are removed from the potential influence of national majorities, and each (minority) segment is enabled to take decisions on matters of exclusive concern to it.

One of the earliest forms of group autonomy on the basis of the personality principle was devised by Karl Renner for the Austro-Hungarian Empire.[41] Contemporary examples are found in the Netherlands and Belgium in relation to religious and linguistic communities. But segmental autonomy also has a measure of de facto application in countries such as Switzerland where the segments are territorially concentrated. In these circumstances it is unnecessary to pursue segmental autonomy on the problematic basis of the personality principle, because it can be more easily institutionalised through a geographic federation, itself a consociational method.[42] As segmental and territorial autonomy are closely related matters, special attention needs to be given to the conceptual and empirical links between consociationalism and federalism.

3. CONSOCIATION AND FEDERATION[43]

Although federalism is a much-defined concept its essential nature remains elusive. The modern tendency is to describe federalism as a process, or in terms of the various reactions to a federal situation, and as a function not of constitutions but of societies.[44] From a legal-institutional point of view a federal system's primary feature is the territorial division of political authority between two formally autonomous sets of institutions, one national and the other regional, the various institutions having some guarantee of

continued existence as institutions and as holders of power.[45] The secondary features of federalism all bear some relation to the first: the constitution
is codified, the legislature is bicameral, and all constituent regions are
entitled to be involved in the process of constitutional amendment—these
are invariable features of the federal systems. The other secondary features
are more variable in nature, namely the over-representation of small states
in the federal chamber, and the degree of decentralised government deriving from the first federal principle.[46] Finally, it is a federal characteristic
that the judiciary resolves conflicts between governmental authorities and
upholds the supremacy of the constitution, which in many cases includes a
bill of rights.

It is appropriate in the present context to refer to two types of federalism
which are possible in a heterogeneous or plural society. In the first, an
asymmetrical federation, the boundaries between the federal units predominantly coincide with those between the different segments. In the second, a
symmetrical federation, the two types of boundaries are predominantly
cross-cutting. There is a dispute as to when the federal formula, which
constitutes an attempt at resolving territorial diversity and conflicts of
interest, will also contribute to the resolution of communal diversities.[47]
Lipset,[48] on the one hand, suggests that where the national differences are
reproduced at the unit level in a symmetrical federation it is easier to
resolve intergroup problems on a small scale and with local variations, but
that where federal boundaries coincide with subcultural differences a disruptive and conflict-prone situation can arise.[49] Lijphart, on the other hand,
argues that the optimal arrangement is for the boundaries to coincide in an
asymmetrical federation so as to translate the national heterogeneity into
unit homogeneity. He is viewing this aspect of federalism consistently from
the consociational perspective, which holds that conflict can be reduced
where there are clear dividing lines between antagonistic groups, and particularly where these are reinforced by state boundaries.[50] Switzerland
provides an example of an asymmetrical federation, while the United States
and Austria are examples of symmetrical federations, though these classi-
fications are necessarily relative. In both views federalism is seen to have a
useful purpose in the context of a plural society, but from fundamentally
different perspectives. There is, however, basic agreement on the fact that
in both the symmetrical and asymmetrical forms federalism serves to prevent, through the dispersement of authority, a single ethnic or racial group
from dominating the political system through its control of the centre.
Reference should also be made to the concept of 'corporate federalism'
because of its affinity to consociationalism. Conventionally federalism is
understood in terms of a territorial division of power, but some writers,
such as Friedrich,[51] extend its meaning to include a non-territorial arrangement where autonomy is extended to corporate groups, instead of geographically defined regions. Friedrich applies the term 'corporate federalism' to the short-lived Cyprus constitution of 1960. The relevance of the
extended definition is that it leads on to the consociational model, because
the federal 'corporate units' correspond to the consociational 'segments'
upon which the latter system is based.

It is clear that the consociational and federal models coincide in many respects, most evidently in that they both involve the distribution of governmental power among a number of institutions in the country. Some authorities have jurisdiction over the whole country and the component units are entitled to participate in their decisions, while others have more limited jurisdiction, either territorial or personal, and provide the basis for the decentralisation of functions. Both systems are formally anti-majoritarian, though in differing ways and degrees, and both provide a formula for resolving disputes between the various authorities, and for amending a normally rigid and supreme constitution. In other respects the two models overlap, but do not coincide. The federal upper chamber usually displays some characteristics of a grand coalition, and the coalition principle tends to be applied in the formation of the federal executive, though not to the same degree as in the consociational model. Proportionality tends to be applied to some extent in the federal model, for example in the composition of the federal chamber, but it is a pervasive feature of the consociational model. Similarly, the principle of consensuality has less application in the federal model, though constitutional rigidity provides a legislative veto in respect of constitutional amendments.[52] The number of component units in either system could be as low as two, but the federal model can accommodate more units than the consociational model, which becomes susceptible to immobility or deadlock with a large number. The jurisdictional complications inherent in non-territorial units also act as a practical limitation on their number. The two systems show clear divergences in so far as the segments in the consociational model are defined in terms of common personal characteristics or interests, while the regions in the federal model are territorially defined; jurisdiction is based on the personality and territorial principles respectively. A second divergence lies in the fact that a federation need not be democratic as is the case, by definition, with consociational democracy.[53]

In summary, a consociation will also be a federation when the segments are geographically concentrated and the boundaries between the federal units follow segmental boundaries as far as possible, and where the other federal principles, such as bicameralism, are applied. Conversely, a federation will also be a consociation when the first three consociational principles are applied, the federation is asymmetrical and consists of the appropriate number of small component units, and it provides a decentralised system of government. Federal theory embodies all the consociational principles in rudimentary form,[54] and the concept of 'corporate federalism' highlights the affinity between the two. On the above criteria Switzerland can be classified as both a federation and a consociation, and there can exist a number of federal and consociational combinations, as illustrated by the case of Belgium.[55] Here the religious and socio-economic cleavages were resolved along consociational lines through bargaining and compromise, with each segment having its own organisational infrastructures, but a federal decentralisation was required to accommodate the French–Dutch ethno-cultural cleavage, which became increasingly salient in the 1960s. As Heisler observes,[56] '. . . for some purposes Belgium could be thought of as a federal entity consisting of three units, while for other purposes it is comprised of [sic] only two'. While the consociational techniques were insufficient to manage ethnic differences, their experience facilitated the transition to a federal regime.

A further element can be introduced into the discussion of federalism and consociationalism by showing the affinities between these two systems and liberal corporatism. Reference was made earlier to the modern trend away from pluralism to corporatism and neo-corporatism,[57] as evidenced, inter alia, by the collaboration between business and organised labour in certain areas of economic policy-making. In an illuminating article[58] McRae extends Lijphart's earlier analyses by identifying five basic similarities between corporatism, consociationalism and federalism in democratic settings. The most important of these is the fact that

> 'the total load of government is shared, either formally or informally, between a central government and at least one other level, or arena, of interest intermediation and decision-making'.

While the three systems have this basic similarity, they differ as to the kind of issue that is removed from the central political arena, and offer alternative modes of response to the problem of governmental overload. But corporatist, consociational and federal systems all have in common

> 'a certain minimum disposition among élites towards collaborative or co-operative, rather than authoritative or majoritarian, modes of decision-making in order for the system to function . . .'.

In this sense they all repudiate the majoritarian assumptions of the Westminster constitutional system. Combinations of the three systems are also possible in a single polity. McRae suggests that of the four 'classic' consociational democracies only Belgium cannot also be regarded as neo-corporatist, while Lembruch describes the consociational democracies as 'extreme examples' of liberal corporatism.[59] Ultimately, however, corporatism provides an alternative interpretation of political life to consociationalism.[60]

4. CONSOCIATIONALISM IN PRACTICE

In the preceding description consociational democracy has been presented mainly as a theoretical model. In its empirical form four 'classic' cases of consociationalism have been identified by McRae,[61] all among developed Western democracies—the Netherlands, Austria, Belgium, and Switzerland. In each case a temporal qualification indicates the key period of consociational accommodation—in Austria during the period of Catholic–Socialist coalitions from 1945 to 1966, in Belgium since the First World War, in the Netherlands from 1917 to 1967, and in Switzerland from 1943 to the present.[62] Examples of consociational systems outside Europe are Lebanon from 1943 to 1975, Malaysia from 1955 to 1969, Cyprus briefly between 1960 and 1963, Surinam from 1958 to 1973, the Netherlands Antilles since 1950, and Colombia from 1958.[63] Lijphart describes two other countries as 'semi-consociational' democracies, namely Israel since 1948 and contemporary Canada,[64] each of which has several consociational features. Nigeria, which was referred to as the main example of consociationalism by the first modern writer in the school,[65] could at best be labelled semi-consociational during the period 1957–1966.[66] Of local relevance is Zimbabwe, whose independence constitution incorporated several consociational institutions and devices.[67] In the light of the earlier comparison of federalism and consociationalism it is noteworthy that of the above cases all save Lebanon, Cyprus, Israel, Surinam and Zimbabwe are also federations or semi-federations, which indicates that the conceptual links between the two systems are reflected in practice.

But consociationalism remains a disputed concept, even in respect of Switzerland which is often held out as its prime example. As far as the nature of Swiss society is concerned, Bohn argues that it is not, on the evidence, fragmented into isolated and competitive segments and that, particularly from the ethnic perspective, the social structure is best accounted for by the open pluralist model.[68] Other writers[69] also allude to the presence of cross-cutting cleavages in Switzerland and suggest that stability is a result of the 'remarkable consensus' in Swiss society, and not its consociational regulation of conflict. As far as its institutional features are concerned it is pointed out that at both national and subnational levels Switzerland has one of the most extensive systems of direct democracy in existence, and that the referendum and popular initiative through which it is effected are decidedly non-consociational in character.[70] Because of the possibility of direct majority rule provided by these institutions it is argued that Switzerland provides no support for the theory of consociational democracy, despite the existence and important function of such consociational devices as proportionality and the grand coalition.[71] The classification of other 'consociational' systems has also been challenged in the literature.

In reality many political systems contain a mixture of co-operative and competitive institutions of conflict-regulation. While the consociational systems have a preponderance of the former over the latter,[72] there are numerous non-consociational systems which contain at least some consociational devices. Nordlinger points out that wherever conflict is successfully regulated in divided societies one or more of these devices is invariably employed, although not always the whole range.[73] These factors have led Steiner to suggest that, instead of classifying countries as consociational, it might be more appropriate to take decision-making for individual conflicts within countries as the units for classification.[74] This would lead to a more accurate and useful system of classification because distinctions could be drawn between issues resolved along co-operative and competitive lines within each country, and comparisons could be made not only between but also within countries. It would also lead to an investigation beyond general constitutional arrangements to concrete decision-making situations. It is the case however, that where consociational devices are only selectively applied they need not have consociational outcomes, and could even increase the influence of majorities and diminish the likelihood of co-operation.

It is evident from the survey above that many cases of consociational democracy have been of short or limited duration, and that others have ended in failure. The question arises as to whether this is attributable to the weakness of the consociational techniques and the inappropriateness of the basic principles of consociationalism. An answer to the question is complicated by the fact that the total sample of cases is relatively small. Lijphart has argued in respect of the Netherlands and Austria that consociationalism made itself superfluous by its very success, and that these countries were able to shed it in favour of stable and democratic majoritarian systems.[75] In these circumstances, he says, the termination of consociationalism cannot be equated with its failure.[76] The interruption of consociationalism by the Lebanese civil war is attributed partly to the international nature of the Lebanese conflict and the intervention of external forces; the consociational experience before this interruption is regarded as having been moderately successful, despite the over-rigid application of some consociational devices.[77] The consociational features embodied in the 1960 Cyprus constitution were unable to prevent civil war and the eventual partition of the country, and this consociational experiment can be classified as a failure. Nevertheless it has been argued that the external intervention by Greece and Turkey jeopardised the precarious political stability and that the easy availability of the veto power contributed to the political breakdown.[78] A further problem in Cyprus was that consociationalism was only reluctantly agreed to by the Greek majority, which far outnumbered the Turkish minority.[79] The consociational school argues, moreover, that despite the failures consociationalism remains the only feasible alternative to a majoritarian system for a divided plural society—other than partition, or the permanent suppression of minorities. The choice, it submits, is between consociational democracy and no democracy at all.

5. FAVOURABLE AND UNFAVOURABLE CONDITIONS FOR CONSOCIATIONALISM

From the record of the consociational systems commentators have identified various conditions which are favourable and unfavourable for its operation, although the views on this aspect tend to be widely diverging, and at times conflicting.[80] Where agreement does exist, it is invariably pointed out that the favourable conditions are neither necessary nor sufficient for successful consociationalism, and the converse applies to the unfavourable conditions. A distinction can be drawn between conditions that are attitudinal, such as those relating to élite behaviour, and those that are objective, such as the social structure and physical features of a country. Self-evidently the former can be changed more easily over time than the latter.

(a) Favourable conditions

As consociationalism has been described mainly from the perspective of élite behaviour it is not surprising that, while all political systems require prominent élite leadership, this is a crucial condition for successful consociationalism. Leaders should accept at least some basic national symbols and be committed to the maintenance of the system; they should be willing and able to transcend the divisive cleavages in society through over-arching co-operation and compromise; and they should be sufficiently strong to take their followers with them, which requires that they (at least) appear to be accommodating popular demands. The leadership should be relatively stable, in that a high circulation of leaders is not conducive to the strong and effective hegemony needed within the segments and the trust and co-operation needed in respect of intersegmental relationships. The corollary of structural élite predominance is a citizenry that accepts the position and predominance of élites and is relatively apolitical and acquiescent. Besides these conditions relating to non-élites, there should also be at the mass level some loyalty to the national system[81] and a minimal consensus on the rules of the game.

Among the more objective favourable conditions are a multiple balance of power among the plural society's segments, a multi-party system through which each segment is represented by its own political party, and distinct lines of cleavage between the subcultures and internal political cohesion within them.[82] The country should be relatively small in size and population, since co-operation, and the governing process generally, becomes more complicated on a large scale,[83] and a perception of external threats against a small country can be conducive to internal cohesion and co-operation.[84]

The most disputed of the favourable conditions for consociationalism is that of a prior tradition of élite accommodation, which has given rise to a debate in the literature between Daalder and Lijphart.[85] This has led to two divergent approaches to consociationalism,[86] each with a different consequence for the system as a normative model. The issue is whether consociationalism is essentially a product of earlier political traditions, or whether it can be created through the deliberate efforts of leadership élites. Daalder argues that the historical tradition of compromise and co-operation is crucial for a successful consociational arrangement in the modern period; consociationalism is seen not as a response to the dangers of subcultural divisions, but as the reason why these never became disruptive. Lijphart, particularly in his early writings, stresses the voluntaristic, rational and purposive aspects of élite behaviour in establishing a consociational system: at a particular moment in history élites consciously decide to counteract the threats of political and cultural divisions through mutual accommodation based on power-sharing and compromise—the 'self-denying hypothesis', which stands in contradistinction to the theory of the plural society.[87] The difference between the two relates both to timing and causal relationships.[88] While the debate has not been satisfactorily resolved, the viewpoints need not be regarded as irreconcilable. Lijphart concedes that even in Austria, where Daalder's theory seems least applicable in view of the fact that a civil war preceded the consociational accommodation, the grand coalition was not a purely intellectual conception since the principle had been applied at the Länder level during the first republic. Nevertheless he argues that one should not shift from a voluntarist position to one of complete determinism.[89] Daalder concedes that the consociational model may be relevant for developing nations without a history of élite accommodation, provided they have at least some earlier pluralist traditions.[90] This issue affects the potential relevance of consociational democracy for South Africa. If consociationalism depends on a tradition of political accommodation and a special élite culture its implementation in societies without these features is likely to be difficult. This would be the case in South Africa, with its stark historical absence of accommodationist politics. But if consociationalism depends on intelligent choices by particular élites at a critical juncture in a divided nation's history, then it could serve as a normative model for societies such as South Africa. Any attempt to apply consociationalism prescriptively to South Africa must inevitably adopt the latter view, rather than that based on historical determinism.

(b) Unfavourable conditions

Apart from the absence of the above conditions various other factors unfavourable for consociational politics are referred to by the writers. These include a high degree of socio-economic inequality within a country, and the presence of external threats which are not perceived in the same way by the different segments. In the Third World context it is suggested that modernisation is an unfavourable condition because of the increasing socio-economic demands it generates and its tendency to break down traditional attitudes of political deference. There is ambivalence over the extent to which the structure of a society's cleavages, their quality, and the degree of politicisation they give rise to, can be unfavourable conditions.[91] While in consociational theory the absence of cross-cutting cleavages is not generally regarded as an unfavourable condition, the fact that there are cross-cutting cleavages in many of the working consociations, such as Switzerland, has led to the view that the system's success might depend on this factor. As far as the nature of the cleavages is concerned, it has been suggested that if they are based on ethnic identity they may be inauspicious for a consociational arrangement.[92] Even Lijphart concedes that the chances for consociational democracy decrease as the degree of pluralism of plural societies increases.[93]

Different constitutional arrangements can also be highly favourable or unfavourable factors. This matter is dealt with separately in the following section. Unfortunately this survey of favourable and unfavourable conditions has little predictive value since, from a methodological point of view, the conditions are 'empty'.[94] One critical analysis concludes that only two factors, and then with some qualification, have true conditional status: subcultural stability, and élite predominance over deferent followers.[95] Lijphart concedes that the conditions are neither necessary nor sufficient for consociational democracy, but suggests that in aggregated form they give some indication of its viability: the more favourable and the less unfavourable conditions there are, the more likely it is that consociationalism will succeed. But this aggregative treatment is of dubious value if the variables do not have constant values. The system's applicative potential for South Africa cannot therefore be determined from an analytical assessment of the various conditions as they pertain to this country. Lijphart nevertheless suggests that consociational engineering can be attempted 'even where the conditions for it do not appear promising at all'.[96] This attitude highlights the salience in consociational theory of an élite commitment to co-operate:

its existence can compensate for the absence of some favourable conditions, while its absence will prove fatal despite the existence of most favourable conditions.

6. THE OPTIMAL CONSTITUTIONAL FRAMEWORK

Although consociational democracy cannot be identified with any specific institutional arrangement, some constitutional frameworks are more conducive to its success than others. The system is not incompatible with presidentialism, majority or plurality electoral systems, and unitary forms of government, but a better institutional framework is provided by their 'opposites': parliamentary systems (or semi-parliamentary systems with plural executives), list systems of proportional representation, and, in the case of societies with geographically concentrated segments, federalism.[97]

The main advantage of a parliamentary system over presidentialism is that it facilitates the emergence of a coalition cabinet. It is easier for some or all of the parties represented in the legislature to be included (on a proportional basis) in a joint executive, because of the close institutional relationship between the two. Even traditional parliamentary systems have transformed their one-party majority cabinets into coalition cabinets at times of instability or crisis, despite the distortions this involves for the conventions of cabinet government. Presidentialism, on the other hand, entails the predominance of a single, usually popularly elected, leader who is at arm's length from the legislature and has greater institutional freedom in appointing his cabinet. The electoral process tends to make him representative of a particular segment, which, combined with his institutional predominance, provides a less favourable constitutional basis for the emergence of a coalition cabinet,[98] despite the fact that there may have been a measure of coalition-building to secure election. On the other hand, the more formal separation of powers associated with presidentialism has been regarded as a factor which facilitates a coalescent style of government, since élites have more institutional independence from the legislature to co-operate with one another.[99] The semi-parliamentary Swiss system provides a compromise between parliamentarism and presidentialism and what is generally regarded as a highly favourable site for élite co-operation, the federal executive council. Members of the council are elected by the federal parliament for a fixed period during which they vacate their seats in the legislature and do not remain dependent on its support for their continuance in office. The presidency rotates annually among members of the council, in order of seniority, and the president has no greater powers than other members;[100] it is a collegial executive in form and substance. The advantages of this system are that cabinet members can be elected by the legislature on a proportional basis, but once appointed the cabinet has tenure and stability, without the loss of all constitutional controls over it.[101]

As far as electoral regimes are concerned[102] a plurality system operating in single-member constituencies, with its electoral distortions and discouragement of minority parties, is the most anti-consociational of all electoral arrangements.[103] Some refinement can be provided through features such as a second ballot or alternative vote, but because these operate in single-member constituencies the system remains fundamentally majoritarian. The various systems of proportional representation, on the other hand, are designed to allocate seats to all parties in proportion to their electoral strength. In consociational terms they ensure that all segments are represented in common institutions, thereby enabling them to influence decisions according to their proportional strengths. The power of political majorities is mitigated, and minorities are not permanently excluded from office and influence. The list system of proportional representation ensures the most faithful institutional reflection of popular support and gives the greatest degree of control to party leaders. It is therefore the optimal system from the consociational point of view, although most countries using list systems have modified them to give voters a choice between candidates in a more or less effective form.[104] The list systems can operate on a national basis or in several multi-member constituencies, with the former (the 'pure form') being the more proportional of the two.[105] Two broad variations are found within the list systems as far as the calculation of the parties' seats is concerned: the d'Hondt or highest average method, and the greatest remainder method.[106] While the latter tends to favour small parties, and therefore seems preferable for consociationalism, the former is more widely practised in the consociational systems.[107] The other main system of proportional representation is based on the single transferable vote operating in multi-member constituencies. This was devised before the list systems and is more democratic from the voter's point of view because it allows a wider range of choice.[108] The main variations within the system concern the number of seats in each constituency, which has a direct bearing on the degree of proportionality it produces. While the single transferable vote system is not as favourable for consociationalism as the list system, it is designed to make every vote effective and it is more favourable than plurality systems.

Federalism is more favourable than unitarianism for consociational government because its division of power is anti-majoritarian and its multiple sites of political competition reduce the distinction between government and opposition and the competitiveness of the contest between the two.[110] To this postulate must be added the qualification that the federal constitution should give rise in practice to a decentralised system of government. Nwabueze, writing on constitutional government in Africa,[111] holds that the decentralisation of functions makes the question of central control less embittering than it would be in a unitary system. With its limited powers the central government can less easily become 'an instrument of total domination'. Federalism also facilitates the application of the segmental autonomy principle where the segments are geographically concentrated, and in this context is regarded as a consociational method.[112] However, while a federal constitution may be well suited to consociationalism, it could be an obstacle to other objectives such as socio-economic reform, national planning or welfarism, because it is not conducive to uniform development and progress.[113]

In more general terms those constitutional features that place a relatively

high load on central institutions and concentrate the sites of political competition will be less favourable than those that divide and devolve power
and increase the sites of competition.[114] The majoritarian Westminster
model scores badly in terms of all its essential constitutional principles—
parliamentary supremacy, unitarianism, single-party executive, adversarial
two-party system, and plurality elections. It is therefore understandable
that consociationalism has been raised as a justificatory theory for South
Africa's alleged move away from the Westminster system.

7. THE DISADVANTAGES OF CONSOCIATIONAL GOVERNMENT

The promotion of consociationalism as a normative system for divided
plural societies such as South Africa invites an assessment of the disadvantage of this form of government, the feasibility of its procedures and its
political acceptability temporarily aside. Generally its shortcomings derive
from the system's heavy reliance on leadership élites and the premium it
places on co-operation and compromise. Both factors have implications for
its democratic qualities, yet the interaction between consociationalism and
democracy tends to have been inadequately analysed by the consociational
writers.[115] If the democratic quality of a system depends upon the strength
of the structured opposition,[116] periodic alternations in office, or the competitiveness of the electoral system, then consociationalism is democratically deficient in that there is no opposition in the traditional sense,[117] no
alternation in office between government and opposition, and electoral
outcomes are not crucial.[118] From the consociational perspective these
criticisms display a majoritarian bias, and overlook the fact that the consociational pattern of decision-making discards the very assumptions of
majority rule. But also having implications for the democratic qualities of
consociationalism is the factor of structured élite predominance,[119] which
derives from the system's emphasis and reliance on élite co-operation and
such manipulative constitutional features as proportional representation
based on electoral lists controlled by party hierarchies. The crucial role of
élites in the co-operative process requires popular deference to leaders,
acquiescent attitudes to authority, and patron–client relationships between
leaders and followers. The danger that leaders will be regarded as apostates
because of their willingness to compromise can necessitate the suppression
of popular dissent.[120] The system of 'bargaining behind closed doors' by an
élite cartel involves restrictions on popular participation in government and
on access to information, and the possible co-optation of all experts who
might oppose élite decisions. Summit diplomacy implies the depoliticisation
of many issues as far as the electorate is concerned, and élites are in a
favourable position to keep issues off the political agenda if they imply a
threat to the status quo.[121] These features have serious consequences for
the democratic qualities of consociationalism as far as non-élites are concerned, and the notion of democracy as self-government becomes heavily
qualified in the consociational context.

The main practical disadvantage of the counter-majoritarian features of
consociationalism is that they produce slow and ineffective government.

The coalition and veto principles have the potential for completely immobilising government, thereby frustrating attempts to introduce political reforms and favouring the socio-economic status quo. There is an implied assumption that changes of policy are more costly than its continuation, which could lead to the destabilisation of the political system and the rise of private power.[122] Loss of efficiency can be anticipated from the extensive application of the proportionality principle if important appointments are made on this basis rather than on merit. Financial inefficiency can also be expected as a result of the above factors, as well as the multiplication of institutions required for the implementation of the segmental autonomy principle.

While conceding the existence of the above drawbacks, the consociational school argues that they should not be exaggerated. The short-term effectiveness of majoritarian systems, it suggests, is likely to be counterproductive if it leads to instability in the long run. Conversely the consociational model may be slow and frustrating in the short term, but more effective in the long. As far as the democratic shortcomings are concerned, they suggest that these are not so drastic when compared with the democratic prospects of a majoritarian system in a divided society, or with the real (as opposed to the theoretical) democratic qualities of the liberal Western systems.[123] They also point to Austria and the Netherlands as evidence of the relative ease with which consociationalism can be discarded in favour of a majoritarian system.

An additional drawback of the consociational model is its potential for making a plural society more plural.[124] This derives from the institutionalisation of segmental differences and the organisation of politics along segmented lines, which has the tendency of increasing segmental isolation and potential hostility, despite the 'good fences and good neighbours' hypothesis of consociational theory. Furthermore, the assumption that the cleavages in society are static can become a self-fulfilling prophecy. Barry[125] has argued that for these reasons the model should not be used outside its original areas since it might lead to increased polarisation and instability; he suggests that in the particular situations of Canada and Northern Ireland consociational practices might make matters considerably worse. In view of these drawbacks consociationalism should be treated cautiously as a prescriptive model.

8. CONSOCIATIONALISM AND THE CRITICS

While consociational theory has been described as 'among the most influential contributions to comparative politics in the last decade',[126] it remains relatively undeveloped, and its descriptive adequacy and explanatory capacity have been seriously questioned. Early critics were concerned about the type of conflict that might be regulated along consociational lines, and in his analysis Barry concludes that it is doubtful whether consociationalism could be used to accommodate divisions based on ethnic (as opposed to linguistic or religious) identity.[127] This limitation would considerably narrow the range of consociationalism as a normative model. A formal analytical assessment of Lijphart's ideas is provided by Boynton & Kwon,[128] who suggest that his argument is incomplete because accommodation does not necessarily follow from the structure called consociational democracy. They conclude that more is required to guarantee political accommodation and democratic stability in plural societies than is advocated by consociational theory. Criticisms such as these, together with the debates among the consociational writers themselves, have led to attempts to redefine consociational theory so as to enhance its validity.[129] However, in time more penetrating critiques of consociationalism have emerged.

The most comprehensive collection and synthesis of consociational critiques has been provided by Rinus van Schendelen, a Dutch sociologist, who concentrates in particular on the writings of Arend Lijphart.[130] His central concern is the scientific status of the consociational democracy theory, which he evaluates in terms of three criteria. The first relates to the way Lijphart uses and understands five crucial concepts in consociational theory: pluralism, democracy, stability, accommodation, and conditions. Van Schendelen argues that each of these is loosely formulated by Lijphart and based on implicit theoretical thinking. For example, Lijphart defines a plural society as one which is divided by segmental cleavages. But since all societies display diversity in terms of language, class, culture, religion and so on, what form of segmentation is required to constitute a plural society? More particularly, according to what criteria will a division in society be regarded as a cleavage, and a cleavage as segmental? Van Schendelen suggests that these issues are not satisfactorily dealt with by Lijphart. The second factor concerns the essential elements of the consociational model, inter alia the structure of the society, the attitudes and behaviour of the masses, élite responses, and political stability, each of which is analysed by Van Schendelen in relation to the Dutch consociational system. It is suggested that in dealing with these matters Lijphart has resorted to impressionistic methods and inductive reasoning[131] which, in the absence of rigorous empirical research, inevitably weakens his conclusions. Furthermore some writers have pointed to important political variables which have been overlooked by Lijphart as determinants of the Dutch political system: the role of the bureaucracy, the build-up of the state's welfare sector, the changing role of the state, and the international environment. The third factor is the scientific quality of the theory of consociational democracy which Van Schendelen evaluates in terms of its validity, verifiability, predictive power, applicative potential and standing in the community of scholars. Not surprisingly in the light of his preceding analysis he concludes that its scientific qualities are seriously suspect and that Lijphart's consociational thinking requires 'rigorous reconsideration'. Van Schendelen concedes that none of his critics has scientifically disproved Lijphart's entire theory of consociationalism. His main objection is that because of its methodological weaknesses, and the concern with the applicability of consociational theory rather than its validity, Lijphart's own thesis remains largely unproven.

It is understandable in the light of the recent emergence of consociational theory that the debate between its proponents and critics is relatively undeveloped. Nevertheless several competing interpretations of the consociational systems have already appeared. From the marxist perspective a fundamentally different account of political accommodation in the Netherlands is provided by Ronald Kieve.[132] He argues that the religious cleavages in the Netherlands were never so deep and intense as to require consociational arrangements to avert civil war, but they did serve to divide the working-class movement and contribute to the maintenance of the existing relations of production which was more important—as far as the interests of the bourgeoisie were concerned—than the formal consociational arrangements. Moreover the accommodationist arrangements in the Netherlands

'were themselves determined by shifts in the balance of class forces between the bourgeoisie and the proletariat. For that very reason it is not wholly surprising that these arrangements should start breaking down with the intensification of class conflict, that is, precisely during those periods of social and political unrest when they are supposed to be most effective.'[133]

This line of argument can be developed into a more generalised critique of consociational theory from a class perspective, according to which religious, linguistic and cultural cleavages are not fundamental in themselves but are manipulated in the attempt to resolve basic class antagonisms. It is doubtful, in this view, that consociationalism could resolve class conflicts to the advantage of the lower classes.[134]

Other competing interpretations of the consociational systems have been advanced in terms of theories of élite control (Dutch consociationalism is seen as an ordinary case of élitist crisis-management and pillarisation as a product of élite manipulation) and corporatism (the consociational democracies are regarded as 'extreme examples' of liberal corporatism in which political parties and leaders have only a supportive function). All the competing views 'share a disbelief in élite-prudency as the rationale of stability and democracy in plural societies',[135] and give greater emphasis than the consociational school to the struggle for power in political systems. The competing theories do not entirely discredit the prudency theory in all circumstances. But at the least they introduce reservations concerning the use of consociational democracy as a normative system and consociational theory as a legitimising ideology.

9. CONCLUSION

Despite the disputed status of consociationalism it is used in the rest of this work as a basis of analysis for South Africa's constitutional development. It has been referred to mainly as a system of government in which leadership élites play a decisive role, and while it is possible to make power-sharing an institutional requirement it is not possible to legislate for appropriate élite behaviour. As this work operates mainly at the constitutional-juridical level the focus in the remaining chapters is on the extent to which various constitutional developments promote or inhibit a consociational form of government. But the analysis must be seen in the light of the fact that consociationalism cannot be reduced to constitutional factors alone.

The possibility of a consociational option in South Africa was first raised in 1973 in the Sprocas commission report on political alternatives.[136] Since then numerous political scenarios have, expressly or implicitly, incorporated consociational arrangements in different variations and the system has been presented as a normative model for the reconciliation of what are perceived as the two polarised political demands in South Africa—from whites, political separation and continued white domination in the 'common area', and from blacks, an extension of political rights to all citizens in a unitary system of government. Most commentators who have analysed the feasibility of the consociational option in South Africa have reached a negative conclusion because many of the important conditions for its successful operation do not exist in this country, or at least there are serious obstacles to its implementation here.[137] There is no voluntary group membership in South Africa; there is no multiple balance of power among existing groups nor would there necessarily be one among future groups; there are few overlapping memberships among groups; there is no strong tradition of political moderation and co-operation; the country is fairly large in size and population; it has a high international profile; the external threats against it are not uniformly perceived by all inhabitants; and there is a high degree of socio-economic inequality. The social divisions in South Africa are very unlike the vertical divisions in the Netherlands (hence the appropriateness there of the pillarisation metaphor), which implied no hierarchical ordering and relatively little intergroup contact. In South Africa the divisions imposed by law and custom are not only based on factors of ethnicity but are horizontal, which involves a hierarchial ordering and far greater intergroup contact.[138] There is no evidence that consociationalism is suitable in such circumstances. Perhaps the most serious drawbacks to consociationalism in South Africa relate to leadership élites and the restrictions imposed on them. There is a situation of leadership vacuums, non-representative leaders, and externally based élites, none of which has existed to the same degree in the empirical consociations. Even in respect of the leadership élites who are participating in the political process, there does not exist a common commitment to maintaining the integrity of the system and to observing the rules of the consociational game—in short, consociationalism is not accepted as a fundamental norm. A recent study concludes slightly less negatively, albeit somewhat ambiguously, on the prospects of consociationalism for South Africa. The work of Hanf, Weiland & Vierdag[139] examines the objective and perceived factors of conflict in South Africa, in the light of which they conclude that there is no possibility of peacefully creating a unitary state in which there is a full democratic franchise. But as an alternative to unitarianism, on the one hand, and partition, on the other, they find that 'some form of consociational democracy need not be completely excluded'[140] for the resolution of the conflicts in South Africa. As far as the conditions for successful consociationalism are concerned, this study is also more optimistic, though at times, it would seem, unduly so.[141] Thus on the basic structural conditions of consociationalism it concludes:

'. . . we may say that the basic conditions of the group structure in South Africa and the country's international profile are not unfavourable to the emergence of a consociational democracy. While the existing political culture clearly militates against it, the possibility exists that change may occur because serious conflict is recognised to be imminent.'[142]

Of the conditions pertaining to political leadership, they find that the most important are fulfilled, namely the existence of strong and representative leaders, but they refer to the prevailing attitude of the white power-élite as the destructive factor at this level.[143] As far as the conditions pertaining to the population as a whole are concerned, they conclude that these are in part favourable and in part unfavourable, but that the latter could be overcome through incisive changes in economic relations.[144] It is thus primarily a change in attitude by white leaders within the short or medium term that would be needed to ensure the emergence of a system of consociational democracy. But because of the absence of a real threat to white political power during this period, the authors are of the view that the present system of 'unilateral conflict regulation' is as possible, for the foreseeable future, as peaceful change:

> 'Our conjecture about the immediate future is therefore that the white power-élite will not opt for consociation, but for a sham consociation; that is, for a perpetuation of unilateral conflict regulation in forms which only resemble those of a consociational democracy.'[145]

They also suggest that a transition from sham consociation to genuine consociation is possible, but not likely under prevailing circumstances. In subsequent chapters attention is given to the government's 'sham consociation' for whites, coloureds and Indians.

NOTES AND REFERENCES

[1] The word 'consociate' derives from the Latin *consociare*: to associate together, join in fellowship. The term was used by Johannes Althusius (1563–1638) in his work *Politica Methodice Digesta* (1603). Its first modern exponent was David Apter (*The Political Kingdom in Uganda: A Study in Bureaucratic Nationalism* (1961) who (at 24f) defined consociation as a 'Joining together of constituent units which do not lose their identity when merging in some form of union'. He described it as a system of compromise and accommodation, but subject to immobilism because of the need to find agreement on common action. The first writer to use and apply the term systematically was Arend Lijphart, beginning with his articles 'Typologies of Democratic Systems' 1968 *Comparative Political Studies* 3–44 and 'Consociational Democracy' 1969 *World Politics* 207–25. G Lehmbruch (*Proporzdemokratie: Politische System und politische Kultur in der Schweiz und in Oesterreich* (1967) developed the concept independently of Lijphart. Other terms used are *accommodation, contractarianism, amicable agreement* and *konkordanzdemokratie*. In this work the terms 'consociationalism' and 'consociation' are used interchangeably.

[2] K McRae (ed) *Consociational Democracy: Political Accommodation in Segmented Societies* (1974) 5–13.

[3] As exemplified by V Lorwin 'Segmented Pluralism—Ideological Cleavages and Political Cohesion in the Smaller European Democracies' 1971 *Comparative Politics* 141–75 (included in McRae op cit 33–69).

[4] As exemplified, inter alia, by Lijphart in his works referred to below.

[5] The approach adopted by H Daalder in the works cited below.

[6] *The Politics of Accommodation* (1968); the second edition of this work was published in 1975, and a third edition in Dutch, which viewed Dutch consociationalism as a historical phenomenon, only in 1979. For an excellent review of Lijphart's writings, see R van Schendelen 'The Theory of Consociational Democracy: The views of Arend Lijphart and collected criticisms' to be published in 1984 *Acta Politica*.

[7] There were two Calvinist parties.

[8] The most significant is *Democracy in Plural Societies—A Comparative Exploration* (1977); all Lijphart references in this chapter relate to this work, unless otherwise indicated.

[9] Lijphart 1.

[10] Cf Lijphart 'Consociation: The Model and its Application in Divided Societies' 3 (paper presented at the Study Conference on models of Political Co-operation, Queen's University, Belfast, 25–28 March 1981).

[11] However, as A Aunger shows in respect of New Brunswick, all four characteristics can be identified in some systems at the subnational level: *In Search of Political Stability: A Comparative Study of New Brunswick and Northern Ireland* (1981).

[12] On this characteristic see Lijphart 25–36; E Nordlinger *Conflict Regulation in Divided Societies* (1972) 21f.

[13] But cf B Barry 'The Consociational Model and its Dangers' 1975 *European Journal of Political Research* 393 at 405f, who argues that the grand coalition is only an epiphenomenon and that the political willingness to maintain stability is the more important factor.

[14] But cf Aunger (op cit) to the effect that the Westminster system's one-party cabinets are not incompatible with a grand coalition, provided the segments are represented in both major parties.

[15] The grand coalition principle contradicts the theory that in zero-sum conditions coalitions tend toward the minimal winning size. See W Riker *The Theory of Political Coalitions* (1962) 28–32.

[16] A Lewis (*Politics in West Africa* (1965) 68) advocated coalition government by all major parties in preference to the one party systems which emerged in the early years of African independence; in addition he favoured proportional representation in all branches of government, and federalism or a provincial devolution of power.

[17] This so-called 'magic formula' results in two socialists, two Catholics, two liberal-radicals, and one peasants' party representative being elected, by convention, to the federal executive. These numbers have fluctuated according to the respective strengths of the parties and the present quota is of comparatively recent origin. The linguistic segments are also catered for within this formula. See C Hughes *The Federal Constitution of Switzerland* (1954) 108f, and *The Parliament of Switzerland* (1962) 69–83.

[18] Lijphart refers to examples in Belgium, the Netherlands, Austria and Czechoslovakia, but they are also encountered in non-consociational systems such as France.

[19] See D Butler (ed) *Coalitions in British Politics* (1978) 113f; and above 9–10.

[20] Nordlinger op cit 21–2.

[21] See A Rabushka & K Shepsle *Politics in Plural Societies* (1972) 83: '. . . ambitious politicians not included in the multi-ethnic coalition have incentives to generate demand for communal rather than national issues . . . [they] seek to increase the salience of communal issues and then to outbid the ambiguous multi-ethnic coalition'.

[22] Lijphart 36–8; Nordlinger op cit 24–6; R Dahl *Political Oppositions in Western Democracies* (1965) 358.

[23] See D Rae 'The Limits of Consensual Decision-Making' 1975 *American Political Science Review* 1270–94. Rae argues that consensus should not even be a normative criterion, despite its deep liberal roots. The idea that negotiation should continue until a solution acceptable to all participants is found corresponds partly with the *palaver* tradition among some African tribes. See B O Nwabueze *Constitutionalism in the Emergent States* (1973) 168f; W D Hammond-Tooke *Command or Consensus* (1975) 4–75.

[24] J Calhoun *A Disquisition on Government* (American Heritage Series edited by C Gordon Post (1953) 20–31). Calhoun contrasted the numerical or absolute majority with a concurrent or constitutional majority. Writing before the American Civil War he had some support from J Madison *The Federalist Papers* No 10. See further D M Potter *The South and the Concurrent Majority* (1972) for ways in which the South was able to maintain a position of power in the national government through this device, and to prevent, inter alia, the advancement of civil rights.

[25] The failure of the Cypriot consociational constitution has been attributed in part to the over-use of the veto, which was available as a constitutional right.

[26] As Rae (op cit 1280) points out, a majoritarian decision minimises the maximum number of voters who can be dissatisfied with an outcome.

[27] Ibid.

[28] See Lijphart 38–41; Nordlinger op cit 22–4; Dahl op cit 358; J Steiner 'The Principles of Majority and Proportionality' 1971 *British Journal of Political Science* 63–70. The arguments of G Lehmbruch in *Proporzdemokratie* (1967) are summarised and developed in 'A Non-Competitive Pattern of Conflict Management in Liberal Democracies: The Case of Switzerland, Austria and Lebanon' in McRae op cit 90–7.

[29] Steiner op cit 63.

[30] Nordlinger op cit 23. This is facilitated by the fact that the proportional model postpones decisions to the highest level of government where it is easier to effect compromises, though this incurs costs in respect of the concentration of power and administrative secrecy.

[31] e g, there is parity of representation in the Belgian cabinet for French- and Dutch-speaking members, although the latter constitute an overall majority of the population.

[32] For example the United States and Australian senates.

[33] A Lijphart 'Consociation: The Model and its Application in Divided Societies' (op cit) 4.

[34] There are numerous examples of proportionality in practice at different levels of government, some of which are referred to subsequently. To cite a single example: in Belgium political decisions on matters such as industrial development, education and public works projects are taken on a 'proportional' basis. See Nordlinger op cit 24; Steiner op cit 64.

[35] Steiner op cit 63.

[36] Ibid; cf Lijphart 39.

[37] Steiner op cit 63.

[38] See J Steiner 'The Consociational Theory and Beyond' 1981 *Comparative Politics* 339; cf Lijphart's response to these suggestions in the same volume at 355.

[39] Lijphart 41–4; Dahl op cit 358. Nordlinger does not refer to segmental autonomy as a conflict-regulating device, and specifically excludes federalism, with which it is closely related (op cit 31–3).

[40] This feature has been characterised as 'a kind of dissolution of the modern territorial state into a quasi-feudal system'. See G Lehmbruch 'Consociational Democracy in the International System' 1975 *European Journal of Political Research* 377 at 379.

[41] See the references to Renner's work in T Hanf, H Weiland & G Vierdag *South Africa—The Prospects of Peaceful Change* (1981) 385.

[42] The territorial concentration of segments could be conducive to partition or secession which are possible outcomes in divided societies but are, by their nature, alternatives to consociationalism.

[43] See on this section two papers given by Arend Lijphart, viz 'Federal, Confederal and Consociational Alternatives for the South African Plural Society: Theoretical and Comparative Aspects' and 'Consociation and Federation: Conceptual and Empirical Links'. These papers have been included in amended form in, respectively, R Rotberg & J Barratt (eds) *Conflict and Compromise in South Africa* (1980) 51–75, and 1979 *Canadian Journal of Political Science* 499–515. All references to Lijphart in this section are to these two papers, the second being an elaboration of the first. Some of his views have been developed and applied to South Africa in L J Boulle 'Federation and Consociation—Conceptual Links and Current Constitutional Models' 1981 *THRHR* 236.

[44] See e g, U Hicks *Federalism: Failure and Success—A Comparative Study* (1978) 3–19.

[45] See I Duchacek *Comparative Federalism: The Territorial Dimension of Politics* (1970) 192; G Sawer *Modern Federalism* (2 ed, 1976) 1.

[46] D Elazar ('Federalism' in Greenstein & Polsky *Handbook of Political Science* vol 5 101) finds it more appropriate to describe this feature as one of 'non-centralisation'; in practice, however, federalism and decentralisation tend to go together.

[47] Cf Carnell 'Political Implications of Federalism in New States' in Hicks op cit 23f; V Lorwin 'Segmented Pluralism' 1971 *Comparative Politics* 141.

[48] S M Lipset *Political Man* (1959) 61. Lipset's argument is that federalism increases the opportunity for multiple sources of cleavage by adding regional interests to the others which crosscut the social structure; this additional source of crosscutting cleavages is lost when federalism divides a country along the lines of its basic cleavages.

[49] Nordlinger (op cit 31) does not include federalism in his list of conflict-regulating devices, but for a different reason, viz that he regards it as a substantive outcome of the other conflict-regulating practices. See also D Horowitz 'Quebec and the Canadian Political Crisis' 1977 *American Academy of Political and Social Science Annals* 19.

[50] E McWhinney (*Federal Constitution-Making for a Multi-National World* (1966) 41) argues that the successful examples of multiracial societies are those where the different ethnic-cultural communities are conveniently located in territorially distinct units of the country (i e 'horizontal federalism'). He adds that where these groups are not dispersed in this way, the constitutional draftsmen must look beyond the 'classic' federal ideal-types.

[51] C J Friedrich *Trends of Federation in Theory and Practice* (1962) 124. For Friedrich the main advantage of 'corporate federalism' is that it does away with the problem of 'territorial districting'—'The Politics of Language and Corporate Federalism' in J G Savard & R Vigneault (eds) *Multilingual Political Systems, Problems and Solutions* (1976) 233.

[52] Sawer (op cit 15–16) observes that after the creation of the US constitution there was a 70 year dispute as to whether the system was predominantly national or confederal. Those emphasising the latter spoke of the 'concurrent majority' required in congress,

which would have given each region or group of regions a veto power, and the theory of nullification envisaged a reserve power for each region to disregard major decisions affecting their interests. Since 1865 primacy has been given to the national assumptions of the system. The doctrine of the concurrent majority is associated with Calhoun (op cit) who is referred to by several of the consociational writers.

[53] Consociationalism, on the other hand, can also operate undemocratically, as where non-elected leaders are drawn into the process of government on a limited scale.

[54] This is not restricted to theory—e g S Noel ('Consociational Democracy and Canadian Federalism' 1971 *Canadian Journal of Political Science* 14–16) shows that in Canada élite accommodation along consociational lines has taken place in the institutions which are central to the maintenance of the federal system: the federal cabinet, federal boards and councils, and interprovincial conferences.

[55] See M Heisler 'Managing Ethnic Conflict in Belgium' 1977 *American Academy of Political and Social Science Annals* 33 at 38.

[56] Op cit 42.

[57] See above, 11 and the references cited there.

[58] K D McRae 'Comment: Federation, Consociation, Corporatism—An Addendum to Arend Lijphart' 1979 *Canadian Journal of Political Science* 517

[59] G Lehmbruch 'Consociational Democracy, Class Conflict and the New Corporatism' in P Schmitter & G Lehmbruch (eds) *Trends Towards Corporatist Intermediation* (1979) 53 at 58.

[60] Cf Van Schendelen op cit.

[61] K McRae *Consociational Democracy* (1974) 13. A less notable European case is Luxemburg.

[62] See Lijphart 'Majority rule versus democracy in deeply divided societies' 1977 *Politikon* 113 at 119.

[63] On Colombia see R H Dix 'Consociational Democracy—The Case of Colombia' 1980 *Comparative Politics* 303.

[64] Writing in 1973 R Presthus (*Elite Accommodation in Canadian Politics*) found that Canada met most of the functional requisites of consociational politics and that consociationalism was a useful theory in explaining the Canadian political system. He demonstrated how accommodation occurred not only *within* the formal political structure but also *between* government and private political élites; see also Noel op cit. This analysis is not necessarily applicable to contemporary Canadian politics. On the Israel case see Lijphart 129–34.

[65] David Apter *The Political Kingdom in Uganda* (1961).

[66] Lijphart 161–64.

[67] On the Zimbabwe constitution see below, 118–23.

[68] D E Bohn 'Consociational Democracy and the Case of Switzerland' 1980 *The Journal of Politics* 165.

[69] See e g B Barry's important review article of J Steiner's *Amicable Agreement versus Majority Rule: Conflict Resolution in Switzerland* (1974) in 1975 *British Journal of Political Science* 477.

[70] For descriptions of direct democracy in Switzerland see Steiner op cit 18ff and M Mowlam 'Popular Access to the Decision-making Process in Switzerland' 1979 *Government and Opposition* 180.

[71] But cf Mowlam (ibid), who concludes that although many groups have access to the agenda-setting phase of decision-making, élites have the power and resources to turn outcomes against them if the élites so wish.

[72] See G Lehmbruch 'Consociational Democracy in the International System' 1975 *European Journal of Political Research* 377 at 378.

[73] E Nordlinger *Conflict Regulation in Divided Societies* (1972) 117.

[74] J Steiner 'The Consociational Theory and Beyond' 1981 *Comparative Politics* 339 at 455ff.

[75] In the second edition of *The Politics of Accommodation* (1975) he added a further chapter (196–219) in which he adduced reasons for the retreat from consociationalism in the Netherlands and attempted to explain why Dutch politics became less stable when social cleavages began losing their sharpness and political salience.

[76] For a recent rebuttal of the arguments based on the 'failed consociations' see Lijphart 'Consociation: The Model and its Applications in Divided Societies' (op cit) 6–8.

[77] e g the system of proportionality was not made flexible so as to accommodate demographic changes.

70   *South Africa and the Consociational Option*

[78] McWhinney (op cit 76–80) is complimentary of the 'professorial' Cyprus constitution and suggests that its influence in the exacerbation of communal strife was at the most peripheral.

[79] As is pointed out later a dual balance of power is in any case not conducive to successful consociationalism.

[80] See Lijphart 53–103; Nordlinger op cit 42–116; McRae op cit 8–10; V Lorwin 'Segmented Pluralism' 1971 *Comparative Politics* 141; Lehmbruch op cit 377–91; J Steiner *Amicable Agreement Versus Majority Rule* (1974) 269.

[81] Nationalism has not, however, been a prominent feature of the European consociations.

[82] This entails at least three segments and approximate equilibrium among them, so that no compact majority exists and each individual segment is in an overall minority; in this situation working majorities can only be acquired through compromises. See Steiner op cit 253f.

[83] But cf H Daalder 'On Building Consociational Nations: The Cases of Netherlands and Switzerland' 1971 *International Social Science Journal* 355.

[84] This presupposes that the threats are similarly perceived by all groups. Small group research shows solidarity increases within a group under external pressure, and the same applies to states. During World War II Britain deviated from the majority model in setting up an all-party government.

[85] See H Daalder 'On Building Consociational Nations (op cit), 'The Consociational Democracy Theme' 1974 *World Politics* 604 and 'The Netherlands: Opposition in a Segmented Society' in R Dahl *Political Oppositions in Western Democracies* (1965) 188; and A Lijphart 'Cultural Diversity and Political Integration' 1971 *Canadian Journal of Political Science* 1 and 'Majority Rule versus Democracy in Deeply Divided Societies' 1977 *Politikon* 113.

[86] That is, the second and third approaches, referred to at 45 above.

[87] The divergence is revealed by the different conceptions of the Dutch *pacificatie* in 1917; Lijphart describes it as the response to the perils of subcultural divisions, while Daalder emphasises the prior accommodation arrangements and describes *pacificatie* as the prelude (not response) to the development of subcultural interest organisations.

[88] McRae op cit 12.

[89] Lehmbruch (op cit 381–1) suggests that if past violence is perceived as traumatic by all subcultures, it may be an inducement to more peaceful means of conflict accommodation in the future.

[90] Lehmbruch (op cit 379ff) distinguishes between 'genetic' and 'sustaining' conditions of consociational democracy, and suggests that having chosen a consociational strategy under specific genetic conditions, élites may internalise these strategies as norms (in terms of learning theory) thus establishing a routine pattern of conflict regulation which outlives the genetic conditions. The bargaining results will have to be perceived as satisfactory by all groups for this development to occur.

[91] See H Daalder 'The Consociational Democracy Theme' (op cit) 616ff; B Barry 'Political Accommodation and Consociational Democracy' 1975 *British Journal of Political Science* 478 at 488.

[92] See, for example, E Aunger's work *In Search of Political Stability: A Comparative Study of New Brunswick and Northern Ireland* (1981).

[93] A Lijphart 'Majority Rule Versus Democracy' (op cit) at 120.

[94] Van Schendelen op cit.

[95] A Pappalardo 'The Conditions for Consociational democracy; a logical and empirical critique' 1981 *European Journal of Political Research* 365.

[96] Op cit 124.

[97] Lijphart 224.

[98] Lijphart (33) cites as an exception the Columbian arrangement where the presidency alternated between the two main parties; here presidential predominance was modified by proportionality in the temporal dimension. See also R H Dix 'Consociational Democracy—the Case of Columbia' 1980 *Comparative Politics* 303. Alternatively, there could be a power-sharing executive comprising the president and other top office-holders (deputy-president, prime minister, etc) as has been the case in Lebanon.

[99] Cf Dahl op cit 351; the same can be said for the semi-separation of powers in the Netherlands. For a contrary view see C J Friedrich *Trends of Federalism in Theory and Practice* (1968) 29.

[100] His status is that of primus inter pares, as was formerly the case with the Prime Minister in a Westminster system.

[101] Such as 'interpellation'; see art 22 of the Swiss constitution and C Hughes *The Federal Constitution of Switzerland* (1954) 150 and 160.

[102] On comparative electoral systems see E Lakeman *How Democracies Vote—A Study of Majority and Proportional Electoral Systems* (3 ed, 1970); W J M Mackenzie *Free Elections* (1958).

[103] Plurality elections are not necessarily undesirable at the segmental level, since it is primarily intersegmental relationships which are regulated on a proportional basis.

[104] Lakeman op cit 98–103. At 80–9 he describes various semi-proportional systems, but these are numerically insignificant.

[105] This is used in Israel (see E Likhovski *Israel's Parliament—The Law of the Knesset* (1971) 63ff). In the Netherlands the country is regarded as a single unit for the allocation of seats. The national list system was used in the internal Namibian elections in 1978, and effectively in the 1979 and 1980 pre-independence elections in Zimbabwe. It is interesting that Lijphart (*The Politics of Accommodation* (2 ed, 1975) 214) attributes the breakdown of the Dutch politics of accommodation partially to its countrywide system of proportional representation.

[106] Mackenzie op cit 78–80.

[107] Such as Belgium and the Netherlands; other countries include the Federal Republic of Germany, Italy and Luxemburg (with a small variation). See G Hand, J Georgel & C Sasse (eds) *European Electoral Systems Handbook* (1979). In Switzerland the list system is used but the provision for *panachage* allows voters to choose candidates on opposing lists.

[108] It was developed in England in the 1850s by Hare and was promoted by J S Mill *Representative Government* (edited by H B Acton, 1972) at 263ff but denigrated by Walter Bagehot *The English Constitution* (The World's Classics ed, 1974) 132–40. It came to be used in English-speaking countries other than Britain—Northern Ireland, Canada, Australia and most consistently in the Republic of Ireland (see Hand, Georgel & Sasse op cit 121–39). For a contemporary critique see G Doron 'Is the Hare Voting Scheme Representative?' 1979 *The Journal of Politics* 918.

[109] The greater the number of seats per constituency, the more proportional the electoral outcome.

[110] See Dahl op cit 351.

[111] B O Nwabueze *Constitutionalism in the Emergent States* (1973) 112.

[112] See above, 51–4.

[113] See I Duchacek *Comparative Federalism—The Territorial Dimension of Politics* (1970) 120.

[114] There may seem a contradiction between the emphasis on (conspiratorial) élite accommodation in the consociational model, and the desirability of a division and devolution of power. The aim of the latter features, however, is primarily to ensure that no single élite group attains a hegemonial position which could result in a zero-sum political process, and not necessarily to encourage non-élite political participation which might remain low even in a devolved political structure. Cf J Steiner *Amicable Agreement Versus Majority Rule* (1974) 259ff.

[115] Cf H Daalder 'The Consociational Democracy Theme' 1974 *World Politics* 604 at 617.

[116] But cf Dahl's (op cit 387–401) epilogue on the desirability of structured opposition in a democratic system. He suggests that the 'government-versus-opposition' notion is an idealised concept and a deviant phenomenon in Western democracies which show no single prevailing pattern of opposition (op cit 332). Cf O Kirchheimer's earlier 'The Waning of Opposition in Parliamentary Regimes' 1957 *Social Research* 127.

[117] However, there could still be a majority government confronted by an opposition in a consociational system, provided each group is a coalition and not constituted along the lines of the major cleavage. E Aunger, in *In Search of Political Stability: A Comparative Study of New Brunswick and Northern Ireland* (1981), shows how the grand coalition principle can be incorporated in a one-party cabinet.

[118] Consociationalism puts a premium on the non-circulation of leaders.

[119] Cf C B Macpherson's description of the 'pluralist élitist equilibrium model' of democracy in *The Life and Times of Liberal Democracy* (1977) 77–82.

[120] See C Young *The Politics of Cultural Pluralism* (1976) 83; I Lustik 'Stability in Deeply Divided Societies: Consociationalism versus Control' 1979 *World Politics* 325 at 334; cf Nordlinger's (op cit 74–8) argument for élite predominance.

[121] Cf S Lukes *Power: A Radical View* (1974) 16–20.

[122] See D Rae 'The Limits of Consensual Decision-Making' 1975 *American Political Science Review* 1270 at 1280; also M Heisler 'Managing Ethnic Conflict in Belgium' 1977 *American Academy of Political and Social Science Annals* 33 at 38.

72 South Africa and the Consociational Option

[123] Lijphart gives specific attention to the *quality* of Dutch democracy during the period of accommodation in *The Politics of Accommodation* (2 ed 1975) 177–80; cf Macpherson (op cit) 82–92.

[124] Cf V Lorwin 'Segmented Pluralism' 1971 *Comparative Politics* 141 at 158.

[125] B Barry 'The Consociational Model and its Dangers' 1975 *European Journal of Political Research* 393.

[126] G B Powell 'Review of Arend Lijphart: Democracy in Plural Societies' 1979 *American Political Science Review* 295.

[127] B Barry 'Political Accommodation and Consociational Democracy' 1975 *British Journal of Political Science* 471.

[128] G R Boynton & W Kwon 'An Analysis of Consociational Democracy' 1978 *Legislative Studies Quarterly* 11.

[129] e g J Steiner 'The Consociational Theory and Beyond' 1981 *Comparative Politics* 339.

[130] R van Schendelen 'The Theory of Consociational Democracy: The views of Arend Lijphart and collected criticisms' to be published in 1984 *Acta Politica*.

[131] See the references in Van Schendelen op cit. See also A J Venter 'n Kritiese Ontleding van die Konsosiasiemodel van Arend Lijphart (unpublished MA thesis, University of South Africa, 1980) 101–3.

[132] R A Kieve 'Pillars of Sand: A Marxist Critique of Consociational Democracy in the Netherlands' 1981 *Comparative Politics* 313.

[133] Ibid 332.

[134] See L Graziano 'The Historic Compromise and Consociational Democracy' 1980 *International Political Science Review* 345.

[135] Van Schendelen op cit.

[136] Sprocas Report No 10 *South Africa's Political Alternatives* (1973) 163–6.

[137] e g L Schlemmer 'The Devolution of Power in South Africa: Problems and Prospects', paper presented at the conference on Intergroup Accommodation in Plural Societies, Cape Town, 1977, and 'Social Implications of Constitutional Alternatives in South Africa' in J A Benyon (ed) *Constitutional Change in South Africa* (1978) 266; H Adam & H Giliomee *The Rise and Crisis of Afrikaner Power* (1979) 288ff; Royal Institute of International Affairs *A Survey of Proposals for the Constitutional Development of South Africa* (1980).

[138] See L Thompson & A Prior *South African Politics* (1982) 107f.

[139] T Hanf, H Weiland & G Vierdag *South Africa—The Prospects of Peaceful Change* (1981), originally published as *Südafrika, friedlicher Wandel?*

[140] At 381.

[141] e g at 389 the authors suggest that 'if South Africa were to adopt an acceptable form of conflict regulation it would achieve a low profile in international politics'. It is not self-evident, however, that consociationalism would be regarded internationally as an *acceptable* arrangement, and it would probably not be if it excluded external black leaders; the work seems to underestimate the degree to which political issues in South Africa have become internationalised.

[142] At 391.

[143] At 393.

[144] At 394.

[145] At 412.

4 South Africa's Constitutional Background

1. INTRODUCTION

This chapter comprises an historical overview of the main constitutional developments in South Africa during the seven decades since Union.[1]* Its purpose is to provide the background against which the current phase of constitutional developments is taking place; these developments are dealt with in subsequent chapters although some aspects are referred to briefly in this chapter. Two different sorts of constitutional development can be identified within the period referred to. The first concerns the evolution in South Africa's constitutional status from colonial and dominion subordinacy to republican independence, a transition of only indirect relevance to this work.[2] The second concerns the internal changes in constitutional structures and processes; here, despite various inconsistent and contradictory developments, there are several clearly discernible constitutional trends, and in many respects the government's constitution of 1983 involves their continuation and, in institutional terms, their culmination.

The latter developments have been well documented in the literature.[3] They are dealt with here in terms of their affinity or otherwise to the Westminster constitutional system, an approach that provides some clarity to one aspect of the current constitutional debate. Ever since the Theron report[4] focused on the assumed 'Westminster nature' of the South African constitution it has become politically and intellectually fashionable to describe present constitutional developments as a movement away from the Westminster system to an arrangement better suited to South Africa's plural society. More recently consociational concepts have been introduced in the promotion of various constitutional alternatives to South Africa's 'Westminster system'. The analysis in this chapter shows that these suppositions are faulty in that South Africa's imported version of the Westminster model deviates in fundamental respects from the original. This approach also illustrates the extent to which the majoritarianism that is closely associated with the Westminster model has influenced the South African constitutional system. The extent of the Westminster influence gives an indication of the system's variance with the principles of consociationalism, though clearly the non-Westminster constitutional features are not necessary consociational in nature. It will appear subsequently that while consociational concepts have been invoked to justify the new constitution it perpetuates many of the Westminster and the non-consociational features of the past.

2. WESTMINSTER FEATURES OF THE SOUTH AFRICAN CONSTITUTION[5]

(a) Parliamentary supremacy

The drafters of the Union constitution had several constitutional traditions from which to draw[6] and opted for the British notion of parliamentary supremacy, of which the Cape, Natal and to a lesser extent the Transvaal Republic had experience, in preference to the Orange Free State precedent of a rigid constitution with guaranteed rights and judicial review.[7] This Westminster principle was to be the most important feature of the constitutional order and was to have far-reaching political consequences.

Until the passing of the Statute of Westminster in 1931[8] the legislative capacity of the Union Parliament was qualified by the subordinate constitutional status of the country. The British Parliament retained legislative supremacy over the Union, including the right to amend its constitution; the Colonial Laws Validity Act of 1865[9] precluded the Union Parliament from legislating repugnantly to an Act of the British Parliament extending to the country; and there was a territorial limitation on the Union's powers, though its extent was not clear.[10] The Union's position of subordinacy involved other derogations of sovereignty: the Governor-General, a British Government appointee, could reserve Bills for the Crown's consideration, and the Crown retained a power of disallowance.[11]

The Union's constitutional subordinacy was not, however, reflected in political practice and the prevailing conventions regulating British–dominion relationships led to a gradual increase in the political independence of the dominions. It was nevertheless considered necessary to remove the legal limitations on the dominions' legislative competence, and this was effected by the Statute of Westminster, whose main significance was that it gave juridical force to prevailing practice. The statute (i) provided that no Act of the British Parliament should apply to a dominion unless requested by the latter; (ii) repealed the Colonial Laws Validity Act, provided that no future legislation of a dominion would be void for its repugnance to the law of England or any existing or future British Act, and empowered the dominions to repeal or amend British statutes; and (iii) empowered the dominion parliaments to legislate with extra-territorial effect.[12] To avoid problems that may have arisen from the repeal of this British statute, the Union Parliament incorporated the relevant provisions into South African municipal law in the Status of the Union Act, which described the Union Parliament for the first time as having 'sovereign legislative power in and over the Union'.[13] This Act also ended the legislative limitations implicit in reservation and disallowance.[14]

A remaining limitation on the Union Parliament's competence was the procedural requirement contained in the entrenched sections,[15] although the prevailing view before the constitutional crisis of the 1950s was that the entrenching procedure was ineffective.[16] The crisis was to have an ironic outcome: it confirmed the juridical efficacy of the entrenching procedure,[17] but illustrated how easily it could be subverted by the principle of parliamentary supremacy. The principle was reinforced in 1956 in the wake of the crisis through a constitutional amendment that precluded the courts from invalidating legislation other than that affecting the entrenched sections.[18] In so far as parliamentary supremacy denotes the absence of legislative rivals to Parliament and a judicial testing-right over legislation, the Union Parliament was legally supreme subsequent to the passage of the Statute of Westminster and the constitutional crisis. From a juridical point of view, however, sovereignty was divided between Parliament as constituted under s 63 and under the proviso to s 152 of the South Africa Act.[19] In terms of the 'new view' of parliamentary supremacy, which came to prevail in South Africa,[20] the legislature had to comply with the provisions of the constitution which for the time being regulated its composition in order to render its enactments effective. When the Union became a republic in 1961[21] the principle of legislative supremacy was assigned to a new legislature, differently composed.[22] The republican Parliament was again described as having 'sovereign legislative authority' in and over the Republic,[23] and the provision first adopted in 1956 was retained[24] to ensure that the courts could review only legislation relating to the entrenched clauses.[25] It remains necessary for the constituent parts of Parliament to function as constitutionally prescribed,[26] in accordance with the 'new view' of supremacy.[27]

The principle of parliamentary supremacy requires in South Africa, as in the Westminster system, that there are no geographical or functional areas from which parliamentary authority is legally barred and, since Parliament operates on a majoritarian basis, from which the parliamentary majority is precluded from intervening. As applied in South Africa the principle has three important corollaries. The first is the legal dependence of the judiciary on the legislature, and the absence of any substantive legislative testing-rights for the courts.[28] The second is the unitary, as opposed to federal, nature of the constitutional system, despite the 'federal characteristics' which commentators have been wont to identify in the constitutions of the Union and the Republic.[29] The 'federal' division of competence implicit in the provincial system was always susceptible to unilateral transformation by the central parliament and never gave rise to a federal system of government in practice. Thirdly, the constitution is highly flexible, save for the remaining entrenched clauses.[30] These features testify to the relative absence of institutional restraints in South Africa on the power of electoral majorities. The party controlling Parliament has been able to enact far-reaching constitutional changes while leaving intact the fundamental principle of parliamentary supremacy. There have been amendments affecting the franchise, the composition of the constituent parts of Parliament, the status and powers of the provincial governments, and the control and operation of political parties. There have been major innovations in the form of separate, subordinate authorities for coloureds and Indians, and a system of territorial decentralisation leading to the self-government and partition of the homelands. Recently Parliament has had the legal competence to prolong its own life, abolish one of its component parts, amend the entrenching procedure, limit its geographical jurisdiction, and enact a constitutional amendment having retrospective effect for twenty years.[31] Finally, it has been possible to enact such pervasive features of the living constitution as the Population Registration Act [32] and the Group Areas Act,[33] which will remain indispensable features of the government's new constitution. Even though the *de jure* institution of parliamentary supremacy has developed into a form of *de facto* executive supremacy[34] the principle has maintained a focal significance in the constitutional system.

(b) Parliamentary government

Having preferred the Westminster notion of parliamentary supremacy to that of a legislature limited by the constitution, it was not surprising that the delegates at the National Convention should have opted for a parliamentary executive as well.[35] The principle of the parliamentary executive had been introduced in the Cape in 1872 and involved the transfer of the executive function from the imperial government to a committee that enjoyed the support of the locally elected lower house. In this context the term 'responsible government' was used to denote the responsibility of the colonial government to the colony's inhabitants and not the metropolitan power. In endorsing the cabinet system for the Union the drafters gave little consideration to the alternative executive systems of the United States or the Boer republics.[36] The South Africa Act, however, provided only a 'fragmentary statutory basis for responsible government',[37] namely the requirement that no minister could hold office for more than three months unless he was or became a member of either House of Parliament.[38] The implications of this system of government were not spelled out but had to be sought in the conventions of the English constitution, which was the main source of South African constitutional law. Some conventions were enacted[39] and others came to be incorporated by reference,[40] but a third group was not specifically referred to in the Union constitution. The Governor-General's duty to act on the advice of the executive council, an essential feature of parliamentary government, was statutorily prescribed[41] to prevent difficulties arising from the Westminster-derived diffusion of executive power between the heads of state and government. The conventions of joint and individual ministerial responsibility came to be observed 'within elastic limits'[42] to give further support to the system.

The Republican constitution also provided a fragmentary basis for responsible government by requiring ministers to be members of the Senate or House of Assembly within three months of assuming office. In 1980 the period of grace was extended to twelve months,[43] and with the abolition of the Senate that year ministers were compelled to be elected or nominated members of the House of Assembly only. The State President's duty to act on the advice of the executive council was statutorily prescribed,[44] as were some other conventions, while the remainder were given statutory recognition without being enacted.[45] The most important among the last group is the State President's duty to appoint the leader of the majority party in the House as Prime Minister, and the other ministers on the latter's advice. However, the constitutional conventions associated with the Westminster system, in particular the principles of joint and individual ministerial responsibility, have never assumed great significance in South Africa. According to the theory of parliamentary government the executive is responsible to the people through the mediation of the legislature, and the efficacy of the system depends materially on the representative nature of the latter. The fact that the South African Parliament is largely unrepresentative has caused inevitable distortions in this theory, and the convention of ministerial responsibility has undergone substantial modification in scope and significance in the light of political events of the late 1970s.[46] The conventions have also been structurally weakened through the increased period of grace for cabinet ministers, and the introduction of nominated members of parliament.[47] The political responsibility of the government is significantly less in South Africa than in the Westminster system itself, and parliamentary government has amounted in practice to complete domination of the legislature by the cabinet,[48] with little notion of balance between the two.[49] The concentration of power in the cabinet, the rise of bureaucratic power, and the emergence of corporatism,[50] have led to further distortions in the theory and practice of parliamentary government and contributed to the legitimacy crisis which the state system faces in the 1980s.

(c) The electoral system

The South African electoral system,[51] the restricted franchise apart, has always been modelled on the Westminster precedent of single-member constituencies operating according to the plurality principle.[52] As has been shown,[53] this is a thoroughly majoritarian system which exaggerates the representation and influence of majority parties, and there has been no exception to this tendency in South Africa.[54] The absence of any form of proportional representation has also denied parliamentary representation to smaller parties. The electoral system has in the past given rise to two dominant parties within parliamentary politics and the party system has had similar political consequences to those of its British progenitor. In recent years, however, there has not been the alternation-in-power phenomenon associated with Westminster political practice, and it is doubtful that a two-party system prevails today, but for reasons largely unconnected with the electoral system.

A local variation on the Westminster electoral system is the loading of urban and the unloading of rural constituencies.[55] This constitutional feature distorts electoral outcomes further, in that parties with predominantly rural support can convert their electoral strength into a disproportionately high number of parliamentary seats, while the converse applies to urban-based parties. Despite manifest objections to the system,[56] it has endured since the time of Union. Further inter-provincial distortions have resulted from the provision in 1980 for each province to have its own electoral quota for the purposes of constituency apportionment to replace the national quota.[57] At the same time the number of constituencies in each province has been pegged, irrespective of future inter-provincial demographic fluctuations.[58] The net effect of these arrangements is that a rural seat in a relatively depopulating province can have less than half the voters of an urban seat in a province with a relatively expanding population.[59] But despite these variations, the South African electoral system performs the same basic function as its counterpart in the Westminster system: it produces a government-versus-opposition dichotomy and an adversarial political context. It is not designed to produce what systems of proportional representation produce, namely the translation of electoral support into parliamentary strength. In this sense it is a predominantly majoritarian and anti-consociational institution.

(d) Bicameralism

A less enduring feature of the Westminster model in South Africa was bicameralism, which came to an end with the abolition of the Senate in 1980.[60] Like the House of Lords the Senate was never directly elected, it was designed to serve as a chamber of review, and it was subordinate to the elected house.[61] But unlike the Lords the Senate was partly elected (albeit indirectly[62]), and was, at various periods of its existence, intended to perform functions additional to that of reviewing legislation. The more salient of these were to represent and safeguard provincial interests,[63] to represent groups excluded from the franchise, and to safeguard the entrenched sections.[64] At the time of the Senate's demise in anticipation of the government's new constitution it was generally agreed that none of its four functions had been adequately performed. In particular it never significantly mitigated the majoritarian aspects of the constitutional system, nor did it assume the consociational character of some federal upper chambers.

(e) Constitutional conventions

The influence of the Westminster system is apparent in relation to the main conventions of the South African constitution,[65] although the tendency in South Africa has been to enact the important conventions,[66] as it has been with other Westminster exported models.[67] This has resulted in the conventions proper being not so numerous in relation to the codified parts of the constitution, as is the case in Britain. Apart from this inconsequential difference, the conventions in South Africa are significantly weaker than their British counterparts,[68] as has been alluded to in the discussion of parliamentary government. This may be partially attributed to the fact that they do not have the same rationale, which in Dicey's well-known terms is to give effect to the will of the true political sovereign, the majority of the people.[69] But it is also a function of the South African political culture and the fact that many of the conventions are seldom applied in practice, with the result that their continued status as conventions and their exact scope are no longer self-evident.[70] It can also be said of the conventions that they do not materially qualify the majoritarian aspects of the constitution.

3. NON-WESTMINSTER FEATURES OF THE SOUTH AFRICAN CONSTITUTION

By virtue of its origins and history the South African constitution embodies two variations on the Westminster paradigm which do not have the practical significance of the non-Westminster features discussed below. The first is its codified nature, the only significance of which is that it has enabled the entrenchment of two constitutional provisions.[71] For the rest the constitution is as flexible as its Westminster counterpart and the usual ancillary features of codification, such as rigidity and a bill of rights, have been assiduously eschewed. The second is that native institutions such as the presidency and Senate have not enjoyed the status and prestige of their

Westminster counterparts;[72] in Bagehot's quaint terms they have not attracted the same 'motive power' as the 'dignified parts of government' in the British constitution.[73] This difference is of little significance in the everyday working of the constitution, but is inclined to assume significance at times of political or constitutional crisis.[74] The other departures from the Westminster model are of a more substantial nature and have had important political implications.

(a) The franchise

The most obvious and significant variation on the Westminster model in South Africa has been the restricted franchise.[75] In most western political systems ruling parties sought to broaden the base of their electoral support by enfranchising new strata of the population, democracy becoming a fulfilment of the liberal state.[76] The modern history of the parliamentary franchise in Britain began with the Reform Act of 1832 and within just under one hundred years the franchise had become the right of all British residents of eligible age.[77] Political rights were extended first on the basis of property qualifications, then on the basis of residence to all males, then on a uniform basis to men and women over twenty-one years of age, and finally to all adults over eighteen years. The final stage of electoral reform was the abolition of plural voting in 1948, since when there has been a universal and equal franchise. The development involved a gradual but purposive widening of the franchise, until the principle that the Commons should represent 'property and intelligence' had been replaced by the principle of equal citizen representation. In South Africa a contrary process occurred with periodic retractions of political rights in the central government, save in respect of white women and minors.

Since the introduction of self-government in the Cape in 1853 the parliamentary franchise in South Africa has always been qualified in one or more ways.[78] The original Cape franchise had no race or colour determinant and extended to all British subjects who owned property of a certain value or received a certain annual remuneration. The economic qualifications were amended subsequently and in 1892 an educational requirement was introduced for the first time. The effect of the qualifications was to produce a predominantly white electorate. In Natal the franchise was originally non-racial and based on economic criteria, but subsequent qualifications effectively excluded black, and later Indian, voters. The franchise in the Free State Republic extended to all burghers of the state, who by definition had to be white and have additional residential or property qualifications. The constitution of the South African Republic forbade equality between whites and persons of colour, and both citizenship and the franchise were restricted to the former, but later even naturalised citizens were excluded from the rolls. Property qualifications were relevant to the attainment of citizenship through naturalisation, and not to the franchise directly. In all four territories women were denied all political rights.

One of the well-known compromises of the pre-Union Convention was the retention of the franchise arrangements in each colony for the purpose of electing members to the House of Assembly from each of the new provinces.[79] The franchise issue was never properly resolved because the Convention was unable to agree on a uniform franchise for the whole country. The Union Parliament was empowered to prescribe future franchise qualifications, subject to the special procedure for legislation disqualifying existing electors in the Cape.[81] There was also provision that no person could be removed from a voters' roll by reason only of factors of race or colour, and this safeguard was also entrenched.[82] Even before political rights were further restricted the significance of the qualified franchise in the Cape and Natal provinces was affected by three factors. First, the qualifications relating to electors did not apply, *mutatis mutandis,* to members of the Union Parliament, who were required to be 'of European descent'.[83] Secondly, in establishing delimitation quotas the white population only was taken into account,[84] which resulted in fewer seats being apportioned to the Cape (in which most coloured voters were resident), and a reduction in the relative value of the Cape vote. Thirdly, in 1930 Parliament enfranchised white women only,[85] without any qualifications and, together with the subsequent removal of income and property qualifications for white males,[86] this led to a substantial reduction in the strength and significance of the coloured franchise.[87]

The subsequent qualifications to the franchise were all 'racially' based. In 1936 blacks were removed from the common parliamentary rolls,[88] except for the few in Natal who remained eligible.[89] In 1946 those Indians on the general rolls were deregistered,[90] and coloured voters were removed by the Separate Representation of Voters Act of 1951,[91] which was validated in the wake of the constitutional crisis.[92] Since then the parliamentary franchise has been restricted to whites,[93] for whom there is a system of universal, in the sense of non-qualified, franchise. The right to be elected corresponds with the right to elect.[94] Subsequent extensions of political rights have been in respect of the separate and subordinate political institutions referred to below, introducing a new type of 'qualified franchise' for coloureds, Indians and blacks.

Besides derogating from the representative functions of the central Parliament, the non-universal franchise in South Africa has distorted the operation of the Westminster principles of parliamentary supremacy and parliamentary government, and has served to deny any form of rational-legal legitimacy to the constitutional system. Because the Westminster system implies a universal franchise it was rejected by the government as a normative model, since even a gradual extension of the franchise was perceived to involve a threat to its political hegemony. Instead it followed each retraction of the franchise with various forms of communal representation in joint, and subsequently separate, institutions, and these came to provide the inspiration, and institutional basis, for its constitutional dispensation of the 1980s.

(b) Communal representation in corporate authorities

(i) *Blacks*

Upon their exclusion from the general parliamentary franchise in 1936, blacks in the Cape were placed on a communal roll to elect three white members to the House of Assembly and two to the Cape Provincial Council.[95] The existing franchise qualifications remained in force while this form of indirect representation endured, but it was discontinued in 1959.[96] Communal representation for blacks was also introduced in the Senate in 1936,[97] with four white senators indirectly elected by blacks in four electoral divisions.[98] These senators held office for five years regardless of any prior dissolution of the Senate. In 1951 the government was empowered to increase the number of black-elected senators to six,[99] but this power was never exercised and the system as a whole was also abolished in 1959,[100] since which date blacks have had no representation, direct or indirect, in the central political institutions. The principle of ethnic differentiation among blacks was never applied while they were represented in common authorities.

(ii) *Coloureds*

The history of coloured persons' communal representation in parliament was similar to that of blacks, but extended over a different time-period.[101] Upon their removal from the common electoral rolls coloured voters in the Cape were registered on separate rolls to elect four white representatives to the House of Assembly and two to the Cape Provincial Council.[102] This representation was terminated by the Separate Representation of Voters' Amendment Act of 1968,[103] which coincided with the creation of the Coloured Persons Representative Council. Thereafter there was no further coloured participation in common authorities, until the establishment of the President's Council in 1981. There was never any separate representation of coloured voters in the Senate. Statutory provision was made in 1951 for an additional white senator to be nominated on the ground of his 'thorough acquaintance' with the reasonable wants and wishes of the 'non-European' population in the Cape,[104] and this provision was retained in the Republican constitution until its repeal in 1968;[105] there was also provision for half of the nominated senators to be acquainted with the interests of the coloured population,[106] but juridically these conditions were not peremptory and they had no political significance.

(iii) *Indians*

In the Cape Province Indians were on the same voters' roll as coloured persons and shared their electoral fate, but in Natal, in which the majority were resident, no Indians could register as voters after Union.[107] Because of their pre-existing virtual exclusion from the franchise, Indians were never actively disfranchised by the Union Parliament and there was not the same compulsion to establish compensatory communal representation in common institutions as there was for blacks and coloureds. When legislation was enacted for this purpose the arrangement was stillborn. In 1946 provision[108] was made for Indians in the Transvaal and Natal to elect three white members to the House of Assembly, and for those in Natal to elect two members, who could be white or Indian, to the local provincial council. The franchise was restricted to males who satisfied certain educational and income requirements. Provision was also made for Indian voters to elect one white member to the Senate, and for the appointment of an additional white senator to represent their interests. The scheme was boycotted by Indians,[109] and the provisions of the statute dealing with representative matters were repealed shortly after the National Party came to power in 1948.[110]

Communal representation in common institutions is a non-Westminster constitutional feature that is encountered in the consociational systems of government.[111] The South African versions, however, proved to be no more than transient arrangements in the movement towards communal representation in separate political institutions. Contemporary policy statements[112] justified them in terms of 'baasskap' or 'apartheid' concepts, in which the overt emphasis was on the exclusion of non-whites from institutional bases of power. Subsequent policy statements gave greater emphasis to the notion of 'separate development', which was to involve the creation of the separate communal institutions described below. For several manifest reasons the system had little political impact.[113] The minimal representation extended to non-white groups afforded them no prospect of materially influencing the political process; the system of representation operated on a vicarious basis in that the 'representatives' of these groups were for the most part white, and black and coloured leaders could not themselves be participants; and the insecurity of the various arrangements in the face of parliament's supremacy further diminished their constitutional significance and political credibility. Despite this negative history the principle of communal representation in joint institutions has been fundamental to the government's constitutional strategies of the late 1970s and early 1980s.

(c) **Communal representation in separate institutions**

In conjunction with the restriction of representation in the central legislature to whites, the institutional basis of the government's separate development policy began to emerge with the creation of separate constitutional authorities for coloureds and Indians. In so far as these developments involved a devolution of authority from Parliament to subordinate bodies they evidenced a deviation from the Westminster model, but this form of devolution took place within the departmental structure, which Wiechers describes as a process of 'departmental deconcentration of activities'.[114] For blacks the government had earlier instituted a communal assembly at the national level of government, and when the process of constitutional partition had begun to take effect, it instituted local authorities. In all these developments ultimate control was retained by the relevant minister and Parliament, and the broad constitutional framework was left intact. An important feature was the system of race classification, regulated predominantly by the Population Registration Act,[115] which became an indispensable determinant of the constitutional and political process.

(i) *Coloureds*

In 1943 an advisory coloured council was created under the wing of the Department of Social Welfare,[116] which was at the time responsible for administering coloured persons' interests. The council consisted of twenty-five nominated members and had only advisory powers. It met four times a year. After differences with the government on matters of principle the members resigned in 1950 and the council was dissolved shortly afterwards. The same statute which disfranchised coloured voters,[117] made provision for a similar, but this time partly representative, institution, namely the Union Council for Coloured Affairs,[118] consisting of fifteen nominated members and twelve elected by enfranchised coloureds, with an executive committee of five. The nominal concerns of the Council were to advise the government on matters affecting coloured persons, to act as an intermediary between this group and the government, and to carry out other functions assigned to it by the government.[119] The Council was officially inaugurated in 1959 and held regular meetings *in camera* under the nominated chairman. It failed to have much impact because of its limited powers, its widespread rejection by coloured organisations and community leaders, and because of the continued, albeit indirect and limited, coloured participation in 'white' politics.[120] The Theron Report describes the period of its operation as a 'transitional phase' in the constitutional development of coloured persons.[121]

Provision was made for a successor to the Union Council in 1964, but the implementation of the Act was delayed and it was amended before it took effect.[122] In terms of the amended Act a Coloured Persons Representative Council (CPRC) could be instituted, consisting of forty members elected by coloured voters and twenty nominated by the State President, all of whom had to be coloured persons.[123] The cautious blend of elective and appointive members ensured substantial government influence in the Council, and was to be a controversial feature for the duration of its existence. All coloured persons over the age of twenty-one who were South African citizens and not subject to any disqualification were liable to register as voters to return the elected component. The Council's tenure would be five years but it might be dissolved by the State President at any time. It was empowered to elect from its members a chairman and deputy chairman, as well as four members to the executive, which would be presided over by a chairman designated by the government.[124]

The CPRC was brought into existence by proclamation in 1969,[125] the year in which coloured representation in parliament was discontinued. During its eleven-year existence the Council, and its executive, had three nominal functions. The first was to legislate, the Council having law-making competence in respect of finance, local government, education, community welfare and pensions, rural areas and settlements, agriculture, and any other matters delegated by the State President.[126] The jurisdiction of the Council was founded on the personality principle[127] and was not territorially based, an arrangement which invited jurisdictional problems, particularly as it was never clear whether laws of the Council would prevail over other forms of subordinate legislation.[128] The Council's legislative competence over the designated matters was described as being equivalent to that of Parliament, although it clearly could not legislate repugnantly to existing statutes.[129] In fact the Council's subordinate status was strongly evident in respect of its law-making powers, since ministerial approval was required prior to the introduction of legislation,[130] the central government retained a legislative veto,[131] and subsequent Acts of Parliament would override its laws. In addition the minister could regulate the sessions, proceedings and all other matters relating to the Council's functioning,[132] and Parliament, by virtue of its continued supremacy, could withdraw powers or terminate its existence—which it subsequently did. The Council's legislative inefficacy was demonstrated by the fact that in its eleven years of existence it passed only a handful of laws.[133]

The executive functions of the Council were carried out by its executive committee,[134] which was also empowered to exercise all the functions of the Council, short of legislating, when it was not in session. The management of finance was assigned to the chairman, other portfolios being allocated among the members in the chairman's discretion. The most important function of the executive related to the annual budget. It prepared estimates of expenditure for submission to the Minister of Coloured Relations who, in consultation with the Minister of Finance, determined the amount which Parliament would be petitioned to appropriate. From the total funds allocated by Parliament the Council could make its own appropriation by resolution.[135] The executive committee was in political control of those functions allocated to the Council, and their administration was entrusted to an Administration of Coloured Affairs, the bureaucratic arm of the CPRC which was headed by a commissioner appointed by the central government. Matters outside the executive's purview continued to be administered by the Department of Coloured Relations.[136] Although the system provided some basis for administrative decentralisation, the Minister of Coloured Relations, who was accountable to the central Parliament, remained in overall control of coloured affairs.

The third statutory function of the Council and its executive was to advise, and make recommendations to, the central government on matters affecting the economic, social, educational and political interests of coloured persons, and to serve as a link and means of contact and consultation between the government and coloured persons through the mediation of the minister.[137] This open-ended function implied an attempt to overcome some of the shortcomings in the powers and status of the CPRC and its executive by prescribing informal consultation and liaison as methods of influencing the government on matters affecting coloured persons. The structural deficiencies were not, however, to be easily remedied in this way and the Theron Report found severe inadequacies in the advisory function of the Council.[138]

The creation of separate and subordinate political institutions for coloured persons was an important step in the institutionalisation of the policy of parallel development, which implied the greatest possible political separation between whites and other groups.[139] The policy was justified on the basis that distinctions could be drawn between matters in which the interests of coloured persons are decisive, matters in which the interests of whites are decisive, and matters of common interest. The first category was to be regulated by the CPRC, through which the political rights of coloured persons would be exercised, while the second and third categories would continue to be regulated by the central and regional white institutions. The same assumptions were to underlie the government's 1977 constitution, which purported to transform the CPRC into a coloured parliament, and its executive into a coloured cabinet, thereby fulfilling a vision which had predated the creation of these bodies.[140] But the institutional continuity implicit in this process was broken in 1980 when the CPRC was dissolved, following requests for such a step from its majority and minority parties.[141]

The failure of the CPRC to gain legitimacy, and its eventual disestablishment, can be attributed to its basic constitutional characteristics—its unrepresentative composition,[142] the restraints on its legislative powers, the inadequacy of parliamentary-type privileges,[143] the absence of a satisfactory territorial jurisdiction, its dependent fiscal status, and the insecurity of tenure of the Council and its subsidiary institutions. The Council's subordinacy and political limitations were further underlined when provision was made during its lifetime for additional far-reaching ministerial intervention in its activities. To ensure the provision of revenue for the services controlled by the Council in the event of the majority Labour Party's rejecting the budget, provision was made in 1972 for the executive committee alone to appropriate money, and failing this the Minister of Coloured Relations.[144] After the Labour Party's election successes in 1975 the minister was empowered to exercise any function of the executive,[145] its chairman, or the council, if such party failed to do so; alternatively the minister could delegate the function to 'any other person', which he subsequently did on several occasions.[146] These developments aggravated the lack of credibility already affecting the Council as a result of various factors—the fact that it was unilaterally imposed by the government, that it was perceived to be part of a divide and rule strategy, and that it was intimately related to the system of race classification, residential and educational segregation, and other discriminatory practices. The failure and dissolution of the CPRC was a prominent symptom of the legitimation crisis in South Africa.

(ii) *Indians*

Separate communal authorities for Indians were slower in developing than those for coloured persons and they never had the same political salience—a function partly of the lower profile of the Indian franchise. The government conceded the failure of its repatriation scheme for Asians only in 1962,[147] and it then pursued the same constitutional policy as for coloured persons, articulating similar assumptions about exclusively 'Indian interests'.

In 1964 a National Indian Council was established consisting of twenty-one nominated members, and presided over by the Secretary for Indian Affairs. In its early years the Council was an extra-constitutional body and had only advisory powers. After becoming the South African Indian Council in 1965, it was given statutory recognition in 1968.[148] Its size was increased to a maximum of twenty-five, all members being ministerially appointed Indians representing the Cape Province, Natal and Transvaal.[149] The Council could appoint its own chairman and elect four members to the executive committee, the fifth member and chairman of which would be appointed by the minister.[150] The Council had neither legislative nor executive competence, and its statutorily defined powers were to advise the government on matters affecting the economic, social, cultural, educational and political interests of the Asiatic community, to make recommendations on these matters, and to serve as a link and means of contact between the government and this group.[151]

Subsequent legislation empowered the State President to increase the SAIC's size to thirty members, to specify the number of appointed and elected members, and to prescribe the qualifications of candidates and voters and the election and nomination procedures.[152] These administrative competences highlight the degree of discretionary control which has always existed over non-white constitutional development. In 1974 the Council was duly enlarged to thirty members, with parity of strength between the government nominees and those elected by electoral colleges comprising members of Indian local authorities, local affairs committees, management committees and consultative committees.[153] Elections were held in the same year, and an elected member was appointed chairman of the council's executive. In 1976 the minister delegated all powers vested in him in regard to education and social welfare to the executive committee,[154] which could then deal with these matters in so far as they affected Indians, but without legislating thereon. In this form the Council had an inferior constitutional status to that of the CPRC but it was to be some time before its legitimacy was subjected to the direct test of popular elections.

In what proved to be the first statutory step in the implementation of the government's new constitution, legislative provision was made in 1978 for significant changes in the composition of the Council.[155] These included an increase in its size to forty-five members, the majority of whom would be directly elected, an extension of its term of office from three to five years, an adaptation of the qualifications of members to resemble those pertaining to the House of Assembly, and the introduction of a Westminster-type executive.[156] This statute anticipated the draft Constitution Bill of 1979[157] which, other than for a change in nomenclature,[158] made provision for a representative assembly and responsible cabinet along the lines described. Constitutional and political continuity was again apparent in this intended transformation, implying a transition from representative to responsible government in a process of 'internal communal decolonization'. But for administrative and political reasons there were numerous delays in the elections for the new Council, and the terms of office of the appointed and indirectly elected members were periodically extended. Elections were eventually held in November 1981 and it was clear from the response of the Indian electorate that the SAIC would have the same legitimacy problems as the defunct CPRC.[159] The Council convened for the first time early in 1982, but with no greater powers than its predecessor.

(iii) *Blacks*

The establishment of separate communal authorities for blacks has taken place in terms of three different objectives: first, to compensate for the termination of black representation in common authorities; secondly, to institutionalise black political participation in the homelands system in furtherance of separate development policy; and thirdly, to provide limited involvement in government in the 'common area' at the local level. All three developments involve variations on the Westminster pattern, the first and third being dealt with in this section, and the second in that following on partition.

When black voters were removed from the common electoral rolls in 1936, apart from provision being made for their separate representation in parliament, the Natives Representative Council was established as a compensatory institution.[160] The NRC had a complement of twenty-three:[161] seven official members, comprising the white Secretary for Native Affairs and six 'chief native commissioners'; four black members nominated by the government, one for each of four electoral areas; and twelve black members elected by designated black authorities.[162] The Council had neither legislative nor executive powers, and its functions were solely advisory, as with other bodies of its kind. It was empowered to consider and report on proposed legislation in so far as it affected blacks, and other matters referred to it by the minister, and it could recommend to Parliament or a provincial council legislation which it considered to be in the interests of blacks.[163] Parliamentary or provincial legislation could ostensibly be delayed for the Council's consideration, but only if the minister certified that the enactment would specially affect black interests;[164] the minister's decision was based on his unfettered discretion, and this provision proved to be a dead letter. Long before its abolition in 1951[165] the Council had proved to be inadequate, ineffectual and unacceptable to blacks, and had, of its own volition, adjourned *sine die*.[166] In the light of subsequent developments its most significant feature was that it nominally catered for all blacks, with no regard to ethnicity or language. There has been no comparable successor to the NRC, but in 1980 the Schlebusch Commission recommended the establishment of a black citizens' council to consult with the non-black President's Council.[167] No indication was given of the proposed composition and functions of this body, but it called to mind the failed NRC. The government accepted the recommendation, but abandoned the concept in mid-1980 because of its unequivocal rejection by black leaders.

Between the early 1950s and 1971 the statutory foundations of the homelands policy were laid by the South African Parliament, and this resulted in the process of constitutional partition from the mid 1970s onwards. The government's new constitution has always been premised on all the homelands eventually attaining legal independence, but the Community Councils Act of 1977 heralded a partial departure from previous constitutional developments for blacks, and implied a contradiction of the premise.[168] It both made provision for permanent local authorities with some measure of political autonomy for blacks outside the homeland areas, and abandoned the principle of ethnic differentiation among blacks which had been consistently applied, not only in respect of the homelands but also the predecessors of the new bodies.

Since 1923 provision has been made for blacks resident within the jurisdiction of white local authorities to have some involvement in local government. In that year black Advisory Boards were created for locations or villages under the control of urban local authorities.[169] They usually comprised three members elected by registered occupiers of property in the location or village concerned, and three members and a chairman appointed by the 'parent' local authority. They were empowered to consider and report upon matters affecting blacks in the urban area, and on other matters referred to them by the minister or relevant local authority.[170] The Advisory Boards did not have legislative or executive powers and were gradually replaced by the Urban Black Councils, for which statutory provision was made in 1961.[171] The Councils were established by local authorities at the request of an existing Advisory Board, or on the direction of the minister after consultation with the black community in the area, and they could be instituted for specified residential areas or for members of specified 'national units'. The local authority determined the Council's size and its method of election or selection.[172] The Councils had the same functions as the Advisory Boards, but there was provision for the conferment of additional executive powers by the local authority, after consultation with the relevant provincial administrator and with the concurrence of the minister.[173] In practice few of the additional powers were ever conferred and the Councils remained predominantly advisory bodies with little greater significance than those they succeed. These Councils were in turn replaced when the Community Councils system came into operation in 1977.[174] Community Councils are elected by black residents within their jurisdiction, without ethnic differentiation, and those eligible to vote and stand for office include not only South African nationals but also nationals of the independent homelands.[175] The Act comprises broadly enabling provisions which confer extensive administrative powers on the minister in relation to the establishment and dissolution of Councils. The minister may determine the size of each Council and its method of election,[176] and, after consulting the Administration Board and Council concerned, make regulations relating to its tenure, committees, service conditions, financial affairs, and incidental matters.[177] The conferment of substantive powers and duties on Community Councils is also a matter of ministerial discretion, and in theory considerably greater powers can be conferred on these authorities than on their predecessors,[178] including most powers hitherto exercised by the Administration Boards.[179] The objective of the scheme was for the Councils eventually to act independently of the boards, whose functions would decline as the Council system expanded.[180]

In 1982 the system of black local government was further augmented in an attempt to place it on a footing similar to white local government.[181] The minister is now empowered to establish town and village Councils to replace the Community Councils in certain areas, the new system to be controlled from Pretoria by a Director of Local Government.[182] The local Councils will be directly elected by eligible blacks within their jurisdiction, the most important electoral requirements being nationality of the Republic or a homeland, and residence rights in the area.[183] The Act provides that each authority shall have such functionaries as a mayor, town clerk and executive (management) committee.[184] Powers and functions over an extensive list of scheduled matters are conferable on the Councils, including the right to make by-laws and impose levies; extensive duties can also be imposed on them, including the preservation of law and order.[185] Their financial powers are carefully circumscribed by statute and controlled by the central government.[186] In overall terms the new scheme envisages a general upgrading of the status of black local authorities, including the possibility of qualifying Councils being awarded 'city Council' status.[187]

The open-ended nature of many provisions of the Community Councils and Black Local Authorities Acts provides the basis for a measure of autonomy on matters of local concern, though subject to the overall control of the central government.[188] The extent to which the Councils achieve municipal status and local autonomy is largely dependent upon how the minister exercises the powers conferred by the Act. 'Municipal status' is a diffuse concept, embracing varying situations—from those in which local authorities have secured powers and independent sources of revenue, to those in which they have delegated powers and are dependent on central or regional authorities for their income. As far as the black local authorities are concerned it is clear that their financial dependence on the central government would have a decisive bearing on their autonomy. Their future political role will also depend on the extent to which they are affected by the legitimacy problems affecting the other institutions of separate development.[189] The constitutional significance of the system is that the institutional basis for a decentralisation of competence to blacks in the 'common area' which it provides, countervails both the homelands policy and the logic of the government's new constitution.

(d) Partition[190]

The legal foundations of territorial separation, and eventual partition, can be traced back to the Land Act of 1913,[191] but it was only in the 1950s that the policy of separate development came to be consistently pursued in its political dimension. With the abolition of the Natives Representative Council in 1951 the principle of ethnic differentiation among blacks came to be a major determinant of black constitutional development. From a legal-institutional point of view there was a consistent evolutionary development from the early tribal authorities through to constitutional independence, but when the government's policy was first given institutional form it was not intended to culminate in partition.

The Black Authorities Act of 1951[192] introduced a three-tier system of local administration for blacks. At the base of the pyramid were 'tribal authorities',[193] consisting of the local chief or headman and appointed tribal councillors. These bodies were empowered to administer the affairs of the tribe, assist the chief or headman, advise the government on matters affecting the inhabitants of the area, and perform other functions assigned to them. Their powers were to be exercised according to traditional laws and customs. Where two or more tribal authorities existed a co-ordinating 'regional authority' could be established,[194] headed by the senior chief and including the heads of the various tribal authorities and other appointed members. These bodies could provide educational, health, agricultural and other services, subject to ministerial direction, and could levy rates and exercise delegated legislative powers.[195] At the apex of the system were the 'territorial authorities'[196] whose members were drawn from the regional authorities within their jurisdiction. The powers and functions of these bodies were not statutorily defined but a broad enabling provision[197] envisaged the delegation to them of powers relating to the administration of black affairs. The territorial authorities were subsequently replaced by the various homeland institutions.

The implementation of this scheme was not to be immediate, and it was the object of extensive opposition from blacks. While purporting to revive traditional features of African public law it tended to re-establish tribalism and increase the power of appointed chiefs at the expense of elected leaders.[198] The subordinate status of the various authorities, the restrictions on their powers, and their jurisdictional limitations, did not constitute an attractive alternative to direct participation in the central legislature. However, once the Ciskeian and the Transkeian General Councils had accepted the system it became established throughout the country, the first territorial authority being instituted in the Transkei in 1957. The 1951 legislation established the first separate authorities for blacks and permitted a certain measure of territorial decentralisation, and it was an early milestone on the road to partition.

In 1955 the Tomlinson Commission [199] called for an acceleration in the separate development programme, and although the government never responded effectively to its economic recommendations, it soon gave further statutory effect to its policy of political separatism. In what has been described as 'the decisive year in the evolution of Nationalist policy towards the African',[200] the government in 1959 both terminated black representation in Parliament and provided the statutory framework for the homelands system.[201] The legislation of that year reinforced the principle of ethnic differentiation in the black constitutional process by identifying eight 'national units',[202] each of which came to be associated with a separate territorial area—the future homelands or national states. The powers and functions of the existing territorial authorities were augmented,[203] and in both the preamble to the 1959 Act and the parliamentary debates reference was made to the goal of evolutionary self-government—and even of ultimate independence.[204] Closer liaison with the central government and other 'common area' authorities was envisaged through the provision for a commissioner-general to represent the government in each unit, and for the nomination of urban representatives by the territorial authorities.[205]

By 1970 geographical homelands had been set aside for all the national units identified in the 1959 legislation,[206] and in each case a territorial authority was created. The next stage of constitutional development was that of 'self-government' which was regulated by the National States Constitution Act[207] for all the homelands other than Transkei. The latter was the subject of separate legislative treatment and for historical and other reasons proceeded more quickly through the stages of self-government to independence.[208] Transkei's constitutional development was the model for the other national states.

Analogies have been drawn between the constitutional development of the national states and traditional forms of colonial evolution to independence from the imperial power. The local process has been described as one of 'internal decolonisation',[209] but the description is essentially innappropriate. At the first stage of development[210] the national state acquires, at the request of the relevant territorial authority, its own constitution, a legislative assembly and executive,[211] and legislative and executive competence in respect of matters specified in the schedule to the Act. Central government control is retained through a repugnancy provision, a legislative veto power, and the assembly's financial dependence on Parliament.[212] In addition the minister can resume executive control over any matter to ensure continued governance in the area.[213] The first phase has been passed by all the national states.[214] At the second stage, that of 'self-government',[215] the legislative assembly is empowered, within its sphere of competence,[216] to legislate repugnantly to Acts of Parliament, and central legislation on scheduled matters does not apply within the self-governing territory[217]—but this clearly does not detract from Parliament's legislative supremacy, nor is the veto right affected.[218] The state legislatures can appropriate revenue through their own enactments at this stage, and they acquire personal jurisdiction to make laws with extraterritorial, though intra-republican, effect. Another innovation at the self-government stage is that a high court can be instituted with the jurisdiction of a provincial or local division of the Supreme Court, from which appeals can be taken to the South African Appellate Division.[219] There are also changes of nomenclature, such as 'cabinet' and 'cabinet minister' for 'executive council' and 'executive councillor' respectively, and the introduction of some of the symbols and trappings of self-government, such as flags and anthems.[220]

From the Westminster perspective the 1971 Constitution Act provides the institutional basis for an atypical ethnic-territorial decentralisation of functions. What the system does not entail is the simultaneous participation of the 'self-governing' regions in the central political institutions, so that any suggestion that it involves a federal process would be inappropriate.[221] Even the notion of regional autonomy requires substantial qualification in the light of the political and financial controls retained by the central government over the self-governing national states. Parliamentary supremacy, and therefore overall constitutional control, is clearly unaffected by the delegation of legislative and executive competence to the state authorities, while a more incongruous example of central control is found in the retention of s 25 of the Black Administration Act 38 of 1927,[222] which empowers the State President to legislate by proclamation for homelands on matters not vested in their legislative assemblies.[223] The decentralising potential of the homelands system would have been enhanced had the National States Constitution Amendment Bill of 1977[224] been enacted. This provided for a third stage of self-government short of independence, to be known as 'internal autonomy'. In constitutional terms it would entail additional legislative competence for the relevant state, with the exclusion of only expressly reserved matters, such as foreign affairs and defence. The state would be able to create its own administrative departments, commensurate with its legislative capacity, and provide for the election and designation of its head of government. 'Internal autonomy', however, would have been something of a misnomer: the central government would have retained a legislative veto, and its prior approval would have been necessary for the introduction of a Bill which would incur expenditure which could not be defrayed from the territory's consolidated revenue fund. An 'internally autonomous' state would also not have been able to change its own constitution, which would have remained subject to unilateral amendment by the republican parliament. The significance of the Bill was that, within the framework of the government's constitutional policy, it suggested a *via media* for the national states between subordinate dependence and legal independence, that its decentralising effect would have been in conflict with the centralising trend affecting provincial powers, and that its conception of regional autonomy is at variance with the Westminster model.[225] Despite its failure to appear on the statute book its resuscitation had seemed a possibility for those homelands which would not accept independence; but since Ciskei took this step the possibility has become more remote.[226]

The final statutory stage in the partition process consists of the Status Acts,[227] which confer constitutional independence on the national states. Juridically the transition is effected by proclaiming the relevant entity a sovereign and independent state, by renouncing Parliament's legislative competence over the territory, and by removing the constitutional limitations which had previously restricted the homeland legislature and empowering it, from the effective date, to enact its own constitution.[228] In each case the legislature of the national state has enacted a local constitution on the day of independence, to take effect from the same moment as the Status Act. The constitutional transition of the various territories to independent republican status is characterised by legal continuity and an absence of constitutional autarchy for the homeland states.[229]

One of the most significant features of the homelands policy and partition is that of citizenship, which is also a key factor in the South African Government's response to the legitimacy crisis. In the present context only a brief outline can be given of the statutory provisions regulating black citizenship[230] and their main implications. In the process it is convenient to distinguish between the terms 'nationality', as denoting the continuing legal relationship between an individual and the particular state of which he is a national, and 'citizenship', as denoting the (possibly fluctuating) public-law status (in terms of political, civil and social rights) of an individual within a particular political community.[231] Nationality stresses the international, and citizenship the municipal, aspect of the same notion: state membership.[232] But the terms do not always overlap because although all citizens of a state will *ipso facto* be nationals, the converse is not necessarily true.

Since 1970 citizenship of one or other national state has been ascribed to all South African blacks on the basis of birth, descent, domicile, and linguistic or cultural association. The nationality of such persons is unaffected at this stage and it is expressly provided that they will not be regarded as aliens in the Republic.[233] However, their citizenship status indicates that their political rights will be exercised exclusively through the relevant homeland authorities. The Status Acts build on the existing citizenship arrangements in that they denationalise all those who were citizens of the relevant home- land before independence, and confer on them, and additional groups, nationality of the new state.[234] The process has been described as the most comprehensive transfer of nationality that legal draftsmanship could achieve.[235] The system is of a self-perpetuating nature in that all future generations of blacks having the statutorily prescribed association with an independent national state will be classified as aliens according to South African municipal law, regardless of their place of birth, residence or employment, or of how real their link with that state might be. South African nationality can be regained by denationalised blacks only if they were formerly nationals of the Republic (which excludes future post- independence generations) and, after ministerial approval, are granted citizenship of a non-independent homeland, such as KwaZulu.[236] But the regained nationality will be forfeited when that state acquires independence.

Among the many issues raised by these provisions are problems of statelessness and dual nationality, but these have yet to become acute because the criteria on which the new states have conferred nationality has largely corresponded with those on which South Africa has denationalised. Should a homeland unilaterally narrow its criteria in the future the problem would become more immediate.[237] Problems of statelessness could also arise in international law if the denationalisation process is held to be in violation of international-law principles,[238] if blacks born and resident in the Republic are not regarded as having the necessary 'genuine link' with a homeland to qualify as its nationals,[239] or if the international community refuses indefinitely to recognise the independence of the homelands.

The most important consequence of these citizenship arrangements is that the political rights of South African blacks come to be exercised in the institutions of the respective homelands, and by denationalised blacks in those of the legally independent states. If the citizenship policy is logically pursued all blacks will in time become 'statutory aliens',[240] and the system will have an important legitimising function in that it vindicates the denial of political rights to blacks on the apparent basis of nationality, and not race or colour. In the words of well-known commentators, 'the semantics of inter- national law are being used to create fictions on levels of constitutional development so as to solve vexing political problems'.[241] The system also affords the state new mechanisms of control in matters such as movement and establishment. Thus for the removal of statutory aliens from urban areas resort can be had to deportation procedures which take place without the prior hearing or subsequent judicial review which pertain to influx control procedures.[242] On the other hand the national–alien distinction has not been consistently applied in other areas, such as residence rights and participation in local authorities, where 'statutory aliens' are in a slightly more advantageous position than foreign aliens.[243] The distinction is rigidly maintained in respect of political rights, but not where it would be dysfunc- tional to the economic system. In overall terms the citizenship arrangements for blacks are an essential key to an understanding of South Africa's constitutional politics, and a crucial, albeit latent, factor in the government's new constitution.

From this juridical outline of the homelands system it is apparent that it involves several variations on the unitary Westminster model, although paradoxically it has led to the establishment of new Westminster systems in the national states themselves.[244] In terms of the main themes of this work the creation of self-governing homelands has, *ex facie* the constitutional provisions, some affinity with the consociational principle of segmental autonomy. However, closer investigation reveals that the affinity is only superficial and the outcome of the homelands policy, namely partition, is decidedly non-consociational. In terms of the work's main subtheme it can be said that these constitutional developments have not ameliorated the legitimacy crisis in South Africa. Here reference can be made to the government's own plans for a constellation of states and forms of regional organisation, both of which involve new forms of post-partition relationships with the national states designed to resolve some of the political and economic problems that have been unaffected, or even aggravated, by constitutional independence. These new relationships embody forms of quasi-consociationalism, and are dealt with subsequently.

(e) Decentralisation: The provincial system

The system of provincial government which was incorporated into the Union constitution evidenced at the time a significant variation on the Westminster theme in that it provided the institutional basis for a substantial decentralisation of functions, and it was understandable, in the light of pre-Union history, that the constitution should defer in this way to the locally perceived interests and needs of the new provinces.[245] While the British political system has not, in its modern history, been as strongly centralised as some other countries with unitary constitutions,[246] decentralisation in South Africa was the result of indigenous, non-Westminster constitutional features. Provincial government has always comprised locally elected legislatures[247] and centrally appointed officials,[248] with the provincial councils, successors to the colonial legislatures, enjoying original legislative authority.[249] Provision is made for decentralised executive power to be exercised by the administrator—a central government representative—and the other members of the executive committee, who are elected by the provincial council for a fixed term and are not accountable to it as in a parliamentary system.[250] The separate identity of the provinces has also been recognised in the composition of the controlling central institutions, inter alia in the erstwhile method of electing senators (which involved provincial councillors as well as parliamentarians) the equal representation of the provinces in the Senate, and subsequent over-representation of the smaller provinces, and the existing over-representation of the smaller provinces in the House of Assembly. Electoral divisions have never been permitted to straddle provincial boundaries.[251]

Although they provided a basis for decentralised government, the provincial authorities were always subordinate institutions in that they exercised their powers within a framework of control, or potential control, by the central government.[252] This has led to the South African constitution being traditionally classified as unitary, a characteristic it shares with the Westminster system. The essence of unitarianism, from a juridical point of view, is that sovereignty is undivided, regardless of whether government itself is centralised or localised. Several commentators have described South Africa's unitarianism in qualified terms, by reason of the 'federal' division of legislative competence and the 'federal' composition of the former Senate; but the qualification tends to overlook the extent of the provincial authorities' constitutional subordination.[253] Nor did the provincial system ever give rise to the 'federal process', in the sense of a unitary state becoming differentiated into a federally organised whole.[254] The recent unsuccessful attempts to devolve power in Britain showed some similarity to the provincial system in South Africa in that they would have left the Westminster Parliament's sovereignty unaffected.[255]

While the basic structure and framework of provincial government has not changed much since its inception, modifications within this structure have left the provinces with diminished status and powers. The trend has been towards a gradual, but unequivocal, centralisation of power, as the national government has both directly usurped powers formerly vested in the provincial councils,[256] and begun to co-ordinate policy through administrative and financial controls in areas nominally within provincial jurisdiction. The provinces have become 'implementors of national policy rather than formulators of specifically provincial politics',[257] despite various pleas for 'special status' provinces or regions within the country. By the time the government's new constitution was first mooted in 1977 the provincial system had become a hollow framework and provincial government only a nominal variation on the Westminster model. In the early formulations of the constitution the provincial system was left intact, although the logic of the new dispensation implied an even more diminished role for the provincial authorities. Subsequent formulations were more consistent and portended, albeit indirectly, the demise of the provincial system.

(f) The Rule of Law

Whereas the Westminster system grew up out of a constant recognition of the Rule of Law this has not been the case with the South African constitution, thus implying a significant distinction between the two. In the first place the Rule of Law in South Africa[258] has not generally had a normative influence on Parliament in the exercise of its legislative powers, and it has never emerged as an effective qualification on the principle of parliamentary supremacy. Any conflict between the two principles has invariably been resolved in favour of the supremacy of a Parliament which has not felt constrained from making legislative incursions on substantive and procedural rights. Secondly, the extensive discretionary powers of the executive in South Africa, and its imperviousness in many cases to judicial control, involves a violation of the Rule of Law, as arbitrary and uncontrolled power is fundamentally inimical to the doctrine. Thirdly, although an independent judiciary exists in South Africa, the doctrine of parliamentary supremacy has permitted both direct and indirect incursions into judicial independence and the judiciary's powers, and the courts do not perform the same role in enforcing the Rule of Law, and the human rights standards which it implies, as they do in the Westminster system.

In short the Rule of Law doctrine has shallow roots in the South African constitutional system. This is aggravated by the fact that even when the doctrine is recognised, it is often accorded the narrower meaning of 'government according to law', or the principle of legality,[259] thus stripping it of any notions of substantive justice. When seen cumulatively with the other deviations from the Westminster model this factor has had its most striking impact in South African constitutional law in matters relating to the protection of fundamental rights and liberties. The absence of a vigorous Rule of Law doctrine has gone hand in hand with the absence of a bill of rights and other constitutional guarantees of fundamental freedoms. There is no mitigation of the majoritarianism of the constitutional system from this source.

4. CONSOCIATIONALISM AND THE CONSTITUTIONAL BACKGROUND

It is possible to identify in South Africa's constitutional history several institutions and practices that show some affinity with the principles of consociationalism. However, the quasi-consociational features have existed both functionally and temporarily in isolation from one another, and have not had the significance and consequence of such features in a fully or semi-consociational system. More particularly they have not significantly mitigated the majoritarian effects of the Westminster and non-Westminster features described above, nor have they induced a system of power-sharing in the consociational sense of the term. Nevertheless it is relevant to describe briefly the most salient of these features to complete the account of South Africa's constitutional background.

There was some evidence of the *grand coalition principle* in South Africa in the composition of the provincial executive committees before 1962.[260] The four-member committees were elected by provincial councillors on a proportional basis, which allowed for the participation of more than one party represented in the council. In one instance, though it was atypical, a committee comprised members from four different parties.[261] The system had been modelled on the Swiss federal executive,[262] but its efficacy as a consociational institution was impaired by the absence of other consociational features, such as the mutual veto. The system was subsequently altered in accordance with the majoritarian Westminster cabinet system.[263] In a non-institutionalised form the principle was evident in the political coalition of 1933 in which cabinet seats were equally divided between the two parties,[264] and which led subsequently, after their electoral successes, to fusion. Within the limited framework of white politics this arrangement can be seen as an attempt to avoid the implications of majoritarianism and the government–opposition dichotomy and to effect a more coalescent and consociational style of government. In the absence of institutional support, however, the co-operation was of relatively short duration and in 1939 the adversarial model was reverted to. Finally, the inter-cabinet council which was established in 1976 as an extra-constitutional body displayed some features of an inchoate 'grand coalition'. The council consisted of members of the white cabinet and the statutory Indian and coloured executive councils, and its main function was to provide a forum for the discussion of matters of 'mutual interest'. But it had neither legislative nor executive authority, and its informal influence proved to be negligible because it met irregularly and infrequently and had little credibility among the leadership élites whom it was designed to incorporate consociationally into the political system. The council ceased to meet after a relatively short period, although in the early formulations of its constitutional proposals the government seemed intent on building on its foundations.

There has also been some evidence in the South African constitution of the *proportionality principle* serving as a basis of representation but its significance has been attenuated by a preponderance of majoritarian elections. The National Convention considered a system of proportional representation for parliamentary elections, but preferred the plurality principle in single-member constituencies.[265] Proportionality was, however, the basis on which the provincial executive committees were originally composed,[266] although the principle was distorted by the fact that the provincial councillors who elected the executive were themselves elected on the same majoritarian basis as parliamentarians. The popular electoral strength of parties was not, therefore, reflected in the composition of the executive committees. The same distortion pertained to the election of senators, who were elected on a proportional basis by a majoritarian-constituted electoral college.[267] This system further benefited the majority party in each province since it was able to fill casual provincial vacancies, whether or not the vacating senator was from that party. Finally, the original parity of provincial representation in the Union Senate, and the subsequent over-representation of the smaller provinces in the Union and Republican Senates,[268] may also be seen as variations of the principle of proportionality. The principle has never, however, been used as the basis of allocating resources, public appointments and other 'spoils' of government, and where found in its attenuated form has not effected any significant deviation from the principle of majority rule within the white constitutional system.

The *veto principle* has had very limited formal application in the South African constitution in relation to the entrenching procedure. This originally extended a power of veto to a minority of one-third of the members of the combined House of Assembly and Senate, and since 1980 of the House alone, in respect of legislation affecting the entrenched sections.[269] The veto delayed the enactment of the Separate Representation of Voters Act in 1951,[270] but it was statutorily circumvented in subsequent developments; since then its scope has been reduced and it has had less practical significance. The convention of joint ministerial responsibility implies some form of consensual decision-making in the cabinet, and a type of informal veto principle,[271] but with a quite different function to that of the mutual veto in the consociational democracies. This feature can therefore be said to be generally absent from South Africa's constitutional tradition.

As far as *segmental autonomy* is concerned, the terminology of separate development converges to some extent with that of consociationalism. In South Africa the provision at various times for separate black, Indian and coloured authorities, each set having personal jurisdiction over members of the relevant group, shows an apparent affinity with the principle of segmental autonomy, and has been officially justified in terms of consociational-type concepts of 'self-determination' and 'group autonomy'. It has been suggested that the policy of separate development has provided the structural basis for minority groups to control and regulate matters of exclusive concern to them, as does the segmental autonomy principle in a consociational system. But at the institutional level, and apart from any evaluation of the policy of separate development itself, there are three basic flaws in this line of reasoning. First, it is misleading to speak of the segmented authorities as being 'autonomous', by reason of their constitutional subordinacy, their minimal powers, and the political and economic factors circumscribing those powers. Secondly, the 'segments' recognised by the South African constitution are statutorily defined[272] and are not necessarily based on perceived common interests. Only the withdrawal of the many prohibitions on free political association would ensure the emergence of genuine segmental identities, among which the present divisions might or might not be prominent. The issue of segmental identity would require resolution before any of the consociational devices could be authentically employed. Thirdly, the provision for 'autonomous segmental' institutions has not been accompanied by provision for joint participation in central institutions on matters of common concern, as is provided in the grand coalition of the consociational model. In the case of the national states, moreover, 'segmental autonomy' has led to partition[273] and has 'internationalised' the claim of the independent states and their citizens to a joint say on matters of common concern.[274] While the premises of separate development and consociationalism may be similar in regard to this principle, their outcomes are widely divergent.

5. CONCLUSION

This overview of the main constitutional developments in South Africa since the time of Union provides the background to the current phase of constitutional politics and reveals a basic dichotomy within a single overall constitutional system. On the one hand is a set of Westminster-type institutions which accommodate the 'white' political process. Here are encountered three important features of the Westminster system—the supremacy of parliament, the parliamentary executive, and the plurality electoral system. As far as the constitutional allocation of competence is concerned there is a winner-takes-all system at one decisive site of political competition: the party that gains a majority of seats in the parliamentary elections controls both the legislature and the executive, which leads to control and influence in vast areas of the administrative state. At this level the constitution is thoroughly majoritarian without the compensation, even within the limits of 'white politics', of the alternation of majorities and Rule of Law principles which characterise the Westminster model. There is a tendency to regard this system as the constitution proper,[275] which has led to the misleading view that South Africa has had a slightly modified Westminster constitution. On the other hand are the political and administrative institutions for coloureds, Indians and blacks, subordinate in all respects to their 'white' counterparts. When these institutions are taken into account it becomes inaccurate to describe the constitutional system as Westminster-based, because they involve a non-universal franchise, functional decentralisation and partition, and a distortion of the conventions and other principles of the Westminster model. The constitutional system provides democracy for one category of citizens and authoritarian rule for the other. The ability of the white electoral majority to dominate the overall majority has given rise to a form of minority rule and unilateral conflict regulation,[276] which has contributed to the legitimacy crisis facing the state system in South Africa.

In its response the state has used some consociational concepts to provide an alternative justifying theory for its reforms and has resorted to consociational engineering to create a new dichotomy between blacks and non-blacks. The government's new constitution is an important manifestation of this strategy. However, neither South Africa's constitutional history, nor the existing constitutional system, reveals much in the way of consociational institutions and practices. The Westminster characteristics in South Africa have had an anti-consociational effect on the political process, but so too have the non-Westminster features such as the restricted franchise and the absence of the Rule of Law, since consociationalism assumes both a representative system of government and a deep sense of constitutionalism. While a transition to authentic consociationalism would require at least fundamental institutional changes, the government's present constitutional strategies involve many continuities with the past.

NOTES AND REFERENCES

[1] This chapter updates the analysis of L J Boulle 'The Second Republic: its Constitutional Lineage' 1980 *CILSA* 1–34.

[2] See on this theme H May *The South African Constitution* (3 ed, 1955) 30–43; H Hahlo & Ellison Kahn *South Africa: The Development of its Laws and Constitution* (1960) 128–75;

[3] The authoritative text on the South African constitution is Marinus Wiechers *Staatsreg* (3 ed, 1981). Of historical importance are H May *The South African Constitution* (2 ed, 1949 and 3 ed, 1955), Hahlo & Kahn op cit; verLoren van Themaat *Staatsreg* (2 ed, 1967). More synoptic contributions are found in Hosten, Edwards, Nathan & Bosman *An Introduction to South African Law and Legal Theory* (1977) 588–634 and R Goldblatt 'Constitutional Law' in *The Law of South Africa* (1978) vol 5 3–48. On the constitutional politics of South Africa see D Worrall (ed) *South Africa: Government and Politics* (2 ed, 1975); A de Crespigny & R Schrire (eds) *The Government and Politics of South Africa* (1978); C Niewoudt, G Olivier & M Hough (eds) *Die Politieke Stelsel van Suid-Afrika* (1979); L Thompson & A Prior *South African Politics* (1982).

[4] See below, 129–31.

[5] See Boulle op cit 2; A Cilliers 'Die Westminster-sisteem en Suid-Afrika se Konsepgrondwet' 1979 *Obiter* 86; D van Wyk 'Westminster-stelsel—*Requiescat in Pace?* of: kan 'n luiperd sy kolle verander?' 1981 *THRHR* 105; D du Toit 'Geskiedkundige oorsig van Suid-Afrikaanse konstitusionele modelle met besondere verwysing na die Westminster-staatsmodel' in S Jacobs (ed) *'n Nuwe Grondwetlike Bedeling vir Suid-Afrika—Enkele Regsaspekte* (1981) 8.

[6] See L M Thompson *The Unification of South Africa* (1960) 97–109 and 480–3; C J R Dugard *Human Rights and the South African Legal Order* (1978) 14–36.

[7] In *S v Gibson* (1898) 15 *Cape LJ* 1 the Free State Court confirmed the supremacy of the constitution, but the Transvaal Court's attempt to do the same (Kotze CJ in *Brown v Leyds NO* (1897) 4 Off Rep 17) was less successful.

[8] 22 Geo V, c 4.

[9] 28 and 29 Vict, c 47.

[10] May op cit (3 ed) 24.

[11] Sections 66 and 65 of the South Africa Act (9 Edw 7, c 9), respectively. See *R v McChlery* 1912 AD 196; *R v Ndobe* 1930 AD 484.

[12] See ss 2–4.

[13] Section 2 of Act 69 of 1934.

[14] Except in respect of the matters referred to in s 10.

[15] Sections 35, 137 and 152 of the South Africa Act.

[16] See Stratford J in *Ndlwana v Hofmeyer NO* 1937 AD 229: 'Parliament . . . can adopt any procedure it thinks fit; the procedure express or implied in the South Africa Act is . . . at the mercy of Parliament like anything else . . .'; see May op cit (2 ed) 33 (where he refers to the two-thirds majority rule as being 'legally as dead as the proverbial dodo'); Hahlo & Kahn op cit 154; Dugard op cit 29.

[17] The second Harris decision (*Minister of the Interior v Harris* 1952 (4) SA 769(A)) remains the authoritative curial pronouncement on the entrenchments.

[18] Section 2 of the South Africa Act Amendment Act 9 of 1956.

[19] Centlivres CJ in *Harris v Minister of the Interior* 1952 (2) SA 428 (A) (the first Harris decision).

[20] The first Harris decision was influenced by the 'new view' and in turn provided judicial authority for it. Among those who uphold this view are B Beinart 'Sovereignty and the Law' 1952 *THRHR* 101; May op cit (3 ed) 25; J van der Vyver 'The Section 114 Controversy—and Governmental Anarchy' (1980) 97 *SALJ* 363; Wiechers op cit 33–7 and 333–40; G Barrie 'Die gebondenheid van die parlement aan die reg rakende sy struktuur en funksionering' 1981 *TSAR* 46: P Loubscher 'The Foundation of Sovereignty—Parliament as a Law-making Body' (1981) 98 *SALJ* 529. For other authorities, and contrary views, see Hahlo & Kahn op cit 154.

[21] Republic of South Africa Constitution Act 32 of 1961.

[22] Ellison Kahn 'The New Constitution' (1961) 78 *SALJ* 244 at 272.

[23] Constitution Act s 58(1).

[24] Constitution Act s 59(2).

[25] Sections 108 and 118 of the constitution, s 118 as amended by s 1 of Act 74 of 1980. Despite changes to the various quorums of the Appellate Division effected by Act 46 of 1980, the quorum of 11 judges has been retained for appeals in which the validity of an Act of Parliament is in question (s 12(1)(b) of the Supreme Court Act 59 of 1959). See *S v Tuhadeleni* 1969 (1) SA 153 (A); *S v Marwane* 1982 (3) SA 717 (A).

[26] That is, according to s 24, or s 118 (and before the abolition of the Senate s 63) of the Constitution Act; see *S v Hotel and Liquor Traders' Association of the Transvaal & others* 1978 (1) SA 1006 (W).

[27] The question of whether s 114 of the constitution contains a 'manner and form' provision was settled in the negative in *Mpangele & another v Botha & others (1)* 1982 (3) SA 633 (C) and *(2)* 1982 (3) SA 638 (C) despite the contrary *obiter* in *Cowburn v Nasopie (Edms) Bpk* 1980 (2) SA 547 (NC) at 554. Unfortunately the issue was not canvassed by the courts as adequately as might have been expected.

[28] *S v Tuhadeleni* (supra). In *Cowburn v Nasopie (Edms) Bpk en andere* (supra) Van der Heever J suggested *(obiter)* that s 59(2) imposed only a limited limitation on the courts' review powers. This was in relation to the possible invalidity of the Status of Bophuthatswana Act 89 of 1977, for non-compliance with s 114 of the constitution. Wiechers argues that the courts did have such a right at common law (*Staatsreg* (3 ed) 334–9).

[29] e g the equal representation of the provinces in the former Senate, and s 114 of the Constitution (and its predecessor, s 149 of the South Africa Act)—see C Schmidt 'Section 114 of the Constitution and the Sovereignty of Parliament' (1962) 79 *SALJ* 315. A 'federal' interpretation of s 114 was given *(obiter)* in *Cowburn v Nasopie (Edms) Bpk en andere* (supra) but the fate of s 114 was soon sealed.

[30] Sections 108 and 118 of the Constitution Act.

[31] These matters are all dealt with below.

[32] Act 30 of 1950.

[33] Act 36 of 1966.

[34] See J van der Vyver 'Parliamentary Sovereignty, Fundamental Freedoms and a Bill of Rights' (1982) 99 *SALJ* 557 at 575.

[35] L M Thompson *The Unification of South Africa* (1960) 198–202.

[36] Thompson op cit 199.

[37] Hahlo & Kahn op cit 129.

[38] South Africa Act s 14(1). This was the usual arrangement in the dominions; s 14(1) followed the wording of art 64 of the [Australian] *Commonwealth Act* of 1900. The 'period of grace' derives from the British convention—S A de Smith *The New Commonwealth and its Constitutions* (1964) 101.

[39] e g ss 22 and 56 of the South Africa Act.

[40] See s 4(3) of the Status Act 69 of 1934.

[41] South Africa Act ss 3 and 13.

[42] Hahlo & Kahn op cit 131.

[43] Section 1 of Act 70 of 1980 amended s 20(3) of the constitution.

[44] Unless expressly stated or necessarily implied otherwise—s 16(2).

[45] Constitution Act ss 7(5) and 16(3).

[46] e g the 'information affair'. For the Erasmus Commission's observations on ministerial responsibility see the Report of the Commission of Inquiry into Alleged Irregularities in the Former Department of Information (RP 113/1978) para 11.345–9.

[47] See below, 165–6.

[48] W H B Dean (*The Riots and the Constitution* (1976) 15) suggests that the sole contemporary function of Parliament is to provide the executive with the legislation it requires to effect its policy and that the idea of the legislature controlling the government is obsolete. See also Olivier 'The Executive' in De Crespigny & Schrire op cit 17–31.

[49] See the examples in J van der Vyver 'Parliamentary Sovereignty, Fundamental Freedoms and a Bill of Rights' (1982) 99 *SALJ* 557 at 579ff.

[50] See H Adam & H Giliomee *The Rise and Crisis of Afrikaner Power* (1979) 77–195; L Baxter 'Constitutionalism, Bureaucracy and Corporatism' in L J Boulle & L G Baxter (eds) *Natal and KwaZulu: Constitutional and Political Options* (1981) 75 at 85ff.

[51] On the South African electoral system and process see J Faris 'Elections' in *The Law of South Africa* (1970) vol 8 283–378.

[52] South Africa Act s 32*(a)* and RSA Constitution Act s 40(1).

[53] See above, 6.

[54] See K Heard *General Elections in South Africa 1943–1970* (1974) 236f. The discrepancies in the 1981 general election can be depicted as follows (the first column indicates the seats won by the respective parties, and the second the seats they would be entitled to in a proportional system).

National Party   131—95
Progressive Federal Party   26—31/2
New Republic Party   8—12/3
Herstige Nasionale Party   0—25

Of the 151 constituencies contested 12 were won by candidates with only a relative majority of votes. See also T Hanf, H Weiland & G Vierdag *South Africa—The Prospects of Peaceful Change* (1981) 119–26.

[55] South Africa Act s 40(3) and RSA Constitution Act s 43(4).

[56] The deliberate inequality in the weight of votes conflicts with one of the implied meanings of 'one person one vote'. See I Duchacek *Rights and Liberties in the World Today—Constitutional Promise and Reality* (1973) 194.

[57] By s 1 of Act 28 of 1980 which amended s 43(1) and (2) of the Constitution Act. See below, 159–60.

[58] Section 40(2). The number of seats allocated to each province was not amended after the general reregistration of voters in 1979–80 and the appointment of the 1980 delimitation commission.

[59] The provincial quotas adopted by the 1980 delimitation commission were: Cape—12 626; Natal—13 283; OFS—12 863; Transvaal—15 433. In the 1981 general election the constituency with the most voters was Bezuidenhout (Transvaal) with 17 308, and with the least Prieska (Cape) with 8 720 House of Assembly Questions and Replies vol 5 col 255–9 (26 February 1981). See below, 160–2.

[60] Act 101 of 1980. As Thompson (op cit 203) observes, the Convention showed little enthusiasm for an upper chamber.

[61] This is a corollary of responsible government which requires governmental support in the elective house. The conventional subordinacy of the House of Lords was codified in the Parliament Acts of 1911 and 1949 (1 and 2 Geo 5, c 13 and 12; 13 and 14 Geo 6, c 103) while the South African Senate's subordinacy was implicit in s 63 of the South Africa Act but made explicit by s 7 of the Senate Act 53 of 1955, which amended s 63 and was retained in the republican constitution (s 63) until its repeal in 1980.

[62] South Africa Act ss 24 and 25, Constitution Act s 28.

[63] This follows from the initial parity of provincial representation in the Senate, followed by the over-representation of the minority provinces.

[64] As provided in s 152 of the South Africa Act, and s 118 of the Constitution Act, until amended by s 1 of Act 74 of 1980.

[65] The description of the South African conventions given by Marinus Wiechers *Staatsreg* (3 ed) 172–86, is the most complete, save for some omissions relating to ministerial responsibility.

[66] See ss 7(3), 16(2), 20(3), 26 and 64 of the Constitution Act.

[67] Cf M de Merieux 'The Codification of Constitutional Conventions in the Commonwealth Caribbean Constitutions' 1982 *International and Comparative Law Quarterly* 263.

[68] This is not to overlook the fact that several British conventions have also been weakened by recent political events.

[69] See A V Dicey *An Introduction to the Study of the Law of the Constitution* (10 ed with introduction by E C S Wade 1959) 429. For Dicey the electorate was synonymous with the people.

[70] There are various examples relating to ministerial responsibility; reference can also be made to the convention that if a government is defeated in the House the State President should dissolve Parliament: this was not followed in 1939 when preference was given to an alternative convention.

[71] The southern African and English courts have, however, intimated that the form of a constitution is important—*Madzimbamuto v Lardner-Burke NO* 1968 (2) SA 284 (RAD) at 428–9; *The Bribery Commissioner v Ranasinghe* [1964] 2 All ER 785 at 796.

[72] See M Wiechers 'Grondslae vir Politieke Ontwikkeling in Suid-Afrika' in J Coetzee (ed) *Gedenkbundel—H L Swanepoel* (1976) 103.

[73] W Bagehot *The English Constitution* (2 ed, 1872) (World's Classics ed (1928) 3–4).

[74] e g The manipulation of the Senate during the coloured voters' crisis (Wiechers op cit 106), and the position of the State President in testifying before the Erasmus Commission which had to report to him (see G Devenish 'The protection of the dignity and reputation of the state president' 1981 *THRHR* 136).

[75] Cf D Welsh 'The Evolution of South Africa's Constitutional Structure' (unpublished paper, Cape Town, 3 February 1978) 7.

[76] C B Macpherson *The Real World of Democracy* (1966) 10.

[77] See J Harvey & L Bather *The British Constitution* (1966) 49–61.

[78] On the franchise see Hahlo & Kahn op cit 53ff; Wiechers op cit 299ff; C J R Dugard *Human Rights and the South African Legal Order* (1978) 17ff.

[79] L M Thompson *The Unification of South Africa* (1960) 109–26, 212–26.

[80] South Africa Act s 36. The Cape forwent the right of non-whites to stand for election to Parliament.

[81] South Africa Act s 35(1). There was no restriction on amending the qualifications, and the special procedure was not required when white women were enfranchised by Act 19 of 1930, although this diminished the value of the coloured vote.

[82] Section 35(2) of the South Africa Act as entrenched by s 152.

[83] South Africa Act ss 44*(a)* and 26*(a)*, for the House and Senate respectively. Non-whites were theoretically entitled to sit in the Cape and Natal provincial councils—s 70(2).

[84] Section 24 of the South Africa Act regulated the initial allocation of seats until membership of the House of Assembly reached 150, which occurred in 1931. From then s 41 was applicable, and based the quota on the number of white adults in the Union. This was amended by Act 55 of 1952, which provided that the delimitation should be based on the number of registered white voters.

[85] The Women's Enfranchisement Act 18 of 1930.

[86] Franchise Laws Amendment Act 41 of 1931. Before this enactment all males in the Cape were subject to the property qualifications; thereafter coloured males remained so, but white males and females did not. For the numbers of respective voters see Hahlo & Kahn op cit 165.

[87] It was also affected when white voter registration became compulsory (Act 20 of 1940) and it became necessary for coloured voters to register before a magistrate, policeman or electoral officer (Act 50 of 1948).

[88] Representation of Natives Act 12 of 1936. This necessitated an amendment to s 35 of the constitution which was effected by s 44 of the Representation Act. See *Ndlwana v Hofmeyr NO* 1937 AD 229.

[89] The Electoral Act 46 of 1946 retained this limited franchise for blacks, but it was abolished by Act 46 of 1951.

[90] Asiatic Land Tenure and Representation Act 28 of 1946.

[91] Act 46 of 1951.

[92] By Act 9 of 1956. See *Harris v Minister of the Interior* 1952 (2) SA 428 (A); *Minister of the Interior v Harris* 1952 (4) SA 769 (A); *Collins v Minister of the Interior* 1957 (1) SA 552 (A).

[93] As regulated by Act 46 of 1946 until superseded by the Electoral Act 45 of 1979. The Electoral Laws Amendment Act 30 of 1958 extended the franchise to whites between 18 and 20 years.

[94] See s 46 of the RSA Constitution Act.

[95] Representation of Natives Act 12 of 1936. For a description of the electoral process see May op cit (3 ed) 104–6.

[96] The Promotion of Bantu Self-Government Act 46 of 1959.

[97] Representation of Natives Act. Since 1910 the constitution had provided (s 24(ii)) that four of the eight nominated senators should be thoroughly acquainted with the wants and wishes of the 'coloured races'.

[98] On the electoral process see May op cit (3 ed) 101–4.

[99] Bantu Authorities Act 68 of 1951 s 19, read with the Schedule.

[100] Section 15 of Act 46 of 1959.

[101] The best account of the general history of coloured political rights is to be found in chapter 16 of the Theron Report. (Report of the Commission of Inquiry into Matters Relating to the Coloured Population Group (RP 38/1976).) See below 129–31.

[102] Sections 8(1) and 11(1), read with s 6(2) of the Separate Representation of Voters Act 46 of 1951.

[103] Act 50 of 1968. The Commission of Inquiry into Improper Political Interference and the Political Representation of the Various Population Groups (the Muller Commission, RP 72/1967) recommended the termination of this system because of the establishment of the CPRC.

[104] Section 7 of Act 46 of 1951.

[105] Section 28(1), repealed by s 5 of Act 50 of 1968.

[106] Section 29(2)*(b)*.

[107] See Wiechers op cit 299f.

[108] Asiatic Land Tenure and Indian Representation Act 28 of 1946. The first chapter imposed restrictions on the acquisition and ownership of fixed property by Indians and the second chapter, dealing with representation, could be seen as a quid pro quo.

[109] See Hahlo & Kahn op cit 165.

[110] Section 2 of Act 47 of 1948.

[111] Some countries in which it has been adopted are India, New Zealand, Indonesia, Cyprus, Lebanon and Zimbabwe. See Duchacek op cit 101–8; E McWhinney *Federal Constitution-making for a Multi-National World* (1966) 27–31; S A de Smith *The New Commonwealth and its Constitutions* (1964) 117–21.

[112] See the statements of Prime Ministers D F Malan, J G Strijdom and H F Verwoerd in M Horrell *Laws Affecting Race Relations in South Africa* (1978) 9–10. The government's constitutional programme was further buttressed at this time by the Population Registration Act 30 of 1950, the Group Areas Act 41 of 1951, and the Reservation of Separate Amenities Act 49 of 1953.

[113] For an inside account see Margaret Ballinger *From Union to Apartheid* (1969) 27–140; the author was a 'native representative' for 23 years.

[114] Wiechers in Coetzee op cit 107.

[115] Act 30 of 1950.

[116] This followed a minority recommendation (para 1159) of the Commission of Inquiry into the Cape Coloured Population of the Union (Wilcocks Commission, UG 54 of 1937). The majority recommended (para 1158) that the franchise provisions in the Cape should be extended to the other provinces. This was not the last time that a commission's recommendations would be ignored. See the Theron Report op cit ch 16; Wiechers *Staatsreg* 428–33.

[117] Act 46 of 1951 ss 14–19, as amended by Act 30 of 1956.

[118] Section 14. The original s 14 envisaged a 'Board for Coloured Affairs' consisting of eight elected and three nominated membes with substantially the same powers as those of the Council, but with no executive committee.

[119] Section 18(1)*(a)–(d)*.

[120] See Vosloo & Schrire 'Subordinate Political Institutions' in De Crespigny & Schrire op cit 88.

[121] Op cit ch 16 para 16.50.

[122] Coloured Persons Representative Council Act 49 of 1964, as amended by Act 52 of 1968. The legislation was delayed pending the Muller Report (op cit), the recommenda-

tions of which resulted in the Prohibition of Political Interference Act 51 of 1968, the abolition of coloured representation in the Assembly, and the creation of the CPRC.

[123] See ss 1–5.

[124] Sections 14(1) and 17*(a)*.

[125] Proclamation 77 of 1969 in *GG* 2347 of 3 April 1969.

[126] Section 21(1), read with s 17(6)*(a)*. Agriculture was added by Proc R185 of 1973 (*GG* 3989 of 3 August 1973).

[127] Powers were conferred 'in so far as they affect Coloured persons'.

[128] Theron Report op cit para 17.104–17.107. But cf R Goldblatt in vol 5 *The Law of South Africa* 41.

[129] Section 25(1).

[130] Section 21(2). Approval could only be granted after consultation with the Minister of Finance and the provincial Administrators (the latter presumably to avoid conflicts with provincial ordinances).

[131] This was nominally exercised by the State President—s 23.

[132] Sections 15 and 26. On the additional controls exercised by the central government see Vosloo & Schrire op cit 90.

[133] Wiechers op cit 431.

[134] Section 17(6).

[135] Section 22(1) and (2)*(a)*. In anticipation of appropriation by the Council the chairman could authorise the urgent issue of moneys.

[136] In 1951 a division of coloured affairs had been instituted within the Department of the Interior; it acquired departmental status in 1959 and in 1962 its own minister. In 1969 some functions were taken over by the Administration of Coloured Affairs.

[137] Section 20(1)*(a)*, *(b)* and *(c)*, read with s 20(3).

[138] Op cit para 17.109–17.112.

[139] The Prohibition of Political Interference Act, enacted in the same year that the Council was created (Act 51 of 1968), prohibited members of one 'population group' from being members of, or rendering assistance to, or addressing any meeting of, a political party to which members of any other 'population group' belonged (s 2).

[140] Theron Report op cit para 17.1 and 17.71.

[141] By the South African Coloured Persons Council Act 24 of 1980. In terms of s 4(1) the Council was deemed to have been dissolved, but s 4(2) made possible its future reconstitution.

[142] After the first elections in 1969 the government nominees created a legislative majority out of an electoral minority.

[143] There was a qualified freedom of speech (s 16 of Act 49 of 1964) but this fell short of that conferred on Parliament by the Powers and Privileges of Parliament Act 91 of 1963, and on the provincial councils by s 75 of the Constitution Act. Cf *Leon v Sanders NO* 1972 (4) SA 637 (C).

[144] Section 22 of the main Act, as amended by s 6 of Act 99 of 1972.

[145] Other than the power to legislate.

[146] Section 22A of the main Act, as inserted by s 2 of Act 32 of 1975; on several occasions the minister permitted authorisation of the budget by the replacement chairman.

[147] See the Minister of Indian Affairs in Senate Debates vol 3 cols 503–20 (8 February 1962). The RSA Constitution Act vested in the State President the 'control and administration . . . of matters specifically or differentially affecting Asiatics throughout the Republic . . .' (s 111).

[148] The South African Indian Council Act 31 of 1968.

[149] Sections 1 and 2. At Union entry of Indians into the Free State was prohibited, and their residence there remains prohibited.

[150] Section 7(1), read with s 10(1)*(a)*.

[151] Sections 13(1) and 18(1)*(b)*.

[152] SA Indian Council Amendment Act 67 of 1972.

[153] Proclamation R167 of 3 September 1974 (*Reg Gaz* 2031).

[154] In terms of s 10A(4) (GN R7 of 2 January 1976 (*GG* 4945)); s 10A(4) also provided that powers might be delegated by a provincial executive committee, but this never occurred.

[155] SA Indian Council Amendment Act 83 of 1978.

[156] Section 10; the State President would appoint the majority party leader as chairman, and the other members on the latter's advice.

[157] See below, 151–7. During the second reading the minister said the new Council was designed to fit into the new dispensation. House of Assembly Debates vol 17 cols 8186–7 (30 May 1978).

[158] 'Chamber of Deputies' for 'Indian Council'.

[159] The highest turn-out was 20,5% of registered voters (Red Hill, Natal) and the lowest 1,8% (Fordsburg, Transvaal). In Natal, with the majority of voters, the average poll was 10,15% of registered voters. See 1981 *Survey of Race Relations* 17–21.

[160] Representation of Natives Act 12 of 1936. See M Wiechers *Staatsreg* (3 ed) 435ff.

[161] Section 20.

[162] Such as the general council of the Transkeian territories.

[163] Section 27.

[164] Section 26(3).

[165] By Act 68 of 1951 (s 18).

[166] For a critical evaluation of the Council see M Ballinger *From Union to Apartheid* (1969) 141–218; see also H May *The South African Constitution* (3 ed) 497–500.

[167] See below, 134 and 163.

[168] Cf the comments of S Bekker in F van Zyl Slabbert & J Opland (eds) *South Africa: Dilemmas of Evolutionary Change* (1980) 33–4.

[169] Black (Urban Areas) Act 21 of 1923 s 10, to be replaced by the Black (Urban Areas) Consolidation Act 25 of 1945 s 21; see Hahlo & Kahn op cit 798–802.

[170] Section 21(2)*(a)* of Act 25 of 1945.

[171] Urban Black Councils Act 79 of 1961.

[172] Sections 2 and 3. Act 49 of 1970 dispensed with non-elective members.

[173] Section 4.

[174] Community Councils Act 125 of 1977. Within three years 250 councils had been established. See Wiechers op cit 391–3.

[175] Section 3(4) and (5).

[176] Section 3. If fewer than the required members are elected the minister may appoint members. This provision was introduced by Act 28 of 1978 to prevent electoral boycotts from frustrating the arrangement. Council elections were the subject of dispute in *Moleko v Minister of Plural Relations and Development* 1979 (1) SA 125 (T); *Scott & others v Hanekom & others* 1980 (3) SA 1182 (C); *Nkosi & others v Khumalo & others* 1981 (1) SA 299 (W); *Singapi & others v Maku & others* 1982 (2) SA 515 (SE).

[178] Section 5. Section 5(1)*(n)* allows the minister to confer power over 'any matter, whether or not it is connected with the matters referred to in this subsection' on a council—an enabling provision of the broadest kind.

[179] The Administration Boards were introduced in 1971 (Act 45 of 1971) to assume the powers and functions of local authorities relating to black affairs in urban areas, and resorted under the then Department of Bantu Administration (now Co-operation and Development). Twenty boards were created, but the number was reduced to fourteen in 1979. See *Mbaso v West Rand Administration Board & another* 1982 (3) SA 977 (W).

[180] Cf the Riekert Report (*Report of the Commission of Inquiry into Legislation Affecting the Utilization of Manpower* RP 32/1979) paras 210–11. See below, 131–3.

[181] See the Black Local Authorities Act 102 of 1982.

[182] Sections 2 and 3.

[183] Sections 6–8.

[184] Sections 10, 11, 20 and 30.

[185] Sections 23–8, read with the schedule.

[186] Sections 39–48.

[187] Section 2(1)*(c)*. See below, 218.

[188] Cf Wiechers op cit 392: 'In effek is die blanke parlement en minister besluitnemend, en die gemeenskapsraad prinsipieel uitvoerend.'

[189] In the first elections for the Soweto Community Council, politically the most salient, there were no nominations in many wards. In the contested wards the percentage polls averaged 6%, and by-elections had to be held to achieve a full complement. See 1978 Annual Survey of Race Relations 341f.

[190] See Wiechers op cit 435–42 and 502–24. For a comprehensive juridical approach to this topic see F Venter *Die Staatsreg van Afsonderlike Ontwikkeling* (1981). Among the critical works on the constitutional politics of the homelands are G Carter, T Karis & N Stultz *South Africa's Transkei—The Politics of Domestic Colonialism* (1967); P Laurence *The Transkei—South Africa's Politics of Partition (1976)*; J Butler, R Rotberg & J Adams *The Black Homelands of South Africa: The Political and Economic Development of Bophuthatswana and KwaZulu* (1977); J Dugard *Independent Homelands—Failure of a Fiction* (1979); N Stultz Transkei's *Half Loaf—Race Separatism in South Africa* (1980);

and more journalistically B Streek & R Wicksteed *Render unto Kaiser—A Transkei Dossier* (1981). For the views of homeland leaders see K Matanzima *Independence My Way* (1976); L Mangope *A Place for All* (1978); and M Buthelezi *Power is Ours* (1979).

[191] The Natives Land Act 27 of 1913. (See W B Harvey & W H B Dean 'The Independence of Transkei—a Largely Constitutional Enquiry' 1978 *Journal of Modern African Studies* 189.) This was followed by the Native Trust and Land Act 18 of 1936 which established a trust to purchase land earmarked as 'native reserves', constituting 13,7% of the country's surface area.

[192] Act 68 of 1951.

[193] Sections 2–4. In practice most councillors were appointed by the chief and Commissioner.

[194] Sections 2–6. See May op cit (3 ed) 190–1.

[195] Subject to a central veto—s 5(2).

[196] Sections 2–7.

[197] Section 7(1). However, far-reaching powers in respect of black affairs remained vested in the central executive.

[198] See W D Hammond-Tooke *Command or Consensus—The Development of Transkeian Local Government* (1975) 198–225. Even by chiefs, who stood to benefit, the system was regarded with suspicion.

[199] *Report of the Commission for the Socio-Economic Development of Bantu Areas within the Union of South Africa* (UG 61/1955). See further below, 127–9.

[200] H Kenney *Architect of Apartheid H F Verwoerd—An Appraisal* (1980) 160, and referred to in Wiechers op cit 439.

[201] The Promotion of Bantu Self-Government Act 46 of 1959.

[202] Section 2(1): The North-Sotho, South-Sotho, Swazi, Tsanga, Tswana, Venda, Xhosa, and Zulu units.

[203] Section 12; legislative powers were conferred, and powers in respect of the administration of justice and the imposition of taxes.

[204] House of Assembly Debates vol 16 cols 6215–17 (20 May 1959) and col 6730 (27 May 1959); see also the government's White Paper (3 of 1959) that accompanied the bill.

[205] Sections 2–5.

[206] With the exception of the Swazi group; the South Ndebele national unit was recognised in 1972.

[207] Act 21 of 1971.

[208] Transkei Constitution Act 48 of 1963; see on this aspect J Dugard *Human Rights and the South African Legal Order* (1978) 91.

[209] Cf Wiechers op cit 502; L J Boulle *The Changing Constitution* (1979) 35f; Laurence op cit 65.

[210] Chapter 1 (ss 1–25) of Act 21 of 1971.

[211] The executive's method of appointment is determined by the central government, enabling it to decide such fundamental issues as whether the executive should be parliamentary or not. See W H B Dean 'Whither the constitution?' 1976 *THRHR* 266 at 268.

[212] Sections 3 and 8; however, Act 12 of 1978 enabled the legislative assemblies to appropriate money themselves (s 14).

[213] Section 25.

[214] Save for KaNgwane.

[215] Ch 2 (ss 26–36) of Act 21 of 1971.

[216] Among the matters expressly excluded are defence, explosives, ammunition, posts, police and the Constitution Act itself.

[217] Section 30(3). Uncertainty over this matter was resolved by the Appellate Division in *S v Heavyside* 1976 (1) SA 584 (A). See also *S v Memke* 1976 (4) SA 817 (E); *S v Machebele* 1978 (1) SA 569 (T); *S v Matsana* 1978 (3) SA 817 (T); *S v Kunene* 1979 (2) SA 1153 (N); *S v Sambe* 1981 (3) SA 757 (T); and F G Richings 'The Applicability of South African Legislation in the Self-Governing Bantu Territories' (1976) 93 *SALJ* 119.

[218] Section 31. It has been suggested that in the light of the conventions operating within the former British Commonwealth the State President might come to act on a homeland cabinet's advice when taking a decision on legislation of an assembly. See N J J Olivier 'Implications of Constitutional Development in KwaZulu/Natal for the Rest of South Africa' in L J Boulle & L G Baxter (eds) *Natal and KwaZulu—Constitutional and Political Options* (1981) 57 at 68; but cf the editors' rejoinder, ibid n 8.

[219] Section 34.

[220] Sections 27–29.

[221] However, in *Government of KwaZulu v Government of RSA & another* 1982 (4) SA 387 (D) the court dealt with the question of KwaZulu's *locus standi* along quasi-federal lines.

[222] By s 30(4) (read with s 30(3)). M Wiechers (*Administratiefreg* (1973) 39) describes this as a 'Henry VIII' clause. See *R v Maharaj* 1950 (3) SA 187 (A).

[223] On the extent to which Act 21 of 1971 impliedly repeals the State President's s 25(1) powers see *Government of RSA & another v Government of KwaZulu & another* 1983 (1) SA 164 (A).

[224] B91–'77. See the government's *Explanatory Memorandum* WP 9–'77.

[225] The arrangement would not be unlike that of the associated states, e g Puerto Rico and the United States. Puerto Rico is not a member of the US federation but is subordinate to the US in that its delegated powers of autonomy can be unilaterally revoked. Puerto Ricans are US citizens and are subject to Federal laws, but do not vote in Federal elections or pay Federal taxes. See Duchacek op cit 184.

[226] The Quail Report (*Report of the Ciskei Commission*, 1980) outlined a number of advantages for the Ciskei in 'internal autonomy' as an interim step towards independence, or some other alternative constitutional status. See below, 134–6.

[227] Acts 100 of 1976 (Transkei), 89 of 1977 (Bophuthatswana), 107 of 1979 (Venda) and 110 of 1981 (Ciskei).

[228] The Status Acts (ss 1 and 3) assume that Parliament can limit its sovereignty.

[229] Cf K C Wheare *The Constitutional Structure of the Commonwealth* (1960) 89; E Kahn 'The New Constitution' (1961) 78 *SALJ* 244 at 252ff.

[230] Transkei Constitution Act (ss 7–8); National States Citizenship Act 26 of 1970; and the Status Acts (s 6 and schedule 8).

[231] See D P O'Connell *International Law* vol 2 (2 ed, 1970) 670ff; M Akehurst *A Modern Introduction to International Law* (4 ed, 1982) 81ff. South African writers tend now to use the terms in these senses. See Wiechers op cit 344ff; Venter op cit 206ff; C Schmidt 'Citizenship and Nationality' in *The Law of South Africa* 1977 vol 2 260; H Booysens *Volkereg—'n Inleiding* (1980) 108.

[232] P Weis *Nationality and Statelessness in International Law* (2 ed, 1979) 4–5.

[233] Section 2(4) of Act 26 of 1970.

[234] Section 6(1) read with Schedule B of each Act.

[235] The Quail Report op cit 43.

[236] Section 3 of Act 26 of 1970 as amended by s 1 of Act 13 of 1978.

[237] See W H B Dean 'A Citizen of Transkei' 1978 *CILSA* 57–67; W Olivier 'Statelessness and Transkeian Nationality' 1976 *SAYIL* 143–54 and ''n Juridiese evaluasie van burgerskap' 1979 *TSAR* 212–25 and 1980 *TSAR* 22–31, 127–51.

[238] See J Dugard 'South Africa's "Independent" Homelands: An Exercise in Denationalisation' 1980 *Denver Journal of International Law and Policy* 11.

[239] As laid down in the *Nottebohm* case 1955 ICJ Reports 4.

[240] See the well-known statement of Dr C Mulder (House of Assembly Debates vol 2 col 579 (7 Feb 1978)), then a government minister.

[241] M Wiechers & D H van Wyk 'The Republic of Bophuthatswana Constitution' 1977 *SAYIL* 85 at 86. See also *Ex parte Moseneke* 1979 (4) SA 884 (T), *SA TV Manufacturing Co (Pty) Ltd v Jubati & others* 1983 (2) SA 14 (E).

[242] Sections 44–45 of the Admission of Persons to the Republic Regulation Act 59 of 1972 allow the minister to order the deportation of aliens 'in the public interest'; the discretion is protected by a clause ousting the court's review jurisdiction. The Nyanga squatters were deported in terms of these provisions in 1981. A fair hearing is required for removals under s 29 of the Black (Urban Areas) Consolidation Act 25 of 1945; see *S v Nkabinde* 1967 (2) SA 157 (T); *S v Mangena* 1978 (4) SA 585 (T); *Moeca v Addisionele Kommissaris, Bloemfontein* 1981 (2) SA 357 (O).

[243] Dugard loc cit.

[244] This is something of an overstatement since only the Transkeian constitution can be labelled a Westminster (and South African) imported model, the others being majoritarian presidential or semi-presidential systems. See below, 124–5.

[245] See L M Thompson *The Unification of South Africa* 248–60. On the provincial system see H May *The South African Constitution* (3 ed) 359–96; M Wiechers *Staatsreg* (3 ed) 397–424.

[246] See above, 10.

[247] South Africa Act ss 70–73; RSA Constitution Act ss 68–71.

[248] The most important is the administrator who has legislative and executive functions, but members of provincial administrations are also centrally appointed: South Africa Act ss 68–69; RSA Constitution Act ss 66–67; *Stander v Administrator, Natal & others* 1960 (1) SA 320 (N).

[249] Laid down in *Middelburg Municipality v Gertzen* 1914 AD 544; see also *Brown v Cape Divisional Council* 1979 (1) SA 589 (A); *In re Pennington Health Committee* 1980 (4) SA 243 (N).

[250] However, s 76(2) of the constitution was amended (s 4 of Act 99 of 1982) to allow the premature removal of an executive committee member by resolution of the provincial council; this was ostensibly aimed at a Transvaal MEC who had defected to the Conservative Party, but his subsequent resignation obviated the need for a resolution.

[251] Sections 40–42 of Act 32 of 1961.

[252] Cf W Vosloo & R Schrire in A de Crespigny & R Schrire (eds) *The Government and Politics of South Africa* (1978) 79; among the contemporary constitutional controls are the repugnancy provision (s 85), the veto power over provincial ordinances (s 89), the legislative supremacy of Parliament (s 59(1)), the provinces' financial dependence (s 88(2)), the central appointment of the administrator (s 66), the restricted powers of the provincial councils (s 84(1)), and the flexibility of the constitution (s 118).

[253] Cf K C Wheare *Federal Government* (4 ed, 1963) 30f. The view that s 114 of the constitution is a federal feature cannot be sustained in the light of *Mpangele & another v Botha & others (1)* 1982 (3) SA 633 (C) and *(2)* 1982 (3) SA 638 (C).

[254] With the early predominance of party over provincial interests in Parliament the relative strengths of the provinces lost importance and the 'federal flavour' of the constitution was lost; in the constitutional crisis voting followed party lines, and there was no attempt by the Cape representatives to retain the system which their predecessors had striven to entrench.

[255] See above, 10.

[256] e g in respect of Black Education (Act 47 of 1953) and Indians Education (Act 61 of 1965).

[257] Vosloo & Schrire loc cit.

[258] On which see A S Mathews *Law, Order and Liberty in South Africa* (1971); J van der Vyver *Seven Lectures on Human Rights* (1976) 106ff; J Dugard *Human Rights and the South African Legal Order* (1978) 37–49; M Wiechers *Staatsreg* (3 ed, 1981) 140ff.

[259] See the references in Dugard op cit 41–5.

[260] South Africa Act s 78 read with s 134, and the original s 77 of the RSA Constitution Act.

[261] In the Transvaal in 1917: Hahlo & Kahn op cit 177.

[262] Which A Lijphart (*Democracy in Plural Societies* (1977) 31) describes as one of the best examples of the grand coalition in its prototypal form. Cf R H Brand *The Union of South Africa* (1909) 80; H May *The South African Constitution* (3 ed) 369.

[263] By Act 28 of 1962.

[264] See May op cit (3 ed) 135; this arrangement conformed to Nordlinger's 'stable governing coalition' in that the coalition was formed prior to elections. Less striking examples of the coalition principle are the Unionist Party's 'merger' with the South African Party in 1920, the Nationalist–Labour pact which came to power in 1924, and the support of the Afrikaner Party for the National Party after the 1948 election.

[265] See Brand op cit 63–74.

[266] Cf the original s 134 of the South Africa Act.

[267] Except during the period 1955 until 1960; see s 30 of the Constitution Act until its repeal by Act 101 of 1980.

[268] South Africa Act ss 24 and 25; Constitution Act s 28.

[269] South Africa Act s 152; Constitution Act s 118.

[270] Act 46 of 1951.

[271] See the then Prime Minister's description of cabinet decision-making—House of Assembly Debates vol 10 col 4552 (12 April 1978); and below, 213n69.

[272] By the Population Registration Act 30 of 1950 and National States Citizenship Act 26 of 1970.

[273] Partly because of this possibility Nordlinger (op cit 32), unlike Lijphart, does not include segmental autonomy as a conflict-regulating device.

[274] However, N Stultz (*Transkei's Half Loaf—Race Separatism in South Africa* (1980) 150) describes the post-independence relations between Pretoria and Umtata as more closely resembling the consociational ideal—in that they require bargaining from independent power bases. See below, 219–20.

[275] J C Bekker 'Rewriting the Textbooks: a re-evaluation of some traditional South African constitutional law assumptions' 1979 *CILSA* 272.

[276] See T Hanf, H Weiland & G Vierdag *South Africa—The Prospects for Peaceful Change* (1981) 45–6.

5 The Broader Constitutional Context in Consociational Perspective

1. INTRODUCTION

Before analysing the government's constitutional proposals against the background of the existing constitution, it is appropriate to take account of other constitutional perspectives in southern Africa. The object of this chapter is to provide a comparative analytical framework for that which follows. Attention is given to matters relevant to the consociational theme at the conceptual, empirical and specialist levels, namely the constitutional policies of internal political parties, constitutional arrangements generated by political actors, and constitutional recommendations of commissions of enquiry, respectively. The choice of topics is somewhat eclectic and is restricted by the comparative scope of this work. No attention is given to the numerous constitutional scenarios which have been drawn for South Africa—ranging from radical forms of partition, to military dictatorships of various persuasions, to unitary socialist systems[1]*—except where these are implicit in the subject-matter being dealt with. The alternative perspectives referred to can lay no particular claim to relevance in terms of their probable influence on current constitutional developments. Constitutions, as has been observed,[2] are autobiographical and correspondingly idiosyncratic—they tend, like codes, to reflect the personality and intellectual background of their drafters—and South Africa's new constitution is proving to be no exception. Nor should the 'constitutional copycat'[3] theorem be extended beyond its narrow limits. The various political, empirical and intellectual factors are included less in terms of their potential relevance to the country's future constitutional development than in terms of the need to widen the comparative scope of the analysis.

2. THE PARTY POLICIES

The constitutional policies of the National Party have been institutionalised over the past thirty-five years, and a modern part thereof is enshrined in the government's new constitution. These matters are dealt with in the previous and following chapters respectively. Among the other internal parties with constitutional policies are:[4]

(a) The Progressive Federal Party

The constitutional policy of the official parliamentary Opposition comprises two basic components.[5] The first relates to the constitutive phase of the constitutional conference. The convention is seen as a solution to the legitimacy problems affecting the existing constitution and official constitutional processes. It would accommodate all significant political groups which did not advocate violence at the time of its inception,[6] and its main

* The Notes and References to this chapter commence on page 140.

function would be to devise a new constitution for the country on a consensus basis. It would stand in an advisory relationship to Parliament, which would be responsible for the phased introduction of the new system and would thereafter terminate its legislative supremacy. Other political institutions would remain intact during the constitutional deliberations, but it is envisaged that the government of the day would systematically amend discriminatory laws and ameliorate various socio-economic inequalities.

The second part of PFP policy comprises the substantive constitutional proposals which the party would submit to the national convention. Their most salient features by South African standards are a general adult franchise and the absence of any reference to racial or ethnic factors. There is a strong sense of constitutionalism, as evidenced by a constitutional court which could uphold the constitution and enforce an entrenched bill of rights, as well as an ombudsman. Comparatively the proposals conform more to the liberal-democratic tradition of constitutionalism than do other constitutional models in circulation in South Africa.

In institutional terms the proposals indicate an attempt to incorporate several consociational features into an orthodox federal arrangement.[7] There would be a constitutionally-secured division of competence between a federal legislature and various state assemblies, supplemented by the secondary federal characteristics: bicameralism,[8] equal state representation in the upper chamber, the right of the states to change their constitutions unilaterally and to participate in the amendment of the national constitution, and the institutional basis for decentralised government.[9] The composition of the member states of the federation would be regionally, and not communally, based, giving rise to a territorial-federal as opposed to a corporate-federal arrangement. The non-discriminatory nature of the proposals indicates that state boundaries would be drawn so as to create a symmetrical federation and not to translate national heterogeneity into relative state homogeneity.[10] Nevertheless there are indications that communal factors would carry some weight in this process. The recommendation that the states be relatively small in size would, given the legacy of residential segregation in South Africa, tend to create an asymmetrical arrangement. Furthermore the boundaries commission appointed by the convention would be required to take into account, inter alia, the 'community of interests of the population' and the 'desirability of a high degree of homogeneity'. Finally, the commission would be required to look specifically at existing semi-autonomous areas (that is, self-governing homelands) to ascertain whether, with appropriate boundary adjustments, they could provide a suitable basis for federal states. These factors indicate the possibility of a partially asymmetrical federation emerging in the short term, the furthest concession the proposals make to the consociational principle of segmental autonomy.

The other consociational principles are applied consistently in the PFP constitutional plan. The federal executive would accommodate a grand coalition, its chairman (the Prime Minister) being elected by the federal assembly,[11] and the members being appointed by the chairman in proportion to party representation in the assembly, and after consultation with party leaders. Membership of the cabinet would be incompatible with continued membership of either federal chamber, the resultant semi-separation of powers being a favourable feature for consociationalism.[12] The close affinity of this arrangement with the Swiss federal executive (which Lijphart regards as a prototypal grand coalition[13]) is further evidence of the compatibility of consociational principles with a conventional federal constitution; in the case under discussion, however, the power-sharing aspects of the federal executive would be constitutionally prescribed. The Senate, besides its conventional federal composition, would cater for the consociational incorporation of cultural groups through registered cultural councils.[14] This type of functional representation would be an innovation in the South African context, although it has various precedents in the empirical consociations.[15] In addition a federal Finance Council, comprised of representatives of the federal and state governments and non-government experts, would constitute a type of third chamber. Its main function would be to examine federal and state budgets and to determine the amounts of revenue and loan funds which each state could claim from the federal treasury. Its decisions would be enforceable, unless overridden by majorities in both the federal assembly and the state government concerned. As in Canada, these proposals would introduce the grand coalition principle into the institutions which would be central to the maintenance of the federal system.[16] Proportionality as a basis of representation is envisaged for all legislative bodies, federal and regional, as well as for the federal executive.[17] The veto power would vest in any minority of ten or fifteen per cent in the federal assembly, on all decisions other than those relating to money bills, matters of administrative detail, and the election of the Prime Minister; it would also operate in the federal executive, although it is not clear on what basis. The veto would avail groups of states in respect of constitutional amendments,[18] and both individual states and cultural councils in respect of legislation affecting their particular interests. It would also operate within state institutions.[19]

From this survey it is clear that the consociational elements inherent in federal theory are jointly and severally accentuated in the Progressive Federal Party's constitutional policy, which endorses the Lijphart view that consociational democracy should, if possible, be introduced in a federal form.[20] Inevitably the proposals would involve in practice the same problems that are associated with federal and consociational systems of government in circumstances demanding rapid socio-economic reform, most pertinently inefficiency, immobilism and entrenchment of the status quo, through their emphasis on consensuality and on constitutional, as opposed to majoritarian, democracy.

(b) The New Republic Party

As opposed to the open-ended emphasis in the PFP's proposal for a national convention, the New Republic Party stresses in its constitutional policy[21] the need to use existing institutions as a point of departure in future constitutional developments. Its policy can be categorised as an elaboration of the government's own constitutional plan.[22]

The NRP accepts the existence of 'four main groups' in South African society as presently defined by statute, namely whites, Indians, coloureds and blacks. For constitutional purposes it makes a further distinction between 'homeland blacks' and 'non-homeland blacks',[23] and advocates the incorporation of the latter, together with whites, Indians and coloureds, into a corporate-federal political structure, reminiscent of the defunct United Party's race federation. Each of the four groups would have its own institutions at the local, provincial and national levels of government, and there would be joint consultative machinery at each level. The allocation of functions would be done according to the 'principle of subsidiarity'—that is no function would be allocated to a higher authority if it could be carried out efficiently by a lower one. At all levels each group would have control over its own legislative, executive and administrative authorities, at the apex of which would be the four group parliaments. In addition there would be various 'federal' authorities with specified powers over matters affecting all groups: a bicameral legislature with chambers of equal status,[24] an executive committee elected on a proportional basis by members of the legislature with a rotating chairman[25] (who would also be head of state), a federal judiciary, and a financial committee. The constitution would be highly rigid, amendments requiring approval by the federal legislature, and referendum support from a majority of voters and concurrent majorities within at least three groups. A further 'confederal' arrangement would accommodate the 'federal republic' and the various homelands.[26] This would consist of joint decision-making bodies to deliberate on matters of common interest, but the proposals provide no organisational detail on these matters.[27] Powers would be delegated to the confederal authorities by the member states, and exact relationships would be defined in a series of treaties. The NRP describes its constitutional policy as involving a 'federal-confederal' arrangement for South Africa.

There are several consociational elements in the NRP constitutional proposals, but these do not require specific elaboration. The scheme has a close affinity with the government's new constitution and its constellation proposals, the major point of difference being the position of 'urban blacks'. In overall political terms, its appropriateness, feasibility and significance for the legitimacy crisis in South Africa can be evaluated on a similar basis as the government's constitutional policies.

(c) The Labour Party

In 1978 the Labour Party executive of the Coloured Persons Representative Council appointed the Du Preez Commission to investigate alternative constitutional proposals, which could serve as a basis for negotiation with the government. The report of the commission[28] was tabled in the CPRC, where it was unanimously accepted after the Opposition had left the chamber.[29] The Labour Party was thus predominantly responsible for the initiation, drafting and endorsement of the commission's report, and it became its official constitutional policy.

The Du Preez Report provides critical analyses of the government's constitutional proposals of 1977, the PFP's federal constitution, past and proposed forms of partition, theories of pluralism, and the principle of majoritarianism. Brief reference is made to consociationalism and its significance for future constitutional developments, but the system is rejected on the ground that the South African society is not deeply divided to the point of disintegration and therefore in need of remedial consociational treatment. The nature of the conflict in South Africa is depicted as being not ethnic or cultural, but 'horizontal'—that is, political, social and economic— and the conflict is seen as being susceptible to constitutional containment only through 'a process of democratisation'. Recurring reference is made to the fact that it is the abuse of the Westminster system in the past, and not the system itself, which has been the fault, and the report suggests that, if properly utilised to give effect to popular political sovereignty, the Westminster system would be an ideal constitutional model for the future.[30]

In its own recommendations the commission advocates a unitary system of government based on a general principle of non-discrimination.[31] In effect it endorses a fully-democratised version of the South African constitution as it existed in 1980. This would involve a universal adult franchise and common electoral rolls to elect members to an enlarged House of Assembly. All members of the Senate would be indirectly elected by parliamentarians and provincial councillors, and the Senate would function as a chamber of legislative review. The executive would be drawn from the majority party in parliament with traditional Westminster forms of responsibility. The State President would continue to be elected at a joint session of both legislative chambers and serve as head of state. Provincial councils would be retained, with no greater powers or security of tenure than at present. Judicial independence from the other branches of government would be sought by empowering the judiciary itself to appoint new members to its ranks. The system would not only incorporate basic Westminster constitutional principles but would also involve a substantial degree of institutional continuity with the past, save that the political system would become fully inclusive.[32]

Three variations on the Westminster paradigm are evident in the Labour party proposals, one of which is a consociational characteristic, namely proportional representation in parliament and the provincial councils. For parliament the extreme form of proportionality would be used, there being a single country-wide constituency with electors voting for political parties and not candidates. The only qualification would be a five per cent popular support requirement before a party could share in the distribution of seats, a threshold designed to prevent political fragmentation. The electoral system is justified on the grounds that it would prevent a minority party from gaining a majority of parliamentary seats, obviate the time-consuming process of redelimiting the country to accommodate the newly enfranchised voters, and prevent the exploitation of *de facto* 'racially' exclusive constituencies, a legacy of years of residential segregation. But extreme proportionality increases the prospects of a multi-party system, a fact which reveals a basic inconsistency in the Du Preez proposals: the Westminster system is adopted as a normative model, but the proportional electoral system would not give rise to the two-party system which is responsible for many of its features.[33] It would be difficult to form a single-party cabinet, yet the proposals insist that executive authority would be the sole prerogative of the parliamentary majority and that the principle of proportionality should not apply in the formation of a cabinet. The other two Westminster variations are not inherently consociational, but also reveal internal contradictions in the proposals—the constitution would be supreme and highly rigid, and there would be an entrenched bill of rights. These features imply a judicial testing-right which is inconsistent with the notion of the political supremacy of the electorate, to which continual emphasis is given in the report. While the principles of popular democracy and Diceyan notions of sovereignty are espoused, the institutional recommendations imply a system of rigid constitutionalism.

Save for the proportional electoral system, the Labour Party's constitutional proposals have little significance from a consociational point of view. At the time of their promulgation the antipathy between them and the government's constitutional policies highlighted the legitimacy problems facing the state, since the Labour Party had received a substantial majority of electoral support during the tenure of the CPRC. But despite this discrepancy the party opted in early 1983 to participate in the government's constitution. While this was a controversial decision among coloured persons, leading to several resignations among prominent party members, the party's constitutional policy lost much of its significance in the process.[34]

(d) Inkatha[35]

In common with other black organisations, Inkatha has not adopted a fixed constitutional position but has formulated a set of principles as a basis for future negotiation.[36] In terms of existing constitutional trends the most salient principle concerns the status of the homelands: the maintenance of the geographical integrity of South Africa is regarded as a non-negotiable factor in future constitutional developments, and homeland independence as a violation thereof. Deriving from this stance are demands for one nationality, one citizenship, and one economy. Inkatha makes common cause with other groups which regard a representative national convention as the only legitimate forum for determining the constitutional future of the country. Its own constitutional proposals are presented in the most basic terms, as involving 'power sharing within one political system'. No particular form of power-sharing is proposed nor is any institutional detail provided. But a future constitution would have to involve 'the repeal of discriminatory laws as a first step towards political normality', the repeal of the 'political interference' laws, the creation of a 'truly free enterprise' economic system, and the legal entrenchment of minority rights. There would be a justiciable bill of rights based on the Inkatha 'Statement of Belief'.[37] As far as the homelands are concerned, these would be consolidated and given provincial status, provided there was 'regionality without ethnicity'.

Because of their generalised nature it is not possible to provide a consociational analysis of the Inkatha constitutional principles. The references to power-sharing and minority rights do not in themselves indicate a commitment to a consociational form of government. Moreover, power-sharing seems at times to be understood in terms of communal representation by blacks and whites in common institutions, which contradicts the repeated disavowal of any constitutional reference to factors of race or ethnicity. On the whole the principles uphold traditional concepts of liberal-constitution-alism. Their significance was superseded with the publication of the Buthelezi Report which recommended a consociational form of government for Natal and KwaZulu[38] and was subsequently accepted by Inkatha.

3. THE EMPIRICAL CONSTITUTIONS

(a) The Turnhalle constitution

Of some comparative relevance for South Africa was the proposed con-stitution for Namibia which emanated from the Turnhalle constitutional conference in 1978. Previously constitutional developments in the territory had been under the direct control of the South African Government.[39] This had resulted in the establishment of a legislative assembly and ancillary institutions for the white electorate, each having a similar constitutional status to the corresponding provincial authority in the Republic. For blacks the statutory foundations had been laid for the establishment of homelands according to the South African precedent, and by 1977 the first stage of self-government had been attained by four of the statutorily defined black groups. For coloured persons a partially elective advisory council had been established for those not accommodated in the Coloured Persons Represen-tative Council. Before the Turnhalle conference the internal constitutional structure of the territory resembled that of South Africa in many respects.

The Turnhalle conference[40] was held between September 1975 and November 1977 and attended by eleven invited delegations, each of which purported to represent a different 'ethnic' group.[41] For the most part delegates were drawn from the institutions created by the South African Government. At its first session the conference issued a 'Declaration of Intent'[42] and resolved that decisions of the conference and its committees would be taken by consensus. The most prominent function of the confer-ence was performed by the constitution committee, whose third draft con-stitution was accepted in plenary session and incorporated in a petition to the South African Government requesting the institution of a provisional government according to its terms.[43] Appropriate legislation was prepared for Parliament but international developments prevented its enactment. The Turnhalle conference was terminated and as a 'national convention' exercise proved to have little impact, although its achievements were significant in the light of the territory's political history. Its failure may be attributed to the exclusion of a major political force in the country, the South West African Peoples' Organisation, to the internationalisation of the Namibia issue, and to several features of the constitution itself. The exercise also highlighted the futility of embarking on a constitutive constitu-tional phase before the holding of free elections and the identification of authentic leaders.

The Turnhalle constitution survived the conference's demise when it was incorporated into the policy of the Democratic Turnhalle Alliance, a grouping of political parties that had attended the conference. It provided for three levels of government—central, 'communal' and local—and a functional distribution of authority based on the separation of powers doctrine.[44]

At the local level representative 'ethnic' authorities would exercise standard powers of local concern, and co-ordinating metropolitan bodies would be created where ecessary. At the second level would be eleven elected legislatures (the 'representative authorities'), one for each group. These bodies were an extension of previous separate development institutions such as the homeland authorities, the council for coloured persons, and the white legislative assembly. Each representative authority would have its own executive, and would have personal jurisdiction over members of the relevant group. They would also nominate members to the central legislature (the 'national assembly'), a unicameral body with sixty seats, of which forty-four would be divided equally among the eleven groups, and the remainder would be allocated proportionately.[45] Authority on matters of manifestly national concern would vest in the assembly, while the representative authorities would have original legislative competence over other not insubstantial matters,[46] legislation on these matters prevailing over repugnant enactments of the assembly.[47] However, the division of powers between the two levels of government would be flexible, and liberal provision was made for the delegation of authority in either direction. The national assembly would operate on a qualified-majority basis, all decisions requiring overall majority support, and in addition concurrent majorities within each ethnic delegation. A veto exercised in the assembly could be reversed by the relevant representative assembly, but where exercised by more than three groups it would be conclusive.

Executive power at the central level would vest in a president and ministers' council, the former nominated by the South African Government for the interim period and having the predominantly ceremonial powers of a head of state.[48] Each group represented in the national assembly would be entitled to nominate one member to the ministers' council, and to remove him at the group's discretion.[49] The chairman of the council would be elected by, and remain responsible to, the assembly at large, but his tenure would depend on continued membership of the assembly, and therefore on the confidence of the relevant representative authority as well. Decisions in the council would be taken by consensus, unless it was unanimously agreed that an ordinary or a two-thirds or a three-quarters majority vote would suffice for a particular decision.[50] These principles would apply to all decisions, and no institutional mechanism was provided for resolving deadlocks.

The Turnhalle constitution vested judicial power in a Supreme Court, the members of which would be appointed by the ministers' council and would have security of tenure, subject to dismissal by resolution of the national assembly. Apart from customary judicial functions, the court would have a testing-right over legislation enacted by the national assembly, representative authorities and local bodies, which could be invalidated for excess of jurisdiction. A separate constitutional court[51] would advise the various legislatures, at their request, whether proposed legislation was compatible with the declaration of fundamental rights contained in the constitution. An adverse finding by the court would have to be tabled in the appropriate legislature, but could not avert enactment.[52] The bill of rights was based on the Basic Rights of the Federal Republic of Germany and was a significant innovation, even in its unenforceable form, in the southern African context. Provision was also made for a rudimentary ombudsman-figure who could investigate complaints of alleged infringements of the bill of rights resulting from administrative practice or action, and mediate, if necessary, with the appropriate authority.[53]

This constitution displayed many characteristics of liberal-democratic constitutionalism such as the general adult franchise, separation and division of powers, checks and balances, independent judiciary, bill of rights and constitutional rigidity. In institutional terms it showed some similarity with the Westminster model, but avoided its thoroughgoing majoritarianism through several consociational features. The grand coalition principle would be evident in the composition of the ministers' council, as would variants of the proportionality principle in the form of minority over-representation in the assembly, and parity of group representation in the council. The mutual veto would be available in a slightly qualified form in the assembly, but in its extreme form in the council. The principle of segmental autonomy would be institutionalised along separate development lines among the eleven groups on the basis of the personality principle. From the federal perspective this could be seen as a form of 'corporate federalism', supported by the secondary federal characteristics.[54] Save for one qualification, namely that the 'segments' would be statutorily defined and not the product of free political association, the Turnhalle constitution displayed all the main features of the consociational model. The qualification, however, was critical, and affects any comparison of the Turnhalle constitution with consociationalism or other constitutional systems. The consociational features, moreover, portended slow, inefficient and expensive government, not an attractive option for a newly independent state. Even among the Turnhalle participants they were the cause of serious divisions, and in the case of the smaller and less prosperous groups the realization of any degree of meaningful self-government would have been unlikely.[55]

Since the termination of the Turnhalle conference the constitutional development of Namibia has been delayed, pending negotiations between South Africa and the international community.[56] In terms of a wide enabling provision the State President was empowered to legislate for the territory by proclamation with 'a view to the eventual attainment of independence'.[57] This power was delegated to an administrator-general[58] who conducted an internal election for a constituent assembly,[59] which was subsequently converted into a national assembly with extensive legislative powers.[60] In addition a ministers' council was established with the same functions and relationship with the assembly as envisaged in the Turnhalle constitution. These bodies were both controlled by the Democratic Turnhalle Alliance from their inception. The national assembly promoted the notion of elected second-tier authorities, corresponding to those envisaged in the Turnhalle constitution, and elections were held for most groups towards the end of 1980.[61] While international attempts to secure a Namibian settlement in terms of United Nations Security Council resolution 435 of 1978 were unsuccessfully pursued,[62] the DTA-controlled national assembly continued to legislate by proclamation and the ministers' council to act as the territory's cabinet. In 1981 the national assembly was increased in size to seventy-two members, and the ministers' council to fifteen. However in that year, and increasingly in 1982, the DTA began to fragment and lose political support, and in early 1983 Pretoria resumed direct control of Namibia through the office of the administrator-general. The period of quasi-consociational government inspired by the Turnhalle conference was of relatively short duration and it seems unlikely that the conference and its constitution will have much impact on the long-term developments in Namibia.[63] In retrospect the episode can be seen as an attempt to reserve substantial political power for the white minority despite the trappings of constitutional reform, and to reinforce the socio-economic status quo.

(b) **The Rhodesian-Zimbabwean constitutional transition**

Despite the socio-political upheaval attending it, the constitutional transition from Rhodesia to Zimbabwe displayed a high degree of institutional continuity and did not change the fundamental nature of the state system. It involved the political control of Westminster-type institutions being transferred gradually from whites to blacks. Black attention tended to focus on parliament throughout the transition, but as this body became more representative white attention tended to shift to the bureaucracy and armed forces. Different consociational devices were used at different stages of the transition, affecting the majoritarian bias of the constitutional system in different ways.

The modern constitutional history of Zimbabwe[64] began with the 1961 constitution of Southern Rhodesia which became effective while the territory was still part of the Central African Federation. This was the first of many arrangements during the 'fancy franchise' era[65] which purported to involve blacks in the political system, while retaining political control in white hands. It provided for a legislative assembly of sixty-five members, of whom fifty would be elected by 'A' roll and fifteen by 'B' roll voters. While both rolls were nominally open, the 'A' roll qualifications[66] rendered it predominantly white, and the system amounted in practice to communal representation for blacks and whites in the unicameral parliament.[67] Constitutional amendments required a two-thirds legislative majority, a number within reach of the white component. Some amendments also required the British Government's assent, or that of the country's four 'racial' groups expressed in separate referenda—the latter 'concurrent majority' implied a type of mutual veto, but the procedure was never used in practice. Legislation could be delayed by a constitutional council for a six-month period for non-compliance with a detailed declaration of rights.[68] Apart from these qualifications, and the dependent status of the country, the constitution was of the Westminster export variety. On dissolution of the federation, South-

ern Rhodesia resumed all functions previously vested in the federal authorities and the 1961 constitution remained intact, save for the establishment of
a local appeal court.

Shortly after the unilateral declaration of independence in 1965,[69] a new
constitution was ratified by the legislative assembly. It dispensed with all
forms of external control, to accord with the government's view of the
country's independent status, but as far as the internal distribution of
authority was concerned the old constitution was re-enacted almost in its
entirety. After several years of unsuccessful negotiations between Rhodesia
and Britain, the Whaley Commission was appointed to consider a new
constitution for the country. Its recommendations were partly incorporated
in a draft constitution which was approved in a referendum in 1969, at which
the white electorate also voted in favour of republican status. The republican constitution[70] eliminated all constitutional ties with Britain, but retained the essentially British structure of government. The President assumed the Crown's functions as head of state,[71] and executive power was
vested in a Prime Minister and cabinet drawn from and responsible to the
legislature, according to Westminster rules and conventions.[72] Parliament
became bicameral for the first time, with a dominant lower house[73] comprising fifty directly elected white members and eight black members
elected by an electoral college of traditional and elected leaders.[74] The
Senate comprised ten whites elected by the white members of the House,
ten black chiefs (five each from Matabeleland and Mashonaland) elected by
the Council of Chiefs, and three (later five) senators appointed by the
President.[75] The principle of communal representation in the legislature
was more strongly enforced than before, because of the colour determinants
of the voters' rolls and membership of either House. There was provision
for the number of blacks in the House to be increased in proportion to the
amount of income tax paid by blacks, until there was parity of representation for blacks and whites,[76] but in practice the electoral arithmetic was not
materially affected.

Among the other obvious Westminster features, the principle of legislative supremacy was most prominent in the republican constitution.[77] The
Declaration of Rights was made non-justiciable,[78] and the Constitutional
Council was disestablished. Statutory measures incompatible with the Declaration could only be temporarily delayed by the Senate Legal Committee,[79] and the latter could not scrutinise money or constitutional bills,[80] nor
delay bills certified by the Prime Minister to be in the national interest.[81]
Furthermore, the Declaration would not exclude the differential treatment
of persons if such treatment would 'promote harmonious relations'.[82] There
were therefore few legal restraints on the white-controlled political institutions. The gross under-representation of blacks in the legislature, the existence of majority party cabinets, and the absence of a veto power, ruled out
an institutional basis for a consociational type of government. A veto was
available to the black legislative minority only in respect of constitutional
amendments, which required an affirmative vote of two-thirds of the total
membership of each House, but even this could be circumvented if a bill
which had not achieved the two-thirds majority in the Senate was re-

submitted to that body and approved by a simple majority.[83] The two-thirds majority in each House was peremptory in respect of amendments to the 'specially entrenched provisions', but these, and various entrenched provisions in other statutes,[84] were essential for the retention of the political and economic status quo, so that constitutional rigidity favoured the white minority. The overall picture was of a predominantly majoritarian Westminster-type constitution, whose variations on the Westminster paradigm, particularly those relating to the franchise and composition of parliament, served to secure minority domination—the antithesis of consociationalism.

During the operation of this constitution attempts were made to reach a constitutional settlement acceptable to the white government, internal and external black leaders, and Britain.[85] In March 1978 an 'internal agreement' was signed in Salisbury, following talks between the government and leaders of three black political groupings within the country.[86] The agreement can be regarded as a type of consociational pact among internal élites acting in terms of the self-denying hypothesis, but it was not a self-conscious 'union of opposites', in the consociational sense, because of the absence of the Patriotic Front, one of the major parties to the conflict. It provided for a transitional government consisting of an Executive Council, comprising the four signatories to the agreement,[87] and a Ministerial Council, comprising equal numbers of black and white ministers.[88] This involved the consociational incorporation of black leaders into the existing system of government, on an informal extra-constitutional basis. Effective control remained with whites as the new authorities stood in an advisory relationship to the existing parliamentary institutions, although during the transition several discriminatory statutes were amended or repealed. The pairing of ministers in the allocation of cabinet portfolios, and the rotation of the Executive Council chairmanship (that is proportionality in the temporal dimension), can be seen, within the limits of the system, as attempts to provide a basis for power-sharing by the black participants. However, the consociational aspects of the transitional government contributed to its undemocratic and authoritarian qualities because of the unrepresentativeness of the black members and the gross over-representation of whites in the new bodies. They also had no material impact on the legitimacy problems affecting the state.

The Zimbabwe-Rhodesian constitution was drafted by an all-party committee and enacted by the outgoing Rhodesian Parliament.[89] After general elections had been held earlier in the year,[90] it came into effect on 1 June 1979. In broad outline the new system was similar to its republican predecessor, but for the first time consociational institutions became a prominent feature of the country's constitutional order—communal representation in the legislature, over-representation for the white minority, an institutionally required coalition executive, and a substantial veto power. For the House of Assembly white and black voters were entitled to elect twenty and seventy-two members respectively;[91] this component served as an electoral college for the election of eight additional white members from sixteen candidates nominated by the twenty elected whites.[92] The Senate consisted of ten black and ten white senators elected by the respective sections of the House, and ten chiefs elected by the Council of Chiefs. For the first time the black majority in the country acquired a majority in parliament. As far as the executive was concerned the President was required for the first five years to apportion cabinet posts among the parties represented in the House.[93] This arrangement introduced elements of a grand coalition into an otherwise Wesminster cabinet, and resulted in the appointment of five white ministers to the first national government.[94] There was no constitutional provision for a minority veto in the cabinet. A substantial veto was available in respect of the legislative process and constitutional amendments, and 'black majority rule' entailed an end to Westminster notions of parliamentary supremacy.[95] While normal enactments required ordinary legislative majorities, the constitutional provisions relating to the head of state, executive, legislature, judiciary, service commissions, finance, declaration of rights, and entrenched procedure itself, required affirmative votes of at least two-thirds of the senators and seventy-eight members of the House to be amended,[96] which gave an accessible and conclusive veto to the white parliamentarians as far as the composition and functioning of the main institutions of government were concerned. Various non-constitutional statutes were also specially entrenched in this manner.[97] Other constitutional amendments required only a two-thirds majority in each House, and if the Senate failed to provide this majority it could be overruled after a delay of six months. One consequence of these amending procedures would have been the perpetuation of the prevailing level of white representation, and therefore the white veto, in parliament for at least ten years,[98] after which a commission of review might recommend a reduction in the number of white seats. Although such recommendation might be implemented by a simple majority vote in the Assembly,[99] the composition of the review commission would safeguard white interests,[100] so that even these amendments would require white approval. Additional white control would have emanated from various other commissions regulating the judiciary, public service, prison service, police force and defence forces, since commission members, as well as the permanent heads of the services and other functionaries such as the Attorney-General and the Auditor-General, would require senior experience for minimum periods (in most cases five years) before the enactment of the constitution.

Besides these limitations on the new government the Declaration of Rights was once more made justiciable,[101] although pre-existing laws were beyond its reach. The government was therefore both constrained by discriminatory Rhodesian laws and prevented by some of the Declaration's provisions (for example in relation to private property) from innovating certain socio-economic reforms. Although the Zimbabwe-Rhodesian constitution provided the institutional basis for constitutional and consociational government, these very features were highly contentious because they restrained and limited the power of the popular and legislative majorities, and were seen as aggrandised devices for protecting minority white interests. Although a coalition form of government prevailed for the constitution's short duration, the absence of a major interest group ensured that the legitimacy problems remained substantially unresolved.

The independence constitution was accepted by the Zimbabwe-Rhodesian Government and the external black parties at the Lancaster House conference, held between 10 September and 15 September 1979 under British chairmanship.[102] After a return to legality,[103] Britain resumed direct rule over the country. It enacted the Zimbabwean constitution through order-in-council,[104] and made legislative provision for the attainment of independence.[105] Elections were held under British supervision during February 1980,[106] and the constitution became operative on 1 April that year.

A substantial degree of institutional continuity is again evident in the new constitution, although there has been a significant movement towards majoritarianism in the removal of many legal restraints imposed by its immediate predecessor. The main innovations relate to the composition of the legislature and executive. White representation in the House has been reduced to twenty members elected on a constituency basis by voters on the white electoral roll, the other eighty members being elected by voters registered on the common roll.[107] The composition of the Senate and its method of election has been retained, save that the number of non-chief black senators has been increased from ten to fourteen, and provision is made for an additional six senators to be appointed by the President on the Prime Minister's recommendation.[108] There is no longer a formal prohibition on the formation of single-party Westminster executives and the coalition features of the Zimbabwe-Rhodesian cabinet have been omitted from the constitution.[109] Nevertheless the coalition principle was strongly evident in the first Zimbabwean cabinet.[110]

While the more limited white participation in the legislature and executive have reduced the capacity of the white minority to influence decision-making in these bodies, constitutional rigidity again provides some security. The constitution is 'supreme law', and legislation inconsistent with its provisions will be void to the extent of the inconsistency.[111] The ordinary legislative process, which operates on a simple majority basis,[112] and constitutional amendments, which require the approval of seventy members in the House and two-thirds of the Senate (subject to Senate disapproval being overruled by the House) cannot be delayed by the white minority.[113] The requirement of unanimity in the House to amend the specially entrenched constitutional provisions, however, affords the white legislative minority an absolute veto power. This will endure for ten years in respect of amendments affecting the Declaration of Rights, and for seven in respect of the composition and functions of the legislature, after which the ordinary amending procedure will apply. The content of the Declaration of Rights, and its method of enforcement,[114] has not been changed significantly in the new constitution, but a broad judicial discretion to overrule official reliance on the savings clauses in many provisions of the Declaration has been introduced. A law or action can be held to be in contravention of the declaration if reliance on the savings proviso could not be 'reasonably justifiable in a democratic society'.[115] This innovation imposes additional, though slightly vague, restraints on the government.[116] Finally, white influence in the bureacracy has again been ensured, though in less conspicuous form, in the requirements pertaining to the composition of the commissions controlling various branches of the administration, as well as the qualifications of prominent officials.[117]

In institutional terms the transition from Rhodesia to Zimbabwe was characterised by a remarkable degree of continuity as the political system became progressively more inclusive. Within a broadly liberal-democratic constitutional framework the main changes related to the franchise, the racial composition of parliament, the availability and effect of the veto power, and the legal status of the bill of rights. The virtual exclusion of blacks from the political institutions of the Rhodesian state ensured that the main constitutional issue during the period under discussion was perceived by the political actors as being black participation, and its extent, in these institutions. In the constitutional debate blacks and whites were regarded as cohesive groups—from the consociational perspective, as communal segments. This factor, apart from any others, mitigated against the emergence of a fully consociational arrangement because the black/white demographic realities excluded any possibility of a 'multiple balance of power'.[118] There was also little prospect of segmental autonomy because of the sparsity of whites in a large territory. Nevertheless consociational devices were in evidence during the transition. Those emanating from the internal agreement and the Rhodesia-Zimbabwean constitution were not successful because the legitimacy problem had not been resolved. Their stringent qualification of majority rule may have even exacerbated the conflict during this unrepresentative phase of government. But once the accommodation of legitimacy had been reached at Lancaster House the position changed significantly. The agreement was strongly consociational—a self-conscious 'union of opposites', in which accepted leaders reached a constitutional compromise which was more acceptable to all than a continuation of the political and military conflict. It was still not possible to make the constitution fully consociational, because of the reasons previously stated. Nevertheless it was possible to include in the independence constitution several consociational devices, such as the over-representation of whites in parliament and the legislative veto, and although these created certain tensions they were politically successful during the early years of independence, partly because the basic legitimation problem had been overcome. For the same reason it was possible to form a coalition cabinet without any institutional inducement, although this is also attributable to the statesmanship and moderation displayed by the Prime Minister. During 1982 the coalition was weakened by the dismissal of Nkomo, and the possibility of a one-party system was mooted from government quarters. However, in respect of the critical consociational accommodation the Rhodesian-Zimbabwean constitutional experience has some comparative relevance for South Africa.[119] Consociational devices cannot in isolation resolve fundamental political conflicts, but they can be invoked to sustain a pre-existing political accommodation.

(c) The national states

The conferment of legal independence on the national states in South Africa, and the enactment of an independence constitution in each case, has led to the existence of several new constitutional regimes on the subcontinent. The first example was not promising from a comparative point of view, as the relevant model for Transkei was the South African constitution. It has been said of the Transkei constitution that it is impossible to detect 'any feature adopted or adapted from the numerous constitutional experiences elsewhere in the new nations of sub-Saharan Africa or Asia'.[120] The constitutions of the other national states proved to be marginally more exotic and, without providing a detailed description of the various systems, three matters of comparative relevance can be referred to, though their significance for the consociational theme is only indirect.[121]

(i) *Semi-presidentialism*

While the Transkei constitution provided for the traditional Westminster diffusion of executive power between the heads of state and government, and relied on Westminster constitutional theory to resolve possible conflicts between the two, Bophuthatswana, Venda and Ciskei adopted semi-presidential systems, in advance of South Africa's own move to a species of presidentialism. Although the three systems are not identical, the Bophuthatswana model serves as a representative example. The Bophuthatswana President is elected for a five-year term by members of the National Assembly sitting as an electoral college and must himself be a member of the Assembly. He is subject to dismissal during his term of office on impeachment by the Assembly, and is eligible for re-election unless the Assembly expressly resolves to the contrary. The presidency combines the roles of head of state and head of government, although in the latter capacity the President is required to consult the executive council, which he appoints from the ranks of the legislature. There is no statutory provision for a Prime Minister, and the Speaker of the assembly serves as acting President when the office is vacant.

The significance of this arrangement from a consociational point of view is that the semi-separation of powers which it entails is a favourable institutional feature for consociational government.[122] The system is not fully presidential, in that the President has no mandate separate from that of the legislature and is constitutionally limited in choosing ministers;[123] but in relation to the grand coalition principle it combines the advantages of both presidentialism and parliamentarism. The fact that the President is elected for a five-year term, and that he and the cabinet are not dependent on the continued support of the legislature, provides the institutional leeway for a coalition cabinet to act as a 'conspiratorial élite cartel' and to effect compromises for which they would not be directly accountable in parliament. The fact that ministers must for the most part be chosen from the legislature facilitates the formation of a grand coalition, in that all parties represented in parliament can be drawn into the cabinet. The major disadvantage of this arrangement is the predominant institutional position of the President. Unlike the Swiss system, with which it has several similarities, there is no rotation of the presidency, and this militates against the emergence of a collegial cabinet. And in practice the respective presidents dominate the political process and the system of government is unconsociational. Of comparative relevance for South Africa is the fact that an isolated consociational feature can be of little significance in itself in the face of predominantly countervailing forces.

(ii) *Traditional and modern combined*

The four independence constitutions afford significant recognition to traditional leaders in the legislature, and purport to balance their authority and power with that of the representative leaders.[124] In all cases the unicameral legislature comprises both elected members and chiefs, with the proportion of the latter ranging from fifty per cent in Transkei to sixty per cent in Ciskei.[125] In all cases other than Transkei the President can nominate members to the legislature, which further weakens the position of the elected members. As ordinary members of parliament chiefs can aspire to ministerial rank. From the consociational perspective the prominence of chiefs in these constitutions draws attention to those neglected principles of African public law according to which consensuality was an important feature of the political decision-making process, and authority had to be consensually legitimated.[126] These principles have a greater affinity with consociationalism than Westminster majoritarianism, and are to some extent evident in the constitutions under discussion. In terms of the Bophuthatswana constitution the component parts of the legislature must jointly and severally approve a motion for the removal of the President, a mutual veto device aimed at promoting 'obligatory conciliation' between the traditional and modern elements.[127] The concurrent majority principle is also applied in the legislative process if thirty members of the National Assembly petition the Speaker for a decision to be taken separately by the elected and *ex officio* components of the House; in this situation the veto is effective for a full year.

In the comparative African context, however, the status and potential influence of chiefs in the homeland systems of government is strikingly unique.[128] In those African states which uncharacteristically opted for bicameralism there was even an avoidance of placing chiefs in a weak upper house, in spite of the initial attraction of this arrangement.[129] In the more preponderant unicameral systems there was seldom express provision for traditional leaders and, where there was, never to the same numerical extent as in the homeland constitutions.[130] It is also an historic reality that the chiefs in South Africa lost much of their traditional prestige and status when they came to be incorporated into the 'Bantu authorities' system,[131] where they represented the white bureaucracy, often against their own people. With the advent of homeland self-government chiefs became salaried administrators of the respective homelands and susceptible to administrative removal, so that it became misleading to characterise them as traditional or natural leaders. In all cases they have exercised considerable influence on the pre-independence power-structure, and in some their presence has had a crucial bearing on the acceptance of independence itself.[132]

In terms of the independence constitutions chiefs continue to be dependent for their appointment and power on the governments of the national states.[133] In these circumstances they hardly qualify as the representative leaders required for authentic consociationalism and, whatever their individual proclivities towards coalition politics, the institutional reality is that their collective strength places chiefs in a good position to obstruct any legislation which directly or indirectly threatens their office or vested interests. It is furthermore ironical that the chiefs have been accommodated in legislative authorities, when the chief's original position was that of an upholder of tradition and seldom a legislator or initiator of change.[134] When seen in the wider socio-political context neither the mutual veto device referred to earlier, nor the use of 'traditional' elements of African public law, has any real significance for consociationalism.

(iii) *Constitutionalism and a bill of rights*

Both the Bophuthatswana and Ciskei constitutions embody an institution alien to the Westminster and South African constitutional traditions, namely a bill of rights. In content they are both modelled on the European Convention on Human Rights, and the rights therein may be broadly classified as liberal.[135] They purport to benefit all inhabitants of the territories, whether nationals or aliens, but nationals of the homeland states domiciled outside the respective jurisdictions (and most pertinently those in South Africa) derive no bill-of-rights benefits in their places of residence and employment. In each case the bill of rights is complemented by a rigid constitution which is described as the 'supreme law' of the territory, indicating strict adherence to one of the elements of constitutionalism.

As far as the status of these 'fundamental' rights is concerned, only the Bophuthatswana constitution renders them binding on the legislative, executive and judicial branches of government and permits their enforcement by the Supreme Court; the Ciskei constitution, by contrast, expressly provides that laws of the national assembly will not be invalid for contravention of its bill of rights.[136] In terms of section *eight* of the Bophuthatswana constitution a person may apply to court in the appropriate manner to enforce any of the constitution's fundamental rights, and the court is empowered to adjudicate in such matters and issue the necessary orders. The rights and freedoms contained in the declaration may be restricted only by a law of parliament with general application, but not to the extent that a right or freedom is totally abolished or encroached upon in its essence.[137] As any legislative restriction of a fundamental right would amount to a constitutional amendment, it would have to be effected in terms of the rigid amending procedure.[138] The supremacy and rigidity of the constitution, the bill of rights, and the system of judicial review which they imply, are prominent innovations in the South African constitutional context. Their relevance to the theme of this work is that consociationalism assumes a high degree of constitutionalism, and unless the government commits itself to the principle of constitutional government, which it has yet to do, it will be unable to introduce a consociational system.

The Bophuthatswana bill of rights, and its ancillary features, not only provided for South Africa a contiguous comparative model of constitutional government but also introduced a new, albeit temporary, constitutional function for the South African Appeal Court. The court was constituted as the final appellate tribunal for all decisions of the Bophuthatswana Supreme

Court, on the same basis as appeals from the South African provincial divisions. This meant that the Appellate Division would be the ultimate upholder of the constitution and enforcer of its provisions on fundamental rights, a situation of some irony in view of the alien nature of this function in the South African and Westminster constitutional traditions. The relationship between the Bophuthatswana Supreme Court and the South African Appellate Division (terminated in 1982) was analogous to that between the latter and the Judicial Committee of the Privy Council up to 1950, an analogy which was expressly drawn by the Bophuthatswana Court.[139] As far as constitutional review was concerned, this was also an alien function for the Privy Council when it acted as appellate tribunal on certain constitutional matters emanating from the dominions, in particular the federal states of Canada and Australia,[140] and in this capacity it was accused of 'incurable positivism'.[141] From the South African point of view the arrangement afforded the court an opportunity to reassess its approach to statutory interpretation in the circumstances of a wholly different constitutional order, and in the only constitutional matter which came on appeal the majority of the court showed an awareness of the need to interpret fundamental constitutional provisions differently to other statutes.[142] However, the opportunity for further experience in this capacity was denied the court when Bophuthatswana abolished the right of appeal to the South African Appellate Division in 1982.[143] If a charter of rights were introduced in South Africa, as well as other legal limitations on government, the norms of constitutionalism could be served only by a fresh judicial approach to the interpretation of this special type of statutory provision.[144]

4. THE COMMISSIONS

While several commissions of enquiry have over the years made a significant contribution to the constitutional and political debate in South Africa, their recommendations have not had a uniform impact on constitutional developments. Apart from those which have been rejected outright by the government,[145] some have been accepted but not implemented for financial or political reasons, and others have been accepted but implemented in ways not intended by the relevant commission. Despite their meagre practical influence a description of some of the more important recommendations serves to broaden the comparative background against which the government's constitution is analysed. The commissions could be distinguished with regard to whether they are official or non-official, or deal with national or sub-national matters, but here they are treated chronologically and related to the consociational theme.

(a) The Tomlinson Commission[146]

The terms of reference of the Tomlinson Commission were to report on a comprehensive scheme for the rehabilitation of black areas with a view to developing them within a social structure in keeping with black culture and based on effective socio-economic planning.[147] The commission gave a wide interpretation to these terms, as is evident from its recommendations.

These were based on its perception of the fundamental dichotomy facing South Africa, namely the complete integration, or the separate development, of the two main racial groups.[148] Its recommendations involved a consistent endorsement of the latter option, and suggested various steps for the practical realisation of separate development for blacks and whites, involving the full-scale development of black areas to provide for a diversified economy and the creation of development opportunities there. It recommended the consolidation of existing black areas on an ethnic basis into seven blocks, in which blacks would be gradually incorporated into the administrative process and there would be black political development. It was argued that if the financial recommendations relating to this programme were conscientiously carried out there would be dramatic increases in the proportion of the black population living in black areas.[149] The commission was of the view that its socio-economic development programme would derive its driving force from the prospects it would offer blacks for forms of political expression.[150] As a first step in political development blacks would assume responsibility for village boards, town councils and municipalities; thereafter administrative responsibility could be increased on a regional basis, and this might evolve into a type of provincial system in each of the seven black areas, with locally elected 'provincial governments'. No reference was made to the possible independence of these areas. As a corollary to this local and regional political involvement blacks would lose any claim to political rights in non-black areas, into which they would be allowed entry only as temporary migrant workers.[151] The Tomlinson Commission saw its development programme as the 'logical implementation of state policy as laid down in 1913 and 1936', a reference to the Acts of those years which restricted the use and occupation of land by blacks to certain specified areas.[152] The partial segregation established by those measures would now be supplemented by the economic development of black areas and a gradual accretion of political rights, so that separate development, as envisaged by the commission, would lead to the geographical, economic and political separation of blacks and whites.

In its White Paper the government accepted some and rejected other parts of the report.[153] It rejected as impracticable and unacceptable the consolidation of the various black areas into cohesive blocks, as well as the majority view that white entrepreneurs should be allowed to establish industries in the reserves and that 'white' capital be used for economic development.[154] Those recommendations that were accepted were never funded over the years according to the commission's estimates, and the administration was never capable of carrying out the measures necessary for the projected economic development.[155] As a result the social and economic reorganisation of the reserves, which was essential for the attainment of 'ultimate separate development', was never pursued along the lines recommended by the Tomlinson Commission.[156]

The government, however, did not see economic underdevelopment as irreconcilable with the development of political institutions in black areas, and the vague guidelines in the Tomlinson Report were vigorously pursued as far as the constitutional development of the homelands was concerned.

The Promotion of Bantu Self Government Act of 1959,[157] an elaboration of the earlier Black Authorities Act,[158] became an important statutory step in the implementation of separate development policy and the homelands programme, and the preamble to this Act revealed the influence of the Tomlinson Report. In its strategy to reduce the number of blacks who could demand political rights in the Republic, emphasis came to be placed in the ensuing years on the forms of political structures and constitutions,[159] so that legal independence was eventually attained without the 'reorientation of the economic structure' which the commission perceived to be necessary to alter the process of integration.[160] The legitimacy crisis of the 1980s may be partially attributed to the outpacing of social and economic realities by constitutional developments, and the failure of ultimate separate development. The government's 'constellation of states' and 'regional economic organisation' strategies may be seen as its response to the inadequacies of the black homelands.

In advocating a re-evaluation of various commission reports Wiechers[161] has suggested that the recommendations of the Tomlinson Commission, as well as those of the Fagan and Theron commissions, 'point to kinds of consociational arrangements which include elements of federalism and group accommodation'. Reference has already been made to the lines of convergence between separate development and consociationalism. The consociational aspects of separate development, however, have been conceived and implemented on an authoritarian basis in terms of statutory concepts of ethnicity. The many restrictions on genuine leaders and the meagre resources of the homelands preclude any genuine form of consociational accommodation among élites of equal strength. Even the 'segmental autonomy' of homeland blacks is severely circumscribed by financial and political factors, so that the Tomlinson Report cannot be regarded as implying a form of consociationalism for blacks and whites.

(b) The Theron Commission[162]

The Theron Commission had wide-ranging terms of reference relating to the development of coloured persons in the social, economic, political and cultural fields. While it was empowered to make recommendations on these matters, the Prime Minister emphasised shortly before the release of the report that the commission had not been appointed to devise an alternative policy for coloured persons but to suggest ameliorations which could be effected in terms of the government's policy.[163] The government in fact rejected several of the key social and political recommendations of the commission which came into conflict with its own policies for coloured persons.

Of the one hundred and seventy-eight recommendations made by the Theron Commission, only one had a direct bearing on the constitutional question of political rights for coloured persons.[164] In view of the subsequent misrepresentations of this recommendation it is appropriate to quote it in full:

'Since the Coloured population has no direct share or say in the decisive legislative institutions of the Republic of South Africa (ie Parliament, provincial councils, municipal councils and rural local authorities), and the successful development of the alternative measures taken for purposes of Coloured representation and self-determination is being hampered by strong opposition from the vast and effective majority of Colorureds, as well as by constitutional anomalies which in the opinion of the Commission cannot be eliminated satisfactorily and adequately, the Commission recommends that:

(a) with a view to the further extension of the political civil rights of Coloureds and the creation of opportunities for more constructive participation and co-operation, provision be made for satisfactory forms of direct Coloured representation and a direct say for Coloureds at the various levels of government and on the various decision-making bodies;

(b) with a view to the implementation of the proposal above, a committee of experts be appointed to make more detailed proposals in regard to the organisational and statutory adjustments required, provided that due regard shall be had to all the problems and considerations set forth fully in Chapters 17 and 21 of this report;

(c) in the process of constitutional adjustment it will have to be accepted that the existing Westminster-founded system of government will have to be changed to adapt it to the specific requirements of the South African plural population structure.'

The first part of this recommendation was approved by a majority of eleven commissioners to seven, but was not accepted by the government in its White Papers,[165] since it implied a major deviation from prevailing policy. In its new constitutional proposals, first publicised the following year, the government underlined its rejection by providing for an increase in the status and powers of the Coloured Persons Representative Council and avoiding coloured participation in the dominant political institutions. This involved a continuation of, rather than a deviation from, past constitutional trends. The second part was nominally accepted by the government, but instead of appointing the committee of experts envisaged in the report, it formed a cabinet committee whose findings formed the basis of the government's 1977 constitution.[166] The third part was more enthusiastically accepted by the government and has been continually restated in various forms since 1976, despite its faulty characterisation of the South African constitution. A persistent feature of the subsequent reformulations of the recommendation has been the reversal of the commission's priorities. Emphasis has been given to the need to move away from Westminster, in contrast to the commission's own emphasis on the need for a direct coloured voice in government, which has often been ignored. This phenomenon gives (unwitting) support to the dissenting minority of commissioners, for whom the need to move away from the Westminster system was a point of departure, and not a corollary.

The Theron Report had no immediate effect on the constitutional development of the Republic because of its implications for the government's existing policy. Nor was the government prepared at the time to accept other recommendations which would have involved changes to important subsidiary features of the constitutional system—amendments to group areas legislation, termination of the mixed marriages prohibition, the opening of separate amenities, and the unification of separate administrations. However, the 1982 formulations of the government's constitution involved a partial vindication of the main political recommendation of the Theron Commission in that it provided for the consociational incorportion of coloured persons into the new parliament, and into composite bodies at other levels of government. Furthermore by focusing on the shortcomings of the Westminster model the Theron Report emphasised the need for a new normative system of government, and this led to the arrogation of the emerging theory of consociationalism. In retrospect the commission can be seen as significant stimulus towards constitutional reform and a quasi-consociational option for whites, coloureds and Indians.

(c) The Wiehahn and Riekert commissions

In 1977 the government appointed two commissions of enquiry whose reports were to influence the government's political strategy in the late 1970s and early 1980s. The Wiehahn Commission[167] was required to investigate the country's labour legislation as administered by the Department of Labour and Mines.[168] The Riekert Commission[169] was charged with enquiring into all legislation directly or indirectly affecting the economic use of manpower, excluding that being investigated by the Wiehahn Commission; it was to examine statutes with a close bearing on constitutional matters for blacks, such as the Community Councils Act, the Black (Urban Areas) Consolidation Act, the Group Areas Act, and the Black Trust and Land Act.[170]

The Wiehahn Commission, which has been described as the most representative that the National Party government has ever appointed,[171] issued a series of reports beginning in 1979, of which the first was the most significant.[172] It recommended the repeal of most statutes which discriminated in the field of industrial relations, and advocated a unified system of collective bargaining and complete freedom for workers in their choice of trade union. In the statutory developments which followed the report a National Manpower Commission was created to investigate labour matters and make appropriate recommendations, an industrial court was instituted to replace the industrial tribunal, statutory job reservation was abolished, the registration of black trade unions was permitted, and provision was made for the general inclusion of blacks in the system of collective bargaining.[173] Subsequently the government accepted the Wiehahn strategy of regulating all employees in South Africa, regardless of race or nationality,[174] by providing for the inclusion of both alien blacks and those denationalised by homeland independence. It also allowed trade unions to determine whether their membership would be multiracial or not, without the need for ministerial approval.

The report of the one-man Riekert Commission was published in 1979[175] and its stated objective was to provide better and more stable urban black communities. In common with the Wiehahn Report it advocated the repeal of discriminatory legislation, in this case relating to the training and employment of labour. In respect of the influx control laws affecting blacks it did not recommend their abolition, but suggested that entry into 'white' areas should be made dependent on the availability of employment and housing. Part of the Riekert strategy was to give urban blacks preference over migrant workers in regard to existing facilities, and it accordingly recommended some measures to tighten up influx control.[176] The report also recommended increased formal mobility for qualified urban blacks by allowing section *ten* qualifications to be transferred from one urban area to another; however the implementation of this recommendation[177] was not significant as intercity mobility was made dependent on the availability of housing, the shortage of which, in the commission's own findings, was acute. Finally it was recommended that a new composite statute be enacted for the positive development of urban and rural black communities outside the homelands, in replacement of several existing statutes.[178]

The government accepted most of the Riekert recommendations, but their statutory implementation was to be much slower than those of the Wiehahn Commission. In October 1980 three bills[179] designed to give effect to the recommendations approved by the government were published. While they included provisions relating to intercity mobility, leasehold property rights and increased powers of local government for blacks, a closer examination revealed several harsh innovations, such as the prohibition on additional blacks acquiring urban residence rights in the future. The bills did not give effect to the principles on which the Riekert recommendations were premised, and were withdrawn in early 1981 for further investigation.[180] During 1982 the Black Local Authorities Act was enacted,[181] but the Black Community Development Bill and the Orderly Movement and Settlement of Black Persons Bill of that year were not finalised. The latter bills were severely criticised for ignoring the intentions of the Riekert Commission and for introducing more authoritarian forms of state control over blacks.

The Wiehahn and Riekert commissions implied several apparent deviations from the mainstream of constitutional development in South Africa. First, they involved a rejection of the Tomlinson Commission vision of physical and economic separation for blacks and whites, despite the existence of separate political institutions for each group. Both commissions accepted the permanence of blacks outside the homelands and indicated the need for some economic and social development for them in their places of residence and employment. Secondly, they disturbed the neat logic of the government's citizenship arrangements in that the 'aliens' created by the homelands system who qualify for residence rights would be entitled to some non-political rights, such as urban residence, otherwise restricted to nationals. Thirdly, the Riekert Report accepted and reinforced the principle that urban blacks should have political rights in autonomous local government institutions in the 'common area', a change of policy first evident in the Community Councils legislation. However, the government's acceptance of the various recommendations has taken place within the context of its overall constitutional policy. While the changes may be material from the government's perspective, they do not herald fundamental deviations from its constitutional strategy, such as the granting of black political rights of any significance outside the homelands.

From a consociational perspective the Wiehahn and Riekert reforms influenced the state's move towards a pluralist model of conflict resolution in industrial relations. The repeal of discriminatory statutes in this field introduces freedom of choice for workers in joining trade unions and selecting their own leaders. The provision for free collective bargaining between employers and employees creates a type of functional autonomy, corresponding to the segmental autonomy of consociationalism. However, not only does this activity take place under overall state supervision, and at times with overt state intervention, but it must be seen in conjunction with the new authoritarian control forms for blacks and labour generally. While the reforms avail those blacks with urban residence qualifications, they draw a much sharper distinction between this group and those who do not qualify. For the latter the immediate living constitution comprises those institutions regulating and restricting their access to the urban economy, as epitomised by the Orderly Movement and Settlement of Black Persons Bill of 1982. The pattern of quasi-consociationalism for 'insiders' and constitutional authoritarianism for 'outsiders' evident here, applies equally to the government's new constitution.

(d) The Schlebusch Commission

The government's 1977 constitutional proposals were embodied in draft legislation in April 1979[182] and the bill was referred to a joint select committee of both houses,[183] the terms of reference of which were to consider the introduction of a new constitution for the Republic. At the end of the parliamentary session the committee was converted into a commission of enquiry[184] comprising twenty-four members of the House and Senate with equally wide terms of reference. The Schlebusch Commission held public sittings in various centres; witnesses representing a range of political opinions testified before it and a number of memoranda were received.

The commission presented a short interim report in May 1980[185] which introduced several minor variations on the government's 1977 constitution. It followed the Theron Commission in rejecting the Westminster system as a normative model for the new South African constitution:

'. . . the Westminster system of government, in unadapted form, does not provide a solution for the constitutional problems of the Republic and under the present constitutional dispensation the so-called one-man-one-vote system will probably lead to minorities being dominated by majorities and to serious conflict among population groups in the Republic, with disastrous consequences for all the people in the Republic, and does not provide a framework in which peaceful co-existence in the Republic is possible. . . .'[186]

This again involved a faulty assumption as to the Westminster nature of the existing South African constitutional system. The report went on to recommend the abolition of the upper chamber of parliament, which was heralded at the time as a decisive step in the movement away from Westminster despite the fact that that system is fully reconcilable with unicameralism. Several other recommendations were made relating to the entrenched clauses of the constitution, the appointment and role of a Vice State President, the status, composition and functions of a President's Council, and adjustments to the composition of the House of Assembly. Each of these recommendations resulted in statutory amendments which are dealt with subsequently in this work. None of the recommendations was motivated in the report, nor was a government White Paper issued between its publication and the enactment of the constitutional changes shortly thereafter.

Despite the Schlebusch Commission's wide terms of reference, its recommendations symptomatically related only to the constitutional development of non-blacks. Only an oblique reference was made to blacks in relation to a council of 'black South African citizens' which might be established to consult with committees of the President's Council; although the government accepted the recommendation it abandoned the concept after rigorous objection from homeland and other black leaders. As far as political rights are concerned this body implicitly accepted the Tomlinson Commission vision of white–black separation. In respect of the President's Council, however, it partially endorsed the Theron Commission view that coloured persons should participate in joint decision-making bodies, notwithstanding the limited significance of the Council. Finally, the Schlebush Report showed some deference to constitutional legitimacy and the importance of an authentic process of constitution-making in its observation that,

'. . . in the process of designing future constitutional structures there should be the widest possible consultation and deliberation with and among all population groups, in an attempt to raise the level of acceptability of any proposals in this regard. . . .'[187]

At face value these sentiments conflicted with the government's previous assumptions about the constitution-making process, although in reality the Schlebush Commission was itself an unrepresentative body and its own recommendations lacked credibility.[188] The minority report[189] was more expansive in its recommendations on the constitutional process, and emphasised the need for urgent negotiation (as opposed to 'consultation and deliberation') among recognised leaders and representatives of all groups in the country. It recommended that where the unilateral creation of new constitutional structures was imperative, these should be only interim in nature, and should be limited in function to matters relevant to constitutional development. The minority recommended the establishment of an interim 'Constitutional Council', consisting of members of all population groups, in order to advise on the development of a new constitution, and it rejected the establishment of the President's Council in the form recommended by the majority.

(e) The Ciskei (Quail) Commission

In 1978 the Ciskeian Government appointed a commission to enquire into and to make recommendations on the feasibility of independence for the Ciskei, in the light of all relevant political, economic and social considerations.[190] The commission's membership was more specialist than representative, but it did achieve unanimity despite a divergence of political views.[191] Its programme was wide-ranging and included enquiries into education, social welfare, nationality and citizenship, agricultural, economic and fiscal matters, and labour and industry; its report[192] also included attitude surveys of blacks and whites on the various options open to the Ciskei and Ciskeians.

The main constitutional recommendation of the Quail Commission was that the Ciskei should request additional powers from the central government with a view to the attainment of 'internal autonomy' and an eventual federal relationship with the rest of the Republic.[193] On the basis of the attitude surveys, tactical considerations, the question of international recognition, and the size and viability of the Ciskei, the commission advised strongly against the independence option—especially on the same terms that had been imposed on the other national states. In its view independence should be considered only if the following conditions were satisfied: a referendum of all Ciskeians indicated support for it; satisfactory citizenship arrangements were negotiated; additional land was added to the Ciskeian territories; residential and employment rights of Ciskeians in the Republic were preserved; and South Africa agreed to provide equitable financial support.[194] The commission suggested that independence would prove fatal to the emergence of any South African federal arrangement involving the Ciskei and that even a loose association, such as a confederation, should be settled on simultaneously with independence and not thereafter. In regard to the 'constellation of states' concept, which the government began promoting in 1978, the commission recommended that, if this seemed an attractive prospect to the Ciskei, it need not necessarily take independence as a means of attaining it.[195]

From a consociational perspective the significant aspect of the Quail Report was the suggestion of a 'multiracial condominium'[196] consisting of the unconsolidated Ciskei (including the white-owned areas earmarked for future incorporation), the 'corridor',[197] and East London—an area stretching from the Great Fish River in the south to the Great Kei in the north, and from the Stormberg Mountains to the sea. Constitutionally this area would remain part of South Africa and its inhabitants would remain South African nationals for an experimental period of approximately a decade. It would have a high degree of internal autonomy, greater than the self-governing Ciskei, but not as great as an independent homeland, and discriminatory South African legislation would not be enforceable within its boundaries. The form of internal government for the condominium would be negotiated prior to its formation, but an essential feature would be institutionally required power-sharing between blacks and whites. Without offering a constitutional blueprint the report suggested possible ways of achieving this objective.[198] These suggestions display a strong consociational orientation. Fiscal and economic arrangements would be negotiated with the Republican Government, but the system would be based on the premise that, by remaining part of South Africa, the region would gain an appropriate share of the wealth and resources of the whole country. The economic development of the area would be a prime motivating factor for the condominium arrangement, which would provide all the advantages of increased autonomy without any of the disadvantages inherent in legal independence. Of the several advocates for 'special status' regions within the Republic the Quail Commission was the first to recommend consociationalism at the subnational level of government.

The Quail Report also referred in passing to the desirability of a consociational system for South Africa generally.[199] In an analysis of unitarianism as a constitutional option for the Republic (including the Ciskei), the report compared and contrasted consociationalism with majoritarian and adversarial political systems. In somewhat inconclusive fashion it rejected consociational democracy as a realistic possibility for South Africa on the grounds of its slow and cumbersome procedures and its probable unacceptability (as a species of power-sharing) to whites. But the report went on to suggest that on the basis of the government's commitment to the consociational incorporation of coloureds and Indians into the 'white' political system, and the marketability of consociationalism as a system for preventing the white minority from becoming powerless vis-à-vis the black majority, consociationalism could over time come to gain greater acceptance among whites. However, the Quail Report had little effect on the eventual terms of Ciskeian independence,[200] let alone on the government's national or regional constitutional programmes.

(f) The Lombard Commission

In 1980 the private sector-appointed Lombard Commission investigated alternative solutions to the problems which the South African Government sought to solve through the 'consolidation of KwaZulu'.[201] In its report it emphatically rejected any consolidation formula as a feasible and acceptable basis for the constitutional independence of KwaZulu.[202] It did so in terms of its perception of the 'basic realities' of Natal and KwaZulu, in particular their economic interdependence.[203] It suggested that future deliberations should move away from the concept of consolidation-related transfers of land towards notions of representative, participatory and legitimate government.

While the Lombard Report had a regional orientation it approached the constitutional question from a national perspective. The search for a new constitutional order in South Africa should be confined to a spectrum of options that,

> . . . do not discriminate politically on grounds of colour as such, but at the same time avoid the spectre of colour majoritarianism in a unitary political system. Solutions might be found for the problems of our "deeply divided society" in approaches that start at the regional level of such problems.'[204]

The 'appropriate constitutional philosophy' for South Africa, for which the report found some justification in pluralist theory,[205] was that of confederal government. Confederalism would permit political power-sharing within southern Africa (including the independent national states) and promote the decentralisation of economic activities. It would resolve the citizenship issue, in that each citizen of the participating states might 'in terms of his subordination to the circumscribed confederal institutions' also claim the protection of certain rights by these institutions.[206] The confederal process would require the devolution of responsibility, authority and power on a meaningful regional basis, with only powers pertaining to truly common functions being retained at the central institutional levels. The constitutional form of the confederal political system would be 'a multilateral agreement between otherwise sovereign governments', with the qualification that each government's obligations under the agreement would be entrenched within its own constitution. The report built on the 'confederal direction' evident in the government's homeland policy, which it described as a mode of political reform. However, among the many issues not illuminated was the 'delicate problem' of defining the borders of the confederal states.[207]

Against this background the Lombard Report examined possible political configurations for Natal/KwaZulu.[208] It suggested that three geo-political areas could serve as the 'building blocks' for the area: the KwaZulu area, the white-owned rural area along the main transport corridors, and the Durban metropolitan area. Three levels of government could exist in the region—the local government level, a subprovincial level serving each of the above-mentioned areas, and the Natal/KwaZulu regional level. At the regional level legislative power could vest in an assembly elected by the three subprovincial authorities which could, in the initial stages, be equally represented; the assembly would have powers over matters common to the region. There could be a fixed-term executive, elected either by popular vote or by the assembly, and a judiciary could be appointed by the assembly or executive and be empowered to invalidate acts of both these bodies. In addition a bill of rights could be incorporated into the regional constitution. Discriminatory legislation would be constitutionally outlawed in the region, although 'group rights' would be expressly recognised in the constitution. It is unclear whether local government would be territorially or communally based, but individuals would have unrestricted mobility, in terms of entry and establishment, within the three subprovincial areas. As far as the constitutional relationship between an internally autonomous Natal/KwaZulu and the Republic is concerned, the report suggested that it could range from a federal arrangement with a 'weak' territorial distribution of power, through to partition with limited bilateral ties.

The Lombard Report's discussion of constitutional alternatives for Natal/KwaZulu was based on general principles and avoided institutional detail.[209] In relation to prevailing constitutional trends its main significance was the emphasis on the need for economic and political decentralisation along territorial-regional lines, as opposed to existing patterns of partition, on the one hand, and centralisation of authority on the other. As with the Quail Report it implied the possibility and viability of regional differentiation in matters of constitutional status and organisation. In the Natal/KwaZulu region, the constitution would be non-racial, and 'race' classification as a basis of political representation would be avoided. There would be a strong spirit of constitutionalism[210] and some resort would be had to consociational devices.[211] Even in the short term, however, the Lombard Report tended to be overshadowed by that of the Buthelezi Commission.

(g) The Buthelezi Commission

In 1980 the Chief Minister of KwaZulu announced the appointment of a commission of enquiry to consider the destiny of KwaZulu and Natal and to make proposals which might 'add a new dimension to the political evolution of South Africa'.[212] Its terms of reference[213] were broad and open-ended, and it was asked to submit recommendations on the constitutional future of Natal and KwaZulu, and to relate these to the constitutional options facing the country as a whole. The commission comprised forty-six members representing a moderately wide range of academic disciplines, economic interests and political ideologies. The members were divided into five specialist working groups,[214] each of which published a separate report, and these were supplemented with the results of extensive attitude surveys and an integrative main report. The commission came to be known after its sponsor and not its chairman.[215]

The Political and Constitutional Committee, unlike the other committees, did not present a combined and integrated report but provided four specialised papers submitted to the committee and a chairman's report summarising their themes and findings. The latter was incorporated into the main report, which also took cognisance of the constitutional implications of the other working groups' findings. The commission unequivocally rejected the separate development option, as well as universal franchise in a unitary state, but provided no constitutional blueprint for the country as a whole. As far as Natal and KwaZulu are concerned its recommendations provide the following picture:[216]

(i) *Natal and KwaZulu would be governed as a single political unit within the republic*

The commission rejected both the independence and the 'federal-confederal' options for the region in favour of a special constitutional status for the combined Natal/KwaZulu entity within the Republic. This would involve the retention and adaptation of representation and participation in the central government, an increased devolution of power from Pretoria, and a new dispensation as far as fiscal relationships with the national government are concerned. However, the report is significantly reticent on all three of these crucial issues and concentrates instead on the internal government of an autonomous Natal/KwaZulu.

(ii) *Natal/KwaZulu would have a consociational form of government*

For its internal governance Natal/KwaZulu would have a legislative assembly elected on a basis of universal adult suffrage through a system of proportional representation; there would in addition be 'minimum group representation' in the assembly. The legislature would elect a chief minister to head the executive branch of government for the region and the chief minister would appoint other members of the executive from the legislature on a proportional basis. There would be a 'totally independent judiciary'. The legislature and executive would have jurisdiction over matters delegated to the region by the central government, and they would be further limited in their activities by a judicially enforceable bill of rights. In the legislative process any minority of a specified minimum size would have an absolute veto on matters affecting individual and group rights, and a suspensive veto on less fundamental matters. There would be a further 'federal' devolution of power to metropolitan and local authorities within the region.

(iii) *The movement to consociationalism would involve the adaptation of existing political institutions in Natal/KwaZulu*

The commission envisaged four successive stages in the establishment of an autonomous consociational system in the region. The first would involve close co-operation between the existing legislative, executive and administrative authorities of Natal and KwaZulu. The second would see the establishment of a single combined executive committee under the co-chairmanship of the Natal Administrator and the KwaZulu Chief Minister and including representatives of all groups; the joint executive would be directly concerned with the process of constitutional change in the region. The third stage would involve the creation of a combined legislature and executive for part of the region (such as the Durban metropolitan area) operating along consociational lines, and this would presage the final stage of a single consociational government for Natal/KwaZulu, by which time the region's relationship with the central government would have been finalised through bilateral negotiations.

The Buthelezi Commission recommendations show the pervasive influence of consociational thinking,[217] as well as a strong sense of constitutionalism. The report recognises and addresses itself to the legitimacy problem facing the state system in South Africa by stressing the importance of the constitution-making process, the need to involve in the political system all those subject to it, and the necessity to transform those areas of the living constitution which have contributed to the problem. But it tends to overlook both the legitimacy and efficiency of the consociational form of government, failing to examine some of the political and socio-economic implications of this system. It also glosses over the essential prerequisites for authentic consociationalism, and deals indifferently with a problem endemic to it, namely the extent to which group identities based on race, colour, ethnicity or other factors, can be expressly accommodated in the constitution. The commission clearly felt the need to move away from such factors as basic determinants of the constitutional order, as the following extract shows:

'In the first instance and for historic reasons only [the Commission] suggests that [the consociational executive] will consist of equal representation of the White South African group . . . , the Black South African group . . . and that there should also be representation of the Indian and Coloured South African communities. These would be the groups which entered into the original consociational agreement. At a later stage the group associations would be found to have changed toward common political and economic interests and by agreement the groups represented on the executive could be varied under an amended consociational agreement. This executive would place before the legislative assembly bills which had been accepted by the consociational executive and would therefore be acceptable to the group.'[218]

But despite the awareness there is a somewhat peripheral treatment of this important issue, and the constitutional debate in South Africa would have been better served had the commission given greater attention to the question of the extent to which constitutional arrangements can take account of colour in order to move away from it.[219] The legitimacy of consociationalism as a political alternative for South Africa would depend in part on how this matter is handled.

Because of their implications for the dominant trends in the constitutional process none of the three commissions advocating autonomous regions within the country with internal systems of consociational government have had any immediate political effect. Of the three the Buthelezi Report enjoyed the greatest moral force because of the commission's genesis and composition. Nevertheless, although its findings were endorsed by Inkatha and the KwaZulu legislature, they received a negative reaction not only from the central government but also from the majority party in the white Natal Provincial Council. In the short term the commission's contribution was mainly academic.

(h) Other commissions

There have recently been three other commissions of enquiry into constitutionally related matters, but in each case the government has directed that the findings be not disclosed. The Van der Walt Committee on the consolidation of the national states[220] was appointed in 1979 and was reported to have completed its findings within two years; their main relevance would be in respect of homeland independence and the government's regionalist policies. The Grosskopf Committee which investigated the three 1980 bills pertaining to 'urban blacks' reported in May 1981 but would appear to have had a limited effect on the Orderly Movement and Settlement of Black Persons Bill of the following year.[221] As far as the departmental Niewoudt

Commission investigating aspects of nationality and citizenship is concerned, there was speculation that it recommended a 'confederal nationality' for all inhabitants of the proposed constellation of states; this would accrue to all citizens of the various member states and would constitute an attempt to overcome problems caused by the denationalisation of homeland blacks and the non-recognition of the national states. It is improbable that any of the commissions recommended fundamental deviations from the prevailing trends of constitutional development, but one or more may have suggested minor adjustments which the government was unwilling to implement, let alone publicise. Another report with constitutional implications was that of the cabinet-appointed Human Sciences Research Council investigation into education.[222] This recommended, *inter alia*, a single department of education and a uniform national educational policy, but with a strong degree of organisational and functional decentralisation. In rejecting this recommendation the government reaffirmed that, in terms of its policy of school segregation, it was essential that each population group have its own education authority or department. It further emphasized that the recommendations on education would be implemented only in so far as they conformed to its own constitutional programme.[223] Finally, the President's Council, which is dealt with in the following chapter, was depicted by the government as a standing commission of enquiry into constitutional matters and began making recommendations in late 1981.

5. CONCLUSION

In this chapter on southern African constitutional matters a comparative background has been provided to the South African Government's constitutional proposals. Because of the diversity of matters surveyed it is difficult to draw a synthesised conclusion. The single theme which the various policies, practices and recommendations have in common is a rejection, in the constitutional context, of unqualified majority rule. Beyond this they display widely diverging responses to questions of legitimacy, constitutionalism and consociationalism. The most consistent acceptance of consociational principles was encountered in the Progressive Federal Party's constitutional policy. However, neither this policy nor the other developments referred to can claim to have had much influence on the government's constitutional programme, despite the fact that it shares with them a rejection of majority rule.

NOTES AND REFERENCES

[1] See e g D Geldenhuys 'South Africa's Constitutional Alternatives' 1981 *South Africa International* 190–227; see also the Sprocas Report No 10 *South Africa's Political Alternatives* (1973), W H Thomas 'South Africa Between Partition and Integration' 1979 *Aussenpolitik* 305, the articles in R Rotberg & J Barratt *Conflict and Compromise in South Africa* (1980), Royal Institute of International Affairs *A Survey of Proposals for the Constitutional Development of South Africa* (1980) and T Hanf, H Weiland & G Vierdag *South Africa—The Prospects of Peaceful Change* (1981).

[2] S E Finer *Five Constitutions* (1979) 21; cf E McWhinney *Federal Constitution-Making for a Multi-National World* (1966) 7.

[3] See I D Duchacek *Rights and Liberties in the World Today—Constitutional Promise and Reality* (1973) 11–14.

⁴ On the 'external' parties see Thomas op cit 315–16, Royal Institute op cit 28–9. While radical opposition groups tend to place more emphasis on liberation as an immediate goal than specific constitutional blueprints the following principles have constitutional significance: Equal franchise rights for all inhabitants; the abolition of racial differentiation; a socialist economic system; alternative strategies for socio-economic development. The ANC also advocates a national constitutional convention. On the constitutional views of Dr Motlana of the Soweto 'Committee of Ten' see Rotberg & Barratt op cit 31–47. The Conservative Party was formed in 1982 and has a similar policy for blacks to that of the National Party, but it would extend the homeland system to include both coloureds and Indians.

⁵ The description which follows is taken from the *Report of the Constitutional Committee of the Progressive Federal Party* (the Van Zyl Slabbert Report), adopted at the federal congress of the party in Durban, 1978. Cf F van Zyl Slabbert & D Welsh *South Africa's Options—Strategies for Sharing Power* (1979).

⁶ The convention would determine whether independent homelands could participate, with a view to being incorporated in the new structures. Blacks denationalised by the Status Acts but domiciled in the Republic would be allowed representation. A judicial commission would ensure the overall representativeness of the convention.

⁷ See L J Boulle 'Federation and Consociation: Conceptual Links and Current Constitutional Models' 1981 *THRHR* 236 at 248–50.

⁸ The chambers would have equal and co-ordinate powers (except in respect of money bills), but as the lower house would elect the Prime Minister and its composition would determine membership of the federal executive, power would gravitate to the lower house as in other non-presidential federal systems.

⁹ The states would have jurisdiction over all matters not 'essentially national'.

¹⁰ See above, 51–3. Discussions of federalism in South Africa are largely concerned with whether the units should be regionally or communally defined. A du Toit *Federalism and Political Change in South Africa* (1974) 17f; L Marquard *A Federation of South Africa* (1971) 71f.

¹¹ This would tend to weaken the federal element in the executive sphere since the federal chamber would have no say in his election.

¹² The proposals refer repeatedly to a separation of powers, but this is misleading from a strict constitutionalist perspective.

¹³ A Lijphart *Democracy in Plural Societies* (1977) 31.

¹⁴ Any 'cultural group' could establish a cultural council to promote its interests, which, on registration with the constitutional court, would be empowered to nominate one member to the Senate.

¹⁵ The best example is found in the Belgium constitution of 1971 which recognises (art 3*(c)*) French, Dutch and German cultural communities, and provides for French and Dutch cultural councils which can issue decrees on cultural and educational matters (art 59(2)). See also I Duchacek *Comparative Federalism* (1970) 1–10.

¹⁶ See above, 69n54.

¹⁷ There would also be a proportional allocation of federal assembly seats among the states.

¹⁸ Amendments would require an affirmative vote in the Federal Assembly and Senate, and two-thirds of the state legislatures.

¹⁹ While the proposals envisage the states deciding on their own forms of government, they stipulate basic requirements of consensus and proportionality.

²⁰ A Lijphart 'Consociation and Federation: Conceptual and Empirical Links' 1979 *Canadian Journal of Political Science* 599 at 414; cf Boulle op cit 254.

²¹ This description is taken from the party's submissions to the Schlebusch Commission, drafted by Prof D J Kriek; they are reticent on several matters of detail.

²² A Lijphart 'Federal, Confederal and Consociational Options for the South African Plural Society' in R Rotberg & J Barratt (eds) *Conflict and Compromise in South Africa* (1980) 51 at 69.

²³ The basis of this distinction is not clear, but the proposals suggest that it could be effected through an amendment to the National States Citizenship Act 26 of 1970. Although the system would depend on 'race' classification, compulsory classification in terms of Act 30 of 1950 would be replaced by 'a system of natural registration'.

²⁴ The lower house would be indirectly elected, each group parliament electing one component; the upper house would comprise an equal number of members nominated by each of the group executives.

²⁵ This would be a collegial body modelled on the Swiss federal executive.

²⁶ The proposals assume the attainment of constitutional independence by all the national states, but no reference is made to the terms thereof, nor to such matters as consolidation.

[27] Passing reference is made to a council of ministers and secretariat.

[28] The report of the commission is dated 14 March 1979.

[29] Debates of the CRC vol 41 (3–5 April 1979).

[30] There are indications that the commission identified the Westminster system principally with unitarianism, as opposed to federalism, although it did go on to recommend a Westminster-type cabinet.

[31] This would necessitate the abolition of all 'race' classification laws and the Prohibition of Political Interference Act 51 of 1968.

[32] Before implementation the constitution would require ratification in a referendum.

[33] Cf S E Finer *Comparative Government* (1970) 158.

[34] Du Preez himself was appointed to the President's Council in 1981. See below, 188n4.

[35] Inkatha Yenkululeko Ye Sizwe, the Zulu National Cultural Liberation Movement headed by Chief G Buthelezi, Chief Minister of KwaZulu.

[36] This description is from the Inkatha memorandum to the Schlebusch Commission, which includes the 17-point 'Statement of Belief'. It appears in W S Felgate 'Co-operation Between Natal and KwaZulu—An Inkatha View' in L J Boulle & L G Baxter (eds) *Natal and KwaZulu—Constitutional and Political Options* (1981) 154–65; see also G Thula 'A Constitutional Alternative for South Africa (Inkatha)' in F van Zyl Slabbert & J Opland (eds) *South Africa: Dilemmas of Evolutionary Change* (1980) 36–45; and 'A Basis for the Constitutional Transformation of South Africa' in R Rotberg & J Barratt (eds) *Conflict and Compromise in South Africa* (1980) 161–9.

[37] Felgate op cit 161–2. This would include equal rights before the law, a redistribution of wealth, the elimination of secrecy in government, due process of law, and the right to form trade unions.

[38] See below, 137–9.

[39] See M Wiechers *Staatsreg* (3 ed 1981) 445–501. The main statute regulating the territory's constitutional affairs was the South West Africa Constitution Act 39 of 1968.

[40] See M Wiechers ''n Kritiese ontleding van die Turnhalle-grondwet vir 'n tussentydse regering' 18 (1977) *Codicillus* 4; L J Boulle 'The Turnhalle Testimony' (1978) 95 *SALJ* 49.

[41] D Prinsloo *South West Africa: The Turnhalle and Independence* (1976) 11ff. The most notable absentee was Swapo, but other groups were also excluded.

[42] This is available in 1976 *CILSA* 277–81.

[43] The white electorate first approved the constitution in a referendum on 17 May 1977 (GN 122/77 in *Official Gazette* 3610 of 5 April 1977). For details see 1977 *CILSA* 231.

[44] See Wiechers op cit; Boulle op cit; 1977 *CILSA* 232–3.

[45] The final distribution would be: Owambo 12, white 6, Damara 5, Herero 5, Kavango 5, coloured 5, Nama 5, Caprivu 5, Bushman 4, Baster 4, Tswana 4.

[46] e g education, social services, roads, forestry, agricultural credit and land use, and environmental control.

[47] In other cases of conflict central legislation would prevail.

[48] His assent to the national assembly's laws would not be required.

[49] The minister need not belong to the nominating group, but would have to be a member of the assembly.

[50] Chapter III s 2(f). The chairman of the council would have neither an ordinary nor a casting vote.

[51] Its three members would be appointed by the ministers' council.

[52] The second draft of the constitution made the bill of rights judicially enforceable, but the conference subsequently amended this.

[53] There is again a similarity with the German constitution (art 93(1)4a) which allows individuals with basic rights complaints against public authorities access to the Constitutional Court.

[54] Because the representative authorities had territorial jurisdiction over land owned by members of the relevant group, the 'corporate federation' could have taken on asymmetrical territorial-federal form in practice. Needless to say there were wide disparities in land ownership among the ethnic groups.

[55] The system of public finance entailed each representative authority having as its main independent source of revenue taxation on the personal income of members of the relevant group; this would have resulted in large discrepancies in the standards of social services. There was considerable pressure from poorly endowed groups to remove matters from the second to the central tier of government, for fear that the well-endowed groups would dominate the system from below.

[56] Mainly in the form of the United Kingdom, United States, Canada, West Germany and France.

⁵⁷ Act 95 of 1977 amended s 38 of Act 39 of 1968.

⁵⁸ Proclamations 180 and 181 of 19 August 1977.

⁵⁹ The elections were held on a nationwide proportional basis and resulted in the Democratic Turnhalle Alliance acquiring eighty per cent of the fifty seats. See 1979 *CILSA* 126. In *Du Plessis NO v Skrywer NO en andere* 1980 (2) SA 52 (SWA) the court decided that a member need not retain membership of the party which nominated him in order to retain his assembly seat. The case was a sequel to the Abolition of Racial Discrimination Act. The decision was confirmed in *Du Plessis NO v Skrywer NO en andere* 1980 (3) SA 863 (A).

⁶⁰ Proclamation AG 21/1979 of 21 May 1979. The validity of this proclamation was challenged in proceedings which were somewhat inconclusive (*Du Plessis v Adminis-trateur-Generaal vir die Gebied van Suidwes-Afrika en andere* 1980 (2) SA 35 (SWA); see also *Beukes v Administrateur-Generaal, Suidwes-Afrika* 1980 (2) SA 664 (SWA)) but a subsequent proclamation placed the legality of the assembly and its laws beyond doubt (Proc 172/779 in *GG* 6618/1979 (13 August 1979), made retrospective to 14 May).

⁶¹ For a summary of these events see 1980 *Survey of Race Relations* 644ff. The assembly departed from the Turnhalle constitution in conferring limited powers on the second-tier authorities and retaining extensive powers itself.

⁶² The most notable attempt was a multi-party meeting in Geneva—see A du Pisani 'Namibia: The Search for Alternatives' 1981 *South African International* 292.

⁶³ Even the DTA eventually accepted the constitutional proposals presented by the five Western powers in October 1981, although these had little in common with the Turnhalle constitution.

⁶⁴ On earlier developments see C Palley *The Constitutional History and Law of Southern Rhodesia 1888–1965* (1966); see also the résume in A Blaustein & G Flanz *Constitutions of the Countries of the World* (1980) and references cited there.

⁶⁵ Cf R Luyt 'African constitutionalism: Constitutions in the context of Decolonisation' in J Benyon (ed) *Constitutional Change in South Africa* (1978) 15 at 19.

⁶⁶ A mixture of income, property and educational requirements.

⁶⁷ A complicated 'cross-voting' procedure allowed voters on one roll to influence to some extent elections held under the other.

⁶⁸ A two-thirds parliamentary majority could reverse the decision. The High Court could also grant redress to petitioners for contraventions of the Declaration.

⁶⁹ On the legality of UDI see M Wiechers *Staatsreg* (3 ed, 1981) 29–30 and 33, and the numerous references cited there.

⁷⁰ Act 54 of 1969, promulgated on 2 March 1970.

⁷¹ Save where otherwise provided he had to act on the cabinet's advice (ss 53, 54 and 57). Somewhat unusually for a Westminster system he was appointed by the executive council—s 3(1).

⁷² Sections 56 and 55(5).   ⁷³ Sections 10, 11 and 42.

⁷⁴ Section 18(2)*(a)* and *(b)*.   ⁷⁵ Section 13(2)*(a)* and *(b)*.

⁷⁶ Section 18(4). The additional members would be alternatively indirectly and directly elected.

⁷⁷ Cf s 30(1).

⁷⁸ Second Schedule; see *Deary NO v Acting President, Rhodesia & others* 1979 (4) SA 43 (R).

⁷⁹ Section 43(1) and (2) read with s 14(5).

⁸⁰ Section 43(6)*(a)* and *(b)*.

⁸¹ Section 45. The certificate also rendered unnecessary Senate approval of a Bill.

⁸² e g s 19(2).   ⁸³ Section 78(1) and (2).

⁸⁴ e g parts of the Electoral and Land Tenure Act.

⁸⁵ See L Sobel (ed) *Rhodesia/Zimbabwe 1971–1977* (1978).

⁸⁶ The United African National Council, the Zimbabwe African National Union, and the Zimbabwe United People's Organisation. For the agreement see 1978 *CILSA* 223. See C F Forsyth 'Conventions *Ex Africa*: The Status of the Rhodesian Internal Settlement' 1976 *Acta Juridica* 295.

⁸⁷ The Prime Minister Mr I Smith, Bishop A Muzorewa (UANC), Rev N Sithole (ZANU) and Senator Chief J Chirau (ZAPO). The chairmanship rotated among the four.

⁸⁸ The cabinet portfolios were held jointly by black and white ministers. This necessi-tated the Constitution Amendment Act 18 of 1978.

⁸⁹ Act 12 of 1979.

⁹⁰ On which see 1979 *CILSA* 249. The black members were elected on a proportional basis and Bishop Muzorewa's UANC won 51 of the 72 seats. All elected white seats were won by the governing Rhodesia Front. Cf Blaustein & Flanz op cit 26.

[91] The first election of black members was held on a proportional (party-list) basis because of the impossibility of delimiting constituencies timeously. The court in *Chikerema & others v UANC & another* 1979 (4) SA 258 (ZRAD) was faced with a similar problem to that in *Du Plessis v Skrywer* (supra) and held that it had no jurisdiction to force the appellants to vacate their parliamentary seats after resigning from the respondent party, which had nominated them. The court found support in the English decision *Amalgamated Society of Railway Servants v Osborne* 1910 AC 87.

[92] For the first and only election the sixteen candidates were nominated by the fifty white members of the outgoing House.

[93] Section 67 read with s 8 of the Third Schedule. Each party with five members in the House would be entitled to representation in the cabinet. In recommending the appointment of ministers from non-government parties the Prime Minister would act on the advice of party leaders.

[94] The first cabinet posts were apportioned as follows: UANC—11; RF—5; ZANU—2; UNFP—2. The constitution prohibited whites, for a five-year period, from forming a governing coalition with any party other than the majority black party. Third Schedule s 8(1).

[95] The constitution itself was 'supreme law' and inconsistent laws would be invalid (s 3).

[96] Section 157 read with the Second Schedule.

[97] Section 160. Among these were the Electoral Act and laws relating to school education and medical services.

[98] Or after the second dissolution of parliament within the ten year period. The equivalent period for the executive was five years.

[99] The Senate's approval would not be required—s 159(6).

[100] Of its five members one would be the Chief Justice and two would be elected by the white parliamentarians.

[101] Section 134. It was a substantial re-enactment of the previous non-justiciable Declaration.

[102] See the *Report of the Constitutional Conference, Lancaster House, London* Cmd RZR 3–1980. Besides the British, the signatories were Bishop A Muzorewa and Dr S Mundawarara of the internal government, and Mr R Mugabe and Mr J Nkomo of the Patriotic Front. See also 1980 *CILSA* 240–1.

[103] The Constitution of Zimbabwe Rhodesia Act (44 of 1979) reversed the declaration of independence and proclaimed the country once more a British dominion. It provided for a governor to assume all legislative and executive powers. The British Parliament enacted the Southern Rhodesia Act 1979, which made provision for the introduction of a new constitution and for the interim governance of the country.

[104] The Zimbabwe Constitution Order 1979 (No 1690), made in terms of s 1 of the Southern Rhodesia Act of 1979. The new constitution was also annexed to Act 44 of 1979 (Rhodesia).

[105] Zimbabwe Act 1979.

[106] The twenty white constituency seats were won by Smith's RF. The eighty black seats were contested on a proportional basis in eight multi-member constituencies, electors voting for parties, not candidates. The seat allocation was ZANU-PF (Mugabe) 57, PF (Nkomo) 20, UANC (Muzorewa) 3. Muzorewa's votes dropped from 64% in the internal elections to 8,1%—commentators attributed this, *inter alia*, to the white constitutional veto and continued white control of the forces and bureaucracy during his tenure.

[107] Section 38(1).

[108] Section 33. The ten senatorships for chiefs were again divided equally between Mashonaland and Matabeleland, despite the numerical preponderance of the Shona tribe in Zimbabwe.

[109] Section 69(1). A coalition between white members of the lower house and any minority black party for the purpose of forming a government was prohibited—s 69(2).

[110] The 'cabinet of national unity' consisted of 23 members, of whom 4 were from Nkomo's PF and two from Smith's RP. This development contradicted the theory that in zero-sum conditions coalitions tend toward the minimal winning side. (W Riker *The Theory of Political Coalitions* (1962) 28–32).

[111] Section 3; cf *S v Tekere & others* 1981 (1) SA 878 (ZAD).

[112] Section 56.

[113] Section 52.

[114] Section 24. Petitioners may approach the Appellate Division for redress, but the court will not adjudicate on academic matters—see *Mandirwhe v Minister of State* 1981 (1)

SA 759 (ZAD). See also *Commissioner of Police v Wilson* 1981 (4) SA 726 (ZA); *Hewlett v Minister of Finance & another* 1982 (1) SA 490 (ZSC).

[115] Section 24(5) read with ss 16(7), 19(5), 29(2) and (4), 21(3), and 22(3)*(a)–(e)*.

[116] Existing laws would be immune from invalidation for non-compliance with the Declaration for a period of five years—ss 25(2) and (3).

[117] Chapter VII.

[118] Blacks outnumbered whites by approximately twenty-five to one.

[119] Cf M Hirsch 'Lessons from Rhodesia for Constitutional Change in South Africa' in F van Zyl Slabbert & J Opland (eds) *South Africa: Dilemmas of Evolutionary Change* (1980) 54–70.

[120] W B Harvey & W H B Dean 'The Independence of Transkei—A Largely Constitutional Inquiry' 1978 *Journal of Modern African Studies* 189 at 213.

[121] See generally M Wiechers *Staatsreg* (3 ed) 502–24. On the Transkei constitution see I Rautenbach 'The Constitution of Transkei' 1977 *TSAR* 199; also Harvey & Dean op cit; Booysen, Wiechers, Van Wyk & Breytenbach 'Comments on the Independence and Constitution of Transkei' 1976 *SAYIL* 1. On Bophuthatswana see M Wiechers & D H van Wyk 'The Republic of Bophuthatswana Constitution' 1977 *SAYIL* 85; on Venda, G Carpenter 'The Independence of Venda' 1979 *SAYIL* 40; and on Ciskei, G Carpenter 'Variation on a Theme—The Independence of Ciskei' 1981 *SAYIL* 83.

[122] See above, 59.

[123] But in all three systems the president can nominate members to parliament; he can also appoint ministers from outside parliament in Ciskei (5) and Transkei (3, since 1982).

[124] See Rautenbach op cit 206f.

[125] In Ciskei there is in fact no constitutional limit on the number of chiefs in the legislature, the appointment of chiefs vesting in the President.

[126] See W D Hammond-Tooke *Command or Consensus—The Development of Transkeian Local Government (1975)* 67–74; B O Nwabueze *Constitutionalism in the Emergent States* (1973) 168f.

[127] Wiechers & Van Wyk op cit 94.

[128] On various African countries see S A de Smith *The New Commonwealth and its Constitutions* (1964) 155–66.

[129] S M de Minón 'The Passing of Bicameralism' 1975 *American Journal of Comparative Law* 236. The Botswana constitution instituted a House of Chiefs with advisory powers but no legislative function. Cf J C Bekker 'Kapteins in die Wetgewende vergaderings van Botswana en Transkei' 1978 *TSAR* 268.

[130] Outside southern Africa only Gambia and Sierra Leone expressly accommodated chiefs in the legislature, most pronouncedly in the latter case with twelve chiefs out of one hundred members. Botswana, Lesotho and Swaziland also made some constitutional reference to chiefs. Bekker op cit 269; W Breytenbach 'Kapteinskap en Politieke Ontwikkeling in die Tuislande' 1975 *Afrika-Instituut Bulletin* 328 at 329. On the position of chiefs in the Zimbabwe Senate see above, 119–22.

[131] By Act 68 of 1951. See Hammond-Tooke op cit 206–15; also N M Stultz *Transkei's Half Loaf—Race Separatism in South Africa* (1980) 50–4.

[132] See P Laurence *The Transkei—South Africa's Politics of Partition* (1976) 63–78. After a constitution amendment in 1982 Bophuthatswana became the only homeland in which elected members outnumbered nominated chiefs in parliament.

[133] See eg s 66 of the Transkei Constitution Act.

[134] Hammond-Tooke op cit 212.

[135] There is a notable absence of the right to form trade unions.

[136] Ciskei Constitution Act s 136.

[137] Section 18.

[138] Section 79. Amendments to the first ten chapters require a two-thirds affirmative vote in the Assembly unless the s 49(3) procedure is petitioned for, in which case a two-thirds majority is required in each component of the Assembly.

[139] *S v Moloto* 1980 (3) SA 1081 (BSC) at 1084D (per Hiemstra CJ).

[140] See E McWhinney *Judicial Review in the English-Speaking World* (2 ed, 1960); L P Beth 'The Judicial Committee of the Privy Council and the Development of Judicial Review' 1976 *American Journal of Comparative Law* 22.

[141] McWhinney op cit 29.

[142] In *S v Marwane* 1982 (3) SA 717 (A) members of the court were in agreement that provisions of the former South African Terrorism Act 83 of 1967 (under which Marwane had been convicted) were repugnant to the Bophuthatswana charter of rights. Whereas the minority held that this repugnancy only invalidated post-independence laws, the majority reversed the court *a quo* (*S v Marwane* 1981 (3) SA 588 (BSC)) in holding that it

also affected those South African laws taken over at independence. The majority judgment referred to *Minister of Home Affairs v Collins MacDonald Fisher* [1980] AC 319 (PC) and precedents in other jurisdictions in relation to the correct approach to fundamental rights provisions, but paradoxically was able to uphold the appeal with a literalist interpretation; the minority adopted a restrictive interpretation and its judgment displayed no sense of constitutionalism.

[143] By the Bophuthatswana Constitution Amendment Act of 1982.

[144] Cf L Barry 'Law, Policy and Statutory Interpretation under a Constitutionally Entrenched Canadian Charter of Rights and Freedoms' 1982 *Canadian Bar Review* 237; J Dugard 'Judicial Power and a Constitutional Court' in L J Boulle & L G Baxter (eds) *Natal and KwaZulu—Constitutional and Political Options* (1981) 189–211.

[145] See above, 103n116.

[146] The Commission on the Socio-Economic Development of Native Areas within the Union of South Africa was appointed by the government in 1950 and presented its report in 1954. An official summary of the report was published in 1955 (UG 61/1955) and all references are to the summary.

[147] *Report Summary* xviii.

[148] On this section see ch 50 of the *Report Summary* (194–208).

[149] The report cites proportions of 60% by 1981 and 70% by 2000 (*Report Summary* 203). While demographic estimates relating to the homelands are notoriously unreliable, C E W Simkims (*The Distribution of the African Population of South Africa* (Cape Town, 1981) gives the percentage of blacks resident in the homelands in 1980 as 54%, probably the most reliable estimate.

[150] *Report Summary* 211.

[151] Here the Tomlinson Report differed from the earlier Fagan Report (*Report of the Native Laws Commission, 1946–48* (UG 28/1948)) which recognised that total segregation, in the sense of partition with population transfers, was impossible, and recommended acceptance of the full implications of a permanent urban black population. For an approving account of the Fagan Report see H Brotz *The Politics of South Africa* (1977) 132–50.

[152] The Natives Land Act 27 of 1913, and the Native Trust and Land Act 18 of 1936; *Report Summary* 195.

[153] White Paper on the Development of Bantu Areas, published in May 1956. On the black response to the report see Carter, Karis & Stultz *South Africa's Transkei* (1967) 18.

[154] It thereby upheld the minority view (of two of the nine commissioners) that white participation in the economic development of the reserves would be contrary to the policy of separate development.

[155] See Butler, Rotberg & Adams *The Black Homelands of South Africa* (1977) 160.

[156] On the contemporary economies of the national states see J Nattrass *The South African Economy* (1981) 190–224. In 1975 the homelands produced 3% of South Africa's total economic output, although they contained 35,8% of the total population.

[157] Act 46 of 1959. See above, 90.

[158] Act 68 of 1951.

[159] Carter, Karis & Stultz op cit 54.

[160] *Report Summary* 194.

[161] M Wiechers 'Possible Structural Divisions of Power in South Africa' in J Benyon (ed) *Constitutional Change in South Africa* (1978) 107 at 115.

[162] The Commission of Enquiry into Matters Relating to the Coloured Population Group was appointed on 23 March 1973 (Proc 81 GN 442) and its report (RP 38/1976) was tabled on 18 June 1976. The commission consisted of twelve whites and six coloured persons.

[163] House of Assembly Debates vol 12 cols 5133–4 (21 April 1976).

[164] Paragraph 178.

[165] Provisional Comments by the Government on the Recommendations of the Commission of Inquiry into Matters Relating to the Coloured Population Group WPS-'76. A second, and 'final' White Paper was tabled in 1977—WPD-'77.

[166] The committee comprised the following ministers' Mr P W Botha (chairman), Dr C P Mulder and Messrs J van der Spuy, O P Horwood, M C Botha, S J Steyn and H Smith (secretary). The coloured commissioners had emphasised that the committee of experts should include coloured persons.

[167] Commission of Enquiry into Labour Legislation and Other Related Matters.

[168] Inter alia, the Industrial Conciliation Act 28 of 1956, the Black Labour Relations Act 48 of 1953, the Wage Act 5 of 1957, the Factories, Machinery and Building Works Act 22 of 1941 and, after its terms had been widened, the Mines and Works Act 27 of 1956.

[169] Commission of Enquiry into Legislation Affecting the Utilisation of Manpower.
[170] Acts 125 of 1977, 25 of 1945, 36 of 1966 and 18 of 1936, respectively.
[171] S van der Horst 'Employment' in S van der Horst & J Reid (eds) *Race Discrimination in South Africa* (1981) 34.
[172] *Report of the Commission of Enquiry into Labour Legislation*—Part I RP 47/1979. The government's response was contained in White Paper W 5/1979.
[173] These changes were effected mainly by the Industrial Conciliation Amendment Act 94 of 1979, which amended the Industrial Conciliation Act 28 of 1956 (now the Labour Relations Act). See W B Gould 'Black Unions in South Africa: Labour Law Reform and Apartheid' 1981 *Stanford Journal of International Law* 99.
[174] Acts 94 of 1979 and 57 of 1981 amended the definition of 'employee' (formerly restricted to whites) in s 1(1) of the Labour Relations Act. For the commission's majority and minority views on this see Wiehahn Report Part I §§ 3.43, 3.63.
[175] *Report of the Commission of Enquiry into Legislation Affecting the Utilisation of Manpower* RP 32/1979. The government's response was contained in White Paper WP T–1979.
[176] eg the fines for employing unregistered blacks were increased by Act 98 of 1979, which amended s 10*bis* of the Black (Urban Areas) Consolidation Act 25 of 1945.
[177] GN R1208 *GG* 7068 of 13 June 1980 (*Reg Gaz* 3018) amended reg 14 of the Black Labour Regulations of 1975.
[178] Such as Act 25 of 1945, the Black Affairs Administration Act 45 of 1971, and the Community Councils Act 125 of 1977.
[179] The Black Community Development Bill, the Local Government Bill and the Laws on Co-Operation and Development Amendment Bill (*GG* 7280, 7281 and 7282 of 31 October respectively).
[180] By the Grosskopf Commission, which had apparently finalised its report by the year's end, although it has yet to be made public.
[181] Act 102 of 1982; see above, 88–9.
[182] Republic of South Africa Constitution Bill *GG* 6385 (vol 166) (3 April 1979).
[183] House of Assembly Debates vol 8 col 3666 (30 March 1979).
[184] GN R1540 (6 July 1979). Regulations applicable to the commission were promulgated in Proc 141 of 1979.
[185] *Interim Report of the Commission of Inquiry on the Constitution* RP 68/1980. See below, 157–8.
[186] § 8*a*.
[187] § 8*(b)*.
[188] See the views of Inkatha in its memorandum to the commission, § 1. (In W Felgate 'Co-Operation Between Natal and KwaZulu—An Inkatha View' in L J Boulle & L G Baxter (eds) *Natal and KwaZulu—Constitutional and Political Options* (1981) 154 at 158).
[189] Annexure B, signed by the four PFP members of the commission.
[190] GN 14 in Ciskei *Official Gazette* 177 (vol 6) (4 August 1978).
[191] The members were G Quail (chairman), P Kilby, C Lalendle, E Marais, R Rotberg, A Snelling, M van den Berg and R Proctor-Sims (secretary).
[192] *Report of the Ciskei Commission* (Conference Associates) 1980.
[193] See §§ 270–275 of the report and above, 91–2.
[194] § 348.
[195] §§ 283–287.
[196] §§ 333–339. The commission was unable to provide precedents for this type of arrangement, other than an Anglo-French condominium in the South Pacific and a former Anglo-Egyptian condominium in the Sudan.
[197] That is the strip of land between Ciskei and Transkei, including Queenstown in the north and East London in the south.
[198] eg a bicameral legislature with whites and blacks represented in separate houses of equal size and status; a universal or qualified (but non-racial) franchise with each voter being able to vote for a black and a white candidate in each constituency; a legislative process involving minority vetoes and the need for close co-operation between the two Houses; and a parliamentary executive with the Prime Minister and cabinet being responsible to both Houses.
[199] §§ 292–293.
[200] For a full discussion of this matter see the parliamentary debates on the Status of Ciskei Bill: House of Assembly Debates vol 9 cols 4933–5159 (2nd reading, 28 September 1981) and vol 10 cols 6293–6337 (3rd reading, 9 October 1981). The government's earlier response to the report had seemed favourable—House of Assembly Debates vol 12 col 5864 (7 May 1980).

[201] *Alternatives to the Consolidation of KwaZulu: Progress Report* Bureau for Economic Policy and Analysis, University of Pretoria, Special Focus No 2 (1980)—better known under the name of its final editor, Prof J A Lombard. The commission was appointed by the South African Sugar Association and the Durban Chamber of Commerce, and consisted wholly of academics.

[202] The commission's views can be seen as a partial extrapolation of the Prime Minister's earlier statements on consolidation. House of Assembly Debates vol 1 cols 241–4 (7 February 1979) and summarised at page 5 of the report.

[203] See section II of the report.

[204] Lombard Report 7. The rejection of majoritarianism is sparsely motivated: '. . . majoritarianism under the present unitary constitution of the Republic is an extreme world . . . beyond the bounds of realism. The various social cohesions in South Africa are deeply divided and, as in all other "deeply divided societies", majoritarianism has no chance of a democratic outcome.'

[205] Pluralist language was used in various parts of the report (e g at 7 and 38).

[206] Amidst this circumlocution the report seems to be recommending a 'confederal nationality', in terms of which citizens of the constituent states would have certain rights, e g to a passport.

[207] Lombard Report 43.

[208] Section IV of the report.

[209] More concrete alternatives were examined at the Workshop on Constitutional Issues in KwaZulu and Natal, University of Natal, 27–28 October 1980. The papers of this conference are included in L J Boulle & L G Baxter (eds) *Natal and KwaZulu: Constitutional and Political Options* (1981), and the edited proceedings in the *Supplement to Natal and KwaZulu* (1981).

[210] The report endorsed the principles of separation and division of powers, and constitutional government generally. However, it used the term 'limited government' in the economic and not the constitutional sense. For Lombard's views on 'limited government' see his *Freedom, Welfare and Order* (1978) 19–40. There was a strong spirit of 'free enterprise' in the report.

[211] The government was reported to have rejected the Lombard proposals because they envisaged a 'power-sharing' arrangement between whites and blacks.

[212] See 1980 *Survey of Race Relations* 50–1.

[212] *Report of the Buthelezi Commission—The Requirements for Stability and Development in KwaZulu and Natal* (1982) vol 1, 34–26.

[214] Constitutional and Political, Economic Development, Planning and Administration, Education and Social Services, and Health.

[215] The chairman was Prof G D L Schreiner, vice-principal Natal University.

[216] See L J Boulle 'The Buthelezi Commission recommendations in the light of current constitutional trends' 1982 *CILSA* 261.

[217] Professor Arend Lijphart was a commission member.

[218] Buthelezi Report (vol 1) 113–14.

[219] This is to paraphrase the well-known dictum of Justice Blackman in *Regents of the University of California v Bakke* 438 US 265 (1978) at 497.

[220] See House of Assembly Debates vol 10 cols 4464–5 (19 April 1979). See also the Laws on Co-operation and Development Act 111 of 1981.

[221] Cf 1982 *Survey of Race Relations* 286–7.

[222] *Report of the Main Committee of the HSRC Investigation into Education* (1981) (the De Lange Report).

[223] Interim Memorandum on the Report of the HSRC on the Inquiry into the Provision of Education in the RSA (October 1981).

6 The Government's 1977 Constitution

1. INTRODUCTION

In this chapter attention is given to the first stage in the evolution of the government's constitutional dispensation, which runs from its early formulations in 1977 to the establishment of the President's Council in early 1981. These developments are collectively referred to as the government's 1977 constitution. Most commentators find the genesis of the 1977 constitution in the Theron Commission report, which advocated direct coloured participation in the existing institutions of government and the appointment of a committee of experts to advise on the statutory amendments necessary to achieve this objective, and recommended that in the process of constitutional change the Westminster-based system of government might have to be modified.[1]* The government rejected the first recommendation in favour of its existing policy of parallel development for coloured persons, but accepted the third, and purported to approve the second. However, it appointed not the recommended committee of experts but a cabinet committee to make proposals on possible amendments to the existing constitution.[2] This response was to have two significant consequences. First, it directed attention to the shortcomings in South Africa's allegedly Westminster-type constitution, and away from the shortcomings in the policy of parallel development, which were the main concern of the Theron Commission. This implied a reversal of that body's priorities. As a consequence the new constitution tended to enshrine the premises of parallel development, namely that whites, coloureds and Indians have different spheres of interest which can form the basis of separate political institutions,[3] and thereby to entrench the very system that had been rejected in the Theron Report. Secondly, it affected the new constitution's legitimacy, because of the way in which it was conceived, formulated and presented. The findings of the cabinet committee were first divulged to the National Party caucus and then to closed sessions of the party's provincial congresses during 1977, before being publicly released on a piecemeal basis. From their inception the proposals constituted part of a party political programme, and were presented as such during the general election in November 1977. Only subsequently were they embodied in the more 'neutral' bill form, but this did not change the earlier negative perceptions of the constitution.

The government's 1977 proposals, which never constituted a definitive constitutional model, made their appearance in three distinct phases, and are dealt with on that basis. Despite an overall consistency, each succeeding revelation introduced subsidiary variations. During the first phase, as appears from the following analysis, the proposals presented a clear constitutional picture with a discernible internal logic, despite various ambiguities and uncertainties, whereas by the third phase the overall plan had become more obscure despite individual parts of it having been given institutional form.

149

* The Notes and References to this chapter commence on page 166.

2.   THE EARLY FORMULATIONS

According to the early formulations of the 1977 constitution there would be three parliaments in South Africa with equal constitutional status and powers, one each for whites, coloureds and Indians.[4] These would be predominantly elective bodies, each sovereign within its sphere of competence. They would each approve their own budget, and have legislative jurisdiction over members of the relevant population group in respect of matters of exclusive concern to it. Each parliament would have its own Prime Minister, a Westminster-type cabinet, and a bureaucracy to administer matters within its jurisdiction. Subordinate to the community parliaments would be separate regional and local authorities for each group. This implied at all three levels the enforcement of classical parallel development in its political dimension. At the 'joint' level of government there would have to be new co-ordinating institutions. There would be an electoral college, comprising members nominated from the three parliaments, with the sole functions of electing the President and, if necessary, discharging him. The presidency would be the most important institution in the new dispensation, introducing for the first time in South Africa[5] an 'executive president'. The President would chair a council of cabinets, consisting of ministers drawn from the three community cabinets, and would ensure that all its decisions were taken on a consensus basis. Members of the council would have executive authority over matters of common concern to all three groups, and since most matters would fall within this category[6] the system implied extensive powers for the council. Legislation on these matters would be initiated by the council of cabinets and submitted to all three parliaments, which together would constitute a composite tricameral legislature. The council of cabinets would also co-ordinate the individual legislative activities of the three parliaments. It would be assisted by two advisory bodies, a presidential council elected by the three parliaments, and a nominated financial council. No express references were made to the judiciary during any phase of the 1977 constitution, save that the appointment of coloureds and Indians to the bench would be entertained. Several other matters were obscurely or incompletely presented in the first phase formulations—the fiscal arrangements, the division of functions between the joint and communal levels of government, the exact composition of some bodies and their modus operandi, the status of prevailing constitutional conventions, the amending procedure, the judicial function, and forms of constitutional responsibility.

In its early formulations some use was made of consociational theory to justify the 1977 constitution. The coalition principle was said to be intrinsic to the council of cabinets, presidential council and financial council; the sizes of the three parliaments and the composition of the joint institutions would be proportionately determined;[7] the consensus principle, which implied a mutual veto power, would apply in the council of cabinets and presidential council; and the three parliaments, with their subordinate institutions, would provide the basis for the segmental autonomy of whites, coloureds and Indians. The system could also be presented as 'democratic', in so far as it implied full citizenship rights for whites, coloureds, and

Indians within the same political system.[8] Consequently the government referred to it as a form of consociational democracy which involved genuine power-sharing among the three involved groups.[9] But although the constitutional proposals had more consociational elements in their first phase than in subsequent phases, they fell far short of the requirements of authentic consociationalism, as is borne out by the analysis below.[10] The government's presentation was based on a generous interpretation and not an analytical evaluation. Even before the draft bill was published there was a shift in emphasis from the notion of power-sharing (magsdeling) to that of dividing power (magsverdeling).[11] The council of cabinets was depicted as a forum for 'consultation and co-responsibility', as opposed to the earlier 'negotiation and power-sharing'. It was said that the sovereignty of the white Parliament would be unaffected, that real power would vest with the (white) President,[12] that members of the council of cabinets would have no executive powers, and that there would be no joint bureaucracy to administer 'common concern' matters. These changes in emphasis reflected the strains that the constitution was generating within the National Party, and presaged its shape in the second phase.

The response of disfranchised groups during the first phase of the 1977 constitution ranged from outright rejection to conditional acceptance as a basis for further negotiation. The Du Preez Report, which rejected it in all material respects, reflected the attitude of the coloured persons for whom it was primarily designed.[13] Nevertheless, acting on a 'mandate' received from the white electorate in the 1977 general election, the government began its piecemeal implementation even before publication of the draft constitution bill, by providing for the changes in the structure and composition of the South African Indian Council described above.[14] This legislation was passed with the new constitutional dispensation in mind,[15] and it provided for a predominantly elective assembly and parliamentary-type executive in anticipation of the later draft bill. The objective was to establish a representative institution, similar to the CPRC, to which powers could be allocated when it was integrated into the new dispensation. For various reasons, however, the first SAIC elections were held only two and a half years after the draft bill's publication.[16]

3.   THE DRAFT CONSTITUTION BILL

(a) General

The draft bill of April 1979[17] introduced a second phase of the government's 1977 constitution, but despite its statutory form the constitution still contained many omissions, uncertainties and complexities. With few exceptions, commentators had difficulty in unravelling the bill, and in elucidating and evaluating the powers of the various authorities and their relationships with one another.[18] But these factors did not obscure the bill's most salient feature, namely its close affinity with the existing constitutional system. In so far as the Westminster model had hitherto applied in South Africa it was left substantially unaffected, and many of the constitutional features anticipated during the first phase were not in evidence. No provision was made for an executive president, the parliamentary form of government was retained, the three legislative assemblies were not accorded equal status, the white House of Assembly retained its legislative supremacy, most powers remained with the white institutions and did not vest at the joint level of government, and equal citizenship rights were not introduced for whites, coloureds and Indians. Many features of the constitution were left wholly intact, including the provincial councils, the state presidency, judicial and financial matters, the constitutional conventions, and the national symbols. Far from heralding a new constitutional order, the draft bill superimposed on the old the few innovations described below. As a consequence it embodied fewer consociational elements than had originally been claimed for the government's constitution.

(b) The institutions of government

The bill regulated institutions at only the 'community' and 'joint' levels of government, and no reference was made to subnational matters, save for the provincial institutions which were left intact. At the community level provision was made for the three predominantly elective assemblies envisaged in the first phase. The existing House of Assembly was retained for whites, with an increase in membership to accommodate twelve indirectly elected and eight nominated members,[19] while for coloureds and Indians the Coloured Persons Representative Council and South African Indian Council were reconstituted as the House of Representatives and Chamber of Deputies respectively, comprising elected, indirectly elected and nominated members in the same proportions as in the restructured Assembly.[20] This arrangement implied the disestablishment of the Senate, as had been indicated in the early formulations of the constitution. Most provisions regulating the House of Assembly were retained, and extended mutatis mutandis to the new assemblies. This included the electoral system, franchise requirements, qualifications for assembly membership, voting, quorum and dissolution matters, and domestic arrangements.[21] Each assembly would have a Westminster-type cabinet and Prime Minister, the latter appointed by the State President in accordance with prevailing conventions and empowered in turn to advise on ministerial appointments and dismissals. Members of the community cabinets would be the 'ministers of the Republic' and would administer the various state departments. Far from the constitution involving a departure from Westminster at this level, it actually replicated Westminster parliamentary institutions for coloureds and Indians in a more consistent application of parallel development policy. The majoritarian bias of the Westminster system was in strong evidence at the community level, and was even strengthened through the provision for non-elected members in the assemblies.

At the joint level of government the bill was more innovative. It provided for all the institutions envisaged during the first-phase formulations, but accorded them a significantly diminished constitutional status and political significance. The presidential office was nominally opened to coloureds and Indians for the first time but the President's functions were left substantially as they had been,[22] as were most ancillary matters relating to the office.[23]

The only new powers related to the appointment of the additional prime ministers and members of the community cabinets, in respect of which he was circumscribed by convention and statute, and to the chairmanship of the council of cabinets, which itself had limited powers. It became apparent that the presidency would not be of the executive type, but of the ceremonial sort associated with a Westminster head of state.[24] However, because the notion of an executive presidency persisted during this phase much attention was given to the new method of electing the State President.

One of the most consistent features in the various formulations of the government's constitutional proposals has been the composition and functioning of the presidential electoral college. The bill confirmed that the 4:2:1 ratio would apply in the college, assuring the white members an overall majority.[25] It also implied, as government spokesmen had earlier intimated, that each component of the college would be elected by the majority party in the respective assembly, and that it would exercise its functions on a simple majority basis.[26] The absence both of minority parties and a qualified majority decision-making procedure meant that in electing and impeaching the president the college would be under the direct control of the majority party in the white assembly.[27] Although the presence of coloureds and Indians in the college was required to legitimise the presidency, their participation on these terms would be more formal than effective. The bill purported to entrench the size and composition of the electoral college by requiring the approval of the three assemblies for their variation,[28] although the juridical efficacy of this provision was questionable.[29] A boycott strategy by coloureds and Indians was pre-empted by a low quorum provision, which was also encountered in respect of other joint institutions.[30] Thus, besides failing to extend executive-type powers to the president, the bill also excluded the possibility of a presidential mandate separate from that of the legislature, an important feature of presidential government. Only in the second phase of the government's constitution was the notion of presidentialism more consistently upheld.

The draft bill's main institutional innovation was the council of cabinets, a successor to the inter-cabinet council, an ad hoc extra-constitutional body.[31] Besides the President, who would chair the council, its membership included the three prime ministers, ex officio, and eleven other ministers appointed by them from the community cabinets—six whites, three coloureds and two Indians.[32] This structure entailed equal representation for whites and non-whites, with the balance of power vesting in the (white) chairman. It also entailed the participation of majority parties only in the council. Although the President was not empowered to dismiss ministers directly, he could do so indirectly by terminating their membership of a community cabinet, after consulting the relevant prime minister. Unanimity was not an institutional requirement in respect of the council's decisions, there being no veto power, but it was depicted as a consensus-inducing forum, with the corollary of joint cabinet responsibility for all its members. This revealed a misguided attempt to project the workings and conventions of one-party parliamentary cabinets on to a composite multi-party executive.[33] It would be particularly inappropriate to hold ministers drawn from three parties, unconnected by a coalition or pact, jointly responsible for council decisions, especially in the light of the political arithmetic of its composition. A further anomaly is that if joint responsiblity also pertained to the community cabinets[34] the potential would exist for individual ministers to be constitutionally responsible for two conflicting decisions.

In the absence of any joint representative or deliberative assembly the council of cabinets was a focal point of attention in the 1977 constitution. But the bill did not bear out the first phase predictions that it would be both a functional political institution and the main forum for consociational accommodation. Although, as is shown below, it was given a significant role in the legislative process it was denied any executive powers and only three functions were expressly allocated to it in the bill—it could activate the President's Council to make recommendations on matters of national interest, authorise ministerial participation in the proceedings of the different assemblies, and provide countersignatures to instruments executed by the President.[35] As provided for in the draft bill the council of cabinets would have been a relatively insignificant body, and several modifications were made to its successors in subsequent versions of the government's constitution when more powers came to be vested at the 'joint' level of government.

In the second phase of the 1977 constitution the position of the President's Council still belied the prominence that it would subsequently assume. The bill provided[36] that it would comprise fifty-five members appointed by the State President, in consultation with the prime ministers, for five-year terms. The main qualifications for membership were mature age and eligibility to register as a voter for the white, coloured or Indian assemblies. The only functions envisaged for the council at this stage were to advise the council of cabinets, at the latter's request, on any matter of national interest, and, in its own discretion, to enquire into any matter relating to such request. It was depicted during this phase as a prestigious consociational-type body that would resolve contentious issues in an élite non-public forum.

(c) **The distribution of competence**

In each of its variations the government's constitution has implied a division of competence between 'joint' and 'community' institutions. During the first phase it was indicated that most powers would be exercised at the joint level of government, and in the absence of a national legislative assembly commentators constructed the theory of a 'tricameral parliament' to accommodate the legislative function. In a symbolic aspect the draft bill encouraged the notion of tricameralism by providing different nomenclature for the white, coloured and Indian assemblies,[37] but in reality the white Parliament's supremacy was left intact.[38] The House of Assembly was vested with original legislative competence, the sole power to appropriate moneys, and the primary power to amend the constitution (which remained highly flexible),[39] and unlike the other assemblies all its laws would be immune from judicial invalidation.[40] The other two assemblies would inherit the law-making powers of their predecessors, which in 1979 entailed very limited competence for the coloured assembly only. In addition the

The Government's 1977 Constitution 155

council of cabinets could confer delegated legislative competence on the coloured and Indian assemblies, or refer a specific piece of legislation to one of them (or the white assembly) for enactment. Legislation affecting only one community would be initiated by the relevant cabinet, and after approval by the assembly would require the assent of the appropriate Prime Minister and the President. According to the tricameral theory 'common concern' legislation, on the other hand, would require the approval of all three assemblies, and it was provided that such bills could be submitted to them all for their consideration. However, differences of opinion on such measures would be referred to the council of cabinets, a joint advisory committee, or the State President, any of which could take a binding decision on the form of the legislation; thereafter enactment by a single assembly would validate the statute. This flexible mechanism for by-passing one or more assembly had the effect of negating the theory of 'tricameralism'. Moreover even this abridged procedure could be circumvented if the council of cabinets, in its discretion, submitted such legislation directly to any one of the community assemblies for enactment. In overall terms the bill would have provided little significant variation in the distribution of legislative competence. The white assembly's predominance in this field was assured, the other assemblies being subordinate to and not co-ordinate with it. Their authority could only be augmented at the pleasure of the president, acting through the council of cabinets. The inevitability of the white community institutions dominating the system was strengthened by the arrangements relating to executive power.

The draft bill was largely reticent on the matter of executive competence but the clue to this question lay in the number of ministers in the community cabinets: seventeen whites, five coloureds and three Indians, in addition to the three prime ministers.[41] Individuals appointed to these cabinets would be the ministers of the Republic,[42] and would have executive authority in that capacity. It is clear from this arrangement that, save for the limited separable matters that could be vested in the other cabinets, most executive powers would remain with the white ministers. All matters of 'national' concern, including the initiation of legislation, would be controlled by white ministers, some of whom would also be members of the council of cabinets. But the council itself would have no executive authority, nor would the 'national' portfolios be distributed among its members in their capacities as council members. The further implications of this arrangement were that it would be predominantly white ministers who would advise the President in the exercise of his functions (for example, in respect of black affairs)[43] and that most state departments would be headed politically by white ministers. The bill did not stipulate, nor did it imply, changes in the composition and functioning of the white-dominated bureaucracy, despite the importance of this institution in modern political systems. While it would have been naïve to expect the draft bill to involve a threat to the dominant group's political position, it is significant that it allowed it to dominate mainly through existing legislative, executive and administrative institutions.

(d) The draft bill and consociationalism

The draft bill contained several consociational elements, and was justified in terms of consociational theory, but it would have given rise to a decidedly less consociational form of government than was anticipated during the first phase of the 1977 constitution.[44] The council of cabinets and its subsidiary institutions implied some scope for the grand coalition principle, the proportionality principle was encountered in the composition of various bodies, and some institutional basis was provided for segmental autonomy. But a closer analysis supports the finding of Hanf, Weiland & Vierdag that,

> '. . . some of the structural features of consociation have been adopted, as well as its vocabulary. But its essence is missing: the regulation of conflict remains unilateral, rather than being worked out by all the parties concerned. Power remains in the hands of the white group.'[45]

There were three major factors that caused the system to deviate fundamentally from the consociational norm, each of which also affected subsequent versions of the constitution.

In the first place there was the exclusion of blacks from the arrangement, impliedly justified in terms of the homelands policy.[46] Apart from the implications of this factor for the representative and democratic aspects of the system, it also rendered it imperfectly consociational in that a major conflict group was omitted from the accommodationist process, in so far as that was provided for. For the dominant group to exclude certain rivals from the political process is a travesty of the consociational norm, although the demographic realities entailed that the government was only able to introduce some consociational elements without losing its dominance provided blacks were excluded completely. There was speculation during 1980 that a fourth assembly for blacks might be established to complete the 'consociational' arrangement, but this was never a serious possibility because of its implications for the arithmetical equilibrium of the government's constitution. The draft bill further formalised the black/non- black dichotomy in constitutional development which had begun to emerge in the preceding years. While authoritarian forms of consociationalism could be created for whites, coloureds and Indians within a common political system, the constitutional programme for blacks catered only for political separatism and partition. The consociationalism/partition duality was subsequently reinforced by the President's Council.[47]

Secondly, even within the ambit of the government's constitution there could be no authentic consociationalism, without a system of free political association. The draft bill incorporated the prevailing 'segmental' definitions which had been statutorily imposed by the dominant group,[48] and which in the case of the residually-defined coloured group had never been popularly accepted. No provision was made for voluntary association on the basis of commonly accepted interests, and the bill implicitly retained the Prohibition of Political Interference Act[49] which proscribes political alliances or co-operation between different groups. While imposed group definitions might be relevant during a constitutive constitutional phase they can be less easily justified in a consociational system of government that assumes the existence of politically homogeneous segments.[50] The constitution's effect of embedding in the political system groups defined in terms of statutory concepts of colour and ethnicity would obstruct the emergence and activism of the genuine leadership élites on which consociationalism relies. To accommodate the emergence of these leaders would require the removal not only of statutory group definitions and restrictions on voluntary political formation but also many other authoritarian features of the constitutional system that restrict, restrain and circumscribe political leaders.

The third major shortcoming, from a consociational perspective, was the absence of an effective veto power for coloureds and Indians.[51] As whites constitute an overall majority of the combined white, coloured and Indian electorate there could not be the multiple balance of power that is a favourable condition for consociationalism. But the draft bill exacerbated the position by reproducing the white demographic majority proportionately in the electoral college, president's council and joint advisory committees. In these institutions coloureds and Indians would jointly and severally be permanent minorities, without the compensation of any veto power. Where coloureds and Indians were overrepresented in a joint institution, namely the council of cabinets, they also had no veto power, as the President was empowered to take binding decisions. Although allowed to participate in these bodies, coloureds and Indians were denied the institutional means of directly influencing the decision-making process, despite the sanguine predictions that consensus would become a fundamental norm of the political process. In Dahl's terms,[52] the constitution would have given rise to a more inclusive political system (in terms of increased citizen participation), but would not have involved greater political contestation because of the new opposition's institutionalised minority status and lack of veto power.

Several other features of the 1979 bill were not favourable from a consociational point of view. The majoritarian electoral systems, majority party cabinets, and exclusion of minority parties from the joint institutions implied a strong majoritarian bias for the whole system.[53] The entrenchment of the composition of the electoral college and the sizes of the three assemblies involved an unfavourable rigidity in the proportionality principle. That principle served to exaggerate, instead of mitigate, the influence of the white majority and was not contemplated as a basis for making public appointments or allocating the 'spoils of government'. As the analysis in the preceding section shows, there was little practical scope for Indian and coloured segmental autonomy. In fact the constitution would have retained that feature of the Westminster system which is most anti-consociational in effect, namely that success in one decisive site—the elections for the white assembly—would permit domination of the whole political system. The consociational elements in the draft bill would have served to incorporate coloureds and Indians into the constitutional system on a differential basis, and to maintain overall white supremacy.

4.   THE SCHLEBUSCH REPORT AND ITS SEQUEL

(a)   The Schlebusch Commission

The government submitted the 1979 draft constitution bill to the Schlebusch Commission of enquiry, whose composition and terms of reference have been described above.[54] A contemporaneous political development of some significance was the abolition of the Coloured Persons Representative Council early in 1980.[55] This signified the collapse of the government's official policy for coloured persons a short period after the exposure of its shortcomings by the Theron Commission. The government decided against establishing the fully nominated Coloured Persons Council, for which statutory provision had been made,[56] and it failed to hold elections for the South African Indian Council by the time the Schlebusch Commission convened. The main significance of these developments was that at the time of the Schlebusch Commission deliberations there were no representative coloured or Indian institutions in existence. It was no longer possible to incorporate such institutions into the white constitutional system, as had been contemplated in the first two phases of the 1977 constitution. The Schlebusch report was therefore forced to recommend the incorporation of individual coloured and Indian élites into the political process through a non-elective body which for the first time came to the fore of the government's constitution, namely the President's Council. For the same reasons it became necessary to institutionalise the 1977 constitution during its third phase on a piecemeal basis.

(b) The Schlebusch Commission's recommendations

Five constitutional recommendations were made in the majority report of the Schlebusch Commission:

(i) That the senate be abolished (although this did not imply the acceptance in principle of unicameralism);

(ii) That, in view of the recommendations on the Senate, the entrenching procedure be placed within the jurisdiction of the House of Assembly alone;

(iii) That a Vice State President be elected on the same basis as the President to serve ex officio as chairman of the President's Council;

(iv) That a President's Council, comprising sixty 'nationally acknowledged experts' appointed by the State President, be established to advise the latter on various matters;

(v) That the House of Assembly be enlarged to accommodate twenty additional members nominated by party leaders on a proportional basis.

The recommendations were all reconcilable with the principles of the 1977 constitution, and involved a selective endorsement of its institutions. The change in emphasis from the two earlier versions of the constitution was necessitated by the disestablishment of the CPRC: it became necessary to focus on the highest tier of government at which the nominated President's Council came into prominence. The office of Vice State President was an innovation and appeared to be designed to add prestige to the President's Council without the State President being overtly drawn into the political arena. Although none of the majority recommendations was motivated in the report all were accepted by the government and were implemented within a short period.

(c) **The abolition of the Senate**

The demise of the upper chamber had been anticipated in the first two phases of the 1977 constitution, which envisaged three unicameral 'parliaments'. Its abolition received the unanimous endorsement of the Schlebusch Commission and became effective on 1 January 1981.[57] It was a first major step in the statutory implementation of the government's constitution and was portrayed as a decisive event in the movement away from the Westminster model, although in reality bicameralism is only a secondary feature of that model. In the light of its history the abolition of the Senate had little practical significance for the political process: its role as a chamber of review had been very limited, it had not been conspicuous in representing the interests of the provinces nor of those excluded from the franchise, and even in its more specialised role as curator of the entrenched sections it had followed the House of Assembly's lead.[58] Nevertheless, in terms of the norms of modern constitutionalism the abolition of the Senate involved a weakening of the checks and balances on governmental power and enhanced the cabinet's control of the legislature in its law-making and other roles. It was also symptomatic of the move away from the principle of representative government in South Africa, in that the successor to the indirectly elected Senate, the President's Council, was a fully nominated body. While the Senate's demise was not widely lamented, some commentators suggested that the Schlebusch Commission was shortsighted in failing to investigate possibilities for its radical reformation during the process of constitutional change, so as to benefit from its institutional legitimacy.[59]

In anticipation of the Senate's abolition the entrenching procedure had been altered[60] to enable the entrenched provisions to be amended by the House of Assembly and State President only, the tradition of rigidity being retained in the requirement of a two-thirds majority in the House. This amendment was presented to a joint sitting of the two houses and approved by the required two-thirds majority[61] and when the Act became effective it relegated the joint sitting procedure, a focal feature of the constitutional crisis in the 1950s, to constitutional history. As this legislation was enacted prior to the abolition of the Senate the entrenched procedure was not required for the subsequent action, which was effected through the normal bicameral process.

The abolition of the Senate was preceded in 1980 by another indirectly related constitutional amendment. The legislation[62] provided that for delimitation purposes a provincial and not a national quota would henceforth be used for determining the median voter-strength of each constituency, subject to the discretionary loading and unloading. The provincial quota system had originally been introduced by the South Africa Act which guaranteed each province a minimum number of seats,[63] regardless of its share of registered voters. But additional seats accrued to the demographically expanding provinces until the various provincial quotas were approximately equal.[64] From 1942 the delimitation commission was empowered to allocate seats interprovincially on a proportional basis[65] and in 1965 a national quota was introduced for the first time.[66] These developments ensured that like constituencies throughout the country would be of approximately equal voter size, as would be the weight of each individual's vote. But in 1973 the number of parliamentary seats in each province was constitutionally pegged[67] and the national quota lost its significance—considerable interprovincial discrepancies arose between the number of voters in similar constituencies because seats could no longer be allocated interprovincially. The 1980 amendment reinforced this arrangement and widely different provincial quotas were used in the subsequent constituency delimitation.[68] To some extent the new arrangement served to compensate the smaller provinces for the minimum representation which they had enjoyed in the Senate.[69] In this sense the overrepresentation of the minority provinces in the central legislature could be seen as a variation of the consociational principle of proportionality. But from a democratic point of view it involved a significant departure from the 'one vote one value' principle,[70] which the consociational model attempts to uphold by converting electoral support into proportional legislative representation. The new arrangement failed to reconcile these conflicting principles in the same way as the Senate, which had provided both minimum representation for all the provinces and additional representation beyond the threshold for the larger ones. While the demise of the Senate was not of direct significance in terms of consociational principles, a related constitutional amendment had some negative implications from this perspective.

(d) The restructuring of the House of Assembly

While a restructuring of the House of Assembly was envisaged during the two preceding phases of the 1977 constitution, the changes effected in 1980 must also be seen in conjunction with the prior abolition of the Senate, for which they provided partial compensation. The size of the House was increased to 177 members and provision was made for the first time for non-elective members of this body.[71] The component of 165 members directly elected on a constituency basis was retained, with four additional members nominated by the State President, one from each province, and eight others proportionately elected by an electoral college comprising the directly elected members. The prevailing qualification requirements were extended to nominated and indirectly elected members. Casual vacancies would be filled by nomination or indirect election, according to the status of the vacating member. These changes involved fewer additional members than those provided for in the 1979 draft bill and the Schlebusch Report.[72] The methods of appointment were in conformity with the bill, save that the provincial factor was dispensed with in respect of the indirectly elected members. The new arrangements were modelled on similar features in the former Senate, and were at times supported in such terms.[73] The government justified the inclusion of nominated and indirectly elected members in the House in terms of the need to accommodate specialists who might be unable to obtain seats by way of ordinary election, and to provide greater participation for otherwise unrepresented groups or interests.[74] Comparative precedents for the proportionately elected component could be found: for example in the Federal Republic of Germany half the members of the Bundestag are voted for directly in plurality based constituency elections, while the other half are indirectly elected through a proportional party-list system.[75] However, precedents for executive-nominated members of a non-secondary legislative body are virtually non-existent, save in respect of South Africa's homeland states.[76]

The above innovations were destined to be applied mutatis mutandis to other legislative assemblies in subsequent versions of the government's constitution, and they have three points of constitutional significance. In the first place they affect the representative nature of the assembly. By conventional democratic standards, whatever justification there might be for non-elected members in a second and secondary chamber cannot be sustained in respect of a unicameral sovereign legislature such as the House of Assembly. This is particularly the case with the nominated members. While the total non-elective component constitutes a small minority within the House, the establishment of the principle renders it easier for the number to be increased by the government of the day. The non-democratic features permit the drafting of experts and technocrats into the legislature in furtherance of the trend away from representative towards managerial government. In terms of this potentiality they complement the government's new-found ability to draw 'specialists' directly into the cabinet for a full year.[77] Nevertheless, it is significant that the constitution prescribes no additional requirements, in terms of qualifications, experience or expertise, for either category of additional members, and the experience of the Senate, and of the early history of this arrangement itself, suggests that party loyalties will predominate over other factors in its application.[78]

The second point is closely related to the first. It concerns the increased scope which the system affords the cabinet and Prime Minister to dominate the legislature, thereby distorting the reciprocal relationships of control and responsibility traditionally associated with the Westminster form of parliamentary government. This factor tends to operate at the level of constitutional theory because the gravitation of power from the legislature to the executive, and the dominance of the latter over the former, are common features of modern systems of government. In terms of the theory the nominated members, and to a slightly lesser extent those proportionately elected by the government, ensure greater control for the cabinet over the legislature, since these members are responsible not to constitutents, but to the government on whom they depend for reappointment. Even the partial separation of powers of a parliamentary system is distorted by this arrangement. The constitutional responsiblity of the cabinet to the legislature, as enjoined by the theory of parliamentarism, must necessarily be affected by these factors. Moreover, the responsibility of the executive to the electorate, as mediated through a representative legislature, becomes more remote when the mediating institution is only partly elected. The overall consequence is a dilution of the principles of constitutional government in this area.

The third point concerns inter-party relationships within the Assembly. The four nominated members in the House of Assembly afford the dominant party an increased parliamentary majority unrelated to its popular support, and where a delicate balance of power exists between government and opposition they could maintain the former in power, despite losses in by-elections or changes of party allegiance which might otherwise unseat it. The position was exacerbated by a subsequent amendment which allowed all non-elected Members of Parliament to retain their seats for up to 180 days after a general election notwithstanding the prior dissolution of Parliament and the holding of the election.[79] This could also lead to a defeated government remaining in power.[80] Apart from the distortions that these factors involve for the Westminster system of parliamentarism, they also have a counter-consociational effect in that they strengthen the majoritarian bias of the constitutional system. As far as the eight indirectly elected members are concerned, their presence would not distort the power-balance within Parliament, save in so far as the majoritarian electoral system distorts the initial representation of political parties, and they reflect this distortion. From a consociational point of view this is a false proportionality. Proportionality can serve a consociational purpose if it exists alongside majoritarianism,[81] but not where it is built on to majoritarianism, in which case it involves merely an extension of the latter. The 'proportionality' principle embodied in these innovations cannot, therefore, be regarded as a consociational element. Cumulatively the changes introduced in the House of Assembly were counter-consociational devices within the white political system.

(e) The Vice State President and President's Council

Effect was given to the Schlebusch Commission recommendation on the Vice State President in the Fifth Constitution Amendment Act of 1980.[82] No provision had been made for this office during the two earlier phases of the 1977 constitution, but it assumed some significance in the post-Schlebusch developments because of the creation of the President's Council, of which the Vice State President was chairman. Apart from functions constitutionally ascribed to the position, it served additional functional and symbolic roles: it provided greater governmental control over the President's Council than would have been the case with a self-appointed chairman, and it extended to that body some of the status and prestige attaching to the presidency.

As far as the qualifications, election, tenure and impeachment of the Vice State President are concerned, the same conditions apply as those pertaining to the State President, and other ancillary matters are also identical. This arrangement involves several deviations from the 1979 draft bill which provided for the chairman of the President's Council to be nominated from its members by the President, who would himself have been elected by a composite electoral college. It was not possible to use this kind of electoral college for the Vice State President, since it depended on the existence of representative coloured and Indian assemblies. Resort was therefore had to the same electoral college used for the presidency, comprising the members of the unicameral white parliament, and in terms of the applicable qualifications the Vice State President would have to be white. The first election resulted in the appointment of a cabinet minister, the former chairman of the parliamentary constitutional commission.[83] The holder of the office has two principal statutory functions: The first is to substitute for the State President when the latter is unable to officiate,[84] in which capacity he succeeds the president of the former Senate. The second is to preside over the President's Council at all times other than when serving as acting State President.[85] One of the contentious aspects of the new office is that the protective scope of s 13 of the constitution has been broadened to include the Vice State President, irrespective of which of the two functions is being performed. This gives rise to the anomaly that the incumbent will be protected in respect of all activities relating to the President's Council, despite its direct role in the political process. However, the office itself only endured while the President's Council performed a constitutive function and it was discarded during subsequent phases of the government's constitution.

In regard to the President's Council there were several deviations from the 1979 draft bill, but the Schlebusch recommendations were substantially adhered to. The Act[86] made provision for a council of sixty members, excluding the Vice State President, to be appointed by the executive[87] for five-year periods, subject to a dissolution of the council within ninety days after a general election.[88] There are three basic qualifications for appointment: a minimum age of thirty years, South African citizenship, and membership of the white, coloured, Indian or Chinese groups,[89] and two incompatibilities: membership of a supra-local legislative body and governmental employment.[90] The reference to Chinese members was an innovation,[91] but the most significant feature of the council's composition is its restriction to non-blacks. The government justified the exclusion of blacks in terms of their different historical constitutional development, and on the grounds that their existing constitutional structures were adequate and their inclusion in the council would involve a duplication of the channels of political communications.[92] The Prime Minister emphasised that even if the President's Council itself recommended the inclusion of blacks, the government would not oblige.[93] The same reasoning had been implicit in the earlier formulations of the 1977 constitution, which in the government's view was designed to complement the homelands' constitutional structures, and not to modify them. The President's Council can therefore be seen as an evolutionary outcome of previous constitutional trends. Its composition confirmed the government's policy that black political rights would be exercised only through the national states, and it highlighted the new black/non-black axis of constitutional development.[94] The only legislative reference to blacks was in respect of the council of 'Black South African citizens', which was regarded by the government as an institutionalisation of the deliberations that have taken place among leaders of non-independent national states, and it was envisaged that consultation would take place between this body and the President's Council through a committee system.[95] The exclusion of blacks from the President's Council also had implications for subsequent constitutional developments in that the government designated it as a vehicle for constitutional change, in which capacity it would inevitably see constitutional issues in black/non-black terms. Subject to the above factors the government's discretion in the appointive process is of the broadest kind. The council was intended to comprise experts in

various disciplines and recognised community leaders, but no such qualifications are statutorily prescribed.

Provision was made for the President's Council to be divided into standing committees for constitutional affairs, economic affairs, planning and
community relationships, multiple membership of committees being permitted. The council has jurisdiction over its rules and orders, subject to a
statutorily provided no-quorum arrangement.[96] Its terms of reference
proved to be wider than those contained in the draft bill, but it is still
restricted to an advisory role. In the first place it can furnish advice to the
State President, either at his request, or in its own discretion if it considers a
matter to be of public interest. Within its limits this empowering provision is
of a broad kind and the cabinet can make use of the council in respect of any
matter, regardless of under whose jurisdiction it normally falls. Reports of
this nature must be tabled in the House of Assembly within fourteen days of
receipt by the State President. A secondary function of the council is to
advise any supra-local legislative body, at the latter's request, on draft
legislation. In this capacity it would serve as a constitutional council, but its
opinion is not binding and does not have to be tabled before the legislation
is enacted. Despite its very limited role in the legislative process, and the
fact that the council is predominantly an instrument of the executive, the
government soon extended to it a wide range of powers and privileges
normally associated with sovereign Westminster parliaments.[97] Not only
are members afforded freedom of speech in relation to council matters, but
the council can summon witnesses to appear before it, and failure to
respond can result in a criminal conviction.[98] In the performance of their
functions the council and its committees are empowered to consult with
individuals or state institutions, and to establish consultative committees for
this purpose. Despite these competences the inferior constitutional status of
the President's Council is ensured by its legal subordinacy to the white
Parliament, and its dependence on the white executive and bureaucracy to
give political effect to its recommendations. These factors have had serious
implications for its credibility.

The President's Council was first instituted in 1981,[99] and was divided
into five standing committees,[100] of which the most prominent is the constitutional committee. By the government it was regarded as the most important product of the several constitutional amendments of 1980. It was
conceived as a consociational-type body—a 'grand coalition' of white, coloured and Indian élites, which could depoliticise contentious issues and
resolve them along accommodationist lines. Its consociational pretensions
have been symbolically emphasised—the council's seating is arranged in
concentric semi-circles, rather than in an (adversarial) horse-shoe shape,
and little physical provision has been made for the media and public.[101]
Plenary meetings are held in public, but the committees, in which its main
work is done, conduct most of their sessions in camera. But several structural features expose its consociational limitations: its unrepresentative composition, its limited powers, and the absence of proportionality and a veto
system. Comparisons with other consociational institutions, such as the
Dutch Social and Economic Council, have limited relevance: while these

may also be nominated advisory bodies, they exist alongside representative institutions and are functionally specialised, whereas the President's Council was created as a substitute for representative institutions, and one of its most salient functions is that of deliberating on basic constitutional matters. Any 'consociational accommodation' achieved by the council could only have a contingent political relevance, because effective power continues to vest in the white political institutions. Nevertheless the council did herald a new constitutive phase in the South African constitutional process and is referred to again in the following chapter.

(f) Changes in parliamentary government

An additional constitutional amendment of 1980 was not directly related to the 1977 constitution, but it fitted into the post-Schlebusch report trends. In the Westminster export models it has been customary to enact the British convention requiring ministers to be members of the legislature, the principle going to the heart of parliamentary government.[102] Varying periods of grace are allowed for ministers to secure membership of Parliament if they are not already members on appointment. In South Africa this period has traditionally been three months,[103] but there has been no bar on indefinite reappointments, after nominal interludes, for such periods. However, during the grace period ministers were denied participation in parliamentary proceedings as well as normal parliamentary privileges, and with the government's ability, where necessary, to nominate such ministers to the Senate the facility was not extensively used.

The 1980 amendment[104] extended the period of grace to twelve months and allowed non-legislative ministers to participate in parliamentary proceedings (save for voting) and to exercise the normal parliamentary powers and privileges.[105] The amendment was motivated in terms of the need to introduce persons with exceptional ability or talents directly into the cabinet, without the inconvenience and disruption of their contesting an election immediately thereafter.[106] It served to extend further the Prime Minister's discretion in making ministerial appointments, despite the fact that the flexibility formerly afforded by the Senate had been retained in the government's new ability to appoint members directly to the House.[107] The twelve-month period and nomination procedure could be used cumulatively, and the cabinet could contain a significant proportion of non-legislative ministers and nominated Members of Parliament. In terms of conventional constitutional theory the new arrangement gives the cabinet greater independence vis-à-vis the legislature, and tends to blur the lines of ministerial responsiblity. However, some control has been provided in that ministers cannot be reappointed under this system (regardless of their actual period served),[108] and by virtue of their participation in Parliament they are subject to the normal forms of parliamentary control of ministers.

The deviation from the principles of parliamentary government introduced by this amendment should be seen in the light of the other constitutional changes of 1980: the transition to unicameralism, the provision for non-elected Members of Parliament, the creation of the nominated President's Council, an increase in the size of the cabinet,[109] and changes in the state administration.[110] Together they contributed to the general movement away from representative government towards a centralised managerial system. In the following year the State President was empowered to assign any statutory power conferred on an individual minister to any other minister for any reason, and the Prime Minister was empowered to assign his own powers and functions to other ministers on the same basis.[111] The extension of executive power without the introduction of new devices for controlling and checking the exercise of such power, implies a movement away from the principles of constitutional government. In so far as these developments involve the concentration of power in the white cabinet they have also been anti-consociational in effect.

5. CONCLUSION

The analysis in this chapter reveals several variations and changes in emphasis in the different stages of the 1977 constitution. Paradoxically, the first formulations embodied an almost comprehensive constitutional model, whereas by the later stages the constitution had become more open-ended and diffuse, despite its partial implementation. Nevertheless in all its versions the 1977 constitution revealed at least three basic consistencies. First, it left unaffected the existing constitutional structures for blacks. Secondly, it sought to provide a new institutional framework for the government's prevailing policies for non-blacks. And thirdly, it showed a commitment to some consociational structures for the purpose of incorporating coloureds and Indians into the white constitutional system as junior partners. In so far as the constitution was premised on the need to move away from the Westminster system the developments during this period were somewhat contradictory. Some of the ancillary features of the Westminster model were removed, but more fundamental features were retained and even strengthened. Those constitutional amendments actually enacted strengthened the position of the politically dominant group, in particular by concentrating power in the executive, thus attesting to its intention of remaining in control of the process of constitutional change. Although these developments were a response to the legitimation problems facing the state system, the largely negative response they evoked from political outsiders showed that questions of legitimacy remained fundamentally unresolved. This period of constitutional activity set the stage for the new constitutive phase which followed.

NOTES AND REFERENCES
    [1] See above, 129–31.
    [2] See above, 146n166; some outside experts were consulted by the committee.
    [3] See M Wiechers 'Current Constitutional Proposals—A Critique' (paper presented at 28th Summer School, University of Cape Town, 8 February 1978) 8, and above, 84–5.
    [4] The main sources at this stage were party publications (e g G Terblanche MP (ed) *The New Political Dispensation for White, Coloured and Indian* (1977), and *Questions and Replies on Constitutional Plan* (1977); see also Pro-Nat (November 1977—Information sheet of Cape National Party) and The Department of Information *South Africa's New Constitutional Plan* (1978)), parliamentary debates (see House of Assembly Debates vol 1 cols 19–384 (30 Jan–3 Feb 1978), the censure debate; vol 5 cols 2254–2306 (3 March 1978); vol 10 cols 4548–4555 (12 April 1978)), and communications by government spokesmen (e g 'The South African government's 1977 constitutional proposals' by D Worrall in J A Benyon (ed) *Constitutional Change in South Africa* (1978) 127–35).

⁵ That is since the Boer republics, a comparison made in the media.

⁶ See Worrall op cit 128.

⁷ The pervasive 4:2:1 ratio was based on the mid-1976 population estimates of 4 320 000 whites, 2 434 000 coloureds and 746 000 Indians; the comparable figure for blacks was 18 629 000. Coloureds and Indians would be overrepresented in the council of cabinets with 4 and 3 members respectively, as against 7 white ministers and the (white) President.

⁸ Cf House of Assembly Debates vol 4 col 1474 (20 February 1978), vol 9 col 3923 (1 March 1978), vol 16 col 7923 (26 May 1978).

⁹ See eg Worrall's (op cit 132–4) references to E Nordlinger's *Conflict Regulation in Divided Societies* (1972).

¹⁰ See below, 156–7.

¹¹ See House of Assembly Debates vol 1 col 34 (30 Jan 1978), vol 10 cols 4546–8 (12 April 1978) and the discussion in Benyon op cit 152–9.

¹² The 'De Gaulle option' was referred to frequently during the first phase, and a cabinet minister referred to the Indian and Coloured parliaments as 'talking shops'.

¹³ See above, 112–14.

¹⁴ See above, 86.

¹⁵ See House of Assembly Debates vol 17 col 8186 (30 May 1978). The earlier Indians Electoral Act 122 of 1977 regulated the SAIC elections.

¹⁶ See above, 105n159.

¹⁷ *Government Gazette* 6386 (3 April 1978).

¹⁸ See on the draft bill N J J Olivier 'Die Regering se Konstitusionele Voorstelle' (unpublished paper, Cape Town 1979); M P Vorster & H P Viljoen 'Die Nuwe Grondwet-like Bedeling in Suid-Afrika' 1979 *TSAR* 201; G Devenish 'A Critical Evaluation of the Theoretical and Political Implications of the New Constitutional Proposals' (University of the Western Cape, 1979); M Wiechers *Staatsreg* (3 ed, 1981) 218–21; and the contributions in S C Jacobs (ed) *'n Nuwe Grondwetlike Bedeling vir Suid-Afrika* (1981).

¹⁹ Draft bill s 27; of the 12, three would be elected by the MPs in each province, along the lines of the Senate; the Prime Minister would nominate the other eight, two from each province.

²⁰ That is 82, six and four members respectively for the House, and 40, three and three for the Chamber. Sections 49 and 52 of the bill.

²¹ Sections 49(2) and 50, and 42(2) and 53 of the bill.

²² Sections 7, 19, 20, 21, 58 and 104; see Vorster & Viljoen op cit 204f; M Wiechers 'Die uitvoerende staatshoof: enkele opmerkings' in Jacobs op cit 139–43.

²³ The period of office was reduced from seven to five years.

²⁴ If this were not the case the retention of s 13 of the Constitution Act 32 of 1961 (protecting the presidential dignity and reputation) would have been anomalous (cf s 13 of the bill).

²⁵ Section 8(1)*(b)*. There would be 50 white, 25 coloured and 13 Indian members.

²⁶ Sections 9(5) and (6).

²⁷ Wiechers (op cit 141) described the State President as 'niks anders . . . as die handlanger van die Blanke parlement nie'.

²⁸ Section 8(1)*(d)*.

²⁹ In the light of s 111 of the bill read with s 77.

³⁰ Section 8(1)*(b)*; cf ss 16(2) and 23(7).

³¹ See above, 96–7.

³² On the council of cabinets see s 16 of the draft bill.

³³ See S C Jacobs ''n Juridiese analise van die konstitusionele voorstelle vir 'n nuwe grondwetlike bedeling in Suid-Afrika' in Jacobs op cit 88 at 98.

³⁴ All ministers would be bound by an oath of secrecy—s 19(4). See below, 200.

³⁵ Sections 45, 44(2) and 18(1) respectively.

³⁶ See the draft bill ss 23–25.

³⁷ That is, House of Assembly, House of Representatives and Chamber of Deputies, which, so the argument ran, together constituted a national parliament. On the importance for constitutionalism of the skilful handling of symbols see C J Friedrich *Constitutional Government and Democracy* 4 ed (1968) 168f.

³⁸ See generally s 26 of the bill.

³⁹ Sections 20(1)*(a)*, 91(2) and 111 respectively; the other assemblies could amend the constitution if empowered to do so by the council of cabinets.

⁴⁰ Section 55. It is noteworthy that provincial Ordinances would be void if repugnant to laws of the Assembly (s 79) but not, by implication, if repugnant to laws of the other two bodies.

[41] Section 19(1) of the draft bill.

[42] Section 19(2).

[43] Section 104.

[44] See L J Boulle 'The New Constitutional Proposals and the Possible Transition to Consociational Democracy' in F van Zyl Slabbert & J Opland (eds) *South Africa: Dilemmas of Evolutionary Change* (1980) 14–35, and 'Federation and Consociation: Conceptual Links and Current Constitutional Models' 1981 *THRHR* 236; W B Vosloo 'Consociational Democracy as a means to accomplish peaceful political change in South Africa: an evaluation of the constitutional change proposed by the National Party in 1977' 1979 *Politikon* 13; A Lijphart 'Federal, Confederal and Consociational Options for the South African Plural Society' in R Rotberg & J Barratt (eds) *Conflict and Compromise in South Africa* (1980) 51–76.

[45] T Hanf, H Weiland & G Vierdag *South Africa: The Prospects of Peaceful Change* (1981) 412.

[46] See the preamble to the draft bill.

[47] See below, 175.

[48] Section 112 incorporated the definitions contained in the Population Registration Act 30 of 1950.

[49] Act 51 of 1968.

[50] Where political organisation does not follow 'segmental' boundaries (as in South Africa) significant minorities within each 'segment' will be excluded from the joint power-sharing institutions, particularly when, as in the government's constitution, the majoritarian principle is applied at the intra-segmental level. Thus the 'grand coalition' would be a coalition of majority parties only, to the exclusion of opposition parties. Furthermore leadership-élites would be conscious of the need to preserve their 'majority' status, which might inhibit them from agreeing to compromise arrangements—this problem would not be so acute where each segment was represented by a single political party.

[51] Lijphart op cit 68.

[52] R Dahl *Polyarchy—Participation and Opposition* (1971) 5ff.

[53] Majoritarianism at the intra-segmental level is acceptable in a consociational system, provided the segments are based on voluntary association. Where they are statutorily defined it has the effect of excluding minority parties from the joint institutions, where they might have an important brokerage role. It is, however, a reality of South Africa's constitutional politics that the National Party will not provide the basis for collusion between white opposition and non-white parties, for fear of being outvoted; during all three phases of the 1977 constitution the government has sought to strengthen its own institutional position within 'white' politics, while providing a limited basis for contestation with the new coloured and Indian 'opposition'. The same applies to the 1983 constitution.

[54] At 133–4.

[55] The South African Coloured Persons Council Act 24 of 1980; see above, 85.

[56] Act 24 of 1980, ss 1–2; see above, 104n141.

[57] Section 16 of the Republic of South Africa Constitution Fifth Amendment Act 101 of 1980 repealed those sections of the constitution relating to the Senate; in terms of s 37(1) of the Act s 16 came into operation on 1 January 1981.

[58] See above, 78.

[59] See the earlier warning of M Wiechers in 'Grondslae vir Politieke Ontwikkeling in Suid-Afrika' in J Coetzee (ed) *Gedenkbundel H L Swanepoel* (1976) 102.

[60] Section 1 of the Republic of South Africa Constitution Fourth Amendment Act 74 of 1980, which amended s 118 of the constitution. See M Wiechers *Staatsreg* (3 ed, 1981) 267–8.

[61] In terms of s 63 of the Constitution. In fact all parties approved the three readings of the bill. See the Debates of the Joint Sitting of the Senate and the House of Assembly cols 1–43 (21–2 May 1980).

[62] The Republic of South Africa Constitution Third Amendment Act 28 of 1980, which was the first of the 1980 amendments to come into operation. The fact that this amendment was passed before publication of the Schlebusch Report was criticised in the debates (eg House of Assembly Debates vol 8 col 3391 (24 March 1980)).

[63] Sections 33 and 40 of the South Africa Act; this resulted in the following interprovincial distribution of constituencies: Cape Province 58, Natal 12, Orange Free State 14, Transvaal 37. Natal and the OFS were both overrepresented. For a more extensive analysis of this issue see the author's thesis 319–21.

[64] By 1931 the House had increased to the maximum size permitted, namely 150 members. See H J May *The South African Constitution* (3 ed, 1955) 82.

[65] The Electoral Quota Consolidation Act 30 of 1942. The provincial quotas were retained but lost their significance since each approximated a notional national quota. The system was retained in the republican constitution, ss 40, 42 and 43.

[66] The Constitution Amendment Act 83 of 1965; the quota was calculated by dividing the total number of voters in the country by 165 (the increased number of seats in the House). The only deference to the provinces was that constituencies could not straddle provincial boundaries.

[67] That is, Cape Province 55 seats, Natal 20 seats, Orange Free State 14 seats, Transvaal 76 seats—The Constitution and Elections Amendment Act 79 of 1973, s 81 of which substituted a new s 40 in the Constitution. Section 83 provided for the first time that the large-size constituencies could be unloaded to 70 per cent of the quota.

[68] See above, 101n59.

[69] However, it was perceived by political commentators as a product of the internal divisions within the National Party, as it threatened the influence of the conservative faction whose strength lay in the now underrepresented Transvaal.

[70] See I Duchacek *Rights and Liberties in the World Today* (1973) 194.

[71] The Republic of South Africa Constitution Fifth Amendment Act 101 of 1980, which amended s 40 of the Constitution Act. An additional member for Walvis Bay was provided for in Act 99 of 1982 (s 2).

[72] Draft bill s 27(1)*(b)* and *(c)* and Schlebusch Report 7, respectively.

[73] See, e g, House of Assembly Debates vol 16 col 8057 (4 June 1980).

[74] See House of Assembly Debates vol 16 cols 8037–8, 8740 (4 June 1980).

[75] G Hand, J Georgel & C Sasse *European Electoral Systems Handbook* (1979) 58ff.

[76] See above, 125–6.

[77] See below, 165.

[78] The first election of members by the electoral college took place on 22 January 1981 and resulted in the return of seven additional government members and one from the official opposition. Of the former, six were ex-Senators and one a party organiser; the Opposition member was a political researcher and former MP. The four nominated members were all active National Party politicians. After the 1981 general election, the government chose two members with 'special expertise'. See H Rudolph 'Nominated Members of Parliament and the Demise of the Entrenched Sections' (1981) 98 *SALJ* 346 at 348. However, once appointed these members have security of tenure—cf the former s 33(3) of Act 32 of 1961.

[79] South Africa Constitution Amendment Act 40 of 1981 (s 1).

[80] See the example in Rudolph op cit 350.

[81] The West German electoral system allows each voter a second vote for the party of his choice, irrespective of whether there is a party candidate contesting the constituency in which he is entitled to vote. The proportional allocation of seats from party lists thus bears a close arithmetical relationship to the popular support of the parties.

[82] Act 101 of 1980 which inserted a new s 10A in the Constitution Act.

[83] Mr A L Schlebusch.

[84] Section 11 of the Constitution Act.

[85] The new s 10(A)(3) of the Constitution Act.

[86] Section 34 of Act 101 of 1980 inserted Part VIIIA in the Constitution Act (ss 102–106).

[87] That is, the State President acting on the advice of the white cabinet; in terms of the draft bill (s 23(1)) he would have had to consult the three prime ministers.

[88] Section 105(1). This arrangement is reminiscent of the Senate and allows a new government to reconstitute the council.

[89] As with the bill, but unlike the first phase formulations, no quotas for the different groups are stipulated.

[90] Subsequently rescinded by Act 99 of 1982 (s 5).

[91] The first indication that Chinese persons would receive constitutional recognition was in the majority report of the Schlebusch Commission which recommended their inclusion in the President's Council. In 1980 there were 8 000 Chinese in the Republic, most of whom were resident in the Johannesburg–Witwatersrand area. See the *Official Yearbook of the Republic of South Africa* (1980–81) 77. The recognitin was short-lived.

[92] See House of Assembly Debates vol 16 cols 8250–5 (5 June 1980); vol 1 cols 246–7 (28 January 1981).

[93] House of Assembly Debates vol 1 col 30 (26 January 1981).

[94] Some supporters of the council, however, suggested that the exclusion of blacks was a temporary aberration that would be rectified in due course. See the incisive analysis of the leader of the opposition in House of Assembly Debates vol 17 cols 9052–60 (12 June 1980).

[95] Section 104(4)*(b)*. See House of Assembly Debates vol 15 cols 8251–2 (5 June 1980). Shortly after the legislation's enactment the government indicated that the council would not be instituted because of black opposition. See above, 134.

[96] Section 102(7). This proviso was carried over from the draft bill, and its purpose is to prevent boycott tactics from obstructing the operation of the council.

[97] See the Powers and Privileges of the President's Council Act 103 of 1981, which is closely modelled on the Powers and Privileges of Parliament Act 91 of 1963, which in turn shows the influence of the Westminster parliamentary privileges. In the previous year the government had indicated that the council would function very much *unlike* a legislature—see House of Assembly Debates vol 17 col 9126 (12 June 1980).

[98] See ss 2, 3, 11 and 15 of Act 103 of 1981. The contempt provisions could theoretically have limited public debate on its constitutional activities, but they were not invoked.

[99] It consisted of 43 whites, 12 coloureds, four Indians and one Chinese.

[100] Those mentioned in the legislation and a scientific committee.

[101] Verbatim reports of the council's sessions are published in *Hansard* form.

[102] See above, 5.

[103] South Africa Act s 14; RSA Constitution Act s 20(3).

[104] Section 1 of the Republic of South Africa Constitution Amendment Act 70 of 1980, which amended s 20(3) of the Constitution Act.

[105] Sections 2 and 3 of Act 70 of 1980 respectively.

[106] House of Assembly Debates vol 10 col 4562 (22 April 1980), vol 10 col 4713 (23 April 1980).

[107] At the end of 1980 Dr D de Villiers was appointed to the cabinet in terms of the s 20(3) procedure. He lost the Gardens constituency in the April 1981 general election, but remained in the cabinet under the 12-months' provision until he won a by-election later that year.

[108] This qualification was introduced at the committee stage of the bill (see House of Assembly Debates vol 13 col 6425 (14 May 1980)); without it indefinite reappointment for twelve-month periods would have been possible.

[109] From 18 to 20 members: s 11 of Act 101 of 1980.

[110] In 1979 the number of state departments was 'rationalised' from 40 to 22; the number of cabinet committees was reduced from 22 to 6. See 1979 *Survey of Race Relations* 5–6.

[111] Section 3 of Act 101 of 1981, which inserted s 30A in the Constitution. Section 10 of the Interpretation Act 33 of 1957 was appropriately amended.

7 The President's Council in the Constitutional Process

1. INTRODUCTION

The constitutional amendments described in the previous chapter were a prominent milestone in the passage of the government's new constitution. They signified a transition from political hypothesizing to institutional adaptation, and revealed the government's unbroken commitment to its own variant of constitutional reform. They implied clear parameters for the reform process, and had manifest implications for the final shape of the emerging constitution. Despite these factors of ineluctability the government felt impelled even at this stage to introduce a new element into the constitutive process, in part due to the legitimacy problems affecting its reforms. In the ensuing phase of constitutional development the President's Council came to the forefront. The government continued to portray itself as the main originator, executor and monitor of constitutional reform, and it maintained an even tighter control over the political process, but it simultaneously depicted the President's Council as an influential new agent of constitutional development. The apparent conflict between these assertions was unequivocally resolved in practice, as the government's policy always prevailed over discrepant views of the council and the latter had no material impact on those fundamental issues which, from the government's point of view, had been previously determined. The council did, however, make some material contributions on other non-fundamental matters. It was also used by the government in contemplation of two related objectives: to ease the passage of its constitution through a complex alignment of political forces, and to salvage a tenuous legitimacy for its reformist strategies.

During this second phase the government remained committed to the basic principles of the 1977 constitution, despite the difficulties encountered in their implementation. On the incentive of the President's Council the period bore witness to various modifications and adaptations of the original plan, some with constitutional and even political significance, but these fluctuations took place within a framework which had been firmly established during the first phase. The new dispensation would remain restricted to non-blacks and leave intact all the constitutional arrangements for blacks described in this work;[1] all institutional changes would take place within a context of continued political control by the dominant group; and resort would be had to some consociational institutions for incorporating coloureds and Indians into the 'white' political system on a non-majoritarian basis. It remained the official objective to depart from South Africa's 'Westminster model' towards an accommodationist type of political system which was more inclusive than the old, and which both maintained the right

171

to group self-determination and avoided sectional domination. The President's Council made consociational democracy the main legitimating ideology for these proclaimed pursuits.

2. THE PRESIDENT'S COUNCIL'S STATUS AS A CONSTITUTIVE BODY

The formal constitutional status of the President's Council has been described earlier in this work.[2] From the government's point of view the council heralded a new phase in the constitutional process because it provided a permanent and independent constitutional commission of inquiry in succession to the Schlebusch Committee.[3] Through the medium of the council the government for the first time was able to involve individual coloureds and Indians in a collaborative process of constitutional investigation and formulation, and thereby attempt to restore some credibility to a process hitherto lacking in support among those it was primarily aimed at. It was able to point to the participation on the council of several politicians formerly in active opposition to the government, of whom the most conspicuous, in the light of the constitution's genesis, were from the coloured Labour party.[4] The council constituted a 'grand coalition' which, operating on a consensual basis would deliberate on, and assist in implementing, a new constitutional system. In terms of the government's previous policy and principles this new institution, and its proposed role, was a significant innovation, and the high salience officially accorded it implied a potential political threat to various existing institutions. Despite its formal subordinacy it constituted a possible rival to the National Party caucus and congresses in terms of access to and influence over the cabinet, particularly in view of the government's need to improve the council's credibility through being responsive to its recommendations. This would have been not inconsistent with the recent decline in the influence of the caucus and congresses in the movement towards a prime-ministerial and managerial form of government.[5] The possibility existed for a reformist government to exploit the new political space provided by the council against its political adversaries, and even against the recalcitrant forces within its own ranks. This possibility materialised to some extent as far as non-government parties and groupings were concerned and their unity and cohesiveness were unfavourably affected towards the end of the period under discussion. There also appeared to be some dissonance between the council and the National Party caucus and congresses, and the council's contributions to the constitutional debate may have precipitated the break in the party.[6] But the President's Council never threatened to take charge of the constitutional process, nor to displace the government's subsidiary institutions by acquiring an especial influence over the cabinet. Its overall effect on prevailing institutional relationships was relatively slight, despite its high official profile.

The destiny of the President's Council was pre-determined by at least three structural factors. The first was its subordinate constitutional status, in terms of which it was essentially an extension and instrument of the political executive which had created it, determined its composition, and defined its powers and competencies. It had neither the legislative nor administrative means to give effect to its proposals, nor a popular political mandate with which to exert leverage over the government. Its legal and political subordinacy confirmed the government's intention to remain in control of the constitutional process, despite the role it alleged the council to be assuming. Secondly, the actual ethnic, class and cultural interests represented by the council's nominated members entailed that, regardless of the extent of its powers, it was not likely to pose a threat to the dominant group. The government nominated a majority of whites to the council as a whole, as well as to each individual committee, and most of the white nominees, and all the committee chairmen, were in addition government supporters. These factors ensured that the preponderant views on the council would be compatible with, and supportive of, government policy. The absence of blacks on the constitutional committee placed it in some respects in the tradition of the Tomlinson and Schlebusch commissions, and, regardless of other factors, rendered it unlikely that it would transverse the emerging black/non-black axis of constitutional development. More generally the establishment-bias of the council militated against its recommending any fundamental changes to the political economy of the country. Thirdly, the substantive output of the council was affected by its organisation and modus operandi, in particular the system of committees through which it predominantly operated. Generally a committee system relies on well-formulated inputs and draft proposals, which enhances the role and influence of committee chairmen and their staff and advisers. In the council's specific circumstances the system also encouraged a symbiotic relationship with the bureaucracy, in particular with the prime minister's department which had been arranged into distinct branches corresponding functionally with the committees of the council.[7] In the constitutional committee there was an uneven distribution of expertise, those with pro-government inclinations tending to have the greatest specialist training and experience.[8] The committees, and the council as a whole, were subject to directives from the government and the initial instructions set a conservative agenda, inter alia by restricting the constitutional deliberations to whites, coloureds and Indians, and the council deferred to its creator by not deviating from this agenda.[9] Cumulatively these factors indicated from the council's inception that it would not be an independent force for constitutional change.

Although there were no fundamental conflicts between the President's Council and the government there were several points of difference between the two. Several of these, particularly those relating to the executive, were of some significance from a constitutional law point of view. The government was able to prevail on these matters without appearing to be in a self-contradictory position because of the council's nominally independent status, and without apprehending direct political consequences because of its lack of popular support. Nevertheless the government felt impelled to pre-empt the council by giving notice that it would not countenance certain types of constitutional recommendations, such as the incorporation of blacks into the political system, and that recommendations involving 'drastic departures' from prevailing policy would be referred to party congresses.[10] Furthermore it enacted a referendum law in 1982, partly in deference to the white electorate's sovereignty.[11] An early indication of the council's political status was provided by the government's response to its well-publicised recommendation that the District Six and Pageview localities be reproclaimed as coloured and Indian group areas respectively.[12] This proposal would have involved no deviation from official policy but merely a variation in its application, yet it was rejected by the government almost in its entirety. In constitutional matters the council's effectual influence proved to be correspondingly limited.

On the other hand the President's Council served a constructive purpose for the government in providing an ostensibly scientific and objective presentation of its constitution. The reports were presented in an academic and annotated format, and of particular relevance to the state's legitimacy problems were the extensive references to and citations of the literature on pluralism and consociationalism.[13] For the first time the government's constitution was justified within a broad intellectual framework and was less immediately identified with the National Party and its policies. The scientific presentation, however, invited a critique on similar terms, and this exposed the reports as deficient in some respects and disingenuous in others.[14]

3. THE REPORTS OF THE PRESIDENT'S COUNCIL

(a) The first constitutional report

The first constitutional report of the President's Council *(First Report)* was issued in May 1982.[15] It was depicted as primarily a response to the State President's second assignment to the council which read,

'Secondly, the evaluation of the documents and evidence which were submitted to the Commission on the Constitution and which, as has been said, are to be transferred to the Council with a view to advice on the adaptation of constitutional structures in South Africa. Obviously the Council will be able to call for further evidence and documents in this connection.'[16]

The constitutional committee purported to interpret this assignment broadly,[17] but its report did not repudiate or disregard any of the principles underlying the government's 1977 constitution and amounted to a selective endorsement of its institutions. The committee not only defined its position and brief in terms of the historical evolution of the government's constitution, but it inherited as its basic resource material the oral and documentary evidence received by the Schlebusch Commission.[18] The committee was conspicuous in portraying the President's Council as a reform-oriented body, it acknowledged the interrelationship between the social, political and economic aspects of society, and it exhorted the government to issue a reformist declaration of intent in relation to these matters.[19] Much of its report, however, operated at the prescriptive and rhetorical levels and on matters of constitutional substance its proposals implied political continuity and not transformation. There was a discrepancy between the goals which the *First Report* proclaimed and the institutional means it recommended for attaining them.

In the early part of the report the committee disclosed the premises and points of departure which influenced its investigative deliberations.[20] A first category had relatively open-ended implications, without being politically neutral. It included the need for political reform in South Africa, for the attainment of equal rights and opportunities for the country's inhabitants, for the protection of identity and the accommodation of ethnic pluralism, for the elimination of group domination, and for strong yet limited government. A second category, however, was more determinate in its implications, namely that the 'orthodox model of democracy (simple majoritarianism)' would be unviable in South Africa, and that a single political system including blacks could not function democratically in current circumstances.[21] Although these propositions were presented as points of departure they were in fact conclusive of crucial aspects of the constitutional debate. But despite their determinative implications they were adduced with virtually no theoretical or empirical justification. The report's final premise was that a single political system for whites, coloureds and Indians could function successfully as a consociational democracy because of 'the absence of important cultural differences . . . favourable population ratios . . . compatibilities of legitimate interests . . . and convergent political objectives'.[22] Methodologically this again involved a deduction being presented as a presupposition, without substantive justification.

Subsequently in the report the committee referred to the possible democratic solutions to political problems in plural societies, namely assimilation, consociational democracy and partition, and listed six conceivable combinations of these systems for South Africa.[23] Not surprisingly, in view of its earlier 'premises', it favoured 'consociational democracy' for non-blacks and 'multiple partition' for blacks:

> 'The Committee adopted the fourth choice—the continuation of official constitutional policy with regard to Blacks, combined with a consociational system which includes the White, Coloured and Indian communities. In terms of the theoretical basis adopted by the Committee, the two principal responses involved here are *partition* and, obviously, *consociational democracy*.'[24]

In this pronouncement the constitutional committee of the President's Council encapsulated and endorsed the already prevalent trends in South Africa's constitutional politics: it enunciated a more modernised and sophisticated version of the government's policies of parallel development and separate development described above.[25] The 'most serious rival' to this constitutional arrangement would be a combination of partition for blacks in the national states and consociational democracy for blacks outside the national states and non-blacks.[26] The report submitted with reference to Arend Lijphart, however, that several conditions were highly unfavourable for a consociational democracy involving all groups,[27] although it failed to appraise those same factors in respect of the limited form of consociationalism it did advocate.

There was one inadvertent consequence of this part of the *First Report*. The committee's more inclusive re-formulation of the government's constitutional policy refocused attention on the fact that its dichotomous parts are in reality complementary and inter-dependent. The report was forthright in conceding that the success of consociationalism would depend, inter alia, on numerical ratios, and that a comprehensive partition programme would facilitate its emergence.[28] Until this stage in its evolution the government's constitution for whites, coloured and Indians had tended to be viewed in isolation from the constitutional arrangements for blacks and had even diverted attention from the latter's contentious political and economic consequences. The President's Council restored the composite picture in this part of its report. Its juxtaposition of consociationalism and partition highlighted the fact that an evaluation of the government's constitution for non-blacks can only be made in conjunction with its constitutional policy for blacks. However, not only did this fact not impinge on the public consciousness but it was left in abeyance by the constitutional committee itself because it failed to evaluate the homelands system and its many implications. Its endorsement of multiple partition implied an approbation of the economic, social and political consequences of the homelands policy and such integral features as the systematic denationalisation of blacks.[29] Some unease about partition was evident in that the committee limited its endorsement to 'the principle of partition and to the *direction* of official constitutional policy', but the only recommendation it made in this regard was that partition should be ' "fair" and negotiated' and 'accompanied by appropriate measures of consolidation'.[30] It did not augment the justifications traditionally advanced for the homelands system, and even these it assumed without restating. Its general reticence on the inherent features of black separatism allowed this portion of the composite picture it had provided to recede rapidly into the background.

The main institutional recommendations in the *First Report* related to the executive function.[31] The constitutional committee was critical of the 1977 constitution, in its various formulations, for attempting to marry an executive presidency to a parliamentary executive. The report accurately observed that this hybrid arrangement would fail to shift the real locus of power; despite purporting to introduce a non-parliamentary executive it would preserve the cabinet system of government. The committee favoured instead a more classical form of presidential government involving a strict separation of personnel between legislature and executive. It suggested that this would not be so far from the prevailing situation in which power had shifted away from parliament to the cabinet and Prime Minister. It also claimed some support for the system, though without convincing authority, in the fact that presidentialism was 'deeply rooted' in the country's constitutional history.[32] The presidential office would have a seven-year tenure period, and would combine the existing roles of head of government and head of state. The President would nominate a premier, and on the latter's advice ministers and deputy ministers to administer the departments of state. Simultaneous membership of the cabinet and legislature would be incompatible, thereby ensuring the principle of the non-parliamentary executive. Cabinet membership would be open to coloureds and Indians, but unlike earlier versions of the constitution no ratios would be prescribed. The President would be elected by an electoral college, comprising members of the legislature, operating in such a way as to ensure that the executive would be as 'supra-ethnic' as possible;[33] however no details were provided on this system.

These recommendations would provide the institutional basis for the more conventional form of presidentialism favoured by the President's Council.[34] Their objective was to establish a powerful presidency, which the committee regarded as essential for reform and for providing a 'sense of basic security' during the reform process.[35] The President would be empowered, inter alia, to formulate national policy, initiate legislation, dissolve the legislature, and regulate the referendum process. The premier would be concerned with day-to-day administration of the country, the co-ordination of ministers, and the government's relationship with the legislature. The premier and ministers would be responsible to the President alone, and not to the legislature but no attention was given in this report to the question of the President's legal or political accountability.

The executive advocated by the committee was designated as the body which would nurture the consociational democracy into existence. Although the recommendations on the executive had implications for the legislative function, relatively little attention was given to the latter in the *First Report*.[36] The committee was, however, highly critical of earlier versions of the legislative process. It indirectly rejected the 1977 notion of three separate legislative bodies and proposed that a single legislature be internally organised to accommodate the segmental autonomy principle. It recommended that simple majoritarianism be avoided in the legislature when it was exercising its various functions. As an interim measure proposed enactments could be referred routinely to the President's Council,[37] thereby allocating it a quasi-legislative role. The *First Report* contained no further recommendations on the legislature, and none on the administrative or judicial branches. The report concluded with an appeal for a government-initiated declaration of intent which should include an endorsement of the committee's premises and a commitment to a consociational form of government for whites, coloureds and Indians.[38] As far as its limited substantive recommendations were concerned the report proposed several modifications of the 1977 constitution, but not so as to affect its essential principles or the existing power relationships.[39]

The main significance of the first constitutional report of the President's Council was that for the first time in South Africa consociationalism was applied prescriptively by a government-sanctioned authority, albeit only for whites, coloureds and Indians. In the committee's view the institutional arrangements deriving from the government's prevailing policy could be adopted and adapted to constitute a consociational form of government. The committee suggested that if the restricted system operated successfully it could be extended more widely through the political system,[40] but this was regarded as a remote contingency and little attention was given to its implications. The compatibility of the council's views with the requirements of the normative consociational model is assessed below.[41]

Within its scope the main vulnerability of the *First Report* lay in the mutually contradictory nature of its dominant themes. On the one hand it prescribed a consociational form of government, and on the other provided an unfavourable institutional base for it, in the form of a powerful executive presidency. Despite its scholarly pretensions it gave little attention to the optimal constitutional framework for consociationalism,[42] and made only passing reference to such alternatives as a collegial executive.[43] A secondary contradiction inhered in its stated preference for a highly decentralised system of government, but its actual provision for a centralised presidency with increased powers. The committee also indulged in reformist rhetoric at the expense of political realism. For example, while it emphasised the need for the President to be 'supra-ethnic', its institutional arrangements were not designed to prevent sectional domination of the office. Its political optimism amounted to constitutional credulity when it advocated a powerful institution with apparently limited legal and political responsibility, the presidency, on the assumption that it would be indefinitely controlled by benevolent reformists;[44] the history of modern constitutionalism suggests the need for a more circumspect approach to the granting and controlling of political power. One of the main accomplishments of the *First Report* was in fact incidental to its self-defined purposes: it obliquely invited attention to the neglected reality that for any assessment of the government's new constitution it should be viewed not in isolation, but within the totality of the country's constitutional system.

(b) The Bloemfontein guidelines

The government's response to the first constitutional report was contained in the Prime Minister's major policy address to the federal congress of the National Party at Bloemfontein in June 1982.[45] The 'Bloemfontein guidelines' were accepted by the delegates and subsequently endorsed by each of the party's provincial congresses, thus constituting its official updated policy. Predictably they re-affirmed the basic principles of the government's constitutional programme. In so far as the guidelines provided further details on the constitutional arrangements for non-blacks there was some evidence of a departure from the 1977 constitution, due possibly to the motivations of the President's Council. This pertained mainly to the legislative process, where the government for the first time accepted the concept of a single composite legislature in preference to the original triple parliament arrangement; legislation on matters of group concern would require the approval of only the relevant community chamber, while that on matters of common concern would now always require consideration by all three chambers. However this change in attitude by the government was less substantial than it appeared: it could recover control over the legislative process by way of the largely nominated President's Council which, it indicated, would resolve deadlocks between the chambers. The 'Bloemfontein guidelines' also appeared to be influenced by the *First Report* in that they acquiesced in a transfer of executive authority from the white cabinet to a president and mixed council. The guidelines subsumed some of the terminology of consociationalism used in the *First Report*, in particular the segmental autonomy concept; while the term 'power-sharing' had been repudiated in 1977 as appertaining to the liberal opposition, it now had a respectable place in the government's vocabulary.[46] The influence of the President's Council was also apparent in so far as the guidelines affected an indirect commitment to a consociational form of government, as that system was depicted by the council.

In respect of the matter to which the President's Council had devoted most attention, however, the government remained obdurate. In stipulating that ministers might remain in the legislature after their appointment to the cabinet the 'Bloemfontein guidelines' negated the principle of the non-parliamentary executive espoused in the *First Report*. Furthermore, the President's tenure would be co-terminous with that of parliament, subject only to prior removal by the electoral college. These orderings reflected the dominant group's concern to retain a link between the President and the caucus of the majority white party, so that the executive branch would remain within the reach and vicarious control of the latter. It therefore advocated a system which would

'. . . combine those features of the parliamentary executive which tie the fortunes of individual legislators to those of the executive (and so enable the latter to dominate the legislature) and those features of both parliamentary and presidential executives which will give the president the security of tenure of the latter and the capacity of both to whip recalcitrant legislators into line by threatening them with public opprobrium'[47]

The government's authoritative statement on the issue at this stage in the evolution of the constitution implied the quietus of the council's notion of a conventional non-parliamentary executive and strict separation of powers. In respect of this matter the guidelines involved a reversion to the 1977 constitution.

The main innovation in the 'Bloemfontein guidelines' concerned the standing legislative committees, to which the Prime Minister alluded briefly. The government had accepted the principle of a single parliament, but not a unified one, and it proposed that the separately functioning chambers should nominate members to the various committees, which would attempt to promote consensus among them on matters of common concern. The committees were to be of focal importance in all subsequent formulations of the constitution. Beyond this, little institutional detail was provided in the guidelines, although this was now the sixth year in the exegesis of the plan. There was a brief reference to the probable demise of the provincial system, as it had hitherto existed, at the end of the sitting provincial councils' term of office. This again highlighted an enduring ambivalence between the normative and institutional aspects of the government's constitutional position: while formal deference was given to the principle of political decentralisation (on which the guidelines reflected the President's Council's sentiments) the dismantling of the provincial system implied a practical centralisation of power. Despite their discontinuities and insufficiencies, however, the 'Bloemfontein guidelines' contained the clearest official formulation to date of the new constitution.

(c) The second constitutional report

Although its chairmanship had changed in the interim[48] there was a basic continuity in the second report of the constitutional committee of the President's Council *(Second Report)*, released in November 1982.[49] This report was portrayed as a sequel to the first, and it reaffirmed the premises and guidelines enunciated in the former.[50] But there was simultaneously an ostentatious deference to the government's constitutional policies: not only were many references made to the 'Bloemfontein guidelines' in the body of the report, but they were included in their entirety as the main annexure.[51] The influence of the guidelines was, in parts, conspicuous. For example, from its comparative survey the committee concluded that the evidence supported either a single parliament, which could divide into segmental units when necessary, or a tripartite parliament with separate self-contained chambers; without demur, however, it accepted and elaborated on the latter alternative which had been enjoined by the Prime Minister.[52] Nevertheless the *Second Report* did contain direct and indirect criticisms of the 'Bloemfontein guidelines'. The most significant of these related to the executive function, where the committee again commented adversely on the hybrid system which the government had just reaffirmed and belatedly repleaded the cause of the non-parliamentary executive it had advocated in its earlier report.[53] The committee cautioned against the inclusion of nominated and indirectly elected members in the legislature,[54] and against a direct role for the non-elected President's Council in the law-making process,[55] aspects which had also been confirmed by the Prime Minister. It emphasised the desirability of popular and legal controls over the President, and a government-sponsored declaration of intent,[56] both of which had been ignored in the 'Bloemfontein guidelines'. These criticisms, however, had no material effect on the constitution's final shape, a reflection of the contingent status of the council's recommendations and its ultimate impotence in the constitutional process.

The *Second Report* made two main contributions to the development of the emerging constitution. The first related to the division of functions, upon which the whole system depended.[57] For the first time there was an official attempt to specify those matters which would fall within the jurisdiction of the ethnically-exclusive institutions and to distinguish them from those pertaining to the common institutions. The committee's lists confirmed what several commentators had long contended, namely that there can be very few matters of exclusive concern to whites, coloureds or Indians, absent separate territorial jurisdictions for each group.[58] Most matters of consequence, including all aspects of public finance, were included in the common list, and it was recommended that residual non-listed matters should also be regarded as common. There was provision for additional functions to be exercised by the segmental institutions through a system of executive delegation, but it was an arrangement which could have little practical significance. Yet in contradiction of the reality it had been forced to recognise and accommodate the committee continued to premise the legislative function on the principle of segmental autonomy. There was a further, though more subtle, inconsistency in respect of education, one of the most important items on the list of segmental matters. Although the constitutional committee made approving references to the HSRC investigation into education,[59] it did not provide for the single ministry of education recommended in that report.

The other contribution also related to the legislative function, in respect of which the constitutional committee conceded that its 'basic philosophy' was the same as the government's.[60] The *Second Report* provided for the first time in the constitution's history some information on how the tricameral legislature could function in its law-making and budgetary functions.[61] The basic premise of the system would be the equality of the three chambers' powers and responsibilities, all enactments being regarded as an exercise of original legislative jurisdiction.[62] Each chamber would deal conclusively with the legislation and affairs of the relevant segmental group, in the same way as the existing parliament. In respect of common concern matters the committee system proposed by the Prime Minister was elaborated on in the report. All committees, of which there would be five distinct types,[63] would represent the chambers in the ratio 4:2:1. In respect of proposed legislation, permanent standing committees would deliberate on a bill before its second reading, in camera, and during its committee stage, in public. This entailed that apart from the cabinet, which would predominate at the initiation stage, the committees would play the primary role in respect of the principles and detail of a statutory enactment. The chambers would play a secondary role in debating, and ratifying or rejecting, at different stages of the legislative process the measure agreed upon by the relevant committee. The committee system would also be used in the budgeting process.[64] A permanent budget committee would be consulted by the treasury on a limited basis during the preparatory stages of the budget, and would debate the proposals in camera after their introduction in parliament. Each individual vote would be discussed and approved in the appropriate standing committee, referred to above. Parliament would have only a limited consultative function in this process: the budget would be initially tabled at a joint sitting for information purposes only, and there would be various debates on individual votes and the total package. But if parliament failed to approve the budget, or even rejected it in its entirety, it would still become effective after the lapse of a prescribed time-period, provided it had received presidential assent. In dispensing with the requirement of legislative ratification in financial matters the committee was introducing a major deviation in both principle and practice as far as the Westminster and South African constitutional systems are concerned, although the contemporary significance thereof was not as great as it had once been. For the President's Council considerations of practicality and administrative efficiency were paramount, and the budgetary process would be merely a 'technical exercise in financial management'.[65] In this sphere the council contributed significantly to the developing ethos of a managerial style of government.[66]

Unlike the 1979 draft bill, which permitted up to two chambers to be completely bypassed in the legislative process, the committee system advocated in the *Second Report* purported to allow the participation of all three chambers on an equal and regular basis. The actual mechanics of the system, however, did not sustain this supposition. In the first place the report implied that only majority parties would be represented on the committees,[67] although it insisted that each chamber should decide this issue for itself. Secondly, the pre-eminent chairmen of the committees would be appointed by the Speaker,[68] who would in turn be the appointee of the electoral college. Thirdly, if consensus could not be reached the committees would operate on a simple majority basis,[69] notwithstanding the consociational assumptions of the system. These features would ensure the majority group in the white chamber institutional dominance throughout the committee system and detract from the role and status of the coloured and Indian chambers. Finally, even the chambers' residual right to reject legislation could be circumvented if a bill received the approval of at least two chambers, or failing this, was ratified by the President's Council.[70] Only constitutional amendments would be exempted from the truncated procedures, the unentrenched provisions requiring a simple majority in each chamber, and the entrenched provisions a two-thirds majority in each;[71] this could not disadvantage the majority white group, however, as it rendered crucial features of the constitution immune from amendment without its consent.

The implications of the committee system had to be seen in conjunction with those of the executive presidency, to which the *Second Report* added a new dimension.[72] The purview of presidential powers was greater than that contained in earlier formulations of the constitution. Besides the powers previously enunciated it was recommended that the President should also have the reserve power to decide whether matters should be regarded for legislative purposes as common or group-specific, the first time this controversial feature manifested itself. More momentous was the recommendation that the executive President be empowered to suspend the constitutional order when the office-holder deemed appropriate circumstances to exist.[73] This innovation was ostensibly modelled on a provision in the constitution of the fifth French republic[74], but it ironically revived a practice frequently resorted to during the formative stages of the Westminster system.[75] No attention was given to possible legal limitations on this extraordinary competence, and only passing attention to legal and political controls on other presidential powers. Despite its apparent obeisance to the norms of constitutionalism the committee would countenance only a remote form of executive responsibility: the President would be removable on grounds of incapacity or misconduct by a body constituted in the same way as the electoral college,[76] an arrangement which the committee had itself deprecated in its earlier report.[77] It now gave support to a system in which the President would have no popular mandate and would be effectively responsible to only one section of the composite legislature. The constitutional committee also forfeited the chance of introducing some form of checks and balances through the third branch of government. In a section of its report[78] most remarkable for its inferior scholarship and lack of objectivity[79] it rejected the principle of a judicially enforceable bill of rights for the new constitutional system. It justified this stance, in part, in terms of the doctrine of parliamentary sovereignty,[80] which is paradoxically one of the main principles of the Westminster system[81] which was allegedly in the process of being discarded. On the pretexts that 'the use or otherwise of a declaration of human rights has not really become an issue . . .' in South Africa, and that at present 'human rights are to a large extent protected by the substantive law and the law of procedure . . .'[82] it settled for the recitation of certain principles in the constitution's preamble[83] and the entrenchment of a few of its provisions.[84] On this aspect the *Second Report* denoted new powers for the political executive but fewer legal and political controls over their exercise than under the prevailing system.

The government's constitution has always entailed a broadening of the representative base of the political system without undermining the dominant group's institutional position. The 1977 constitution would have perpetuated this dominance through the existing institutions of government, despite the new set of authorities it superimposed on them. The *Second Report*, on the other hand, revealed how the transfer of power to a new set of institutions, in particular the presidency and parliamentary committees, was also compatible with that continued dominance. Its proposals ensured that whenever there were conflicts in the political process the whites would have the institutional means to prevail over others, notwithstanding the premises of the system.[85] The corollary of this factor was that coloureds and Indians would have no institutional means of interrupting or arresting the governing process. In these respects the report provided an accurate preview of the 1983 constitution.

(d) Other reports

Contemporaneously with its first constitutional report the President's Council issued two other reports. The more relevant for constitutional development was the joint report of the committee for economic affairs and the constitutional committee on local and regional management systems in the Republic.[86] It was essentially complementary to the *First Report*, the premises and guidelines of which it adopted. After providing a survey of the prevailing system of local and regional government, as well as the findings of earlier investigations on the subject, it made several recommendations which involved modest adaptations of the local government status quo. The general emphasis was on retaining and extending the system of separate and nominally autonomous local authorites for whites, coloureds and Indians. Where the size of a particular group did not warrant a separate authority its members could be represented on an appropriate (white) authority through various institutional arrangements, such as separate wards or separate voters' rolls. 'Soft' functions would be directly exercised by the elected councils within their local jurisdictions, and 'hard' functions[87] on a metropolitan basis by nominated over-arching authorities operating along consociational lines.[88] At the regional level there would be eight administrative units, but the committee could not agree on the context in which they would operate.[89] One alternative would involve the phasing out of elective provincial councils in favour of regional authorities exercising devolved administrative powers; they would be headed by government-appointed administrators and executive committees under the aegis of a Department of Local Government in Pretoria. The other alternative would involve the retention of elected regional councils and executive committees, incorporating coloureds and Indians, with a centrally-appointed administrator; the councils would have devolved executive powers, but no legislative competence. Either system, in the joint committee's view, would require a reorganisation of the financing of sub-national authorities, with particular reference to the provision of alternative and new sources of independent income.

In important respects these proposals reproduced the government's national constitution at the local level. In particular they were restricted predominantly to non-blacks, they assumed separate voters' rolls and separate residential areas for whites, coloureds and Indians, and they envisaged joint action being taken on a quasi-consociational basis. They had the same propensity for widening the representative base of the local authority system,[90] without threatening the major repositories of political power at this level. They even embodied the same internal contradiction as the national plan, in that they were formally committed to a maximum devolution of power but their institutional arrangements implied new modes of control for the central government. The official response to the proposals was predictably approving, save for some aspects which were implicitly rejected.[91] It seemed at one stage that the government, with the legitimising support of this report, would implement its constitution from the local level upwards, and it committed itself to certain interim changes.[92] However this part of the constitutional picture receded into the background when the institutionalisation of the more salient national aspects got under way in 1983.

The other report was also a joint venture and was drafted by the planning committee and committee for community relations.[93] It dealt with the principles and implementation of the Group Areas Act, and its most important recommendation was that the legislation should be retained pro tem. The report did suggest various procedural changes in the application of the act, and it favoured the representation of 'the various population groups' on the Group Areas Board. But in advocating the consolidation of this legislation with other similar laws it confirmed that its underlying principles are indispensable to the government's constitutional policies.

In early 1983 the science committee of the President's Council issued its first report dealing with demographic trends in the republic and related matters.[94] Its recommendations had no immediate impact on the constitutional process.

4. THE PRESIDENT'S COUNCIL AND CONSOCIATIONALISM

It has been shown in this chapter that the President's Council was the first body consistently to use the notion of consociational democracy and its related concepts to justify the government's constitutional proposals. This aspect of its report was directed at the image of the constitution and it encouraged the government itself to adopt terms such as 'power-sharing' and 'segmental autonomy' in promoting it, although it did so more discreetly and selectively than the council.[95] It is necessary to refer to the extent to which the council's substantive formulation of the constitution was compatible with its justificatory theory.

The constitution of the President's Council incorporated many of the structural features of consociationalism embodied in the 1977 model:[96] the President's Council, a multi-racial cabinet, proportionality in the composition of several bodies, and separate segmental institutions. It was also able to include additional consociational features via its innovative institutions: the parliamentary committees, co-ordinating metropolitan authorities, and decentralised political structures. The committee predicted, with reference to the principles of consociationalism, that the 'supra-ethnic' executive would resolve conflicts through compromise, that the President's Council would be a forum for 'purposive depoliticisation', and that the separate legislative chambers and sub-national authorities would generate autonomous rule-making for the segments. The report, furthermore, proclaimed a strong sense of constitutionalism, which the consociational model assumes. But the three major consociational shortcomings of its predecessors also applied to this formulation of the constitution:[97] black South Africans remained excluded, there was no provision for free political association, and there was no effective veto power for coloureds and Indians. Further shortcomings can be identified by reference to matters of institutional detail. An executive presidency would not be a favourable setting for consociationalism, a factor alluded to above,[98] and would be particularly inappropriate when the office was highly centralised and very powerful, as recommended by the council. Plural voting in the electoral college would constitute a manifestly counter-consociational institution. The exclusion of significant minority parties from the common forums, such as the electoral college, presidential executive and parliamentary committees, would run counter to the grand coalition principle of consociationalism. The structure of the parliamentary committees, their operational procedures, and the dominating position of their chairmen, would not be institutionally conducive to compromise and consensus. Proportionality would be applied too selectively, on the one hand, and too rigidly, on the other, and would be completely neglected as a basis of making public appointments and allocating resources. There would be little practical scope for autonomous rule-making and rule-application, as required by the segmental autonomy principle. At the intrasegmental level the majoritarian principle would be the norm: the *Second Report* implicitly endorsed the existing plurality electoral system although it is inimical to consociationalism and, ironically, one of the most important ancillary features of the Westminster system.[99] Finally, the deference to constitutionalism in the report was not reflected in its institutional arrangements. In these respects the council's model was not compatible with its justificatory theory, and Arend Lijphart reportedly described its form of consociationalism as a travesty of his conception of the system.[100]

As consociationalism does not provide an analytical constitutional model the exposition above might be criticised for over-emphasising institutional factors at the expense of behavioural considerations. It has been shown that consociationalism is ultimately a pattern of elite behaviour emanating from prudent and co-operative leaders, that it cannot be reduced to institutional factors alone, and that it is compatible with a variety of constitutional frameworks.[101] The necessary elite behaviour cannot be effectuated by legal rules and is often the product of political convention and social custom.

The response to such a critique is that convention and custom presuppose either a history of accommodationist practices or a self-conscious pact among competing elites at a particular juncture in a country's history. The former alternative is self-evidently absent in South Africa. It might be argued that the new constitution itself is evidence of the latter, but this would be to disregard at least three critical factors: the constitution has been unilaterally formulated with only a limited use of compliant elites in the later stages of the process, even by participating elites there is no commitment to the maintenance of the system, and the evidence is that among the populace generally the constitution has been more divisive than unifying in its effect.[102] In a context such as this institutional factors become a more important condition for consociationalism, although they could not alone sustain the system. The main institutional flaw in the council's version of the constitution is that it would allow the group which wins the elections for the white chamber to dominate the whole political system through its control of that body, and, consequently, the electoral college, the presidency and executive, the President's Council and the parliamentary committees. As with the Westminster system there would be a single decisive site of political competition, the antithesis of consociationalism. In terms of a legal-institutional analysis of its recommendations the President's Council did not significantly advance the cause of consociational politics.

As far as its democratic aspect is concerned the council's version of the constitution was consistent with its predecessors in that it extended political rights to previously non-franchised coloureds and Indians. While the political system would become more inclusive, however, it would continue to withhold political rights from the majority of the country's subjects, so that from the black perspective it would remain fundamentally undemocratic. But even among non-blacks it would be imperfectly democratic in that the institutional arrangements would entail vast discrepancies in the ultimate weight of the white, coloured and Indian groups' political rights, and there would be no attempt to uphold the 'one vote one value' principle.[103] There would also be extensive restrictions within the system as far as political contestation was concerned.[104] It would assume a minimal alternation in office, the coloured and Indian 'opposition' would be in a structurally weak position, and electoral outcomes would be crucial only for whites.[105] Moreover the political options for coloureds and Indians in particular would be restricted by the constitution's rigidity and division of functions, which together would serve to retain and secure what was beginning to be regarded as the 'bottom line' for whites—separate political institutions, separate residential areas, and separate educational systems. Separatism in these areas implied the retention of a range of discriminatory statutes relating to race classification, group areas, amenities and institutions, and political association, as essential prerequisites for the constitution to succeed on its own terms. Finally the system would also tend to make government more remote from the citizenry by removing it from public forums and making its functionaries less accountable. While democratic shortcomings are a corollary of the consociational method of government they could not be justified on that basis in the system under discussion because of its severe consociational limitations.

5. CONCLUSION

Within the protracted and complex process through which the government's constitution emerged between 1977 and 1983 it is not possible to determine precisely the role and impact of the President's Council. The most important factors affecting it were the institutional conditions of its existence, referred to above, and these predetermined the parameters of its activities: its investigations and recommendations were all reconcilable with the basic principles of the government's constitution. Within these parameters the council was neither servilely submissive nor independently assertive. Some of its recommendations were accepted by the government and made a material contribution to the development of its constitution on matters such as the division of competence, the legislative committee system, and local government arrangements. Others were perceived to have adverse implications for the dominant group and the government was able, in riposte, to reject or ignore them; this pertained particularly to legislature–executive relationships where the government proved more responsive to the sentiments of its caucus and constituency than the submissions of the council. The council thus had a real, though limited role, in the development and revelation of the new constitution. From a constitutional law point of view it contributed to a more comprehensive and refined version of the constitution in 1982 than in 1977, although it had given no attention to the bureaucracy and little to the judiciary.

The main functional role of the President's Council was probably to ease the passage of the constitution for the government. It did so by providing new political space in the form of a nominally independent body set apart from the other institutions and parties involved in the constitutional process. The government could have different parts of the constitution evaluated by the council, and pursuantly debated in public, without appearing closely associated with, or committing itself publicly on, those aspects. Although the council was effectively under the government's control it was able to relieve the latter of some of the pressure being exerted from different directions, by assuming the roles of constitutional commission and draftsman.

Ultimately the council's role was more ideological than functional. It was able to provide authority for the disposition to reject the Westminster and other majoritarian-based systems, although the 1983 constitution had a new-found Westminster bias. By invoking the literature on comparative government, political theory and political sociology, it was able to present in a scientific context a modernised version of the government's constitutional polices as the appropriate vehicle for political and social reform. Although the system was essentially an outgrowth from the constitutional past and its basic features had been predetermined by the dominant group, the President's Council created the impression that it was developing out of a dialectical process, which rendered it less immediately identifiable with the National Party and its policies. Its strategic use of the council highlighted the government's concern about the legitimacy problems which had beset the earlier constitutional process. Whatever the causative relationships might have been the constitution had gained wider acceptance by 1983 after it had been processed through the council than it had enjoyed in 1977, particularly among those who were important for its implementation—individual coloured and Indian leaders, members of white opposition groups, and business managers—although its wider legitimacy problems persisted. While the constitutive role of the President's Council was of brief duration, and its ultimate impact was small, it was not without short-term political significance.

NOTES AND REFERENCES

[1] See above, 86 to 94.

[2] See above, 163 to 165.

[3] On which see above, 133 to 134.

[4] eg Mr S Leon, former chairman of the Labour Party, and Mr L du Preez, chairman of the Du Preez Commission (above, 112–14). Also on the council were erstwhile NRP and PFP politicians.

[5] See above, 165–66.

[6] While there were more deep-seated reasons for the split, the immediate issue over which 18 members left the National Party to form the Conservative Party in March 1982 was that of 'power-sharing', which the President's Council had made a prominent feature of the constitutional debate. The 1977 constitution was said to have avoided any power-sharing, while the 1980 versions involved 'healthy power-sharing'; the CP rejected both varieties.

[7] In 1982 a separate Department of Constitutional Development and Planning was also established.

[8] On the backgrounds and qualifications of the members see PC 3/1982 (cf n 15, below) 11–12. Commentators attributed much of the first constitutional report to the committee's chairman, Dr D Worrall, a political scientist and lawyer and former National Party MP.

[9] As the committee stated, 'Regarding the scope of the recommendations, it is clear from the text of the State President's address that the President's Council, by reason of its composition, is expected in the main to concentrate on matters affecting the White, Coloured, Indian and Chinese communities.' PC 3/1982 (cf n 15, below) 15.

[10] See above, 163.

[11] Referendums Act No 97 of 1982. The Act empowered the State President to conduct separate referenda among whites, coloureds, Indians and/or Chinese on a flexible basis. As the system would be plebiscitory in nature the title of the Act was something of a misnomer.

[12] In an interim report dated 16 September 1981.

[13] eg the works of Crawford Young and Nathan Glazer, and Arend Lijphart and Eric Nordlinger respectively.

[14] See W H B Dean 'The government's constitutional proposals 1982' and L J Boulle 'The likely direction of constitutional change in South Africa over the next five years' in W H B Dean & D Smit (eds) *Constitutional Change in South Africa—The Next Five Years* (1983) 90 and 57 respectively.

[15] *First Report of the Constitutional Committee of the President's Council*, PC 3/1982 (hereafter referred to as the *First Report*).

[16] *First Report* 1.

[17] At 14–15.

[18] At 1–4, passim.

[19] See at 8, 23 and 88 of the report, respectively.

[20] Chapter 3, 13–26.

[21] At 19.

[22] At 20.

[23] At 31–40.

[24] At 40.

[25] At 73–108 above.

[26] At 38.

[27] At 39.

[28] At 46.

[29] On the significance of the denationalisation of blacks in the constitutional politics of South Africa see above, 92–4 and references cited there. See also Boulle op cit 71–4.

[30] *First Report* 41 and 44. The finding of both the Lombard and Buthelezi commissions was that no viable form of partition would be possible in the Natal/KwaZulu region (see above, 136–9).

[31] Chapter 6, 50–61.

[32] At 58–9. Reference was made to the pre-Union constitutional systems of the Orange Free State and South African Republic, but the latter is a particularly inauspicious precedent for presidential government. In reality parliamentarism has deeper roots in South Africa. See L M Thompson *The Unification of South Africa* (1960) 194–7; C J R Dugard *Human Rights and the South African Legal Order* (1978) 14–36; and above 76–7.

[33] *First Report* 59.

[34] However, the President and ministers would be able to participate in the legislature, without voting (61).

[35] At 58. For the committee this necessitated that, '. . . it [the political executive] would have to be seen as not posing a threat to the vital interests of the present dominant group' (59).

[36] See chapter 7, 62–75.

[37] In terms of s 106(1) of the RSA Constitution Act 32 of 1961; cf above, 164.

[38] At 88.

[39] The committee frankly conceded (48) that '. . . the proposed changes to the executive . . . will not in the least disturb existing power relationships'.

[40] At 40.

[41] At 184–6.

[42] See above, 59–61.

[43] In an ambiguous passage the committee referred to Lijphart's negative views on the suitability of a presidential system for consociationalism, but failed to investigate his preference for collegial power-sharing (56–7).

[44] e g, '. . . true to the *leitmotiv* of the state the president should govern in the general interest and not in pursuit of sectional interests' (59); and '. . . [the president] would be in a good position to implement a coherent programme of reform . . .' (58).

[45] Held on 30–31 July 1982. The declaration is hereafter referred to as the 'Bloemfontein guidelines'.

[46] Pre-election propaganda of the National Party that year had dismissed 'power-sharing' as a 'Prog-Fed term'.

[47] Dean op cit 106.

[48] Dr Worrall resigned on his appointment as Australian ambassador and was replaced by Dr S W van der Merwe, former chairman of the Economic Affairs Committee of the council. By the end of 1982 six of the committee's original members had resigned.

[49] *Second Report of the Constitutional Committee of the President's Council on the Adaptation of Constitutional Structures in South Africa*, PC 4/1982 (hereafter referred to as the *Second Report*).

[50] *Second Report* 11.

[51] At 99–116.

[52] At 14.

[53] At 51–3.

[54] At 15–17.

[55] At 64.

[56] At 54–7 and 93–4 respectively.

[57] Chapter 3, 18–39.

[58] The committee's list of exclusive matters comprised cultural life, education (non-tertiary), community planning and development, community residential life, social welfare, the composition of select committees, and matters specifically assigned to a chamber (35). Cf the former CPRC's wider competence—at 83 above.

[59] The De Lange report; see above, 140.

[60] At 10.

[61] Chapter 4, 40–50.

[62] That is like laws of the existing parliament, the provincial councils and the legislatures of the national states, and unlike the subordinate legislation of executive and other legislative bodies. The juridical significance of the distinction is that original legislation cannot be set aside on the ground of unreasonableness, vagueness or uncertainty, and special rules apply to the promulgation, amendment and repeal of subordinate legislation. See ss 10, 16 and 17 of the Interpretation Act 33 of 1957.

[63] That is permanent committees for administrative matters, permanent committees for public accounts, posts and railways, ad hoc committees for privilege matters, permanent legislative committees, and a permanent budget committee (40–1).

[64] See the *Second Report* 43–7.

[65] Dean op cit 96. In the council's words, '. . . a committee-based Parliament is essentially a technical institution in which specialisation and expertise will play a major role' (at 44).

[66] See above, 165–6.

[67] eg at 46, § 4.29. Agitation by the parliamentary opposition on this issue led to an extensive public debate during 1982, and resulted in government assurances that minority parties would be allowed on the committees.

[68] In consultation with the leaders of the three chambers (42).

[69] At 42.

[70] At 67.

[71] At 76–7.

[72] Chapter 6, 54–9.

[73] At 55.

[74] Art 16. The 'De Gaulle option' had frequently been alluded to during the earlier life of the constitution. See above, 167n12.

[75] For example Charles I suspended the constitutional order by ruling without parliament between 1629 and 1640. In relation to the Tudor period Wiechers has commented, 'It is the stated objective of the government's proposals to move away from the Westminster system of government. The truth of the matter is, however, that they represent, especially as regards the proposals concerning the President's powers and functions, a regression to those times in the development of the Westminster system where there was no real parliamentary regime and the king could on his own, without a prime minister, make laws and run the country with his often notorious band of councillors in his *concilium* and *curia regis* and infamous star chamber.' 'The government's constitutional proposals', address to the Natal congress of the Progressive Federal Party, Durban, 16 October 1982.

[76] At 56. This aspect was included in the 1983 constitution. See below, 204.

[77] *First Report* 51, n 7.

[78] Chapter 9, 70–7.

[79] Cf Dean op cit 101; Boulle op cit 79–80.

[80] At 71 and 73.

[81] See above, 7.

[82] At 71 and 76 respectively. As authority for the latter proposition it cited VerLoren van Themaat *Staatsreg* (2 ed, 1967) 128; in the third edition published before the council's report in 1981. Marinus Wiechers describes the South African human rights situation as pitiful ('bedroewend') at 178. No reference was made to the numerous other writings in this field (see above, 108n258), nor to the Cape Town Human Rights Conference (C Forsyth & J Schiller *Human Rights: The Cape Town Conference* (1979)).

[83] eg freedom of religion. The report had earlier stated (76): 'On the face of things, a guarantee with regard to freedom of religion looks innocuous, but this cannot be absolutised either: noisy religious services in a residential area could be a disturbance; pseudo-religions might seek undesirable protection; subversive politics might be carried out in the name of religion.'

[84] Besides the language clause, provisions relating to the sizes of the chambers, electoral college and President's Council, the independence of the judiciary, and certain parliamentary procedures (77).

[85] In the committee's own words, '. . . this system cannot be seen as a threat to the cardinal interests of the currently dominant group whose leaders will have to carry all the constitutional changes into effect' (54).

[86] *Joint Report of the Committee for Economic Affairs and the Constitutional Committee of the President's Council on Local and Regional Management Systems in the Republic of South Africa*, PC 1/1982.

[87] The basis of the soft/hard distinction was whether the function involved small-scale services (parks, recreational facilities, internal reticulation) or large-scale services (water, electricity, professional services) respectively (52 and 84).

[88] Blacks might also be included in this level through their separate local authorities.

[89] Chapter 8, 64–82.

[90] The arrangements implied a principle of 'universal franchise' for non-blacks at the local level, but additional forms of plural voting for owners of fixed rateable property or corporate persons were envisaged. See 107–8.

[91] eg the interim participation of local affairs or management committee chairmen with voting rights on white local authorities. See 1982 *Annual Survey of Race Relations* 28.

[92] Cf M R Sinclair 'The proposals of the constitutional committee of the President's Council' 1982 *International Affairs Bulletin* 26 at 33.

[93] *Report of the Joint Committee Consisting of the Planning Committee and the Committee for Community Relations of the President's Council on the Principles and Implementation of the Group Areas Act, 1966 (Act 36 of 1966), and aspects of the Act which Affect Community Relations*, PC 2/1982.

[94] *Report of the Science Committee of the President's Council on Demographic Trends in South Africa*, PC 1/1982.

[95] Before the formation of the Conservative Party the government tended to emphasise the 'power-sharing' aspects of the constitution in response to its liberal critics, but after the rift it tended to emphasise the 'segmental autonomy' aspects in an attempt to appease traditional government supporters.

[96] See above, 156.

[97] See above, 156 to 157.

[98] At 177. See also 59, above.

[99] See above, 6.

[100] Sinclair op cit 30.

[101] See above, 45–6.

[102] Evidence of its divisive effect on Afrikanerdom is provided by the split in the National Party and the five by-elections in 1982/3 in which the party was outpolled by the combined parties on its right; the constitution also caused discernible strain in both the Progressive Federal and New Republic Parties. During 1983 it polarised the coloured and Indian communities on the issue of whether to boycott or participate in the system.

[103] One of the implied meanings of the universal franchise concept is that each vote should carry approximately the same weight as it filters through the political system. Cf. I Duchacek *Rights and Liberties in the World Today* (1973) 194–7.

[104] This is to use Dahl's defining characteristics of democracy without necessarily adopting his definition. R Dahl *Polyarchy: Participation and Opposition* (1972).

[105] See above, 62.

8 The Constitution of 1983

1. INTRODUCTION

The government made a significant breakthrough in the promotion of its constitution in early 1983 when at a special congress of the coloured Labour Party held in Natal the delegates elected to participate in the system once it had been implemented. The decision was not unanimous and it occasioned several resignations from the party, and even those endorsing participation did not sanction the basic principles of the system. However, despite the inconsistency between these principles and those of the party's own constitutional policy[1]* the leadership set no preconditions for participation. The development was significant because it enhanced the initial prospects of the system's functional viability in respect of the coloured group for whom it was primarily designed. It was also symbolically significant in that several of the coloured leaders who had frustrated the Coloured Persons Representative Council and resisted the President's Council now associated with the government's constitution in its 1983 formulation.[2] This unfamiliar sponsorship engendered additional credibility for the proposals, and the government acted promptly before this support, as well as that in other quarters, should wane. Within nine months the constitution had been adduced in statutory form, processed by a select committee, debated and ratified by the House of Assembly, assented to by the head of state, and endorsed by the white electorate in a referendum. The alacrity of these developments belied the constitution's prior phlegmatic progress.

During the final phase the constitutional process was confined predominantly to the white parliamentary institutions. Whereas the President's Council had been prominent in the previous phase it was now completely bypassed, despite the fact that the Constitution Act surpasses the 'Bloemfontein guidelines' in deviating from its constitutional recommendations. Notwithstanding the council's continued existence the government subsequently claimed to have privately consulted individual coloured and Indian leaders outside its ranks during 1982 and 1983.[3] From the evidence of the final product this consultation appears to have been directed more towards securing a participation commitment than towards modifying the system—the 1983 constitution bears the unequivocal character of the National Party government's policy. Even the justificatory theory provided by the President's Council, which had facilitated the progress of the constitution during its previous phase, came to be discarded during this period.

This chapter comprises an outline of the enactment process of the 1983 constitution and a thematic commentary on its content and main implications, within the scope of the work, but it provides neither a systematic juridical analysis of the Constitution Act, nor a detailed prognosis of its likely political consequences.

192

* The Notes and References to this chapter commence on page 211.

2. THE ENACTMENT PROCESS

The final stage in the emergence of the government's constitution commenced with the introduction of the Republic of South Africa Constitution Bill in the House of Assembly in May 1983.[4] As a statutory instrument the bill bore the appearance of the 1961 constitution, from the style of the preamble to the form of the amending clause. An accompanying White Paper expressly emphasised the theme of constitutional continuity of which the bill was an important expression.[5] This draft, however, was more comprehensive and refined than its 1979 predecessor, a function of the intervening constitutional and administrative processes, although it still regulated only some of the institutions affecting part of the governed. After a nominative debate the first reading was held, with the main opposition parties resisting the bill's passage.

The second reading debate commenced a week and a half later and extended over three days.[6] The responsible minister represented the bill as an embodiment of the Prime Minister's guidelines, and depicted its institutional arrangements as another part of the 'evolutionary constitutional process'.[7] Constitutional change was again premised on the necessity in a plural society to discard the winner-takes-all political process of the Westminster model, the Theron and Schlebusch commissions and President's Council being invoked as authority for the introduction of 'drastic' changes to that system. In its stead there would emerge a political process incorporating 'consultation, negotiation, consensus and co-operation'. But despite these factors of rhetorical consistency there was a discernible change in the government's theoretical orientation. On the one hand the Westminster system was less consistently denounced than in the previous phases, and it was conceded that certain facets of the system would have to be retained.[8] On the other hand the concept of power-sharing was treated more circumspectly, and by some spokesmen even repudiated, and the ancillary terminology of consociationalism was partly avoided.[9] The minister affirmed instead the principles of 'self-determination' in respect of community interests and 'joint responsibility' in respect of mutual interests. The bill would effect political reform by broadening participation in the general democratic process and extending the system of individual self-government. This adjustment involved a partial resurrection of terminology used in relation to the 1977 constitution, and was reinforced in subsequent parliamentary debates. In some areas it also portended substantive changes from the preceding versions of the constitution. The government was, however, consistent in justifying black exclusion in terms of the different and separate existing and proposed constitutional structures for the various 'black nations'; matters of further black political development would be urgently considered by a cabinet committee which had been appointed in February 1983.[10] The bill was opposed in principle by the Progressive Federal Party because of its unilateral formulation and for five matters of substance: permanent black exclusion would be a precondition of the system's operation, the President would be institutionally pre-eminent, the majority white party would have a position of entrenched dominance, discriminatory laws would be a condition of its functioning, and opposition parties would have a vague and ambiguous role.[11] The Conservative Party opposed the bill because of its negative implications for the self-determination principle, and in particular because it would deprive whites of political sovereignty.[12] With the support of the New Republic Party[13] the House approved the principles of the legislation in the second reading.

The bill was thereafter referred to the Select Committee on the Constitution, but unlike its 1979 antecedent was withheld from the President's Council. In its report the committee recommended extensive amendments to the details of the bill and the opposition parties also tabled numerous amendments for consideration during the legislative committee stage.[14] Before its commencement the Assembly debated two motions proposed by the official opposition enjoining it to instruct the House in committee to extend the scope of the bill. The first instruction pertained to a Bill of Rights securing enumerated human rights and freedoms,[15] and the second to a constitutional court with competence to interpret and enforce the constitution, to pronounce on the validity of various presidential decisions, and to uphold the rights constitutionally defined.[16] Both motions were opposed by the other parliamentary parties, the government contending, in emulation of the President's Council, that human rights were adequately protected at common law, that the institutions proposed were not well-suited to providing additional protection, and that innovations along these lines would politicise the judiciary and produce legislative uncertainty. Both motions were defeated in divisions, which were conclusory of the constitution's ambit: it would regulate institutional arrangements but would not mediate state–subject relationships.

The committee stage began on 12 August 1983 and promised a detailed consideration of the bill's individual provisions. On the fifth day debate on the seventh of the bill's 103 clauses was interruped for a government-sponsored guillotine motion.[17] It proposed termination of the debate on 27 August, but a subsequent motion deferred the guillotine for four additional days.[18] The opposition parties all opposed the measure on the grounds of the bill's importance and complexity. By the terminal date thirty-four clauses had been debated and approved and in terms of the standing orders the remainder were ratified seriatim without being discussed. Among the matters affected thereby were the composition and functions of Parliament, the administration of justice, the President's Council, financial matters and the transitional and amending procedures. The time allocation was further affected by mini-guillotines on some individual clauses, and the succession of procedural points, interjections and acrimonious exchanges. In partial compensation the government extended the third reading debate from the customary two to ten hours, exclusive of the minister's reply.[19]

In the government's motivation of the clauses debated the trends evident during the second reading stage were confirmed.[20] The emphasis was placed primarily on the constitution's 'self-determination' aspects, and only secondarily on its 'joint responsibility' features, a reflection of which was found in the substantive arrangements relating to 'own' and 'general' affairs.[21] The 'joint responsibility' concept and its analogues were used consistently instead of 'power-sharing', the term which had caused controversy within Afrikaner nationalism and was now assiduously eschewed by the government.[22] Although the system was justified in terms of its suitability for consensus politics the government expressly repudiated the system of 'consociational democracy' recommended by the President's Council.[23] It was again more equivocal about the abandonment of the Westminster system and justified the retention of several Westminster institutions. The government made little use of the constitutional reports of the President's Council to vindicate the system, whereas the opposition parties occasionally cited them in judgment of the constitution in its latest form. Commentators interpreted these factors, and the accompanying institutional changes, as a compulsive retreat by the government in the face of an ascendant right wing.[24] Conservative resistance to the system generated a renewed emphasis on political stability, administrative efficiency, and white security.

The third reading debate extended from 7–9 September,[25] after which the constitution was approved by 119 votes to 35. The debate was directed predominantly at the referendum campaign, which was then under way, and the contents of the legislation and its justificatory theories received limited attention.[26] In general the parties restated their established standpoints towards the constitution, one of the few innovative issues being that of the 'hidden agenda'.[27] Here the government reiterated its extra-parliamentary announcement that it had no covert plan to introduce blacks into the system after its implementation.

3. ACT NO 110 OF 1983

(a) General

The well-established parameters of constitutional reform have not been disturbed by the 1983 Constitution Act for whites, coloureds and Indians. The legacy of earlier constitutions is exemplified by the provisions which preserve the old national symbols and constitutional conventions in the new system.[28] The statute is most conspicuous in that for the first time in South Africa's constitutional history the right both to elect and to be elected to the national parliament is extended to coloureds and Indians.[29] It is also the first time that the provisions of the population classification legislation pertaining to the three included groups is incorporated referentially into the constitution,[30] although the Act makes conspicuously few overt references to race or colour.[31] The new composite parliament, however, does not constitute a national assembly in the conventional sense and cannot give direct expression to the expanded electorate's will.[32] Despite the assumptions of the system the mediating institutions entail a differential access to political power among the three groups. The constitutional structures for blacks are left wholly intact, thereby reinforcing the prevailing axis of black–non-black constitutional development.

(b) The institutions of government

The 1983 Act provides for the main institutions envisaged in the earlier formulations of the constitution and resolves several terminological issues. With minor exceptions the composition of parliament is the same as that envisaged in 1979 and 1982, the House of Assembly as restructured by the 1980 amendments serving as a model for the other Houses.[33] The designation of the component white, coloured and Indian chambers as House of Assembly, House of Representatives and House of Delegates avoids any reference to colour or ethnicity, implies institutional parity for the Houses, and upholds the notion of a tricameral legislature. Each House elects its own chairman and determines its domestic rules and orders, and a rudimentary basis is provided for a joint committee system linking the three. The composition, functions and procedure of the electoral college are similar to those in the 1979 bill, and it has the additional assignment of electing the Speaker of Parliament, who is also Speaker of the individual Houses.[34] The state presidency combines the roles of head of state and head of government, and the office-holder is empowered to appoint four executive authorities, a national cabinet and a ministers' council for each group.[35] The President's Council is revamped and given extended powers, while the judiciary is left unaffected in its status and composition,[36] although its powers are slightly modified.

From a constitutional law point of view the most salient feature of the 1983 constitution is its flexible distribution of power among these institutions. This is a cumulative consequence of several different features. The most significant division of power, between the 'own affairs' of each group and the 'general affairs' of all three, is not constant but accommodates periodic adjustments; the powers of several institutions can be exercised on a delegated or agency basis by others; definitionally parliament is a flexible institution, as are the electoral college and President's Council to lesser degrees; the transitional arrangements permit a gradual and flexible assignment of power from the old institutions to the new; and some of the constitution's clauses are open-ended or ambiguous. These factors of flexibility preclude a single analytical account of the constitution's distribution of power. From a legal-institutional point of view there is a broad range of permissive power relationships which has given rise to inconsistent, but logically defensible, interpretations of the system. Underlying political realities will determine which of the alternatives are most frequently resorted to in practice. Within this flexible context the state presidency is the focal institution, as can be illustrated in respect of each of the following themes.

(c) Own and general affairs

The basic principle of the government's established policy for whites, coloureds and Indians finds more explicit expression in the new constitution, and is the underlying rationale for the whole system.[37] The 1979 bill empowered the executive to distinguish between matters of exclusive group concern and those of mutual concern through a discretionary assignment of functions, whereas the President's Council proposed a dual list system to afford greater certainty, with non-listed matters being of mutual concern. The 1983 Act incorporates elements of both systems. It provides for the first time a definition of the first category, now designated 'own affairs', in ostensibly wide-ranging terms:[38]

'Matters which specially or differentially affect a population group in relation to the maintenance of its identity and the upholding and furtherance of its way of life, culture, traditions and customs, are . . . own affairs in relation to such population group'.

Augmenting the definition is an appended schedule which specifies a quantitatively substantial number of matters as the own affairs of each group.[39] All other matters are regarded as 'general affairs' of all groups for legislative, executive and administrative purposes,[40] making the own affairs concept definitionally paramount.

The flexibility in this sphere derives firstly from the recurrent provisos in the schedule which subordinate own affairs to general laws, either comprehensively or in relation to norms, standards and financial arrangements. This introduces a repugnancy principle, similar to that pertaining to the central government and the provinces, once an area is occupied by a general law.[41] As general laws include all enactments in force at the commencement of the Act the provisos in themselves imply a limited potential significance for the own affairs concept. However, both the defining provision and the schedule are subject to s 16 of the constitution, which is the second major source of flexibility. It extends to the State President the discretionary power to designate a matter as the own affairs of a specific group. The provision was motivated in terms of the probable future need to rectify deficiencies in the schedule in the light of the definition, thereby expanding the own affairs category.[42] In terms of general legal principles this administrative function must be exercised in the light of the Act's scope and purpose,[43] and in particular the contents of the definition provision. The constitution also purports to circumscribe the discretion: the State President must consult with the national cabinet and may solicit advice from the President's Council;[44] if the decision has legislative implications the Speaker of Parliament and chairmen of the houses must also be consulted to the extent he deems necessary, this limited process being subject to judicial scrutiny;[45] and the decision may not entail that the administrative institutions of one group affect the interests of another.[46] However, all these safeguards are rendered potentially illusory by an ouster clause which excludes the courts' inherent review powers in respect of the State President's decision.[47] Although it would violate the spirit of the arrangement and refute the internal logic of the system the State President could, without legal sanction, declare a demonstrably general affair to be an own affair for specific purposes. Ultimately neither the section 14 definition nor the schedule's list could be invoked juridically to control the State President's wide discretion in this matter, and the only sanction for its abuse would be political.

The own affairs/general affairs distinction is of pervasive importance to the system because it relates to legislation, executive functions and state administration, and it was one of the most contentious issues in the parliamentary debates. It was criticised on the one hand for its apparent bias in favour of own affairs, which would imply unequal social and economic services for coloureds and Indians, and the continued predominance of whites; it would reinforce institutional segregation and social apartheid, by making coloureds and Indians responsible for enforcing discriminatory laws.

On the other hand it was criticised for undermining own affairs by making general laws superordinate in most areas of significance, and in particular in financial matters; the schedule's extensive list of own affairs, in this view, was designed to placate white apprehensions and has no substantive significance. In reality the flexibility and ambiguity of the arrangement precludes a definitive assessment along these lines, and from a legal-institutional point of view either eventuality implied by these seemingly contradictory criticisms would be possible. There are neither any constitutionally-secured own affairs matters, nor any matters which could not be declared such, although both these propositions deny the premises of the system. Both practicality and logic indicate that general laws, which include those of the former white parliament, should regulate most significant areas of social and economic life, although their administration could be delegated to separate white, coloured and Indian authorities. Less important enactments might be certified as own affairs legislation, but this would be somewhat akin to subordinate legislation made in terms of an organic statute. The framers' intentions fail to illuminate the matter as the debate was conducted at a high level of abstraction. However, the State President unquestionably retains the competence to use the own affairs classification, both in furtherance of the Act's objects and on grounds of administrative efficiency or political expediency. While the credibility needs of the system will serve to moderate the exercise of this discretion, where a decision is made in respect of executive or administrative matters there need be no publicity beyond cabinet members and chairmen of the ministers' councils.[48] This constitutes one of the crucial features of the new system.

The government justified the flexibility of the own affairs/general affairs distinction in terms of the need to make future adjustments in this arrangement, but it is indicative of the complex compromises which the system had to accommodate. The concept of own affairs is necessary to justify the basic institutional features of the system, such as separate electoral rolls, three Houses of Parliament and multiple executive authorities, and it finds expression in the definition provision, the schedule, and the State President's discretion. However, as the fate of the Turnhalle constitution showed, the own affairs concept is difficult to sustain within a single geo-political system and the schedule's provisos and the residual provision are a reflection of this reality. Not only is there a tenuous link between the definition and some of the schedule's own affairs matters,[49] but it is difficult to conceive of any non-listed matters which might be identified as own affairs in terms of the definition's guidelines. The constitution, however, had to cater for both justificatory theory and administrative practicality. It also had to reconcile the conflicting demands of the system's internal logic and the need for efficient and effective government; of introducing coloureds and Indians into the political process and retaining control in white hands; of not appearing to entrench apartheid and not appearing to threaten white security. All these interrelated sets of demands had as a consequence an ambiguous and flexible compromise in the central tenet of the constitution, the own affairs/general affairs distinction. Its ultimate significance lies in the inherent variability which it extends to the governing process.

(d) Executive authority

The new executive authorities are the State President, a national cabinet and three ministers' councils.[50] As anticipated, the constitution eliminates the diffusion of executive power between titular and effective heads of government, one of the enduring checks and balances of the Westminster system, and it also omits the office of premier recommended by the President's Council.[51] What was not anticipated was the committee stage amendment to the legislation which requires the members of all executive authorities, other than the State President,[52] to be members of the legislature, or to become so within twelve months of appointment.[53] Although a requirement of this type is axiomatic to the South African constitutional tradition, its presence in the new system involves a significant recantation in the light of the government's pronouncements during the protracted preceding debate. It introduces a closer institutional link than had been anticipated between Parliament and the executives, and vicariously between the State President and the majority white party. It also entails the final repudiation of the President's Council's notion of an executive presidency and separation of powers. It is further evidence of the alluring nature of the Westminster system for the dominant group, although it does not imply an orthodox Westminster cabinet system—the cabinet chairman is a non-parliamentarian, ministers may be drawn from three chambers representing separate electorates, and the flexibility of ministerial selection introduced in 1980 is not affected.

The constitution vests in the State President the ceremonial and prerogative powers associated with a Westminster head of state.[54] As with its predecessor it makes the exercise of certain powers a matter of individual discretion;[55] it purports to retain the conventions circumscribing these powers,[56] but those which are left uncodified will be of uncertain scope and questionable efficacy in the new context. Executive authority in respect of the own affairs of a population group vests in the State President acting on the advice of the appropriate ministers' council.[57] The constitutional provisions relating to the appointment of ministers to these bodies,[58] the Houses' competence to express their lack of confidence in them, each council's ability to have the relevant house dissolved,[59] and the prevailing conventions, indicate that each ministers' council will function as a single-party Westminster-type cabinet, although supernumerary members could be appointed or co-opted from minority parties in each House.[60] In respect of these own affair matters the chairman of each council will have prime ministerial-type status and the State President will be an instrument of the council and act as titular head. In regard to general affairs of all three groups, executive authority vests in the State President acting 'in consultation with' those ministers who comprise the cabinet.[61] Here the legislature designedly replaced the time-honoured phrase 'on the advice of', introducing a greater individual discretion for the President, even in respect of non-reserved matters.[62] As the State President is also the presiding member of the cabinet it is clear that legally and politically he will enjoy substantial predominance over it. Cabinet ministers are appointed at the State President's discretion on a permanent or ad hoc basis, membership being open to white, coloured or Indian parliamentarians.[63] The departmental documents[64] suggested that appointments would be made on a meritocratic and not a majoritarian basis but both the conventions and the government's expressed intentions[65] indicate that majority parties only are to be represented. However, there is no institutional necessity for the national cabinet to constitute a grand coalition, nor even to incorporate the majority party leaders,[66] although it will have extensive powers over general affairs; the 1979 council of cabinets, by contrast, had fewer powers but included majority leaders and equal numbers of white and non-white members.[67] Although there is also an inherent flexibility in this area, the institutional arrangements show more affinity with the Westminster than the consociational model.[68]

The operation of the executive function has been left largely to convention and practice. The principle of collective ministerial responsibility could find application within the ministers' councils but although the government intends it to be applied in its existing form[69] in the cabinet it would be less compatible with the latter's basic features. Not only will the cabinet be a multi-party body unsupported by a prior political coalition or pact, but the President will be in a pre-eminent position to impose 'consensus' on its members; moreover cabinet ministers can retain simultaneous membership of a potentially antagonistic ministers' council and subject themselves to dual oaths of cabinet secrecy.[70] In these circumstances the operation of collective responsibility could be problematic. A conventional form of individual responsibility to the legislature is implied by the parliamentary executive arrangement, but is complicated by the composite nature of Parliament. Cabinet ministers are entitled to speak and respond to questions in all three houses,[71] but as their political base will derive from only one house the others will be unable to call them to account by way of the traditional control mechanisms. Individual responsibility will also be affected by the provision for a highly flexible delegation and re-delegation of executive powers,[72] ostensibly designed to prevent administrative breakdowns. However, as with most modern constitutions the nature of the executive function will depend more on organic developments than legal prescription or the framers' expressed intention. What is clear is that although the government made some legislative responses to allegations of a 'presidential dictatorship'[73] the institutional predominance of the State President makes the office the focal point of the executive function, and the constitutional system as a whole. REFER TO NOTE 73.
P. 213.

(e) Legislative authority

The State President will also assume a pivotal role in the legislative process, despite being no longer a constituent part of Parliament. The constitution vests 'sovereign legislative authority' in the President and Parliament jointly, but the Westminster-associated notion of sovereignty is inapposite in this context because the concept of parliament is not constant.[74] Definitionally it is flexible in so far as Parliament consists either of all three Houses, or of such Houses as are actively functioning,[75] a flexibility designed to nullify the effect of boycotts by the various electorates or their representatives. Functionally it is also flexible in that there are five possible methods by which Parliament can legislate, some of them with subsidiary variations; moreover one procedure involves the participation of the President's Council which is not included in the flexible definition of parliament. This flexibility deprives the sovereignty concept of its conventional significance, although it does denote the judiciary's continued subservience to laws constitutionally enacted.

All legislation has the status of an Act of Parliament and it may be enacted in one of the following ways:

(i) *Own affairs*

Advance presidential certification that a bill deals with the own affairs of a particular group entitles the relevant house alone to deal with it conclusively, subject to the requirement of subsequent presidential assent.[76] Such legislation can be initiated by the appropriate ministers' council, and, by implication, the national cabinet. The House will deal with the measure in terms of established legislative procedures, and may accept or reject it on a simple majoritarian basis.[77] However, its ability to modify the legislation is inherently limited, and to this extent its law-making capacity is deficient: if the State President indicates by subsequent certification that an amendment extends beyond the own affairs of the particular group, the amendment must be abandoned or the legislative process discontinued.[78] An individual House may be presidentially summoned during the parliamentary recess to dispose of own affairs legislation or to conduct other business.[79]

(ii) *General affairs—consensual procedure*

Legislation on general affairs matters can be initiated in the cabinet, and must be ministerially initiated if it deals with taxation or appropriation.[80] The bill is introduced in the Houses of Parliament sitting separately and if approved by simple majorities in all three can be submitted to the State President for validation.[81] The consensual procedure will be viable where a measure is acceptable to each of the ministers' councils and a system of joint committees is designed to achieve consensus among the Houses at important stages in the process.[82] The committees comprise members from all three Houses and may be empowered to function while Parliament is prorogued. There is statutory provision for one standing committee dealing with general affairs, but the establishment of additional committees, and their composition, powers and procedures, will be regulated by joint rules and orders to be drafted by the Houses. The question of minority party participation on the committees has not been constitutionally resolved,[83] but the inevitable predominance of majority parties will co-ordinate this process by facilitating the Houses' acceptance of the legislative agreements which the committees reach. In this option the primary institutions will be the cabinet and joint committees, acting in camera, with the Houses playing the secondary role of publicising the legislation and legitimising it through their endorsement.

(iii) *General affairs—conflict procedure*

Where the general affairs procedure has run its course and there is disagreement among the three Houses on whether to pass a bill, or where more than one version thereof has been passed, the State President has an optional mechanism for resolving the dispute.[84] The matter may be referred to the President's Council, but may also be withdrawn at any stage before the council has disposed of it; in a case of non-referral or withdrawal the bill will lapse. The council, operating through its committees, may propose that Parliament amend the legislation, but it must ultimately decide whether the measure, or which version thereof, should be enacted.[85] The bill is thereafter validated through presidential assent and is regarded for all purposes as an Act of Parliament.[86] In this option the unity of the legislative process is broken by the discretionary intervention of the President and President's Council, and Parliament as a totality is precluded from resolving differences among its constituent parts, even on general affairs matters.[87] The legislation is considered and publicised by all three Houses, but the approval of one House, in conjunction with that of the two non-parliamentary institutions, suffices for its enactment despite the putative equality of the three. Apart from the State President's important role, this procedure reveals the President's Council to have a quasi-legislative function and the near-status of a legislative chamber when it is operationalised.

(iv) *General affairs—expeditious procedure*

Where a general affairs bill has been approved in at least one House of Parliament the State President may direct that it be disposed of by the other Houses, or House, within a specified period of not less than fourteen days.[88] If there is non-compliance with the directive the bill is deemed by constitutional fiction to have been rejected by the relevant House or Houses. In these circumstances the conflict procedure outlined in the previous paragraph may be followed, the principle of constructive parliamentary enactment of the legislation being similarly applicable. The implications of the expeditious procedure are identical to those of the conflict procedure, save that the State President has the additional discretion of suspending the constitutional fiction, and the legislation could become effective without having been introduced or considered in one or two Houses of Parliament.

(v) *Constitutional amendments*

Constitutional amendments will constitute a species of general affairs legislation and the 1983 Act provides three different procedures for their enactment. The tradition of rigidity is retained in respect of the two specially entrenched provisions, the language and amendment clauses,[89] for the amendment or repeal of which a two-thirds majority in each House is required. The ordinarily entrenched provisions impart a lesser degree of constitutional rigidity in that a simple majority in each House is required for their amendment or repeal.[90] These clauses regulate, inter alia, the composition, powers and procedures of the main institutions of government, the 4:2:1 ratio determining the composition of the electoral college, President's

Council and three Houses, the own affairs/general affairs arrangements, and the franchise. The entrenchments exclude the conflict and expeditious procedures and the President's Council's arbitrative role in respect of all the essential features of the constitutional system.[91] In the light of the statutory provisions and case law it is also doubtful that the courts would countenance a constitutional amendment being certified an own affair matter for purposes of avoiding their procedural requirements.[92] It is arguable, however, that in terms of the flexible definition of parliament such amendments could be passed by only the House or Houses actively functioning at the time; as this issue involves a question of sovereignty, it would ultimately require judicial resolution.[93] For all other constitutional amendments any of the general affairs procedures may be employed.[94]

An apparent innovation in the 1983 constitution is the judiciary's enhanced review power in respect of legislation. The courts can investigate and pronounce upon whether the Act's provisions have been complied with in respect of any instrument purporting to be an Act of Parliament.[95] They may not investigate parliamentary rules and orders, nor, where applicable, a presidential certification, and substantive review is explicitly excluded. This ordering reflects a 'new view' conception of parliamentary supremacy,[96] the diversity and complexity of legislative procedures necessitating a more specific elaboration of the prevailing situation. But while it may entail increased judicial involvement in the investigation of some legislative procedures it maintains the subordinacy of the courts to legislation properly enacted.

The above outline presents alternative views of the legislative function. The procedures for own affairs legislation and constitutional amendments, and the consensual procedure for general affairs, give expression to the basic assumptions of the system and to this extent the constitution is more internally consistent than the 1979 bill. But the conflict and expeditious procedures, and the State President's unsupervised discretion to define own affairs, repudiate those assumptions in favour of legislative effectiveness and efficiency, thereby restoring the flexibility of the 1979 model. The practical operation of this dualist system will be determined by political factors, but if it is evaluated in terms of its legal-institutional feasibilities the focus falls persistently on the State President who can initiate legislation and regulate its progress, and, in conjunction with at least one House and the President's Council, can secure the enactment of any law without undue delay. It was therefore unnecessary to include a special procedure for financial legislation as recommended by the President's Council,[97] or a discretionary veto power for the State President after the legislative process has run its course.[98] In the constitution's wider context the legislative arrangements extend ultimate legal supremacy to the majority white party acting through the presidency, House of Assembly, parliamentary committees and President's Council. Both categories of entrenchment restrict its legal capacity to act without external support, but they also exempt it from having the basic constitutional structure statutorily modified without its consent.

(f) **Legislative–executive relationships**

The reciprocal controls between the legislature and executive are an important element of constitutional government. In the absence of a popular election the State President's mandate in the new system will be parliamentary-based, as in the Westminster model. However, as Parliament is a nominative and not a functional entity the mandate is vicariously conferred by the electoral college, which will inevitably be an instrument of the majority party in a single constituent part of Parliament. The legislature's control over the State President is also indirect and limited: the Houses in concert may initiate the removal process, which may be effectuated by a majority vote of the electoral college, but only on the narrow grounds of misconduct or incapacity associated with a titular head.[99] The State President's institutional pre-eminence is the main feature of this mutual relationship.

The tripartite structure of Parliament has more general implications for executive accountability, as alluded to in respect of the principles of ministerial responsibility. Where parliamentary government functions in a bicameral setting, as in the Westminster system, power inevitably gravitates to one house;[100] this is invariably the lower house, from which most ministers are drawn, and its political superiority affords it greater control over the cabinet than the upper house. This propensity could be accentuated by the specific institutional features of the 1983 constitution's tricameral system, rendering the executive politically responsible to the white house, of which most cabinet ministers will be members, and remote from the others. The Westminster similarities do not, however, extend to the formal mechanisms of executive control. A vote of no confidence or the rejection of appropriation measures by the three houses could render the State President's resignation a political necessity, but he has the legal option in these circumstances to dissolve Parliament.[101] Here the constitution purports to codify the Westminster conventions which ensure harmony between the legislative and executive branches but it fuses together the prerogative and political powers which that system divides, thereby making the State President an arbiter in his own cause.[102] There is also no evidence of the external checks and balances on the executive branch associated with presidential regimes.[103] While the executive is a parliamentary body the five-year tenure of its head, and the other factors referred to, ensure that it has only some of the forms of responsibility to the legislature associated with parliamentary government.[104] Conversely the legislature has neither parliamentary nor presidential controls over the executive to their full extent.

The State President's predominance is further accentuated by his potential controls over the legislature. Parliament may be dissolved at any time within its five-year term, a Westminster-type competence usually exercised for political advantage.[105] It must be dissolved if it is in political conflict with the cabinet or rejects cabinet-initiated appropriation measures,[106] unless, as indicated above, the State President resigns. The President may dissolve a constituent part of Parliament individually on the request of the ministers' council in question, where it expresses a lack of confidence in the cabinet or rejects its appropriation measures, or where it does not function because of electoral or representative boycotts.[107] Where a House is in conflict with its ministers' council the State President must either dissolve the House or reconstitute the council.[108] This array of dissolution resources entails extensive institutional ascendancy for the State President in the legislative-executive sphere by combining parliamentary instruments of control with presidential security of tenure. Although a dissolution of Parliament would lead to a subsequent presidential election the Westminster experience identifies this as a powerful potential weapon for the executive head in attaining legislative compliance, which is facilitated by his ability personally to address Parliament collectively or its Houses individually.[109] In the new system, moreover, the general parliamentary election would not constitute a vicarious presidential election because the State President requires the support of only the House of Assembly to secure re-appointment. Whatever the political developments in this field, the harmony between the legislature and executive which the parliamentary system entails will revolve ultimately around the institution of the presidency. While this will ensure governmental efficiency and political continuity it could have negative implications for the political stature of Parliament and the constitutional accountability of the government.

(g) The party system

As with most modern constitutions the 1983 Act makes no express provision for party or caucus systems, despite their prominent role in contemporary government. The constitution implies that party organisation and recruitment will take place within the constraints of the Prohibition of Political Interference Act,[110] thereby preventing the formation of inter-group parties. With one minor exception each group can only be represented by its own members in the electoral college, Parliament, minister's council and President's Council.[111] The institutional arrangements also discourage, without prohibiting, post-electoral pacts among parties from the three participating groups.[112] The party system will thus operate on an intra-group basis and the plurality electoral system will tend to favour the emergence of two dominant parties, and their ancillary institutions, in each house.

The importance of the party system is exemplified by the fact that the constitution empowers the dominant white party to nominate the State President. This has been a constant feature of the system in all its formulations. At least in the short term this will maintain the supremacy of the existing dominant group, but its position will be legitimised by a differently-constituted Parliament and electoral college. The original notion of an executive presidency implied a relatively loose link between the executive head and his sponsor-party, and the President's Council envisaged that his detachment from Parliament, the caucus and the party would facilitate a 'supra-ethnic' role for the incumbent. The reversion to a Westminster-based form of parliamentary government, however, involves a tightening of the links between the various institutions and the government indicated in the parliamentary debates that the State President will remain the leader of both his party and caucus after appointment,[113] although he will not be a

Member of Parliament. The President's security of tenure will facilitate control of the party and caucus which cannot directly dispose of him, but their withdrawal of support would inevitably jeopardise his political survival. Although the interrelationships defy exact description, the strong institutional link between the majority white party, its caucus, the House of Assembly and the executive, as maintained through the institution of the state presidency, exposes the Westminster-bias of the constitution in its final form. It implies a more prominent and active role for the dominant party and caucus than was envisaged in some earlier formulations.

(h) The President's Council

The President's Council has been retained in the 1983 constitution but with a modified form and functions.[114] The qualifications for council membership are substantially the same but provision is now made for only fifteen of its sixty members to be nominated by the State President.[115] Thirty-five members are designated by the majority parties in the three houses in a 4:2:1 ratio, and the remaining ten, as a late concession, are indirectly elected by the minority parties in proportion to their legislative strength.[116] The council no longer has a fixed term of office and must be dissolved after each parliamentary dissolution, to be reconstituted post-electorally.[117] If the State President relinquishes office without a dissolution of Parliament the successor has the option of replacing the nominated component, and when an individual house is dissolved the members designated by it may be recalled by its successor and replaced. The council's advisory powers have been retained and may be exercised on the executive's directive or its own initiative.[118] It may be consulted by the State President on an own affairs/ general affairs dispute, where its advice would not be conclusive, but at best persuasive. If entrusted with the resolution of a legislative deadlock it can suggest amendments to the bill and make other recommendations, but if the presidential reference is not withdrawn it must give a decisive and binding decision on the matter, although it cannot amend the legislation.

While the President's Council recommended that its successor in the new system should be a 'depoliticised' body,[119] the amendments introduced in 1983 draw it more directly into the political process. Its party-based composition renders it less an extension of the executive and more a reproduction of the legislature. In addition the nominated members will inevitably reflect the views of the majority party in the electoral college, the State President being disencumbered of a quota requirement incorporated in some earlier versions of the constitution. These factors entail that the majority white party could directly and indirectly return over half the representatives on the council, and install its nominees as chairman and deputy chairman.[120] The dissolution arrangements generally subordinate the council to the fluctuating political process, and more particularly entitle the dominant white party of the day to acquire majority representation on the council through direct designation and indirect nomination and thereby maintain a compatibility between the two. This capability has obvious implications for the council's political predispositions. The political salience of the council's quasi-legislative function implies a more adversarial decision-making procedure and several of its consociational pretensions have been dispensed with: the constitution prescribes a majoritarian decision-making process,[121] the chairman is now elected from the council's ranks, and the committee system has been de-emphasised.[122] Moreover ministers and deputy ministers can now participate directly in its proceedings in a non-voting capacity,[123] thus affording immediate access to political leaders.

The President's Council's new composition, its quasi-legislative role, its link with Parliament and susceptibility to party-political influences, and its modified procedures, give it a closer affinity than its predecessor to the defunct Senate. While it is a subordinate institution with insubstantial original powers it can be used in a utility role to legitimise the governing process. In this capacity it will be a highly politicised body with significant potential influence in the new system.

(i) Subnational authorities

There is no reference of significance to subnational institutions of government in the 1983 Act, the matter having been deferred for subsequent legislative treatment.[124] The constitution assumes a developed system of local government and according to the first schedule matters of local government within a specific group area are the own affairs of the group concerned.[125] Where administration on a joint basis is necessary at the local level it will be regulated by a general law. The government envisages that the principles of self-determination and co-responsibility will be applied at the local level, which implies an eventual local-scale version of the central government system along the lines recommended by the President's Council.[126]

The constitution does not, however, assume a developed system of regional government. The most salient provincial concerns, such as education, health and local government, are identified as the own affairs of each group[127] and the remainder, by implication, are general affairs. This implies a more extensive doctrine of repugnancy than before and removes any justification for the retention of the provincial system as it has hitherto existed. However, the constitution envisages that provincial functions will remain where they are until they have been gradually reallocated. Provincial ordinances remain in force until amended by the State President or Act of Parliament,[128] and the provincial authorities retain their executive powers until they have been assigned to the appropriate body by the State President in consultation with the relevant provincial executive committee.[129] The provincial institutions are accordingly left intact through the non-repeal of the relevant provisions of the old constitution,[130] which in its attenuated form is styled the Provincial Government Act No 32 of 1961. The indications are that they will make way in time for regional administrative authorities. While the new constitution has been premised on the principle of decentralisation, its distribution of power implies a formally more unitary constitution and a potentially more centralised system of government.

(j) Miscellaneous matters

In keeping with the President's Council's recommendations[131] the consti-tution's preamble has been expanded and some 'bill of rights' terminology is incorporated in its provisions. In South African law a preamble does not constitute an organic part of the statute and it has no primary juridical force; it may, however, be invoked as an intrinsic interpretative aid in cases of statutory ambiguity.[132] As the new constitution might be subject to more judicial interpretation than the old the preamble could acquire a secondary legal significance, although it would have no relevance where the Act is unambiguously clear. There is less prospect of the preamble serving as a normative guide to the courts in their discretionary interpretation of other statutes once the constitution comes into effect. While there are precedents for such a development in 'bill of rights' regimes,[133] it is rendered unlikely by the status of the preamble, the potentially conflictual nature of some provisions,[134] and the unequivocal exclusion of its principles in many exist-ing statutes. The preamble can realistically be regarded as having predomi-nantly a symbolic and not a functional significance.

Financial matters are referred to briefly in the constitution[135] but will be more comprehensively regulated in a separate statute. Public revenue will be generated predominantly in terms of general laws and will be credited to a single state revenue fund. There will be separate accounts for the own affairs of each group, to which funds can be transferred according to formulae, and under conditions, prescribed by general law. As the individual houses cannot impose taxes or raise loans to finance their own affairs they will be predominantly dependent on these unspeci-fied allocations. They will, however, be entitled to produce their own esti-mates of revenue and expenditure and to appropriate moneys from the relevant account accordingly, subject to general law conditions and require-ments. This system denotes a dependent financial status for the three houses, and their ancillary institutions, in their administration of own affairs matters.

The clauses relating to the administration of justice have been retained in identical form in the new constitution, and there will be no modification in the structure, composition or powers of the courts in keeping with the changes to the legislative and executive branches.[136] Although the distribu-tion of power, the jurisdictional arrangements and the constitutional pro-visions themselves imply a more active constitutional role for the courts, no accommodation is made for such a development.

The administrative branch of government has also been overlooked in the Act's provisions. The appointment and removal of public servants continues to be vested in the State President, or his delegate,[137] but there is no reference to the one general affairs and three own affairs bureaucracies which the legislative and executive systems postulate. However, existing laws can be administered as before, even if they relate to coloured or Indian own affairs, until their administration is reassigned by the State Presi-dent.[138] This precludes the possibility of an administrative vacuum pending the reorganisation of the bureaucracy.

(k) Transitional arrangements

The constitution's transitional arrangements entail a substantial measure of legal, political and administrative continuity in the new system. All laws remain in effect until repealed or amended by a competent authority;[139] both internal conventions and external treaties or agreements are similarly unaffected.[140] Ministers and deputy ministers remain in office and they and the existing state departments retain all powers and functions until they have been reassigned, all laws being provisionally identified as general affairs laws for administrative purposes.[141] Provincial laws and authorities are correspondingly retained until the provincial system has been dissipated by administrative decree.[142] The House of Assembly as constituted under the old Act can remain in office for up to five years after the other houses have been first elected, and steps taken by it in the legislative process remain valid.[143] Electoral regulations and domestic rules and orders pertaining to the Assembly remain in force and are extended mutatis mutandis to the other houses; the Assembly may also unilaterally promulgate joint rules and orders for an interim period.[144] Pending a presidential election the existing cabinet may appoint an acting State President from its members with the plenary powers of the office.[145] The constitution itself may be brought into operation on a flexible and piecemeal basis, the State President acquiring the customary antecedent powers necessary for its implementation.[146]

In general terms the transitional arrangements preserve the existing white-dominated institutions of government and their powers, and assume a gradual transfer of functions to the newly constituted authorities. They facilitate stability, continuity and efficiency by permitting the incremental implementation of the system as political and logistical circumstances allow and reducing the possibility of its early disruption or breakdown. Their cumulative effect is also to project many features of the past politico-legal order on to the new system. Of particular significance is the panoply of existing legislation, the amendment or repeal of which will be subject to the constraints of the new system and factors of institutional inertia. In so far as constitutional change has preceded social and economic reform this factor has negative implications for the wider reform process. The new system assumes, moreover, the retention of discriminatory legislation in matters of social behaviour, residence, education and public facilities. These factors underline the institutional legacy of the old constitutional system.

4. THE REFERENDUM

The government indicated early in the emergence of its constitution that any radical changes from its prevailing policies would be referred to the white electorate in a referendum. Appropriate legislation was enacted in 1982.[147] In March 1983 the government indicated its intention to exercise the referendum option, but shortly thereafter the proposal was shelved because of adverse climatic conditions affecting the country.[148] During the committee stage of the constitution bill, however, the Prime Minister announced a specific date and form of enquiry for the referendum;[149] it was also indicated that the appropriate minister would negotiate with coloured and Indian leaders on a mechanism for ascertaining the respective groups' attitudes towards the constitution. The 1982 Act was subsequently repealed in its totality and replaced by a new statute.[150] Whereas the old Act was modelled predominantly on the detailed provisions of the Electoral Act[151] its successor comprises broadly enabling legislation which empowers the executive to regulate by proclamation the most important features of a referendum. The government retains the discretionary competence to determine the date of the referendum, the matters at issue, and the categories of voters to be consulted,[152] and it has the additional discretion to decide on the voting districts, the manner for determining and announcing the result, voter identification requirements and diverse voting arrangements.[153] However this institution may still be used only among whites, coloureds and Indians, as statutorily defined.[154] The State President duly issued regulations in terms of these powers.[155]

The referendum for whites was held on 2 November 1983. Voters could respond affirmatively or negatively to a single question—Are you in favour of the implementation of the Constitution Act, 1983, as approved by Parliament? The votes were counted in fifteen different regions, and in aggregate the affirmative votes numbered 1 360 223 and the negatives 691 577.[156] Although the process was essentially plebiscitory the result disposed the government to indicate that the constitution would become effective in late 1984.

In its final form the constitution does not involve a radical departure from the government's established policies, despite its earlier associations with power-sharing and consociationalism. Nevertheless the referendum could be used to solicit a wider legitimacy for the system, both internally and externally. The constitution was motivated as the best kind of reform possible in the circumstances, and the referendum was presented as a final opportunity for the white electorate to accept reform and avoid conflict. This manifesto secured the government support from across the party political spectrum.[157] Despite the substantial majority, however, the electorate's mandate was somewhat ambiguous: while some affirmative voters interpreted the constitution as an extension and confirmation of the government's traditional policies, others interpreted it as a first liberalising step away from those policies,[158] a discrepancy partially attributable to the system's inherent flexibility and equivocacy. There was a similar dichotomy among the negative voters.[159] The Prime Minister indicated shortly after the referendum that there was no hidden agenda for reform, an apparent confirmation that the system would not be modified after its implementation to include blacks.

The referendum device has manifest advantages for the government in power, including its ability to define political issues in dichotomous terms and to appeal directly to the electorate for non-partisan support. In these respects it conflicts with the consociational notion of consensual rule by competing élites. The 1983 referendum did illustrate the difficulty of coordinating three self-contained electorates; although prominent coloureds and Indians requested separate ensuing referenda the possibility of defeat was a serious risk for the constitution and its credibility. Nevertheless the government has indicated that referenda will be a more prominent feature of the future constitutional process[160] and they will provide some scope for a 'plebiscitory presidency'.

5. CONCLUSION

The relative urgency of the final phase of constitutional development reflected, inter alia, the government's preoccupation with the state's legitimacy problems, causing it to give constitutional reform precedence over socio-economic reform. The 1983 constitution accordingly extends the franchise to coloureds and Indians, and introduces separate and joint institutions of government for the expression of their political rights. However, this occurs within a flexible framework which also constitutionalises the government's established policy, makes aspects of apartheid part of the country's basic law, and countenances continued control by the dominant white group. The system rejects some central recommendations of the President's Council and incorporates certain familiar aspects of the Westminster model. Its most prominent feature is the potential supremacy of the executive head of government and the close link between that office and the majority white party and caucus. It remains to relate the 1983 constitution in its wider context to the main theme of this work.

NOTES AND REFERENCES

[1] As formulated by the Du Preez commission. See above, 112–14.

[2] eg Rev A Hendrickse and Mr D Curry. In October 1983, however, the latter also resigned from the party.

[3] See *House of Assembly Debates* vol 15 col 7382–7 (18 May 1983).

[4] *House of Assembly Debates* vol 13 col 6363–9 (5 May 1983).

[5] See *Explanatory Memorandum on the Constitution of the Republic of South Africa Bill, 1983*, WP 7—'83, 2. Cf E Kahn 'The New Constitution' (1961) 78 *SALJ* 244 at 250.

[6] *House of Assembly Debates* vol 15 col 7045–7 (16–18 May 1983).

[7] Ibid 7045–65.

[8] eg *House of Assembly Debates* vol 15 col 7338–9 (18 May 1983): 'Certain facets of the Westminster system are being retained because we had no option.'

[9] eg *House of Assembly Debates* vol 15 col 7191 (17 May 1983): 'We are not dealing with "sharing of power", we are dealing with "sharing of responsibility".'

[10] See the minister of co-operation and development in *House of Assembly Debates* vol 15 col 7075–86 (16 May 1983).

[11] See the leader of the opposition in *House of Assembly Debates* vol 15 col 7065–75 (16 May 1983).

[12] See the party leader in *House of Assembly Debates* vol 15 col 7086–96 (16 May 1983).

[13] See the party leader in *House of Assembly Debates* vol 15 col 7107–15 (16 May 1983).

[14] At the end of its nine-day sitting the select committee had proposed amendments to 55 clauses, and the preamble and schedule, introduced 3 new clauses, and changed several chapter headings; (*Select Committee Amendments to Republic of South Africa Constitution Bill, B. 91—'83*.) Before the committee stage the opposition parties moved 174 amendments and the government moved others during this stage.

[15] See *House of Assembly Debates* vol 23 col 1181–2 (15 August 1983) and the debate following.

[16] See *House of Assembly Debates* vol 23 col 11371 (16 August 1983) and the debate following.

[17] A colloquial term for an order of the house fixing the time for a bill or part thereof. The government exercised its right of putting amendments after debate had ended. *House of Assembly Standing Orders* no 115(1)(b); see *House of Assembly Debates* vol 24 col 11863–949 (24 August 1983).

[18] *House of Assembly Debates* vol 24 col 12097–125 (25 August 1983).

[19] *House of Assembly Debates* vol 22 col 10968–9 (10 August 1983).

[20] *House of Assembly Debates* vol 23 col 11494—vol 25 col 12912 (17–31 August 1983), passim.

[21] See below, 196–8.

[22] There was constant cavilling by the National and Conservative parties on the 1983 constitution's conformity or otherwise with the 1977 and 1979 versions.

[23] See the minister of constitutional development:
'We often argue incorrectly that what we are trying to do is break away completely from the Westminster dispensation. Surely we do not want to break away completely from it. . . . We have never said that we are exchanging this particular system for another academic model . . . [T]he President's Council recommended a consociational democracy . . . [but] we did not accept that. We accepted elements of a new system, and retained elements of the old . . .' *House of Assembly Debates* vol 23 col 11579 (18 August 1983).

[24] See Prof A du Toit 'Turn to right has already happened', *Natal Mercury* 28 August 1983.

[25] *House of Assembly Debates* vol 26 col 13367–635 (7–9 September 1983).

[26] The term 'power-sharing' was the basis of continued skirmishing between the National and Conservative parties—see *House of Assembly Debates* vol 26 col 13439 and 13559 (7 and 8 September 1983, respectively).

[27] eg *House of Assembly Debates* vol 26 col 13525–6, 13541 (8 September 1983). The 'hidden agenda' reports depicted the system as an initial 'step in the right direction', but contradicted the goverment's overall constitutional strategy.

[28] Sections 3–5 and 88 respectively. Some of the conventions have been explicitly enacted—ss 21(2), 24(3)*(b)*, 27(2)*(b)* and 33(1). During the committee stage the term 'President' was replaced by the familiar 'State President'.

[29] Section 52 regulates the franchise. Between 1981 and 1983 all references to Chinese disappeared from use (cf above, 169n91).

[30] The Population Registration Act No 30 of 1950; s 100(1) of the constitution.

[31] Referred to only in ss 52 and 100, and s 93 in respect of blacks.

[32] In this respect it calls to mind the 'fancy franchise' era in the Rhodesia-Zimbabwe constitutional transition—above, 118.

[33] Sections 37–57; see above, 160–162.

[34] Sections 8–9 and 58. The final Act excludes nominated and indirectly elected parliamentarians from the college.

[35] Sections 6, 19, 20, 21 and 24.

[36] Sections 70–78 and 68–69 respectively.

[37] Sections 14–18. On coloured and Indian leaders' negative attitudes to the distinction (as expressed to the select committee) see *House of Assembly Debates* vol 25 col 12755–6 (30 August 1983). On this aspect the system is similar to the Turnhalle constitution. See above, 115–18.

[38] Section 14(1). Despite its semantic inelegance the legislation's terminology is used throughout the analysis.

[39] Schedule I rw s 14(2). Cf the former CPRC's powers (above, 83) and the Turnhalle constitution's 'own affairs' (142n46).

[40] Section 15.

[41] Cf the education minister's example in *House of Assembly Debates* vol 24 col 12378 (26 August 1983), and contrast the De Lange Commission recommendations above, 140.

[42] See *House of Assembly Debates* vol 24 col 12283–6 (26 August 1983). The definition was also necessary to avoid the circular reasoning in the draft bill which defined general affairs in terms of own affairs, and own affairs in terms of general affairs; however, the Act might perpetuate the error.

[43] *Van Eck NO and Van Rensburg NO v Etna Stores* 1947 (2) SA 984 (A); *Mustapha v Receiver of Revenue, Lichtenburg* 1958 (3) SA 343 (A); *Rikhoto v East Rand Administration Board & another* 1982 (1) SA 257 (W).

[44] Section 16(1)*(b)* rw s 19(1)*(a)* and (2), and s 17(1).

[45] Section 17(2)*(a)* rw s 18(1).

[46] Section 16(1)*(a)*; but see s 14 of Schedule I.

[47] Section 18(2). If there is no presidential decision on a matter it is a general affair, and it could be tested against s 14 and the schedule in terms of s 34(2)*(a)*. However, s 18(3) was introduced during the committee stage to close the loophole (*House of Assembly Debates* vol 25 col 12472–7 (29 August 1983)). The ouster clause would not preserve decisions taken in bad faith or fraud—*Union Government v Fakir* 1923 AD 466, *Narainsamy v Principal Immigration Officer* 1923 AD 673, *Winter & others v Administrator-in-Executive Committee & another* 1973 (1) SA 873 (A), *Honey & another v Minister of Police & others* 1980 (3) SA 800 (Tk SC).

[48] Section 16(2).   [49] e g agriculture and water supply.

[50] Part V, ss 19–29. The office of Vice-State President, introduced in 1980 (see above, 162–3) was not retained.

[51] See above, 176.

[52] Section 7(6). An acting State President, however, would be a serving member of the white house (s 10).

[53] Section 24(3)*(a)*. No substantive reasons were advanced by the minister for the reversal. See *House of Assembly Debates* vol 25 col 12691–5 and 12785 (30 and 31 August 1983).

[54] On the prerogative see *Sachs v Dönges NO* 1950 (2) SA 265 (A), *Tutu v Minister of Internal Affairs* 1982 (4) SA 571 (T). The State President does not, however, possess inherent or residual powers. See W H B Dean 'The Government's Constitutional Proposals—1982' in W Dean and D Smit (eds) *Constitutional Change in South Africa* (1983) 90 at 97f.

[55] Section 19(2); cf s 16(3) of Act 32 of 1961.   [56] Section 88.

[57] Section 19(1)*(a)*. The Bloemfontein guidelines made an ambiguous reference to cabinet committees for own affairs, but the 1983 Act recalled the 1979 bill.

[58] The chairmen and members with portfolio must have the support of the majority party (ss 21(2) and 24(3)*(b)*). However, the appointment of the former is a matter of individual presidential discretion which calls to mind the experiences of the CPRC executive. (See above, 85.)

[59] Section 39(3)*(b)*(i) and (3)*(a)*(iv) respectively.

[60] Section 21(1)*(d)*; deputy ministers could also belong to minority parties (s 21(1)*(c)*).

[61] Section 19(1)*(b)*.

[62] In a departmental memorandum it was stated that this phrase best describes the prevailing system of cabinet decision-making, in which the ultimate decision is formulated by the chairman, and takes account of the fact that the functionary is not an agent but a member of the cabinet. *House of Assembly Debates* vol 25 col 12576–80 (29 August 1983). Consultation, however, does not denote agreement—*R v Mbete* 1954 (4) SA 491 (E), *R v Ntlemeza* 1955 (1) SA 212 (A).

[63] Section 20 rw s 24. There is no limit on the number of ministers or deputy ministers (s 27) who may be appointed.

[64] See *House of Assembly Debates* vol 24 col 12027 (24 August 1983) and the National Party's 'Blue Book' distributed during the referendum (Constitution '83 in a Nutshell, 7).

[65] See *House of Assembly Debates* vol 25 col 12868 (31 August 1983).

[66] The government rejected an opposition amendment providing for ministers' council chairmen to serve ex officio on the cabinet. *House of Assembly Debates* vol 25 col 12603–17 (29 August 1983).

[67] Except for the President. See above, 153.

[68] Even ministerial confirmation of non-reserved presidential actions has been retained (s 24; cf s 29 of Act 32 of 1961).

[69] See the minister's extraordinarily wide interpretation of the doctrine—*House of Assembly Debates* vol 25 col 12585–6 (29 August 1983). Collective responsibility has been strong in South Africa only in so far as it has provided a protective shield for individual ministers.

[70] Section 24(4). (Cf s 20(5) of Act 32 of 1961.)

[71] Section 65.

[72] Sections 25, 26 and 27(4).

[73] e g in restricting the matters on which he can act independently of the cabinet (s 19(2)), narrowing the choice of ministers to parliament (s 24(3)), allowing parliament to convene a joint sitting (s 67(2)), requiring consultation with executive committees before provincial powers are curtailed (s 98(3)*(a)*), inserting a proviso in s 16(1)*(a)*, and making the house quorums inflexible (cf s 63(2) of the draft).

[74] Section 30. Cf G Devenish 'The doctrine of parliamentary sovereignty and the proposed new constitutional proposals' 1979 *THRHR* 85.

[75] Section 37.

[76] Sections 31 and 34 rw s 33.

[77] Section 62.

[78] Section 31(2).

[79] Section 66.

[80] Unless it has been recommended by the State President—s 86.

[81] Section 33.

[82] Section 64.

[83] The latest government indication was that all parties with a 'minimum' legislative representation would be included—*House of Assembly Debates* vol 25 col 12868 (31 August 1983). Cf above, 181.

[84] Section 32(1).

[85] Section 78(4) and (5). In terms of s 78(1) the council could also be informally consulted on the bill.

[86] Sections 32(4) and (5), and 33(1).

[87] Section 67(5) precludes the adoption of any resolution at a joint sitting of Parliament, an option recommended by the official opposition to resolve the disputes in question. See *House of Assembly Debates* vol 25 col 12827–8 (31 August 1983).

[88] Section 32(2).

[89] Sections 99(2) and 89.

[90] Section 99(3).

[91] Section 99(4). As in the Zimbabwe precedent (above, 118–23) the extension of the franchise has resulted in greater constitutional rigidity.

[92] See above, 74, and cases referred to. Despite the ouster clause in s 18(2) the courts are likely to give precedence to the peremptory nature of s 99(2) and (3) and clear wording of s 34(2)*(a)*, and to derive support from the constitutional crisis.

[93] Despite the 'generalia specialibus non derogant' principle, the prohibitory wording of s 99(2) and (3), and the fact that reference is made to 'every House' and not to Parliament, the wording of s 37(2) suggests that it takes precedence. Inaction by one or more house is likely to be judicially condoned more readily than manipulative action by the executive.

[94] Section 99(1).

[95] Section 34.

[96] See above, 75.

[97] See above, 181.

[98] Section 33 requires the State President to ratify legislation unless the Act's provisions have not been complied with.

[99] Section 9.

[100] A matter dealt with by the President's Council (*First Report* 73) with reference to K C Wheare *Legislatures* (1963) 202–3.

[101] Section 39(2)*(b)*.

[102] There must, however, be prior consultation with the cabinet.

[103] See above, 15–16.

[104] This factor invites the courts to show less deference to the principle of ministerial responsibility in reviewing administrative action—see *Sachs v Dönges NO* 1950 (2) SA 265 (A), *R v Lusu* 1953 (2) SA 484 (A), *Kati v Minister of Police & another* 1982 (3) SA 527 (TkSC).

[105] Section 39(1) and (2)*(a)* rw s 19(1)*(b)* and (2).

[106] Section 39(2)*(b)*.

[107] Section 39(3)*(a)*.

[108] Section 39(3)*(b)*.

[109] Section 6(3)*(a)*.

[110] Act 51 of 1968.

[111] The exception (per incuriam?) is the opposition parties' nominees on the President's Council (s 70(2) rw s 71(1)*(c)*).

[112] There is limited scope for opposition parties in the President's Council and parliamentary committees to collaborate with parties from other groups.

[113] *House of Assembly Debates* vol 24 col 12003 and 12077 (24 August 1983). The Westminster-derived s 13 of Act 32 of 1961 (protecting the dignity and reputation of the State President) has been appropriately omitted from the 1983 Act, whereas the 1979 bill retained it (s 13).

[114] Part VIII, ss 70–78.

[115] Sections 70 and 71.

[116] Section 70(2) was introduced in the committee stage but was not debated.

[117] Sections 77 and 71.

[118] Section 78.

[119] See above, 185.

[120] Section 72.

[121] Section 75.

[122] But not discontinued—s 76(1); cf s 104(2) of Act 32 of 1961.

[123] Section 76(2). Opposition parliamentarians are impliedly denied such access.

[124] See WP 7—'83, 9 and 10.

[125] Section 6.
[126] See above, 183.
[127] Schedule I, ss 2, 4 and 6.
[128] Section 98(1) rw s 98(3)*(c)*(i) and (ii).
[129] Section 98(2) and (3).
[130] Schedule 2, Part 1, A 2 and 11.
[131] See above, 182.
[132] *Law Union and Rock Insurance Co Ltd v Carmichael's Executor* 1917 AD 593, *S v Kola* 1966 (4) SA 322 (A). Preambles tend now to be restricted to constitutional-type documents (eg National States Constitution Act No 21 of 1971) and there are precedents for their use in this context—*Harris & others v Minister of the Interior & another* 1952 (2) SA 428 (A). See L C Steyn *Die Uitleg van Wette* (5 ed, 1981) 145–6.
[133] Cf L Barry 'Law, Policy and Statutory Interpretation Under a Constitutionally Entrenched Canadian Charter of Rights and Freedoms' 1982 *Canadian Bar Review* 237.
[134] eg the 'equal protection' and self-determination clauses, and the civil rights and law and order clauses.
[135] Part IX, ss 79–86 and schedule 1, s 11.
[136] Part VII, ss 68–69. Cf Dean op cit 100.
[137] Section 28.
[138] Section 98(1).
[139] Section 87.
[140] Sections 88 and 94.
[141] Sections 102(2)*(a)* and 98(1).
[142] Sections 87 and 98(2) and (3).
[143] Section 102(3), (4), (7), (8) and (9). The population register regulated by the Population Registration Act 30 of 1950 will serve as a voters' roll for the House of Representatives and House of Delegates elections.
[144] Section 102(6).
[145] Section 102(1).
[146] Section 103.
[147] The Referendums Act No 97 of 1982.
[148] *House of Assembly Debates* vol 9 col 4284 (30 March 1983); it was postponed the following month.
[149] *House of Assembly Debates* vol 24 col 11949–50 (24 August 1983).
[150] The Referendums Act No 108 of 1983.
[151] The Electoral Act No 45 of 1979.
[152] Section 2 of Act 108 of 1983.
[153] Section 4.
[154] Section 1(vi).
[155] GN R2053 (16 September 1983) as amended by GN R2341 (19 October 1983) and GN R2416 (27 October 1983).
[156] The percentage poll was 76,02% and there were 10 669 spoilt papers. See GN 874 of 1983 (11 November 1983).
[157] The result also elicited a favourable response from the United States government.
[158] That is National Party supporters, and New Republic Party supporters and big business, respectively.
[159] The Progressive Federal Party depicted it as an extension of the status quo, and the Conservative Party as a first move away from the status quo to majority black rule.
[160] *House of Assembly Debates* vol 25 col 12966 (1 September 1983).

9 Conclusion

1. THE 1983 CONSTITUTION AND CONSOCIATIONALISM

The government's constitution in its final form conforms to its antecedent models in the extent to which it provides a conducive framework for consociational government among whites, coloureds and Indians.[1]* The institutions with consociational-type features are the national cabinet, the President's Council and the joint parliamentary committees, all of which will be multi-party and multi-racial bodies; the latter two also incorporate the proportionality principle in some degree. Other aspects as well display an affinity with consociational precepts. The ordinary procedure for general affairs legislation requires concurrent majorities in the three houses and involves a temporary suspensive veto power for each. The conflict law-making procedure entails the use of a body external to the disputants to resolve deadlocks. The ordinarily entrenched and specially entrenched provisions involve a permanent legislative veto for each house, and minority groups within each house, respectively. The own affairs concept and separate legislative, executive and administrative authorities provide an institutional basis for white, coloured and Indian autonomy on certain matters. Although the government repudiated the system of consociational democracy its preferred principles of joint responsibility on general affairs and self-determination on own affairs imply the routine utilisation of these institutions and procedures. It was indicated, moreover, that the institutional innovations would be complemented by significant changes in political style, and that in particular the accustomed forms of adversarial politics would be replaced in the new system with 'consultation, negotiation, consensus and co-operation'.[2]

Within its flexible structure, however, the constitution embodies another set of institutions which are predominantly counter-consociational in character. These include the plurality electoral systems and unit rule in the electoral college; the majoritarian decision-making processes in the electoral college, three houses and President's Council; the single-party ministers' councils; the political supremacy of a single office-holder, the State President; the high degree of centralisation; the way in which proportionality is applied; the flexibility of executive and administrative arrangements; and the State President's discretion in the own affairs/general affairs domain. Furthermore, the external body utilised in the conflict and expeditious law-making procedures is not an independent non-partisan arbiter but an instrument of the dominant political group. These factors entail that from a legal-institutional point of view the national cabinet need not constitute a broad coalition of leaders or operate on a consensual basis; that the will of one or two legislative houses and a significant proportion of the combined electorate could be contravened; that there are no secured own affairs and that each group is unable to identify its own affairs; that there

216

can be a flexible delegation and re-delegation of functions; and that minority parties might be denied a significant brokerage role. Whatever the system's assumptions it does not preclude the dominant group from resorting to the counter-consociational institutions at any stage and thereby negating the prescribed norms of consensual government on general affairs and self-government on own affairs. In reality the system leaves intact the feature of the Westminster system which the literature consistently deprecates for divided plural societies[3]—one site of political competition determines ultimate control over the whole system. In practical terms success in the plurality-based elections for the House of Assembly will enable the relevant white group to control all those institutions which together ensure political dominance—the Assembly, white ministers' council, electoral college, state presidency, national cabinet, joint parliamentary committees and President's Council. This dominance entails further control and influence in vast areas of the administrative state.

In the light of South Africa's constitutional and political history the most salient feature of the 1983 constitution from a consociational point of view is that neither power-sharing on general affairs nor segmental autonomy on own affairs is an institutional necessity. While consociationalism is ultimately a pattern of élite behaviour and cannot be reduced to institutional terms alone, in the South African context a favourable constitutional framework would be a necessary, albeit not sufficient, condition for consociational government. In the government's predication the essential factors of conciliation and compromise will emerge through organic developments and be sustained by constitutional convention and political custom. Yet the new system is not founded on the accommodation of legitimacy, mutual commitment to its underlying principles, and inter-élite confidence which are necessary for their informal emergence. The prevalence of counter-consociational features assumes the continual breakdown of the normative procedures and the constitution conveniently permits the unilateral regulation of conflict. Despite the credibility needs of the system there will be temptations for the government to follow this line of lesser resistance in all matters which it identifies as politically or strategically important. To the extent that there is consensual and autonomous rule it is likely to be a concessionary and not a negotiational outcome, as was the new constitution itself.

If its basic assumptions are also taken into account the 1983 constitution embodies the additional consociational shortcomings referred to above.[4] The omission of blacks precludes the political inclusiveness which consociationalism presupposes to stabilise the system; in the following section black constitutional arrangements are re-integrated into the picture. The system also distorts the nature of political formation and interest-articulation. The most immediate restraints are the imposed segmental definitions and the prohibition on inter-segmental political activity.[5] By precluding free political association and self-defined interest groups these aspects compel political participation through predetermined channels in a way antithetical to the consociational pattern. Also of relevance, however, are the statutory limitations on freedoms of the person, movement, assembly and political

218 *South Africa and the Consociational Option*

speech and expression,[6] as well as other authoritarian features which the system retains.[7] These factors inhibit the emergence of the representative and effective leadership élites on which consociationalism is intimately dependent. Finally, although consociationalism has negative implications for democratic government the 1983 constitution has the peculiar effect of restricting political options on the disputed matters which it entrenches— inter alia, separate political institutions, educational facilities and residential areas.[8] These in turn imply the retention of a range of contentious accessory statutes.[9] In these areas the constitution's rigidity entails that the courts will assume a new role in safeguarding apartheid principles and limiting demo-cratic choices. Constitutional reform cannot be equated with democratisation.

In overall terms the 1983 constitution incorporates several symbolic forms of power-sharing but retains the facilities for unilateral conflict-regulation which epitomised its predecessor.[10]

2. THE RESIDUAL CONSTITUTION

The new constitution for whites, coloureds and Indians continues to exclude blacks from the country's central political institutions. Although the new authorities will have extensive direct and indirect jurisdiction over them, the only reference to blacks is in an omnibus provision transposed from the Act's predecessor which vests the administration of black affairs in the State President.[11] The many specific statutes which confer discretionary executive powers in this field are also preserved.[12] The future governance of blacks specifically will be a general affairs matter managed by whites, coloureds and Indians jointly, subject to the permitted exceptions. Of the existing state agencies the departments of Co-operation and Development, and Education and Training, will be exclusively concerned with black affairs, including constitutional development. But blacks will be affected generally by developments on most general affairs matters, and could be incidentally affected in respect of own affairs matters. While they will not participate in the new system it will impose upon them no less than the old.

The new constitution also leaves intact that part of the all-inclusive constitutional system designed for a majority of the country's inhabitants.[13] The residual constitution comprises all the black authorities within and outside the national states and implies 'first tier' political rights for all blacks in the homelands and 'third tier' rights for some in the common area. In terms of the political participation of different groups the 1983 changes accentuate the dichotomy between the black and non-black constitutional systems, which was emphasised by the President's Council[14] and is an outgrowth of the government's parallel development and separate develop-ment policies. The distinction operates extensively at the legal-institutional level, partially at the territorial and residential levels, and exiguously at the economic level.

At the legal-institutional level the factor of citizenship exemplifies the extent to which each part of the composite arrangement presupposes and complements the other. The new constitution ostensibly resolves the citizenship status of coloureds and Indians by according them nominally equal political rights with whites and extending the promise of other citizenship rights on an equal, albeit frequently separate, basis.[15] Whatever the extent and practical significance of these rights, it is the first time that full citizenship for coloureds and Indians has been constitutionally implied. The homelands programme, as indicated above,[16] has involved the involuntary loss of South African nationality by different categories of blacks and in the official projections will result in the eventual classification of all blacks as statutory aliens.[17] A loss of nationality, in terms of conventional legal standards,[18] implies the forfeiture by those affected of a claim to the political and other rights of citizenship in the Republic. The national/alien distinction will in time supersede that between non-blacks and blacks at certain levels of South Africa's politics. Concepts of nationality and citizenship could accordingly be invoked to justify both parts of the constitutional whole. The 1983 constitution signifies full citizenship rights for all South African nationals, who in time will be exclusively non-black, while the homeland institutions provide separate citizenship rights for the different statutory categories of black nationals.[19] The rigid demarcation between the two systems can be legitimised in terms of the international law concept of nationality instead of race. Despite the black resistance to the homelands system, concepts of nationality and citizenship are therefore fundamental to the government's overall constitutional strategy. They are directly relevant to the consistent standpoint that its policy does not entail the future incorporation of blacks into the new system, and they indicate the unlikelihood of an official deviation from the homelands policy, such as the establishment of the special status regions recommended by various commissions[20] or the creation of alternative political structures for blacks. The formal resolution of the citizenship issue for coloureds and Indians could even expedite the process of black denationalisation so that the 1983 constitution can be depicted as providing a universal franchise for South African nationals.[21] The system can be seen as a modern reformulation of the franchise compromise of 1910, and as an entrenchment of white/black political apartheid.

While the 1983 constitution and homelands programme reinforce political separation between blacks and non-blacks they do not affect their geographical interspersement or economic interdependence.[22] Despite the government's programmes of resettlement and industrial decentralisation all blacks, regardless of nationality or residence, will remain subject to the ultimate supremacy and control of the dominant political institutions. For blacks the South African constitution has always been undemocratic and authoritarian[23] and the 1983 changes will not affect its essential nature. Black residents of the legally independent states are not nominally subject to the new republican authorities while beyond their jurisdiction, post-partition relationships between the states and Pretoria being conducted between the governments on an 'international' basis. A more formalised relationship between the various authorities was envisaged in the 'constellation of states' concept introduced in the late 1970s.[24] It was indicated that the constellation would be arranged through a series of bilateral and multilateral treaties and would comprise functionally specialised bodies with delegated powers. They would be concerned with forms of economic co-operation and rationalisation and would operate through the member

governments.[25] It has been suggested[26] that such relationships would resemble the consociational pattern in that they would involve bargaining
from independent power bases, would be conducted confidentially among
élites on a consensual basis, and would have attributes of summit
diplomacy.[27] The notion that the homelands provide segmental autonomy
for their nationals could also be extrapolated from this conception. The
segmental autonomy deduction, however, would be basically unsound.[28]
Furthermore in economic terms alone the massive regional inequalities and
overwhelming dominance of the core republic would preclude any notion of
bargaining parity among the parties.[29] While some consociational elements
might be in evidence, the inevitable client-dependency of the national states
undermines the consociational analogy at this level.

The significance of the domestic political rights of the homeland electorates will ultimately be commensurate with the states' economic dependence, aside from factors of internal constitutional structure and civil
liberties. The 'statutory alien' categorisation also affords the Republic additional mechanisms of control or potential control over individuals abandon-
ing a national state for the economic centre.[30] Despite the evidence of some
quasi-consociational features in the inclusive constitutional system, the 1983
innovations do not imply a lessening of authoritarian rule for blacks.
Neither its institutional arrangements nor the international law concepts of
independence and nationality for blacks will lessen the ultimate dominance
of the central government over the historic areas of South Africa and its
inhabitants.

3. CONSOCIATIONALISM VERSUS CONTROL

The government's constitutional strategies of recent years have been
directed both at ameliorating the legitimacy problems of the state and at
stabilising a potentially volatile socio-political situation. They have involved
the use of some consociational structures for the co-optation of various
strata of élites as subordinate partners of the dominant group, but stability
has also been maintained through a high level of coercion. Lustik has
developed a theory of 'control', which incorporates elements of both consociationalism and coercion, to explain the persistence over time of deeply
segmented socio-political systems.[31] Control theory shares with consociationalism the pluralist notion of deep and continuing divisions in society
and intense rivalry between the segments for political and economic resources. But whereas consociationalism involves factors of compromise and
consensus among leadership élites and a coalescent political process, control involves the superiority of one segment which is used to constrain the
political activities and opportunities of others by coercive and non-coercive
means. The dominant group can enforce stability by sustaining this manipulation over time.

Concepts of control and domination are not new in explaining why plural
societies continue to function.[32] However, the conceptual distinctions which
Lustik draws between consociationalism and control are analytically useful
for the theme of this work. The distinctions relate to the following matters:

(i) *The criterion that effectively governs the authoritative allocation of resources*. In the consociational system this is 'the common denominator of the interests of the segments as perceived and articulated by their respective élites', while in the control system it is 'the interest of the dominant segment as perceived and articulated by *its* élite'.

(ii) *The linkages between the segments*. In the consociational system this takes the form of political or material exchanges, that is 'negotiations, bargains, trades and compromises', whereas in the control system the linkage is penetrative in character and the dominant group extracts the property, political support and labour it requires from the other groups, and delivers what it sees fit.

(iii) *The significance of bargaining*. In the consociational system bargaining is 'a fact of political life' and a sign that the system is operating successfully, whereas in the control system genuine bargaining would signal 'the breakdown of control as the means by which the political stability of the system is being maintained'.

(iv) *The role of the official regime* (public service, courts, educational system, police, armed forces). In the consociational system it must 'translate the compromises reached between sub-unit elites . . . into appropriate legislation and effective administrative procedure and enforce these rules without discriminating', whereas in the control system the official regime is the 'legal and administrative instrument of the dominant group'.

(v) *The type of normative justification for the continuation of the political order espoused by the regime's officials*. In the consociational society the system is likely to be legitimised in terms of the common welfare of all groups and 'warnings of the chaotic consequences . . . of consociational breakdown', whereas the control system is likely to be justified in terms of the interests of the dominant group. However, the regime's officials in a control system may have a certain public justification for the continuation of the system, but have a different private or unarticulated justification.

(vi) *The character of the central strategic problem that faces leadership élites*. In the consociational system all élites must effect compromises without jeopardising the integrity of the whole system, and they must maintain sufficient segmental cohesion and discipline to be able to enforce such decisions. But in the control system the different sets of élites have different strategic problems: élites of the dominant group must 'devise cost-effective techniques for manipulating subordinate groups', while those of the subordinate groups must 'cope as satisfactorily as possible with the consequences of subordination' and 'evaluate opportunities for bargaining or resistance'.

(vii) *The appropriate visual metaphor*. For consociationalism this is 'a delicately but surely balanced scale' and for a control system is 'a puppeteer manipulating his stringed puppet'.

Recent constitutional developments in South Africa embody elements of both consociationalism and control. However, Lustik's seven categories highlight the extent to which there is a preponderance of control over consociational features in the inclusive political system.[33] In areas such as industrial relations the control mechanisms are not uniformly cohesive and they do not exclude increasing elements of free-market regulation, to which several constitutional reports and the 1983 constitution's preamble allude, but they nevertheless predominate. As Lustik observes, with reference to Israel,[34] distinctions can often be made within one society between the kinds of relationships affecting different sets of groups. Thus while relationships among whites, coloureds and Indians might develop in the consociational direction, the composite non-black group could maintain a stringent control relationship with blacks. There might be a further distinction between the state's quasi-consociational relationship with the national states and its overtly control relationship with their nationals resident in the Republic. Whatever the fluctuations might be in these relationships the state would retain a range of coercive measures to secure stability.

In view of the limited application of consociational measures in the South Africa context it is appropriate to note Lustik's concluding observation that control might serve as a normative model:

> 'In deeply divided societies where consociational techniques have not been, or cannot be, successfully employed, control may represent a model for the organization of intergroup relations that is substantially preferable to other conceivable solutions: civil war, extermination, or deportation.'

There have been suggestions that the government, in the absence of means acceptable to it for resolving the conflict in South African society, has planned for its indefinite control and containment. Since control at the level of constitutional politics is highly conspicuous it would not be accepted by political leaders in liberal or radical opposition to the dominant group and could not readily resolve problems of legitimacy. Whether the state could induce a significant proportion of the population to accept permanent control as an inevitable condition of society is also doubtful, but is a more complex issue.[35] It is also unlikely that a system of control could be self-sustaining and not resort to increasing coercion.

4. CONSOCIATIONAL PROSPECTS

Institutional continuity is a dominant theme of this work. The 1983 constitution has developed out of a long historical process and despite its structural, procedural and normative innovations, is essentially a fulfilment of the government's evolving policy for whites, coloureds and Indians. In terms of its internal logic and the government's proclaimed intentions it does not constitute a basis for future changes but a culmination of past changes. It also complements the government's established policy for blacks and presupposes the orthodox pursuit thereof in the future. During a period of government-controlled constitutional development changes can only be anticipated within the parameters of these two systems and their citizenship arrangements.

Despite its rigidity minor amendments to the 1983 constitution are inevitable in its early phases, but its inherent flexibility obviates the need for extensive changes. The dominant group would also not countenance amendments which disturb the system's intricate balance of power. As far as blacks are concerned immediate developments can be anticipated in respect of the local authority system described above.[36] In so far as they are situated outside the national states these bodies contravene the principles of orthodox separate development, but the government has indicated that they will be institutionally linked to the homeland authorities and do not signify direct or indirect black participation in the central representative institutions. For the national states tentative developments are likely in the direction of the proclaimed policies of a constellation of states and regionalism,[37] neither of which contravenes the political assumptions of separate development despite their respective confederal and federal implications. The government's ability to control the political agenda entails that all such developments will be based on the established concepts of race and ethnicity.

The constraints within which future developments will occur imply that consociational democracy is a remote option for South Africa. The high point for consociationalism was the first report of the President's Council, and then it served only as a prescriptive model for part of the political system. That the government has indulged in consociational engineering on a limited and selective basis is evidence of its incompatibility with the government's constitutional policies and political strategies. Even within the limited scope of the 1983 constitution the government was unable to accept the institutional implications of the system. Despite consociationalism's potential significance as a legitimising theory instead of presidentialism or the Westminster system, it was ultimately rejected along with the majoritarian-based systems, thereby indicating the limited potential for constitutional reform. Authentic consociationalism would involve the termination of the government's constitutional control and political domination.

As a normative model consociationalism also has only a limited relevance. South Africa, as has been shown,[38] lacks many of the favourable conditions for consociational democracy, and the system is least suited for situations of ethnic diversity and a horizontal ordering of groups. Even the most sanguine assessments of its prospects are cautiously framed and are sceptical about a transition from sham to genuine consociation.[39] The system has, however, been mooted as a political crisis model. This assumes an exacerbation of the state's legitimation problems and an extensive destabilisation of the socio-political system beyond the capabilities of its control and coercive resources. Where the perceived bargaining strengths of the respective parties were approximately equal, élite prudence might induce the 'self-denying hypothesis'. Such a development would have similar implications to the Lancaster House conference[40] and might involve the utilisation of various consociational procedures and mechanisms.

In the light of the state's immense strategic resources, however, this type of scenario involves speculation well beyond the short term. In the immediate constitutional future the emphasis is likely to be on the implementation of the 1983 constitution and the black local authorities system, and the furtherance of the homelands policy. As with the constitutional developments of the past each of these will provide new political space and a range of strategic options for subordinate groups, and to a limited but increasing extent, judicial strategic options as well.[41] The extent to which these options are exploited, whether positively or negatively, will be one of the variables determining the course of subsequent constitutional developments and the future of the apartheid state.

NOTES AND REFERENCES

[1] See above, 156–7 and 184–6.
[2] See above, 193.
[3] See above, 34–5.
[4] See above, 156–8.
[5] Cf Degenaar's pluralist model, above 33–4.
[6] See C J R Dugard *Human Rights and the South African Legal Order* (1978) 146ff; M Wiechers *Staatsreg* (3 ed, 1981) 152f. Since the consolidation of various statutes the most important restrictions are found in the Internal Security Act No 74 of 1982. While restrictions on freedom of movement affect mainly blacks, Indians have restricted access to the Orange Free State and may not reside in that province nor in certain magisterial districts of Natal. See above 104n149.
[7] As Dean ('The government's constitutional proposals 1982' in W H B Dean & D van Zyl Smit *Constitutional Change in South Africa* (1983) 90 at 91) observes, authoritarianism has hitherto hardly touched the central organs of government but might do so with the incorporation of coloureds and Indians.
[8] The Group Areas Act No 36 of 1966 is one of the most contentious statutes which it presupposes. Cf the reasons for the CPRC's failure above, 85.
[9] eg the Population Registration Act No 30 of 1950 and the Prohibition of Mixed Marriages Act No 55 of 1945.
[10] See above, 66.
[11] Section 93; see s 111 of Act No 32 of 1961. The reference to 'Asiatics' has necessarily been deleted and there are other minor modifications.
[12] In terms of s 87—e g the Black Administration Act No 38 of 1927, Black (Urban Areas) Consolidation Act No 25 of 1945 and Black Affairs Administration Act No 45 of 1971.
[13] See above, 86–94.
[14] See above, 175.
[15] Shortly after the referendum the government indicated that coloureds and Indians could shortly be eligible for military conscription.
[16] At 93–4.
[17] Ibid, and 107n240.
[18] This is not, however, to suggest that the denationalisation process is valid in international law. See above, 102nn237 and 238.
[19] At present the distinction operates only in respect of the parliamentary franchise, and not at the local level where statutory aliens have limited political rights. See further L J Boulle 'The likely direction of constitutional change in South Africa over the next five years' in Dean & Smit op cit 57 at 71ff.
[20] e g the Quail, Lombard and Buthelezi commissions. See above, 134–9.
[21] In 1982 the government set in motion a scheme to transfer the KaNgwane homeland and parts of KwaZulu to Swaziland, thereby depriving their residents of South African nationality. The action was invalidated by the courts for non-compliance with the organic statute's procedural requirements. *Government of KwaZulu v Government of the Republic of South Africa* 1982 (4) SA 387 (N); *Government of the Republic of South Africa v Government of KwaZulu* 1983 (1) SA 164 (A).
[22] In this respect it involves a final refutation of the Tomlinson Commission vision. See above, 127–9.
[23] See Dean op cit 90 at 91.
[24] The concept was promoted at the 'Carlton conference' between the government and business leaders. See W H Thomas 'A Southern African "Constellation of States": Challenge or Myth?' 1980 *South Africa International* 113–28; D Geldenhuys *The Constellation of States* (1980). The 'inner constellation' comprising the Republic and national states has been referred to as a species of confederalism (*House of Assembly Debates* vol 1 col 53, vol 9 col 4933–44 (3 August and 28 September 1981, respectively)). The 'grand constellation' was to have included other countries in the subcontinent; its prospects were jeopardised by the creation in 1980 of the Southern African Development Co-ordinating Conference, comprising nine states in the subcontinent, with the aim of lessening economic dependence on South Africa.
[25] At a prominent meeting on 11 November 1982 between the Republic and Bophuthatswana, Ciskei, Transkei and Venda plans for a development bank were drafted.
[26] N M Stultz *Transkei's Half Loaf—Race Separatism in South Africa* (1980) 150.
[27] On the similarities between consociationalism and international politics see A Lijphart *The Politics of Accommodation* (2 ed, 1975) 104, 112–15, and 131–4.
[28] See above, 97–8.

²⁹ See L Schlemmer 'Social Implications of Constitutional Alternatives in South Africa' in J A Benyon (ed) *Constitutional Change in South Africa* (1978) 258 at 270.

³⁰ Boulle op cit 73f and above, 93. The Orderly Movement and Settlement of Black Persons Bill, B 113–82, envisaged only black nationals being allowed to apply for permanent urban residence.

³¹ I Lustik 'Stability in Deeply Divided Societies: Consociationalism versus Control' 1979 *World Politics* 325–44.

³² See M G Smith's concept of 'differential incorporation' (above, 30); A Rabushka & K Shepsle (*Politics in Plural Societies* (1972) 90) refer to the 'dominant majority configuration'. The mechanisms of control also show an affinity with class theory.

³³ See R de Kadt *Democracy and Development—The South African Challenge* (University of Natal, 1981) 6–7:

'. . . the government is not prepared to allow oppositional groups—especially those concerned with attempts to articulate and mobilize black interests—to grow. This means that whatever form of concessionary politics they are likely to engage in will *tend* to be of a manipulative and co-optive sort rather than a kind that is premised on negotiation. The point about a "politics of negotiation" is that it requires the growth of organisations and movements whose interests are in conflict with those of the dominant group and with which the dominant group can bargain over the contents of the latter's rights claims. In other words, the "politics of negotiation" implies a "politics of autonomy" in terms of which interest and pressure groups can emerge free from government tutelage. There seems to be little evidence that the government is making much provision for the emergence of such groups. If anything, it seems as though the strategy for which they are opting is one that involves a substantial amount of control over all political activity—whether on the labour or on any other front. This process of *granting* concessions on its own terms rather than establishing the basis for *negotiating* change seems also to be inherent in the present constitutional reconstruction.'

See also H Adam & H Giliomee *The Rise and Crisis of Afrikaner Power* (1979) 61–82.

³⁴ Consociational techniques are used to stabilise intra-Jewish political relations, but Jewish-Arab relations are conducted on a control basis. Cf above, 54–55).

³⁵ Cf Gramsci's notion of 'hegemony'—*Selections from the Prison Notebooks of Antonio Gramsci* (G Hoare & F Smith (eds) 1971) 12–13.

³⁶ See above 87–9. The latest indications are that they will surpass conventional 'third tier' status. *House of Assembly Debates* vol 13 col 13524 (8 September 1983).

³⁷ Like the constellation, regionalism envisages a rationalisation of economic relationships without disturbing constitutional arrangements, but at various subnational levels. The policy was proclaimed in mid-1980, partially in response to consolidation problems, but it is also a variation on the 'border industry' system. The system envisages eight developmental regions in the country, and the first regional economic growth point was proclaimed in 1980, but there has been little publicity since then.

³⁸ Above, 64–6.

³⁹ See T Hanf, H Weiland & G Vierdag *South Africa—The Prospects of Peaceful Change* (1981) 381–412, and above 65–6.

⁴⁰ See above, 122.

⁴¹ On this theme see Boulle op cit 80–3.

Bibliography of Principal Works

Adam, H & Giliomee, H *The Rise and Crisis of Afrikaner Power* (David Philip: Cape Town, 1979).

Aunger, E *In Search of Political Stability: A Comparative Study of New Brunswick and Northern Ireland* (McGill-Queens UP: Montreal, 1981).

Bagehot, W *The English Constitution* (World's Classics edition, 1974).

Benyon, J A (ed) *Constitutional Change in South Africa* (Natal UP: Pietermaritzburg, 1978).

Berger, R *Government by Judiciary—The Transformation of the Fourteenth Amendment* (Harvard UP: Cambridge, 1977).

Birch, A H *The British System of Government* 4 ed (Allen and Unwin: London, 1980).

Boulle, L J & Baxter, L G (eds) *Natal and KwaZulu—Constitutional and Political Options* (Juta's: Cape Town, 1981).

Butler, D (ed) *Coalitions in British Politics* (St Martin's Press: London, 1978).

Butler, J, Rotberg, R & Adams, J *The Black Homelands of South Africa: The Political and Economic Development of Bophuthatswana and KwaZulu* (University of California Press: Berkeley, 1977).

Carter, G & Herz, J *Government and Politics in the Twentieth Century* 3 ed (1973).

Carter, G, Karis, T & Stultz, N *South Africa's Transkei—The Politics of Domestic Colonialism* (Heinemann: London, 1967).

Dahl, R A *A Preface To Democratic Theory* (University of Chicago Press: Chicago, 1956).

—— (ed) *Political Oppositions in Western Democracies* (Yale UP: New Haven, 1966).

—— *Polyarchy: Participation and Opposition* (Yale UP: New Haven, 1971).

Dean, W H B & Van Zyl Smit, D *Constitutional Change in South Africa—The Next Five Years* (Juta's: Cape Town, 1983).

De Crespigny A & Schrire R (eds) *The Government and Politics of South Africa* (Juta's: Cape Town, 1978).

De Smith, S A *The New Commonwealth and its Constitutions* (Stevens: London, 1964).

De Smith, S A *Constitutional and Administrative Law* 4 ed (Penguin Books, 1981).

Dicey, A V *An Introduction to the Study of the Law of the Constitution* 10 ed (Macmillan: London, 1959).

De Tocqueville, A *Democracy in America* (World Classics ed, 1946).

Duchacek, I *Comparative Federalism—The Territorial Dimension of Politics* (Holt, Rinehart and Winston: New York, 1970).

—— *Rights and Liberties in the World Today—Constitutional Promise and Reality* (ABC-Clio: Santa Barbara, 1973).

Dugard, C J R *Human Rights and the South African Legal Order* (Princeton UP: New Jersey, 1978).

Ehrlich, S & Wootton, G *Three Faces of Pluralism* (Saxon House, 1980).

Finer, S E *Comparative Government* (Penguin, 1970).

Friedrich, C J *Limited Government: A Comparison* (Prentice-Hall: Englewood Cliffs, 1974).

—— *Constitutional Government and Democracy* 4 ed (Blaisdell: Waltham, 1968).

—— *Trends of Federalism in Theory and Practice* (Praeger: New York, 1968).

Funston, R *Constitutional Counter-Revolution? The Warren Court and the Burger Court—Judicial Policy Making in Modern America* (Schenkman: Cambridge, 1977).

Hahlo, H & Kahn, E *The Union of South Africa: The Development of its Laws and Constitutions* (Stevens/Juta's: London, 1960).

Hammond-Tooke, W D *Command or Consensus—The Development of Transkeian Local Government* (D Philip: Cape Town, 1975).

Hand, G, Georgel, J & Sasse, C *European Electoral Systems Handbook* (Butterworth: London, 1979).

Hanf, T, Weiland, H & Vierdag, G *South Africa—The Prospects of Peaceful Change* (Indiana UP: Bloomington, 1981).

Hughes, C *The Federal Constitution of Switzerland* (Clarendon: Oxford, 1954).

Jacobs, S C (ed) *'n Nuwe Grondwetlike Bedeling vir Suid-Afrika* (Butterworth: Durban, 1981).

Johnson, N *In Search of the Constitution—Reflections on State and Society in Britain* (Pergamon: Oxford, 1977).

Kariel, H S *The Decline of American Pluralism* (Stanford UP: Stanford, 1961).

Kuper, L & Smith, M (eds) *Pluralism in Africa* (University of California Press: Berkeley, 1969).

Lakeman, D *How Democracies Vote—A Study of Majority and Proportional Electoral Systems* 3 ed (Faber: London, 1970).

Laurence, P *The Transkei—South Africa's Politics of Partition* (Ravan Press: Johannesburg, 1976).

Lees, J & Shaw M (eds) *Committees in Legislatures—A Comparative Analysis* (Duke, 1979).

Leftwich, A (ed) *South Africa: Economic Growth and Political Change* (St Martin's Press: New York, 1974).

Lever, H *South African Society* (Jonathan Ball: Johannesburg, 1978).

Lewis, W A *Politics in Africa* (Allen and Unwin: London, 1965).

Lijphart, A *Democracy in Plural Societies—A Comparative Exploration* (Yale UP: New Haven, 1977).

——— *The Politics of Accommodation* 2 ed (University of California Press: Berkeley, 1975).

Lipset, S M *Political Man—The Social Bases of Politics* (Doubleday: Garden City, NY, 1960).

MacPherson, C B *The Life and Times of Liberal Democracy* (Oxford UP, 1972).

——— *The Real World of Democracy* (Oxford UP, 1966).

MacRae, K (ed) *Consociational Democracy: Political Accommodation in Segmented Societies* (McClelland and Stewart: Toronto, 1974).

MacWhinney, E *Federal Constitution—making for a Multi-National World* (A W Sijthoff: Leyden, 1966).

Mathews, A S *Law, Order and Liberty* (Juta's: Cape Town, 1971).

May, H *The South African Constitution* (Juta's: Cape Town, 1955).

Nicholls, D *Three Varieties of Pluralism* (St Martin's Press: New York, 1974).

Nordlinger, E *Conflict Regulation in Divided Societies* (Harvard University: Cambridge, 1972).

Nwabueze, B O *Constitutionalism in the Emergent States* (C Hurst: London, 1973).

Rabushka, A & Shepsle, K *Politics in Plural Societies* (Merrill: Columbus, 1972).

Riker, W *The Theory of Political Coalitions* (Yale University Press: New Haven, 1962).

Rotberg, R & Barratt, J (eds) *Conflict and Compromise in South Africa* (Lexington Books: Mass, 1980).

Saul, J & Gelb, S *The Crisis in South Africa—Class Defense, Class Revolution* (Monthly Review Press: New York, 1981).

Sawer, G *Modern Federalism* 2 ed (1976).

Schubert, G *Judicial Policy Making—The Political Role of the Courts* rev ed (Scott & Foreman: Glenview, 1974).

Sedgemore, B *The Secret Constitution* (Hodder and Stoughton: London, 1980).

Slabbert, F van Zyl & Opland, J *South Africa—Dilemmas of Evolutionary Change* (ISER, Rhodes University: Grahamstown, 1980).

Slabbert, F van Zyl & Welsh, D *South Africa's Options—Strategies for Sharing Power* (David Philip: Cape Town, 1979).

Sprocas Report *South Africa's Political Alternatives* (1973).

Steiner, J *Amicable Agreement versus Majority Rule: Conflict Resolution in Switzerland* (University of North Carolina Press: Chapel Hill, 1974).

Strong, C F *Modern Political Constitutions* 8 ed (Sedgwick and Jackson: London, 1972).

Stultz, N *Transkei's Half Loaf—Race Separatism in South Africa* (Yale UP/David Philip: New Haven, 1980).

Theberge, L J (ed) *The Judiciary in a Democratic Society* (Lexington Books: Mass, 1979).

Thompson, L *The Unification of South Africa* (Clarendon Press: Oxford, 1960).

Thompson, L & Butler, J (eds) *Change in Contemporary South Africa* (University of California Press: Berkeley, 1975).

Tribe, L H *American Constitutional Law* (Foundation Press: Mineola NY, 1978).

Van den Berghe, P *South Africa—A Study in Conflict* (Wesleyan UP: Connecticut, 1965).

Vile, M C *Constitutionalism and the Separation of Powers* (Oxford UP, 1967).

Wade, E C S & Phillips, G *Constitutional and Administrative Law* 9 ed (Longman: London, 1977).

Wheare, K C *Federal Government* 4 ed (Oxford UP: New York, 1964).

—— *Modern Constitutions* 2 ed (Oxford UP, 1966).

Wiechers, M *Staatsreg* 3 ed (Butterworth: Durban, 1981).

Worrall, D (ed) *South Africa: Government and Politics* 2 ed (Van Schaik: Pretoria, 1975).

Appendix

REPUBLIC OF SOUTH AFRICA CONSTITUTION ACT, 1983

Act No. 110, 1983

ACT

To introduce a new constitution for the Republic of South Africa and to provide for matters incidental thereto.

(English text signed by the State President.)
(Assented to 22 September 1983.)

IN HUMBLE SUBMISSION to Almighty God, Who controls the destinies of peoples and nations,
Who gathered our forebears together from many lands and gave them this their own,
Who has guided them from generation to generation,
Who has wondrously delivered them from the dangers that beset them,

WE DECLARE that we

ARE CONSCIOUS of our responsibility towards God and man;

ARE CONVINCED of the necessity of standing united and of pursuing the following national goals:

To uphold Christian values and civilized norms, with recognition and protection of freedom of faith and worship,

To safeguard the integrity and freedom of our country,

To uphold the independence of the judiciary and the equality of all under the law,

To secure the maintenance of law and order,

To further the contentment and the spiritual and material welfare of all,

To respect and to protect the human dignity, life, liberty and property of all in our midst,

To respect, to further and to protect the self-determination of population groups and peoples,

To further private initiative and effective competition;

ARE PREPARED TO ACCEPT our duty to seek world peace in association with all peace-loving peoples and nations; and

ARE DESIROUS OF GIVING THE REPUBLIC OF SOUTH AFRICA A CONSTITUTION which provides for elected and responsible forms of government and which is best suited to the traditions, history and circumstances of our land:

BE IT THEREFORE ENACTED by the State President and the House of Assembly of the Republic of South Africa, as follows:

PART I

THE REPUBLIC

Continued existence of Republic of South Africa

1. The Republic of South Africa, consisting of the provinces of the Cape of Good Hope, Natal, the Transvaal and the Orange Free State, shall continue to exist as a republic under that name.

Sovereignty and guidance of Almighty God acknowledged

2. The people of the Republic of South Africa acknowledge the sovereignty and guidance of Almighty God.

231

PART II
NATIONAL FLAG AND ANTHEM

National Flag

3. There shall be a National Flag of the Republic of which the design shall be as set out in section 4.

Design of National Flag

4. (1) The National Flag of the Republic shall be a flag consisting of three horizontal stripes of equal width from top to bottom orange, white and blue on which there shall appear—

(a) in the centre of the white stripe, the flag of the republic of "De Oranjevrijstaat" hanging vertically and spread in full; and

(b) on opposite sides and adjoining the flag referred to in paragraph *(a)*—
　　(i) the Union Jack, as it existed in 1927, horizontally spread in full towards the pole; and
　　(ii) the Vierkleur of "De Zuid-Afrikaansche Republiek" horizontally spread in full away from the pole.

(2) The flags referred to in paragraphs *(a)* and *(b)* of subsection (1) shall all be of the same size and of a shape proportionally the same as that of the National Flag, the width of each of such flags shall be equal to one-third of the width of the white stripe on the National Flag, and the flags referred to in paragraph *(b)* of subsection (1) shall be equidistant from the margins of the said white stripe.

National Anthem

5. The National Anthem of the Republic shall be "The Call of South Africa/Die Stem van Suid-Afrika".

PART III
THE STATE PRESIDENT

The State President and his powers

6. (1) The head of the Republic shall be the State President.

(2) The command-in-chief of the South African Defence Force is vested in the State President.

(3) The State President shall, subject to the provisions of this Act, have power—

(a) to address any House, or the Houses at a joint sitting;

(b) to confer honours;

(c) to appoint and to accredit, to receive and to recognize ambassadors, plenipotentiaries, diplomatic representatives and other diplomatic officers, consuls and consular officers;

(d) to pardon or reprieve offenders, either unconditionally or subject to such conditions as he may deem fit, and to remit any fines, penalties or forfeitures;

(e) to enter into and ratify international conventions, treaties and agreements;

(f) to proclaim or terminate martial law;

(g) to declare war and make peace;

(h) to make such appointments as he may deem fit under powers conferred upon him by any law, and to exercise such powers and perform such functions as may be conferred upon or assigned to him in terms of this Act or any other law.

(4) The State President shall in addition as head of the State have such powers and functions as were immediately before the commencement of this Act possessed by the State President by way of prerogative.

Election of State President

7. (1) (a) The State President shall be elected by the members of an electoral college present at a meeting called in accordance with the provisions of this section and presided over by the Chief Justice or a judge of appeal designated by him.

(b) An electoral college referred to in paragraph *(a)* shall be constituted whenever necessary in terms of this Act, and shall consist of—
 (i) 50 members of the House of Assembly designated by it by resolution;
 (ii) 25 members of the House of Representatives designated by it by resolution;
 (iii) 13 members of the House of Delegates designated by it by resolution,
or, in the case of a particular House, such smaller number of members thereof, if any, as may be so designated by it.

(c) A member of a House referred to in section 41(1)*(b)* or *(c)*, 42(1)*(b)* or *(c)* or 43(1)*(b)* or *(c)* may not be designated as a member of an electoral college or participate in the voting or other proceedings of the House in question in connection with a resolution contemplated in paragraph *(b)* of this subsection.

(d) A House shall designate the relevant members of a particular electoral college as often as it may deem necessary.

(e) An electoral college shall dissolve after disposing of the matters for which it is constituted in terms of this Act.

(2) The election of a State President shall be held, subject to the provisions of subsection (4), at a time and place fixed by the Chief Justice and made known by notice in the *Gazette* not less than 14 days before the election.

(3) The date so fixed shall—
(a) in the case of the first such election, be a date not more than seven days after the commencement of the first session of Parliament after the commencement of this Act;
(b) whenever a general election of members of the Houses has been held after a dissolution of Parliament, be a date not more than seven days after the commencement of the first session of Parliament after the general election;
(c) if the State President dies or for any other reason vacates his office before the expiration of his period of office and his successor in office has then not yet been elected, be a date not more than one month after the office became vacant: Provided that if the State President resigns and intimates in his resignation lodged with the Chief Justice in terms of section 9(4) that he will vacate his office on a day not less than one month after the date of the lodging of his resignation, a date earlier than the day on which the office becomes vacant, shall be so fixed.

(4) If any electoral college removes the State President from office in terms of section 9, it shall forthwith proceed to elect a State President.

(5) No person may be elected or serve as State President unless he is qualified to be nominated or elected and take his seat as a member of a House.

(6) Any person who holds a public office in respect of which he receives any remuneration or allowance out of public funds, and who is elected as State President, shall vacate such office with effect from the date on which he is elected.

Method of election

8. (1) Nominations of candidates for election as State President shall be called for at the meeting of the electoral college at which the election is to take place, by the person presiding at the meeting.

(2) Every nomination shall be submitted in the form prescribed and shall be signed by two members of the electoral college and also by the person nominated, unless he has in writing or by telegram signified his willingness to accept nomination.

(3) The names of the persons duly nominated as provided in subsection (2) shall be announced at the meeting at which the election is to take place by the person presiding at the meeting, and no debate shall be allowed at the election.

(4) If in respect of any election only one nomination has been received, the person presiding at the meeting shall declare the candidate in question to be duly elected.

(5) Where more than one candidate is nominated for election, a vote shall be taken by secret ballot, each member of the electoral college present at the meeting in question having one vote, and any candidate in whose favour a majority of all the votes cast is recorded shall be declared duly elected by the person presiding at the meeting.

(6) *(a)* If no candidate obtains a majority of all the votes so cast, the candidate who received the smallest number of votes shall be eliminated and a further ballot taken in respect of the remaining candidates, this procedure being repeated as often

as may be necessary until a candidate receives a majority of all the votes cast and is declared duly elected.

(b) Whenever two or more candidates being the lowest on the poll have received the same number of votes, the electoral college shall by separate vote, to be repeated as often as may be necessary, determine which of those candidates shall for the purposes of paragraph *(a)* be eliminated.

(7) *(a)* Whenever—

(i) only two candidates have been nominated; or

(ii) after the elimination of one or more candidates in accordance with the provisions of this section, only two candidates remain,

and there is an equality of votes between those two candidates, a further meeting shall be called in accordance with the provisions of section 7, and the provisions of this section shall apply as if such further meeting were the first meeting called for the purposes of the election in question.

(b) If at the third meeting there is again an equality of votes, the electoral college shall dissolve, an electoral college shall again be constituted and the provisions of section 7 and this section shall apply *mutatis mutandis* as if the newly constituted electoral college were the first electoral college constituted for the purposes of the election in question.

(8) *(a)* The Chief Justice shall make rules in regard to the procedure to be observed at a meeting of any electoral college constituted as provided in section 7, including rules prescribing the form in which any nomination shall be submitted and rules defining the duties of the presiding officer and of any person appointed to assist him, and prescribing the manner in which a ballot at any such meeting shall be conducted.

(b) Such rules shall be made known in such manner as the Chief Justice may consider necessary.

Tenure of office of State President

9. (1) The State President shall hold office, subject to the other provisions of this section—

(a) during the continuance of the Parliament from which the electoral college that elected him was constituted; and

(b) after the dissolution of that Parliament, whether by effluxion of time or otherwise, until a State President has, at or after the commencement of the first session of the newly constituted Parliament, been elected as provided in sections 7 and 8 and has assumed office,

but shall be eligible for re-election.

(2) The State President shall vacate his office—

(a) if in terms of section 7(5) he becomes disqualified from serving as State President; or

(b) if he is removed from office under subsection (3).

(3) *(a)* The State President shall cease to hold office on a resolution adopted by a majority of the members present at a meeting of an electoral college constituted as prescribed in section 7 and convened, as so prescribed, by the Chief Justice at the request of each of the three Houses, and declaring him to be removed from office on the ground of misconduct or inability to perform efficiently the duties of his office.

(b) In connection with a resolution contemplated in paragraph *(a)* no debate shall be allowed in the electoral college.

(c) No request in terms of paragraph *(a)* shall be made by any House, except after consideration of a report of a committee of Parliament appointed in accordance with rules and orders contemplated in section 64.

(d) A House shall not adopt a resolution that such a committee be appointed, unless there has previously been submitted to the Speaker of Parliament a petition signed by not less than half of the members of each House and requesting that such a committee be appointed.

(e) In connection with a resolution contemplated in paragraph *(d)* no debate shall be allowed in the House in question.

(4) The State President may resign by lodging his resignation in writing with the Chief Justice.

Republic of South Africa Constitution Act, 1983 235

Acting State President

10. (1) Whenever the State President is for any reason unable to perform the duties of his office, a member of the Cabinet nominated by the State President shall serve as Acting State President.

(2) Whenever—

(a) the State President is unable to nominate a member of the Cabinet in terms of subsection (1); or

(b) the member so nominated is for any reason unable to act; or

(c) the office of State President is vacant and there is no member so nominated or the member so nominated is unable to act,

a member of the Cabinet designated by the remaining members thereof shall serve as Acting State President during the incapacity of the State President or of the member nominated by him, as the case may be, or until a State President has been elected and has assumed office.

(3) *(a)* If a member of the Cabinet serves as Acting State President in terms of a designation under subsection (2) during the incapacity of the State President or of the member nominated by him, and the Speaker of Parliament is at any time of the opinion that neither the State President nor his nominee will be able to resume the duties of his office within 60 days from the date on which his incapacity set in, the Speaker shall in writing inform the Acting State President and the Chief Justice accordingly, and thereupon a member of the Cabinet shall without delay be designated as Acting State President by an electoral college *mutatis mutandis* in accordance with sections 7 and 8.

(b) When the Acting State President so designated by the electoral college assumes office, any nomination or designation made under subsection (1) or (2) shall lapse.

(c) The Acting State President so designated by the electoral college shall serve as such during the incapacity of the State President or until a State President has been elected and has assumed office, as the circumstances may require.

(4) Whenever it is in any of the circumstances mentioned above not possible to nominate or designate an Acting State President, the Speaker of Parliament shall serve as Acting State President.

Oath of office by State President and Acting State President

11. (1) The State President and any Acting State President shall when assuming office make and subscribe an oath of office in the following form before the Chief Justice or any other judge of the Supreme Court:

In the presence of Almighty God and in full realization of the high calling I assume as State President/Acting State President in the service of the Republic, I, A.B., do swear to be faithful to the Republic of South Africa and do solemnly and sincerely promise at all times to promote that which will advance and to oppose all that may harm the Republic; to obey, observe, uphold and maintain the Constitution and all other Law of the Republic; to discharge my duties with all my strength and talents to the best of my knowledge and ability and true to the dictates of my conscience; to do justice unto all; and to devote myself to the well-being of the Republic and its people.

May the Almighty God by His grace guide and sustain me in keeping this oath with honour and dignity.

So help me God.

(2) In the case of the State President the oath shall be made and subscribed by him at a formal function where the Seal of the Republic is handed over to him by the outgoing State President or Acting State President, unless he already has the Seal in his custody.

Salary of State President

12. There shall be paid to the State President out of and as a charge on the State Revenue Fund and apart from any privilege which he may enjoy, such salary and allowances as may be determined from time to time by resolution of Parliament.

Pension payable to State President and State President's widow or widower

13. (1) There shall be paid out of and as a charge on the State Revenue Fund—
(a) to any person who has at any time held the office of State President, an annual pension equal to the annual salary which was payable to him on the day upon which he vacated office;
(b) to the widow or widower of any such person, a pension at the rate of three-quarters of the rate of the pension payable to such a person.
(2) A pension in terms of subsection (1) shall be payable—
(a) in the case of the State President, with effect from the day following that upon which he vacated office;
(b) in the case of the State President's widow or widower, with effect from the day following that upon which such person became a widow or a widower.

PART IV
OWN AFFAIRS AND GENERAL AFFAIRS

Own affairs

14. (1) Matters which specially or differentially affect a population group in relation to the maintenance of its identity and the upholding and furtherance of its way of life, culture, traditions and customs, are, subject to the provisions of section 16, own affairs in relation to such population group.
(2) Matters coming within the classes of subjects described in Schedule 1 are, subject to the provisions of section 16, own affairs in relation to each population group.

General affairs

15. Matters which are not own affairs of a population group in terms of section 14 are general affairs.

Decision of questions on own or general nature of matters

16. (1) (a) Any question arising in the application of this Act as to whether any particular matters are own affairs of a population group shall be decided by the State President, who shall do so in such manner that the governmental institutions serving the interests of such population group are not by the decision enabled to affect the interests of any other population group, irrespective of whether or not it is defined as a population group in this Act.
(b) All such questions shall be general affairs.
(2) The State President may, if he deems it expedient, but subject to the provisions of section 31—
(a) express his decision on any question contemplated in subsection (1) by proclamation in the *Gazette*; or
(b) make his decision on any such question known for general information by such a proclamation, or make it known or cause it to be made known in such other manner as he may deem fit,
and shall advise the Chairman of each Ministers' Council of every such decision.
(3) When the State President assigns the administration of a law to a Minister of a department of State for own affairs of a population group under section 26 or 98 he shall do so in pursuance of a decision under this section that the law, in so far as its administration is so assigned, deals with own affairs of the population group in question.

Reference of questions to President's Council for advice, and consultation on certain matters

17. (1) The State President may refer any question which is being considered by him in terms of section 16 to the President's Council for advice.
(2) (a) Before the State President issues a certificate under section 31 in respect of a bill or an amendment or a proposed amendment thereof, he shall consult the Speaker of Parliament and the Chairmen of the respective Houses in such manner as he deems fit.

(b) Paragraph *(a)* does not apply to the issue of a certificate in respect of a bill or an amendment thereof which has been altered as a result of the consultation in terms of that paragraph.

Validity of State President's decisions on own or general nature of matters

18. (1) Any division of the Supreme Court of South Africa shall be competent to inquire into and pronounce upon the question as to whether the provisions of section 17(2) were complied with in connection with a decision of the State President contemplated in those provisions.

(2) Save as provided in subsection (1), no court of law shall be competent to inquire into or pronounce upon the validity of a decision of the State President that matters mentioned in the decision are own affairs of a population group, or are not own affairs of a population group, as the case may be.

(3) For the purposes of subsection (2), the matters dealt with in any bill which, when introduced in a House, is not endorsed with or accompanied by a certificate contemplated in section 31, shall be deemed to be matters which are not own affairs of any population group by virtue of a decision of the State President.

PART V
THE EXECUTIVE AUTHORITY

Executive authority

19. (1) The executive authority of the Republic—
(a) in regard to matters which are own affairs of any population group is vested in the State President acting on the advice of the Ministers' Council in question;
(b) in regard to general affairs is vested in the State President acting in consultation with the Ministers who are members of the Cabinet.

(2) Except in sections 20*(c)* and *(d)*, 21(2), 24, 25, 26, 27, 33, 39(3), 66 and 98(3)*(b)*, or where otherwise expressly stated or necessarily implied, any reference in this Act to the State President is a reference to the State President acting as provided in subsection (1).

The Cabinet

20. The Cabinet shall consist of—
(a) the State President, who shall preside at its meetings;
(b) the Ministers appointed to administer departments of State for general affairs;
(c) any Minister appointed to perform functions other than the administration of a department of State and designated by the State President as a member of the Cabinet; and
(d) any member of a Ministers' Council designated by the State President as a member of the Cabinet, whether for a definite or for an indefinite period or for a particular purpose.

Ministers' Councils

21. (1) A Ministers' Council shall consist of—
(a) the Ministers appointed to administer departments of State for own affairs of one and the same population group;
(b) any Minister who is a member of the population group in question and who has been appointed as a member of the Ministers' Council to perform functions other than the administration of a department of State;
(c) any Deputy Minister appointed to exercise or perform powers, functions and duties on behalf of any of the Ministers referred to in paragraph *(a)*; and
(d) any Minister of the Cabinet who is a member of the population group in question and who has been co-opted by the Ministers' Council as a member thereof, whether for a definite or for an indefinite period or for a particular purpose.

(2) The State President shall designate a Minister who is a member of a Ministers' Council and who, at the time of the designation, in the opinion of the State President has the support of the majority in the House consisting of members of the population group in question, as the Chairman of such Ministers' Council.

Seal of Republic

22. (1) There shall be a Seal of the Republic, showing the coat of arms of the Republic with the circumscription "Republic of South Africa—Republiek van Suid-Afrika".

(2) The Seal shall be in the custody of the State President and shall, save in so far as may be otherwise determined by the State President, be used on all public documents on which it was required to be used immediately before the commencement of this Act.

Confirmation of executive acts of State President

23. (1) The will and pleasure of the State President as head of the executive authority of the Republic shall be expressed in writing under his signature.

(2) Any instrument signed by the State President acting on the advice of a Ministers' Council or in consultation with the Ministers who are members of the Cabinet, shall be countersigned by a Minister who is a member of the Ministers' Council in question or, as the case may be, a member of the Cabinet.

(3) The signature of the State President on any instrument shall be confirmed as provided in section 22.

Appointment of Ministers

24. (1) The State President may appoint as many persons as he may from time to time deem necessary to administer such departments of State of the Republic as the State President may establish, or to perform such other functions as the State President may determine.

(2) Persons appointed under subsection (1) shall hold office during the State President's pleasure and shall be the Ministers of the Republic.

(3) *(a)* No Minister shall hold office for a longer period than 12 months unless he is or becomes a member of a House.

(b) A Minister of any department of State for own affairs of a population group shall—
(i) be a member of the population group in question; and
(ii) at the time of his appointment as such Minister, in the opinion of the State President have the support of the majority in the House consisting of members of that population group.

(4) A Minister shall before assuming his duties make and subscribe an oath before the Chief Justice or any other judge of the Supreme Court in the following form:
I, A.B., do hereby swear to be faithful to the Republic of South Africa and undertake before God to honour this oath; to hold my office as Minister with honour and dignity; to respect and uphold the Constitution and all other Law of the Republic; to be a true and faithful counsellor; not to divulge directly or indirectly any matters which are entrusted to me under secrecy; and to perform the duties of my office conscientiously and to the best of my ability.
So help me God.

Temporary performance of Minister's functions of office by another Minister

25. Whenever a Minister is for any reason unable to perform any of the functions of his office, or whenever any Minister has vacated his office and a successor has not yet been appointed, the State President may appoint any other Minister to act in the said Minister's stead or office, either generally or in the performance of any specific function.

Assignment of powers, duties and functions of one Minister to another

26. The State President may assign the administration of any provision in any law which entrusts to a Minister any power, duty or function, to any other Minister—
(a) either specifically or by way of a general assignment of the administration of any law or of all laws entrusting powers, duties or functions to such first-mentioned Minister; and
(b) either generally or in so far as such provision, law or laws relate to any population group or matter mentioned in such assignment.

Appointment and functions of Deputy Ministers

27. (1) *(a)* The State President may, subject to subsection (2), appoint any person to hold office during the State President's pleasure as Deputy Minister of any specified department of State or Deputy Minister of such other description as the State President may determine, and to exercise or perform on behalf of a Minister any of the powers, functions and duties entrusted to such Minister in terms of any law or otherwise which may, subject to the directions of the State President, be assigned to him from time to time by such Minister.

(b) Any reference in any law to a deputy to a Minister shall be construed as including a reference to a Deputy Minister appointed under this subsection, and any such reference to a Minister shall be construed as including a reference to a Deputy Minister acting in pursuance of an assignment under paragraph *(a)* by the Minister for whom he acts.

(2) *(a)* No Deputy Minister shall hold office for a longer period than 12 months unless he is or becomes a member of a House.

(b) The provisions of section 24(3)*(b)* shall apply *mutatis mutandis* to a Deputy Minister appointed to exercise or perform any powers, functions and duties on behalf of a Minister of a department of State for own affairs of a population group.

(3) A Deputy Minister shall before assuming his duties make and subscribe an oath, in the form prescribed in section 24(4) but with reference to his office as Deputy Minister, before the Chief Justice or any other judge of the Supreme Court.

(4) Whenever any Deputy Minister is for any reason unable to perform any of the functions of his office, the State President may appoint any other Deputy Minister or any other person to act in the said Deputy Minister's stead, either generally or in the performance of any specific function.

Power to appoint and discharge persons

28. The appointment and removal of persons in the service of the Republic shall be vested in the State President, unless the appointment or removal is delegated by the State President to any other authority or is in terms of this Act or any other law vested in any other authority.

Seat of Government

29. Save as is otherwise provided in section 36, Pretoria shall be the seat of the Government of the Republic.

PART VI

The Legislature

The Legislature and its Powers

Legislature and its powers

30. The legislative power of the Republic is vested in the State President and the Parliament of the Republic, which, as the sovereign legislative authority in and over the Republic, shall have full power to make laws for the peace, order and good government of the Republic: Provided that the powers of Parliament in respect of any bill contemplated in section 31 shall be exercised as provided by that section.

Bills on own affairs of a population group

31. (1) A bill which, when introduced in a House, is endorsed with or accompanied by the certificate of the State President that the bill deals with matters which are own affairs of the population group in question, shall be disposed of by that House, and shall not be required to be, or be, introduced in or dealt with by any other House.

(2) If an amendment of any such bill is proposed in the House in question or adopted by it, and the certificate of the State President that such amendment deals with matters which are not own affairs of the population group in question, is at any time, whether before the bill is passed by the House or after it has been passed by it but before the State President has assented to it, laid upon the Table of the House, the bill shall not or, as the case may be, not again be presented to the State President for his assent unless—

(a) the proposal for the amendment is withdrawn or not agreed to; or
(b) if the bill was passed before the tabling of the certificate, the House has reconsidered the amendment and has adopted in its place an amendment in respect of which the State President's certificate *mutatis mutandis* in accordance with subsection (1) of this section was issued before it was adopted.

(3) A bill passed by a House under subsection (1) or passed by a House and thereafter amended in accordance with subsection (2)(b), shall, when it is presented to the State President for his assent, be endorsed with the certificate of the Chairman of the House that it has been passed and is presented for assent in accordance with this section or, as the circumstances may require, that it has been passed and amended and is presented for assent in accordance with this section.

Disagreement among the Houses

32. (1) If during the same session of Parliament—
(a) one or two Houses pass a bill and the other Houses or House rejects it or is deemed in terms of subsection (2) to have rejected it; or
(b) two Houses pass different versions of a bill and the other House rejects it or is so deemed to have rejected it; or
(c) two Houses pass a bill and the other House passes a different version of it; or
(d) each of the Houses passes a different version of a bill,
the State President may during that session refer the bill or the different versions thereof which have been passed, as the case may be, to the President's Council for its decision: Provided that the State President may withdraw the reference at any time before the President's Council gives its decision.

(2) (a) If—
(i) the State President, by message to a House, has requested that a bill passed by another House and introduced in the House in question or in respect of which notice of a motion for its introduction has been given in that House, be disposed of by that House before a date mentioned in the message, which may not be a date earlier than 14 days after the date of the message; and
(ii) that House has not disposed of such bill before the date mentioned in the message,
that House shall be deemed for the purposes of subsection (1) to have rejected the bill, unless the State President by like message determines otherwise within seven days after the date so mentioned.

(b) A House which has rejected a motion for the introduction of a bill shall be deemed for the purposes of subsection (1) to have rejected the bill.

(3) When a recommendation of the President's Council has been laid upon the Table of a House as provided in section 78(8), the House may deal with the recommendation.

(4) A bill which was referred to the President's Council under subsection (1) and which, in terms of a decision of that Council given during the session of Parliament in which the bill was so referred, is to be presented to the State President for his assent, shall be deemed to have been passed by Parliament.

(5) A bill which is deemed in terms of subsection (4) to have been passed by Parliament shall, when it is presented to the State President for his assent, be endorsed with the certificate of the Speaker of Parliament that the bill is by virtue of a decision of the President's Council so deemed to have been passed by Parliament.

Assent to bills

33. (1) When a bill which—
(a) has been passed by Parliament; or
(b) in terms of section 32(4) is deemed to have been passed by Parliament; or
(c) has been passed by a House in accordance with section 31,
is presented to the State President for his assent, he shall declare that he assents thereto or that he withholds assent, but he shall not declare that he withholds assent unless he is satisfied that the bill has not been dealt with as provided in this Act.

(2) The provisions of subsection (1) of this section shall not affect the State President's powers in terms of subsection (2) of section 31 to issue a certificate contemplated in the last-mentioned subsection in respect of an amendment of a bill

when the bill is presented to him for assent, and to return the bill to the House in question.

Validity of Acts of Parliament

34. (1) A bill referred to in section 33(1) to which the State President has assented shall be an Act of Parliament.

(2) *(a)* Any division of the Supreme Court of South Africa shall, subject to the provisions of section 18, be competent to inquire into and pronounce upon the question as to whether the provisions of this Act were complied with in connection with any law which is expressed to be enacted by the State President and Parliament or by the State President and any House.

(b) Rules and orders of a House and joint rules and orders of the Houses shall not be regarded as provisions of this Act for the purposes of paragraph *(a)*.

(3) Save as provided in subsection (2), no court of law shall be competent to inquire into or pronounce upon the validity of an Act of Parliament.

Signature and enrolment of Acts

35. As soon as may be after any law has been assented to by the State President, the Secretary to Parliament shall cause two fair copies of such law, one being in the English and the other in the Afrikaans language (one of which copies shall have been signed by the State President), to be enrolled of record in the office of the Registrar of the Appellate Division of the Supreme Court of South Africa, and such copies shall be conclusive evidence as to the provisions of every such law, and in case of conflict between the two copies so enrolled that signed by the State President shall prevail.

Seat of Legislature

36. Cape Town shall be the seat of the Legislature of the Republic.

Parliament

Constitution of Parliament

37. (1) Parliament shall consist of three Houses, namely, a House of Assembly, a House of Representatives and a House of Delegates.

(2) If and for as long as any House is unable, during a session of Parliament, to meet for the performance of its functions or to perform its functions—

(a) by reason of a shortfall in the number of its members, or because there are no members, as a result of the resignation of members or the fact that an insufficient number of members or no member was elected at any election of members of such House; or

(b) by reason of the absence of members, or the failure of members to take their seats or to perform the functions of their office, after the State President has by proclamation in the *Gazette* called upon all members of such House to be present in the chamber of such House for the performance of their functions as such members on a day and at an hour mentioned in the proclamation, and that hour and day have passed,

Parliament shall consist of the Houses that are or, according to the circumstances, the House that is able to perform their or its functions, and the provisions of this Act and any other law shall be construed accordingly.

Sessions of Parliament

38. (1) The State President may appoint such times for the sessions of Parliament as he thinks fit, and may also from time to time, by proclamation in the *Gazette* or otherwise, prorogue Parliament.

(2) There shall be a session of Parliament at least once in every year, so that a period of 13 months shall not intervene between the commencement of one session and the commencement of the next session.

(3) The first session of Parliament after the general election of members of the Houses held in pursuance of a dissolution of Parliament, shall commence within 30 days after the polling day of the election.

Duration and dissolution of Parliament or a House

39. (1) Every Parliament shall continue for five years from the day on which its first session commences.

(2) The State President—

(a) may dissolve Parliament by proclamation in the *Gazette* at any time; and

(b) shall so dissolve Parliament, unless he resigns from office, if each House, during one and the same ordinary·session of Parliament—

  (i) passes a motion of no confidence in the Cabinet within any period of 14 days; or

  (ii) rejects any bill which appropriates revenue or moneys for the ordinary annual requirements or services of the departments of State controlled by members of the Cabinet.

(3) Subject to the provisions of subsection (2)—

(a) the State President may dissolve any House by proclamation in the *Gazette* if—

  (i) such House passes a motion of no confidence in the Cabinet; or

  (ii) such House rejects any bill referred to in subsection (2)*(b)*(ii); or

  (iii) any circumstance contemplated in section 37(2) applies to such House; or

  (iv) the Ministers' Council in question requests him to do so;

(b) the State President shall so dissolve any House or reconstitute the Ministers' Council in question if—

  (i) such House passes a motion of no confidence in the Ministers' Council in question; or

  (ii) such House rejects any bill referred to in section 31 which appropriates revenue or moneys for the ordinary annual requirements or services of the departments of State controlled by members of the Ministers' Council in question.

Effect of dissolution

40. Notwithstanding the dissolution of any House in terms of this Act, whether by a dissolution of Parliament or otherwise and whether by effluxion of time or otherwise—

(a) every person who at the date of the dissolution is a member of such House shall remain a member thereof;

(b) such House shall remain competent to perform its functions; and

(c) the State President shall have power to summon Parliament or the House in question for the dispatch of business,

during the period following such dissolution up to and including the day immediately preceding the polling day for the election held in pursuance of such dissolution, in the same manner in all respects as if the dissolution had not occurred.

The Houses

Constitution of House of Assemby

41. (1) The House of Assembly shall consist of—

(a) 166 members, each of whom shall be directly elected by the persons entitled to vote at an election of such a member in an electoral division delimited as provided in section 49;

(b) four members nominated by the State President, of whom one shall be nominated from each province;

(c) eight members elected by the members contemplated in paragraph *(a)* according to the principle of proportional representation, each voter having one transferable vote.

(2) The number of members of the House of Assembly to be elected as provided in subsection (1)*(a)* in each province, shall be as follows:

Cape of Good Hope	56
Natal	20
Orange Free State	14
Transvaal	76

Constitution of House of Representatives

2 (1) The House of Representatives shall consist of—

(a) 80 members, each of whom shall be directly elected by the persons entitled to vote at an election of such a member in an electoral division delimited as provided in section 49;

(b) two members nominated by the State President;

(c) three members elected by the members contemplated in paragraph (a) according to the principle of proportional representation, each voter having one transferable vote.

(2) The number of members of the House of Representatives to be elected as provided in subsection (1)(a) in each province, shall be as follows:

Cape of Good Hope	60
Natal	5
Orange Free State	5
Transvaal	10

Constitution of House of Delegates

43. (1) The House of Delegates shall consist of—

(a) 40 members, each of whom shall be directly elected by the persons entitled to vote at an election of such a member in an electoral division delimited as provided in section 49;

(b) two members nominated by the State President;

(c) three members elected by the members contemplated in paragraph (a) according to the principle of proportional representation, each voter having one transferable vote.

(2) The number of members of the House of Delegates to be elected as provided in subsection (1)(a) in a province, shall be as follows:

Cape of Good Hope	3
Natal	29
Transvaal	8

References to directly and indirectly elected and nominated members of Houses

44. Any reference in this Part to a directly elected member, a nominated member and an indirectly elected member of a House, shall be construed as a reference to a member of such House who, as the case may be and as the context may require, has been elected or nominated or is to be elected or nominated as provided in section 41(1)(a), (b) and (c), respectively, or section 42(1)(a), (b) and (c), respectively, or section 43(1)(a), (b) and (c), respectively.

Alteration of number of members of province

45. Notwithstanding any provision to the contrary contained in this Act, the number of members of any House to be elected in the various provinces as provided in section 41(2), 42(2) or 43(2), as the case may be, shall not be altered until—

(a) in the case of the House of Assembly, a period of five years has elapsed from the last delimitation of its electoral divisions in terms of the previous Constitution; and

(b) in the case of the House of Representatives and the House of Delegates, a period of 10 years has elapsed from the first delimitation of the electoral divisions of the House in question in terms of this Act.

Nomination and indirect election of members of Houses

46. (1) The State President may make regulations in regard to the election of indirectly elected members of a House, including regulations prescribing the manner of voting and of the transfer and counting of votes and the duties of returning officers in connection with such election.

(2) A casual vacancy in the seat of a nominated or an indirectly elected member of a House shall be filled by the nomination or election of a member for the unexpired portion of the term of office of the member in whose stead he is nominated or elected, and in the same manner in which the last-mentioned member was nominated or elected.

(3) A nominated or indirectly elected member of a House who—

(a) remains a member of the House in terms of section 40 up to and including the day immediately preceding the polling day for the relevant election referred to in that section; and

(b) is not elected as a member of the House in question at that election,

shall, during the period which in terms of subsection (4) of this section is applicable in his case, be deemed to have been nominated or elected on that polling day as a nominated member or, as the case may be, as an indirectly elected member of that House, and, in the case of a nominated member of the House of Assembly, from the province from which he was in fact nominated.

(4) Any person who is a member of a House in terms of the provisions of subsection (3) shall cease to be a member of such House in terms of those provisions—

(a) in the case of a person deemed in terms of those provisions to have been nominated from a particular province as a member of the House of Assembly, on the day on which a nominated member of that House is nominated from that province in pursuance of the relevant dissolution of that House referred to in section 40, or, if such a member is not so nominated within the period of 45 days after the polling day of the general election held in pursuance of that dissolution, at the expiration of that period; and

(b) in the case of a person deemed in terms of those provisions to be an indirectly elected member of a House or a nominated member of a House other than the House of Assembly, on the first day on which indirectly elected or, as the case may be, nominated members of the House in question are elected or nominated in pursuance of the relevant dissolution referred to in section 40, or, if no such members are elected or nominated within the period of 45 days after the polling day of the general election held in pursuance of that dissolution, at the expiration of that period: Provided that such person, if he is elected or nominated as such a member but not on such first day, shall be deemed to have remained a member of the House in question up to and including the day immediately preceding the day on which he is so elected or nominated.

Polling day at general elections

47. (1) At any general election of members of the Houses held in pursuance of a dissolution of Parliament, all polls shall be taken on one and the same day in all the electoral divisions of all three Houses throughout the Republic, such day to be appointed by the State President.

(2) At any general election of members of a House held in pursuance of its dissolution otherwise than at a dissolution of Parliament, all polls shall be taken on one and the same day in all the electoral divisions of that House throughout the Republic, such day to be appointed by the State President.

(3) The day appointed by the State President in terms of subsection (1) or (2), shall be a day not more than 180 days after the dissolution of Parliament or the House in question, as the case may be.

Delimitation of electoral divisions

48. (1) At intervals of not less than five years and not more than 10 years, commencing, in the case of the House of Assembly, from the last delimitation of its electoral divisions in terms of the previous Constitution, and, in the case of the House of Representatives or the House of Delegates, from the first delimitation of electoral divisions of the House in question in terms of this Act, the State President shall appoint a delimitation commission consisting of three judges of the Supreme Court of South Africa, which shall, subject to the provisions of section 41(2), 42(2) or 43(2), as the case may be, divide the Republic, for the purpose of the election of directly elected members of the House in question, into the same number of electoral divisions as the number of such members of that House, in such a manner that no electoral division is situated partly in one province and partly in another province.

(2) No judge shall be appointed under subsection (1) as a member of a delimitation commission unless he has served as a judge, whether in a permanent or temporary capacity, for a total period of not less than five years.

(3) In dividing the Republic into electoral divisions in terms of subsection (1) the delimitation commission shall act in accordance with the provisions of section 49.

Method of dividing provinces into electoral divisions

49. (1) For the purposes of the division of a province into electoral divisions of a House, the quota of the province for the House shall be obtained, subject to the provisions of subsection (4), by dividing the number of voters of the House in the province in terms of the current voters' lists, duly corrected up to the latest possible date, by the number of members of the House to be elected in the province in terms of section 41(2), 42(2) or 43(2), as the case may be.

(2) A province shall be divided into electoral divisions of a House in such a manner that each such electoral division shall, subject to the provisions of subsections (3) and (4), contain a number of voters as nearly as may be equal to the quota of the province for the House.

(3) The delimitation commission shall give due consideration to—

(a) community or diversity of interests;

(b) means of communication;

(c) physical features;

(d) boundaries of existing electoral divisions;

(e) sparsity or density of population;

(f) probability of increase or decrease of population;

(g) local authority and magisterial district boundaries,

in such manner that, while taking the quota of voters as the basis of division, the commission may depart from the quota whenever it is deemed necessary, but in no case to a greater extent than 15 per cent more or 15 per cent less than the quota: Provided that in the case of an electoral division with an area of 25 000 square kilometres or more, the commission may reduce the number of voters to a number equal to 70 per cent of the quota.

(4) *(a)* The port and settlement mentioned in the Walfish Bay and St John's River Territories Annexation Act, 1884, of the Cape of Good Hope, and the territory surrounding it and bounded as described in that Act, shall be one of the electoral divisions into which the province of the Cape of Good Hope shall be divided for the election of members of the House of Assembly, and, as such electoral division, it shall be called Walvis Bay until different provision is made under section 50.

(b) The boundaries of such electoral division, as described in paragraph *(a)*, shall not be altered by any delimitation commission, but in so far as may be necessary for the purposes of any provision of this Act or any other law those boundaries shall be deemed to have been settled by such commission.

(c) The provisions of this section in regard to the quota of a province and the number of voters of an electoral division shall not apply in connection with the electoral division referred to in paragraph *(a)*, and in their application at any delimitation of the other electoral divisions in the province of the Cape of Good Hope for the election of members of the House of Assembly—

(i) the port, settlement and territory mentioned in paragraph *(a)* shall be deemed not to be part of that province;

(ii) the voters of that electoral division, in terms of the current voters' list, duly corrected up to the latest possible date, shall be deemed not to be voters in that province; and

(iii) the number of members of the House of Assembly to be elected in that province, shall be deemed not to include a member for that electoral division.

Powers and duties of delimitation commission

50. (1) A delimitation commission, having delimited the electoral divisions of a House, shall submit to the State President—

(a) a list of the electoral divisions, with the names given to them by the commission and a description of the boundaries of each division;

(b) a map or maps showing the electoral divisions into which the provinces have been divided;

(c) such further particulars as it considers necessary.

(2) The State President may refer to the commission for its consideration all matters relating to such list or arising out of the powers or duties of the commission.

(3) The State President shall by proclamation in the *Gazette* make known the names and boundaries of the electoral divisions as finally settled and certified by the commission, or a majority thereof, and thereafter, until there shall be a redivision, the electoral divisions so named and defined shall be the electoral divisions of the House in question in the Republic and the provinces.

(4) If any discrepancy arises between the description of the divisions and the aforesaid map or maps, the description or, if the description has been amended in terms of subsection (5), the description as so amended shall prevail.

(5) *(a)* If the commission is satisfied that any such discrepancy as aforesaid is due to an error in the description of the boundaries of any electoral division, it shall in writing inform the State President accordingly, and submit an amendment of the relevant description, correcting the error and certified by the commission, to the State President, unless the period allowed in terms of paragraph *(c)* for such an amendment has expired.

(b) Subject to the provisions of paragraph *(c)*, the State President shall by proclamation in the *Gazette* make known any amendment submitted to him in terms of paragraph *(a)*, and thereafter, until there shall be a redivision, the boundaries as so amended shall be the boundaries of the electoral division in question, notwithstanding the provisions of subsection (3).

(c) No description of the boundaries of any electoral division shall be amended under this subsection after the date on which the proclamation in respect of the first general election for members of the House in question held after the completion of the relevant redivision is published in the *Gazette* in terms of section 34 of the Electoral Act, 1979.

(6) *(a)* The State President may by proclamation in the *Gazette* alter the name of any electoral division as made known under subsection (3).

(b) The name given to any electoral division under paragraph *(a)* shall, notwithstanding the provisions of subsection (3), be the name of that electoral division until there shall be a redivision.

Date from which alteration of electoral divisions takes effect

51. Any alteration in the number of members of a House to be elected in the several provinces, and any redivision of the provinces into electoral divisions of a House, shall come into operation at the next general election of directly elected members of the House in question held after the completion of the redivision or of any allocation consequent upon such alteration, and not earlier.

Franchise

52. Every White person, Coloured person and Indian who—

(a) is a South African citizen in terms of the South African Citizenship Act, 1949; and

(b) is of or over the age of 18 years; and

(c) is not subject to any of the disqualifications mentioned in section 4(1) or (2) of the Electoral Act, 1979,

shall, on compliance with and subject to the provisions of the Electoral Act, 1979, be entitled to vote at any election of a member of the House of Assembly, the House of Representatives and the House of Delegates, respectively, in the electoral division of the House in question determined in accordance with the last-mentioned Act.

Qualifications of members of Houses

53. No person shall be qualified to be a member of a House under this Act unless he—

(a) is qualified to be included as a voter in any list of voters of the House in question in an electoral division thereof; and

(b) has resided for five years within the limits of the Republic.

Disqualifications for membership of Houses

54. No person shall be capable of being elected or nominated or of sitting as a member of a House if he—

(a) has at any time been convicted of any offence for which he has been sentenced to imprisonment without the option of a fine for a period of not less than twelve months, unless he has received a grant of amnesty or a free pardon, or unless the period of such imprisonment expired at least five years before the date of his election or nomination; or

(b) is an unrehabilitated insolvent; or

(c) is of unsound mind, and has been so declared by a competent court; or

(d) is an officer or other employee in the service of any institution, council or body contemplated in section 84(1)*(f)* of the previous Constitution; or

(e) holds any office of profit under the Republic: Provided that the following persons shall be deemed not to hold an office of profit under the Republic for the purposes of this paragraph, namely—

  (i) a Minister of the Republic, or any person holding office as deputy to any Minister;

  (ii) a person in receipt of a pension from the Republic;

  (iii) an officer or member of the South African Defence Force on retired or half-pay, or an officer or member of the South African Defence Force whose services are not wholly employed by the Republic;

  (iv) any person who has been appointed or has become a justice of the peace under section 2 of the Justices of the Peace and Commissioners of Oaths Act, 1963;

  (v) any person appointed as an appraiser under section 6 of the Administration of Estates Act, 1965, or deemed to have been so appointed;

  (vi) any person who, while the Republic is at war, is an officer or member of the South African Defence Force or any other force or service established by or under the Defence Act, 1957;

  (vii) a member of any council, board, committee or similar body established by or under any law who receives no payment in respect of his services on such council, board, committee or body in excess of an allowance at a rate not exceeding the amount determined by the Minister of Finance by notice in the *Gazette* from time to time for each day on which he renders such services, any reimbursement of travelling expenses and subsistence expenses incurred by him in the course of such services and an allowance in respect of entertaining by him in connection with such services;

  (viii) a member of a commission of inquiry or a committee of inquiry appointed by the State President or the Administrator of a province, or a member of a Select Committee of a House or of a provincial council or a member of a committee of Parliament.

Vacating of seats in Houses

55. (1) A member of a House shall vacate his seat if he—

(a) becomes subject to any disability mentioned in section 54; or

(b) ceases to be qualified as required by law; or

(c) fails for a whole ordinary session of Parliament or of the House of which he is a member to attend without the special leave of that House, unless his absence is due to his serving, while the Republic is at war, with the South African Defence Force or any other force or service established by or under the Defence Act, 1957.

(2) A member of a House who—

(a) is designated or appointed as a member of the President's Council, shall vacate his seat as a member of such House with effect from the date on which he becomes a member of the President's Council;

(b) is elected as a member of a provincial council, shall vacate his seat as a member of such House with effect from the date on which he becomes a member of the provincial council.

Penalty for sitting or voting when disqualified

56. Any person who is by law incapable of sitting as a member of a House and who, while so incapable and knowing or having reasonable grounds for knowing that he is so incapable, sits or votes as a member of the House in question, shall be liable to a penalty of R200 for each day on which he so sits or votes, which may be recovered on behalf of the Treasury of the Republic by action in any division of the Supreme Court of South Africa.

Oath

57. Every member of a House shall, before taking his seat, make and subscribe before the Chief Justice, any other judge of the Supreme Court, the Speaker of Parliament or the Chairman of the House in question an oath in the following form:

I, A.B., do swear to be faithful to the Republic of South Africa and solemnly promise to perform my duties as a member of the House of Assembly/House of Representatives/House of Delegates to the best of my ability.
So help me God.

Speaker of Parliament

58. (1) An electoral college referred to in subsection (1) of section 7 shall, after having elected a State President at a meeting called in accordance with the provisions of subsection (3)*(a)* or *(b)* of that section or those provisions as applied by subsection (7) of section 8, proceed to elect a Speaker of Parliament, who shall be a member of a House.

(2) The provisions of sections 7 and 8 shall apply *mutatis mutandis* and subject to the provisions of subsection (4) of this section in respect of the election of a Speaker.

(3) *(a)* The Speaker shall hold office until his successor is elected in terms of subsection (1), but shall be eligible for re-election.

(b) The Speaker shall cease to hold office if he ceases to be a member of the House of which he was a member at the time of his election as Speaker, and may resign his office or his seat by lodging his resignation in writing with the Chief Justice.

(c) The provisions of subsection (3) of section 9 shall apply *mutatis mutandis* to the Speaker, but for the purpose of such application the words "every Chairman of a House" shall be deemed to have been substituted for the words "the Speaker of Parliament" in paragraph *(d)* of that subsection.

(4) *(a)* When the Speaker is for any reason unable to perform the functions of his office, he shall designate a member of a House to perform those functions as Acting Speaker during his absence or inability.

(b) If the Speaker is unable to designate an Acting Speaker under paragraph *(a)* or when the office of Speaker is vacant and there is no Acting Speaker so designated, the State President shall designate a member of a House to perform the functions of the Speaker during his absence or inability or, notwithstanding the provisions of section 7(3)*(c)* as applied by subsection (2) of this section but subject to the provisions of paragraph *(c)* of this subsection, until a Speaker is elected.

(c) If the office of Speaker is vacant, the functions of that office may not during a session of Parliament be performed by an Acting Speaker for longer than a month unless it is the last session before a dissolution of Parliament, or a session contemplated in section 40.

Functions of Speaker

59. (1) The Speaker of Parliament shall be the Speaker of each of the respective Houses and shall preside at a meeting of a House whenever he deems it necessary or desirable.

(2) The Speaker shall, when presiding at a meeting of a House, be vested with all the powers, duties and functions of the Chairman of the House in question, in so far as they are consistent with any functions assigned to the Speaker by rules and orders approved by all three Houses: Provided that the Speaker may only vote in the House of which he is a member.

Chairmen of Houses

60. (1) Every House shall at its first meeting, before proceeding to the dispatch of any other business, elect a member to be the Chairman of the House, and, as often as the office becomes vacant, the House shall again elect a member to be the Chairman.

(2) The Chairman of a House shall cease to hold office if he ceases to be a member of the House in question and may be removed from office by resolution of that House, and may resign his office or his seat by lodging his resignation in writing with the Speaker of Parliament.

(3) Before or during the absence of its Chairman, a House may elect a member to perform his functions during his absence.

Quorums

61. To constitute a meeting of a House for the exercise of its powers, the presence shall be necessary of—
(a) in the case of the House of Assembly, at least 50 members;
(b) in the case of the House of Representatives, at least 25 members;
(c) in the case of the House of Delegates, at least 13 members.

Voting in Houses

62. All questions in a House shall be determined by a majority of votes of members present other than the Chairman or the presiding member, who shall, however, have and exercise a casting vote in the case of an equality of votes.

Rules of procedure

63. A House may make rules and orders in connection with the order and conduct of its business and proceedings.

Joint committees and rules and orders

64. (1) In this section—
(a) "joint committee" means a committee consisting of members of each of the Houses;
(b) "joint rules and orders" means rules and orders approved by each of the Houses as joint rules and orders in connection with the order and conduct of—
   (i) the business and proceedings of each in connection with joint committees or a particular joint committee; or
   (ii) the business and proceedings of joint committees or a particular joint committee;
(c) "standing committee" means a joint committee which, in terms of joint rules and orders applicable to it, is established for the duration of the Parliament concerned and is competent to exercise or perform some or all of its powers, duties and functions also while Parliament is prorogued.

(2) Joint rules and orders may provide for any or all of the following matters, namely—
(a) the establishment of standing committees on general affairs;
(b) the constitution of any such committee, including its chairmanship and the representation of political parties, including opposition parties, in such committee;
(c) the manner in which and the circumstances under which any matter may be referred to any such committee;
(d) the powers, duties or functions of any such committee in connection with a matter referred to it;
(e) the manner in which any such committee may make any decision;
(f) the submission of any proposal to any such committee by a member of a House who is not a member of the committee;
(g) the operation of a decision of any such committee on a matter referred to it, in relation to any further business and proceedings of a House in connection with that matter;

(h) the order and conduct generally of the business and proceedings of any such committee,

but the preceding provisions of this subsection shall not be construed as defining or limiting in any manner the matters or any matter that may be dealt with or provided for in joint rules and orders or as requiring any matter to be dealt with or provided for in such rules and orders.

(3) Joint rules and orders shall provide for at least one standing committee on bills dealing with general affairs.

Powers of Ministers and their deputies in Houses

65. (1) A Minister who is a member of the Cabinet, and any deputy to such a Minister, has the right to sit and to speak in any House, but may only vote if he is a member of a House and only in the House of which he is a member.

(2) A member of a Ministers' Council who is not a member of any House or of the Cabinet has the right to sit and to speak in the House of which the members are of the same population group as the members of the Ministers' Council in question, but may not vote therein.

Summoning of a House during recess of Parliament

66. The State President may by proclamation in the *Gazette* summon any House for the dispatch of business in connection with own affairs when Parliament is not in session, and may prorogue the House in like manner before the commencement of the next ensuing session of Parliament.

Joint sittings of Houses

67. (1) A joint sitting of the Houses shall be called by the State President by message to the Houses.

(2) The State President may call such a joint sitting whenever he deems it desirable, and shall call such a joint sitting if requested to do so by all three Houses.

(3) The Speaker of Parliament shall preside at such a joint sitting.

(4) The Speaker shall determine the rules and orders for the order and conduct of the proceedings of such a joint sitting.

(5) No resolution shall be adopted at any such joint sitting.

PART VII

ADMINISTRATION OF JUSTICE

Constitution and powers of Supreme Court of South Africa

68. (1) The judicial authority of the Republic is vested in a Supreme Court to be known as the Supreme Court of South Africa and consisting of an Appellate Division and such provincial and local divisions as may be prescribed by law.

(2) The Supreme Court of South Africa shall, subject to the provisions of sections 18 and 34, have jurisdiction as provided in the Supreme Court Act, 1959.

(3) Save as otherwise provided in the Supreme Court Act, 1959, Bloemfontein shall be the seat of the Appellate Division of the Supreme Court of South Africa.

Administrative functions relating to administration of justice

69. All administrative powers, duties and functions affecting the administration of justice shall be under the control of the Minister of Justice.

PART VIII

PRESIDENT'S COUNCIL

Establishment and constitution of President's Council

70. (1) There shall be a President's Council consisting of—

(a) 20 members designated by resolution of the House of Assembly;

(b) 10 members designated by resolution of the House of Representatives;

(c) 5 members designated by resolution of the House of Delegates; and

(d) 25 members appointed by the State President,

or, in the case of members contemplated in paragraph *(a)*, *(b)* or *(c)*, such smaller number of members, if any, as may have been so designated by the House in question.

(2) *(a)* Subject to the provisions of paragraph *(f)* of this subsection, the members of the President's Council appointed under subsection (1)*(d)* shall include 10 persons of whom—

(i) six have been nominated as provided in paragraph *(b)* of this subsection by members of the House of Assembly who were supporters of the opposition parties in that House at the time of the nomination;

(ii) three have been so nominated by members of the House of Representatives who were supporters of the opposition parties in that House at the time of the nomination;

(iii) one has been so nominated by members of the House of Delegates who were supporters of the opposition parties in that House at the time of the nomination.

(b) Any nomination contemplated in paragraph *(a)* shall be made by election, according to the principle of proportional representation whereby each voter has one transferable vote, by the members of the House in question who are supporters of opposition parties in the House and who are present at a meeting of such members called in accordance with the provisions of paragraph *(c)*: Provided that any nomination made in pursuance of an agreement among such members of the House who are present at the meeting shall be a valid nomination for all purposes.

(c) A meeting contemplated in paragraph *(b)* shall take place during a session of Parliament or of the House in question and under the chairmanship of the Speaker of Parliament or the Chairman of the House, at a time and place fixed by the Speaker and made known by him or that Chairman at a sitting of the House, and the date so fixed shall—

(i) in the case of a dissolution of the President's Council, be a date after the dissolution but not more than 14 days thereafter;

(ii) if the House was dissolved otherwise than at a dissolution of Parliament, and at least two members of the newly constituted House who would be entitled in terms of paragraph *(a)* to participate in a nomination have requested the Speaker in writing that such a meeting be called, be a date not more than 14 days after the first meeting of the newly constituted House;

(iii) in the case of a casual vacancy in the President's Council in respect of which a person is to be nominated for appointment and of which notice in writing has been given to the Speaker by the Chairman of the President's Council, be a date not more that 14 days after the date of the notice or, if Parliament or the House is not then in session, a date not more than 14 days after the commencement of the next ensuing session of Parliament or the House.

(d) The regulations which apply in terms of this Act to an election of members of a House in terms of section 41(1)*(c)*, 42(1)*(c)* or 43(1)*(c)* at a meeting of members of the House who may vote at such an election, shall apply *mutatis mutandis* to an election contemplated in paragraph *(b)* of this subsection, except in so far as they are amended or replaced by regulations made by the State President for the purposes of an election so contemplated.

(e) The Speaker shall submit to the State President in writing—

(i) the name of every person nominated in terms of this subsection;

(ii) the date upon which he was nominated; and

(iii) if he has been nominated at a meeting called in terms of paragraph *(c)*(ii) for appointment in the place of a member of the President's Council, the name of the member in question,

and the State President shall appoint the nominated person as a member of the President's Council.

(f) If the Speaker advises the State President—

(i) that a meeting was called in accordance with the provisions of paragraph *(c)* and that a nomination which was required to be made thereat, was not made; or

(ii) that such a meeting cannot be called for the reason that there is no opposition party in the House in question or that there is only one opposition party in the

House with only one member of the House supporting it or that any circumstance contemplated in section 37(2) applies to the House,

the State President may appoint any person deemed fit by him as a member of the President's Council in the seat in question: Provided that the provisions of this subsection shall again apply to any subsequent appointment to the seat in question.

(3) A casual vacancy in the President's Council shall be filled by the designation or appointment of a member in the same manner as that in which the member whose office is vacant was designated or appointed.

Qualifications and period of office of members of President's Council

71. (1) No person shall be qualified to be designated or appointed as a member of the President's Council—

(a) unless he is of or over the age of 30 years;

(b) in the case of a member designated by a House, unless he is a member of such House or is qualified to be elected or nominated and take his seat as a member of such House;

(c) in the case of a member appointed by the State President, unless he is a member of a House or is qualified to be elected or nominated and take his seat as a member of a House:

Provided that the provisions of section 54(e) shall not apply with reference to the qualification of a person to be designated or appointed as a member of the President's Council or to be such a member.

(2) A member of the President's Council shall hold office until the next ensuing dissolution of that Council in terms of section 77, but shall be eligible for redesignation or reappointment.

(3) A member of the President's Council shall vacate his office—

(a) on the dissolution of that Council;

(b) subject to the proviso to subsection (1), if he becomes disqualified to be elected or nominated and take his seat as a member of any House;

(c) if he becomes a member of a House or of a provincial council;

(d) in the case of a member designated by a House which was thereafter dissolved, if the House constituted after the general election held in pursuance of such dissolution, withdraws the designation of that member—

  (i) where it was a dissolution of Parliament, by a resolution adopted before that member vacates his office in terms of paragraph (a) of this subsection;

  (ii) where it was a dissolution of such House only, by a resolution adopted within seven days after the first meeting of the House as reconstituted;

(e) in the case of a member appointed otherwise than in terms of section 70(2) by a State President who thereafter resigned his office or was removed from office or died, if the appointment of such member is withdrawn by the newly elected State President within seven days after having assumed office;

(f) in the case of a member appointed by the State President in terms of subsection (2) of section 70, on the date on which a person nominated under that subsection for appointment in the place of the member concerned, by competent members of the House in question at a meeting of such members called in terms of paragraph (c)(ii) of that subsection, becomes a member of the President's Council by virtue of his appointment in terms of paragraph (e) of that subsection.

(4) A member of the President's Council may resign as such member by lodging his resignation in writing with the State President, who shall, in the case of a member designated by a House, forthwith notify the Chairman of the House in question of the resignation.

(5) The designation or redesignation of a person as a member of the President's Council by a House during the period in which a member's designation may be withdrawn under subsection (3)(d)(i) of this section, shall take effect on the day on which the then existing President's Council dissolves in terms of section 77, and shall be a designation as a member of the President's Council constituted on or after that day.

Chairman of President's Council

72. (1) The President's Council shall elect a Chairman from among its members at its first meeting after its constitution, at which a person designated by the State President shall preside until a Chairman is elected.

(2) The Chairman of the President's Council shall hold office until the dissolution of that Council in terms of section 77 unless he—

(a) ceases earlier to be a member of that Council; or

(b) resigns as Chairman by lodging his resignation in writing with the State President; or

(c) is removed from office as Chairman by resolution of that Council.

(3) The President's Council shall at its first meeting elect one of its members as Deputy Chairman, who shall act in the stead of the Chairman when the Chairman is unable to perform the functions of his office.

(4) When neither the Chairman nor the Deputy Chairman is able to act, the President's Council shall elect one of its members to act in the stead of the Chairman.

Remuneration and allowances of members

73. (1) The members of the President's Council shall receive such remuneration and allowances as the State President may determine, as well as such other benefits as he may determine by proclamation in the *Gazette.*

(2) Such remuneration, allowances or benefits may differ according to the offices held by members in the Council, and according to whether the functions performed by members or attached to such offices are in the opinion of the State President of a full-time or part-time nature.

Quorum

74. The presence of at least 30 members of the President's Council shall be necessary to constitute a meeting of the President's Council for the exercise of its powers.

Decisions

75. All questions at a meeting of the President's Council shall be determined by a majority of votes of the members present other than the presiding member, who shall have and exercise a casting vote in the case of an equality of votes.

Rules of procedure

76. (1) Subject to the provisions of this Act, the President's Council may make rules and orders in connection with the order and conduct of its business and proceedings, the establishment, constitution and powers of committees of the Council and the order and conduct of their business and proceedings.

(2) Any Minister or Deputy Minister has the right to sit and to speak in the President's Council, but shall not vote therein.

Duration of President's Council

77. The President's Council shall be dissolved by the first dissolution of Parliament following the constitution of that Council, but the dissolution of the President's Council shall take effect on the day on which the State President elected after such dissolution of Parliament assumes office.

Powers and functions of President's Council

78. (1) The President's Council shall at the request of the State President advise him on any matter referred to it by the State President for its advice, and may, in its discretion, advise him on any matter (excluding draft legislation) which, in its opinion, is of public interest.

(2) Whenever a matter is referred to the President's Council for its advice or when that Council is of the opinion that a matter is of public interest, it may refer such matter to a committee contemplated in section 76 for advice, and if the Council is not in session, reference of such matter to such a committee for its advice may be effected in accordance with rules and orders made by the Council.

(3) The President's Council may transmit any advice received by it in terms of subsection (2) to the State President as the advice of the Council, whether with or without its comments thereon.

(4) *(a)* When any bill or bills are referred for decision to the President's Council under section 32, it may refer such bill or bills to a committee contemplated in section 76 for investigation and report, and if the Council is not in session, reference of such bill or bills to such a committee for investigation and report may be effected in accordance with rules and orders made by the Council, and the Council may take any such report and any recommendation contained therein into consideration when acting in terms of paragraph *(b)* of this subsection or in terms of subsection (5) of this section.

(b) The President's Council may from time to time advise the State President that any bill or bills so referred to it, be amended or otherwise dealt with in the manner recommended by the President's Council.

(5) Unless the State President withdraws the reference, the President's Council shall decide—

(a) in the case of a bill referred to in section 32(1)*(a)*, either that the bill is to be presented to the State President for assent or that it shall not be so presented;

(b) in the case of a bill referred to in section 32(1)*(b)*, either which one of the different versions of such bill that were passed is to be presented to the State President for assent, or that none of those versions shall be so presented;

(c) in the case of a bill referred to in section 32(1)*(c)* or *(d)*, which one of the different versions of such bill that were passed is to be presented to the State President for assent.

(6) The President's Council or a committee thereof may, for the purposes of the performance of its functions and in its discretion, consult with any person or State institution on any matter, and may for such purpose establish consultative committees consisting of members of the President's Council or such committee, as the case may be, and members of any council established by the State President in terms of any other law.

(7) Advice received by the State President in terms of subsection (1) shall be laid upon the Table in every House that has an interest in it within 14 days after its receipt, if Parliament is then in session, or, if Parliament is not then in session, within 14 days after the commencement of its next ensuing session.

(8) Advice received by the State President in terms of subsection (4)*(b)* and accepted by him, and any decision of the President's Council in terms of subsection (5), shall be laid upon the Table of every House within 14 days after its receipt by the State President.

PART IX

FINANCE

Existing debts and liabilities of the State

79. Nothing in this Act contained shall affect any assets or rights belonging to the State or any debts or liabilities of the State as existing immediately before the commencement of this Act, and all such assets, rights, debts and liabilities shall remain assets, rights, debts and liabilities of the Republic, subject, notwithstanding any other provisions contained in this Act, to the conditions imposed by any law under which such debts or liabilities were raised or incurred, and without prejudice to any rights of security or priority in respect of the payment of principal, interest, sinking fund and other charges conferred on the creditors concerned, and the Republic may, subject to such conditions and rights, convert, renew or consolidate such debts.

All revenues vest in State President

80. All revenues of the Republic, from whatever source arising, shall vest in the State President.

State Revenue Fund

81. (1) There shall be a State Revenue Fund, into which shall be paid all revenues as defined in section 1 of the Exchequer and Audit Act, 1975.

(2) No moneys shall be withdrawn from the State Revenue Fund, except in accordance with an Act of Parliament.

Accounts of State Revenue Fund

82. (1) In respect of the State Revenue Fund there shall be—
(a) a State Revenue Account, which shall, subject to the provisions of paragraph *(b)* and subsection (2), be credited with all revenues and from which shall be defrayed all expenditure and be paid any amounts with which it is charged in terms of this Act or any other law;
(b) the accounts in connection with the administration of own affairs of the different population groups, which may be prescribed by any general law and which shall be credited with all revenues accruing to them in terms of this Act or any other law and from which shall be defrayed all expenditure and be paid any amounts with which they are charged in terms of this Act or any other law.

(2) Where any law dealing with own affairs of a population group provides that revenue mentioned therein shall be paid into the State Revenue Fund or that expenditure so mentioned shall be defrayed from that fund, such revenue shall be paid into, and such expenditure shall be defrayed from, the appropriate account contemplated in subsection (1)*(b)*.

Auditing of accounts of State Revenue Fund

83. The accounts of the State Revenue Fund shall be investigated, examined and audited in terms of the provisions of the Exchequer and Audit Act, 1975.

Payments to accounts of State Revenue Fund

84. In respect of every financial year there shall be paid from the State Revenue Fund into its relevant account—
(a) the amounts calculated in accordance with a formula prescribed by any general law;
(b) any amount appropriated by any general law for that account in respect of the financial year in question; and
(c) any amount to be paid into that account subject to conditions determined by any general law.

Appropriation bill shall not deal with other matters

85. Any bill which appropriates revenue or moneys for the ordinary annual services of the State shall deal only with such appropriation.

Appropriation not initiated by a Minister

86. A House shall not consider any proposal, whether by way of a vote or by way of a resolution, address or bill, for the appropriation of any part of the public revenue or of any tax or impost to any purpose and which has not been initiated by a Minister, unless such appropriation has been recommended by message from the State President during the session in which the proposal is made.

PART X
GENERAL

Continuation of existing laws

87. Subject to the provisions of this Act, all laws which were in force in any part of the Republic or in any territory in respect of which Parliament is competent to legislate, immediately before the commencement of this Act, shall continue in force until repealed or amended by the competent authority.

Continuation of constitutional conventions

88. The constitutional and parliamentary conventions which existed immediately before the commencement of this Act shall continue to exist, except in so far as they are inconsistent with the provisions of this Act.

Equality of official languages

89. (1) English and Afrikaans shall be the official languages of the Republic, and shall be treated on a footing of equality, and possess and enjoy equal freedom, rights and privileges.

(2) All records, journals and proceedings of Parliament shall be kept in both the official languages and all bills, laws and notices of general public importance or interest issued by the Government of the Republic shall be in both the official languages.

(3) Notwithstanding the provisions of subsection (1) an Act of Parliament or a proclamation of the State President, issued under an Act of Parliament, whereby a Black area is declared to be a self-governing territory in the Republic, or a later Act of Parliament or a later proclamation of the State President (which in the absence of any other empowering provision may be issued under this subsection) may—
(a) provide for the recognition of one or more Black languages for any or all of the following purposes, namely—
  (i) as an additional official language or as additional official languages of that territory; or
  (ii) for use in that territory for official purposes prescribed by or under that Act or later Act or by any such proclamation; and
(b) contain provisions authorizing the use of any such Black language outside the said territory for such purposes connected with the affairs of that territory and subject to such conditions as may be prescribed by or under that Act or later Act or any such proclamation.

Equality of use of official languages by provincial councils and local authorities

90. All records, journals and proceedings of a provincial council shall be kept in both the official languages, and all draft ordinances, ordinances and notices of public importance or interest issued by a provincial administration, and all notices issued and all regulations or by-laws made and all townplanning schemes prepared by any institution or body contemplated in section 84(1)*(f)* of the previous Constitution, shall be in both the official languages.

Method of publication of notices, etc., in newspapers

91. Whenever anything is published in a newspaper at the instance of the State or by or under the directions of any institution or body contemplated in section 84(1)*(f)* of the previous Constitution, the publication shall take place simultaneously in both the official languages and, in the case of each language, in a newspaper circulating in the area of jurisdiction of the authority concerned which appears mainly in that language, and the publication in each language shall as far as practicable occupy the same amount of space: Provided that where in the area in question any newspaper appears substantially in both the official languages, publication in both languages may take place in that newspaper.

Offences in respect of National Flag

92. (1) Any person who—
(a) maliciously destroys or spoils the National Flag of the Republic as described in section 4; or
(b) commits any other act which is calculated to hold the National Flag of the Republic in contempt; or
(c) without being authorized thereto (the burden of proof of which shall be upon him), removes the National Flag of the Republic as so described from any place, where it is displayed in terms of instructions or directions issued by any State authority,
shall be guilty of an offence and liable on conviction to a fine not exceeding R10 000 or imprisonment for a period not exceeding five years.

(2) If in any prosecution for an offence referred to in subsection (1) it is alleged that the flag in respect of which the offence is alleged to have been committed is or was the National Flag of the Republic as described in section 4, it shall be presumed, unless the contrary is proved, that the flag in question complies or, as the case may be, complied with the description of the National Flag in that section.

Administration of Black affairs

93. The control and administration of Black affairs shall vest in the State President, who shall exercise all those special powers in regard to Black administration which immediately before the commencement of this Act were vested in him, and any lands which immediately before such commencement vested in him for the occupation of Blacks in terms of any law shall continue to vest in him with all such powers as he may have in connection therewith, and no lands which were set aside for the occupation of Blacks and which could not at the establishment of the Union of South Africa have been alienated except by an Act of the Legislature of a Colony which became part of the Union of South Africa in terms of the South Africa Act, 1909, shall be alienated or in any way diverted from the purposes for which they were set aside, except under the authority of an Act of Parliament.

Certain rights and obligations under conventions, etc., vest in Republic

94. All rights and obligations under conventions, treaties or agreements which were binding on any of the Colonies incorporated in the Union of South Africa at its establishment, and were still binding on the Republic immediately before the commencement of this Act, shall be rights and obligations of the Republic, just as all other rights and obligations under conventions, treaties or agreements which immediately before the commencement of this Act were binding on the Republic.

Transfer of certain executive powers

95. All powers, authorities and functions which immediately before the commencement of the previous Constitution were in any of the provinces vested in the Governor-General or in the Governor-General-in-Council or in any authority of the province, shall as far as they continue in existence and are capable of being exercised after the commencement of this Act, be vested in the State President, or in the authority exercising similar powers under the Republic, as the case may be, except such powers, authorities and functions as are by this Act or any other law vested in some other authority.

Affirmation in lieu of oath

96. Any person who is in terms of any provision of this Act required to make and subscribe an oath may in lieu of such oath make and subscribe a solemn affirmation in corresponding form.

Construction of certain references

97. Any reference in any law in force in any part of the Republic, or in any territory in respect of which Parliament is competent to legislate, immediately before the commencement of this Act—
(a) to any territory, institution or functionary which in terms of the previous Constitution was required to be construed as a reference to the Republic, shall be so construed;
(b) to an institution, body or functionary which in terms of the previous Constitution was required to be construed as a reference to the State President, shall be so construed;
(c) to the House of Assembly or a member thereof, or to an institution or body or a member thereof which in terms of the previous Constitution was required to be construed as a reference to the House of Assembly or a member thereof, shall be construed as a reference to Parliament or the Houses or a House or to a member of a House, as the case may be or the circumstances may require, unless it is inconsistent with the context or clearly inappropriate;
(d) to the Executive Council, shall be construed as a reference to the Cabinet or to the relevant Ministers' Council, according to the circumstances;
(e) to the President's Council, shall be construed as a reference to the President's Council established in terms of this Act;
(f) to the Secretary or the Deputy Secretary to the House of Assembly, or to a functionary which in terms of the previous Constitution was required to be construed as a reference to the Secretary or the Deputy Secretary to the House of Assembly, shall be construed as a reference to the Secretary or Deputy Secretary, respectively, to Parliament.

Administration of existing laws

98. (1) Any Act of Parliament or other law which at the commencement of this Act is administered by a Minister of the Republic or in a department of State controlled by such a Minister and which relates to a matter referred to in section 14 shall, notwithstanding the fact that it relates to such matter, be regarded as a general law for the purposes of this Act until, and except in so far as, its administration is assigned under section 26 to a Minister of a department of State for own affairs of a population group.

(2) Any ordinance of a province or other law which entrusts any power, duty or function to the executive committee or other executive authority of such province established by the previous Constitution and which relates to a matter referred to in section 14 shall, notwithstanding the fact that it relates to such matter, be administered according to its provisions unless, and except in so far as, its administration is assigned to a Minister under subsection (3)*(b)*.

(3) The State President may by proclamation in the *Gazette*—

(a) after consultation with the executive committee of the province concerned, declare that the provisions of Part IV apply to a law referred to in subsection (2) to the extent stated in the declaration;

(b) when he so declares or at any time thereafter, assign the administration of such law to a Minister;

(c) when he so assigns the administration of such law or at any time thereafter, and in so far as he considers it necessary for the efficient carrying out of the assignment by the Minister or in his department or of such law in so far as its administration is not so assigned—

   (i) amend or adapt such law in order to regulate its application or interpretation;

   (ii) where the assignment does not relate to the whole of such law, repeal and re-enact, whether with or without an amendment or adaptation contemplated in subparagraph (i), those of its provisions to which the assignment relates or in so far as the assignment relates to them;

   (iii) regulate any other matter necessary, in his opinion, as a result of the assignment, including the transfer or admission of persons to or in the service of the State or any other person, subject to conditions not less favourable than those under which they serve, and the transfer of assets, liabilities, rights and obligations, including moneys, to or from the State or any other person or body established by law.

(4) Section 26 shall apply *mutatis mutandis* to an assignment under subsection (3)*(b)* of this section, but in such application any reference in that section to a Minister to whom a provision in a law entrusts any power, duty or function shall be construed as a reference to the relevant executive committee or other executive authority referred to in subsection (2) of this section.

Amendment of Act

99. (1) Subject to the provisions of subsections (2) and (3), Parliament may by law repeal or amend any provision of this Act.

(2) No repeal or amendment of the provisions of section 89 or of this subsection or of any corresponding provisions of any law substituted for them, shall be valid unless the bill embodying such repeal or amendment has been agreed to in every House by not less than two-thirds of the total number of its members.

(3) No repeal or amendment of section 7(1)*(b)*, (5) or (6), section 8(5), section 9(1) or (3)*(a)*, section 14 or 15, section 16(1), section 19, 20 or 21, section 23(2), section 30, section 31(1) or (2), section 32(1), (2), (3) or (4), section 33, section 34(2)*(a)*, section 37(1), section 38(2), section 39(1) or (2), section 41(1), section 42(1), section 43(1), section 52, 53 or 54, section 64(3), section 70(1), section 71(1) or (3)*(b)* or *(c)*, section 77, section 78(5), this subsection, subsection (4) of this section or Schedule 1 shall be valid unless the bill embodying such repeal or amendment has been agreed to in every House by a majority of the total number of its members.

(4) A bill embodying the repeal or amendment of any provision mentioned in subsection (2) or (3) of this section shall not be referred to the President's Council for its decision under the circumstances contemplated in section 32(1).

(5) Any reference in a provision of this Act mentioned in subsection (3) of this section, or in the definition in this Act of an expression used in any such provision, to any other provision of this Act not mentioned in that subsection or to any other law, shall be construed as a reference to such other provision or other law as it exists from time to time after any amendment or replacement thereof, and the provisions of subsections (3) and (4) of this section shall not be construed as applying to any amendment or replacement of such other provision or other law.

Definitions

100. (1) In this Act, unless the context indicates otherwise—

(i) "Chief Justice" means the Chief Justice of South Africa;

(ii) "Coloured person" means a person classified as a member of the Cape Coloured, Malay or Griqua group or the group Other Coloureds in terms of the Population Registration Act, 1950;

(iii) "department of State" means a department of State established under section 24;

(iv) "general affairs" means matters referred to in section 15;

(v) "general law" means any law dealing with general affairs;

(vi) "House" means a House of Parliament mentioned in section 37(1) and, in relation to a Ministers' Council, the House whose members are of the same population group as the members of the Ministers' Council;

(vii) "Indian" means a person classified as a member of the Indian group in terms of the Population Registration Act, 1950;

(viii) "own affairs" means matters referred to in section 14, and in relation to—

(a) a population group, matters which are own affairs in relation to that population group as contemplated in that section;

(b) a House or a Ministers' Council, matters which are own affairs of the relevant population group;

(c) a department of State, any department of State established for the administration of own affairs of the relevant population group;

(d) a Minister, any Minister appointed to administer a department of State for own affairs;

(ix) "population group" means the White persons, the Coloured persons or the Indians, and in relation to—

(a) a House, the population group of which the members of the House in question are members;

(b) a Ministers' Council, the population group of which the members of the Ministers' Council in question are members;

(c) own affairs, the population group whose own affairs are in issue;

(x) "previous Constitution" means the Republic of South Africa Constitution Act, 1961, and, in so far as it is not repealed by section 101, the Provincial Government Act, 1961;

(xi) "Republic" means the Republic of South Africa;

(xii) "the Coloured persons", "the Indians" or "the White persons" includes persons who would be classified as Coloured persons, Indians or White persons, respectively, in terms of the Population Registration Act, 1950, had the provisions of that Act applied to them;

(xiii) "White person" means a person classified as a White person in terms of the Population Registration Act, 1950.

(2) In this Act and in any other law, except where it is inconsistent with the context or clearly inappropriate, any reference to a resolution or the approval of, or any other act of or with reference to, Parliament (except any act constituting a law of Parliament), or to a member or a committee or the Tables of Parliament, or to any other matter in relation to Parliament (except any law of Parliament), shall be construed as a reference to a resolution or the approval or other act of, or with reference to, each of the different Houses, a member of a House, a joint committee contemplated in section 64, the Tables of the different Houses or such other matter relating to the different Houses, as the case may be.

Repeal and amendment of laws

101. (1) The laws mentioned in Part 1 of Schedule 2 are hereby repealed or amended as set out in that Part, and the laws mentioned in Part 2 of Schedule 2 are hereby repealed to the extent set out in the third column of the last-mentioned Part.

(2) Notwithstanding the repeal of sections 15 and 15A of the previous Constitution, any pension which but for such repeal would have been payable shall continue to be payable as if such repeal had not been effected.

(3) Notwithstanding the repeal of section 116 of the previous Constitution, any of its provisions which but for such repeal would have been applicable to any matter or person, shall continue to be applicable to such matter or person as if the repeal had not been effected.

(4) Any authority constituted or person appointed or power conferred or anything done in pursuance of powers conferred by or by virtue of any provision of a law repealed or amended by subsection (1), shall be deemed to have been constituted, appointed, conferred or done in pursuance of powers conferred by or by virtue of the corresponding provision of this Act or the relevant provision of such law as so amended, as the case may be.

Transitional provisions

102. (1) If section 19(1)*(b)* comes into operation before the first State President has been elected in terms of this Act and has assumed office, a person designated by the Ministers referred to in subsection (2) of this section from among their number, shall serve as Acting State President, and such or any other Acting State President or the State President may exercise any power conferred upon the State President by this section or section 103 but not yet exercised by the State President referred to in section 103(1) at the commencement of section 19(1)*(b)*.

(2) *(a)* The persons who immediately before the commencement of this Act are Ministers of the Republic or Deputy Ministers in terms of section 20 or 21 of the previous Constitution, shall be deemed to have been appointed as such Ministers or Deputy Ministers under section 24 or 27 of this Act, as the case may be, and the departments of State then administered by such Ministers shall be deemed to have been established under section 24 of this Act as departments referred to in section 20 and to be administered by them under the relevant provisions of this Act.

(b) A reference in any law to the Prime Minister which at the commencement of this Act is not in consequence of an assignment under section 20A of the previous Constitution to be construed as a reference to some other Minister, shall be deemed to be a reference to the State President except in so far as the State President assigns the administration of such law to a Minister *mutatis mutandis* under section 26.

(3) Where any matter which, during the session of Parliament (as constituted under the previous Constitution) immediately preceding the commencement of this Act, was submitted to the said Parliament or the House of Assembly (as so constituted), has not been disposed of before such commencement, Parliament or the House of Assembly, as the case may be, constituted under this Act may continue with the disposal or consideration of that matter, and steps taken by the first-mentioned House of Assembly in connection with that matter, shall be deemed to have been taken by the House of Assembly constituted under this Act.

(4) The House of Assembly as constituted for the purposes of the previous Constitution and in existence immediately before the commencement of this Act, shall be deemed to have been duly constituted for the purposes of this Act, and any person elected or nominated as a member of that House of Assembly and holding office immediately before such commencement, shall be deemed to have been duly elected or nominated to the House of Assembly established by this Act.

(5) The regulations made under section 40(1A) of the previous Constitution shall continue to be of force and to apply to the election of members of the House of Assembly in terms of section 41(1)*(c)* of this Act, and shall apply *mutatis mutandis* to elections of members of the House of Representatives and members of the House of Delegates in terms of sections 42(1)*(c)* and 43(1)*(c)* of this Act, until they are replaced by regulations under section 46(1) of this Act.

(6) *(a)* The rules and orders of the House of Assembly as they exist at the commencement of this Act, shall apply *mutatis mutandis* in connection with the

functions and proceedings of the House of Representatives and the House of Delegates, unless and until the House in question provides otherwise.

(b) Rules and orders approved by the House of Assembly before the commencement of this Act as joint rules and orders of the Houses and published in the *Gazette* before such commencement by the Secretary to Parliament, shall after such commencement be deemed to be joint rules and orders approved by each of the Houses as contemplated in section 64, until, and except in so far as, they are replaced by rules and orders which have in fact been so approved: Provided that any rules and orders so published shall lapse on the expiry of a period of two years after the commencement of the first session of the first Parliament constituted under this Act.

(7) The first session of the first Parliament constituted in terms of this Act shall commence within 21 days after the polling day or the last polling day of the first general election of members of the House of Representatives and the House of Delegates, according to whether the poll in respect of those Houses is held on the same day or on different days.

(8) For the purposes of the application of section 39(1) in relation to the first Parliament constituted in terms of this Act, its first session shall be deemed to have commenced on a date determined by the State President referred to in section 103(1) by proclamation in the *Gazette*, which may not be a date earlier than the date of the first meeting of the House of Assembly which existed immediately before the commencement of this Act, or later than the day on which that first session actually commences.

(9) For the purposes of the first delimitation of electoral divisions of the House of Representatives and of the House of Delegates the words "voters of the House in the province in terms of the current voters' lists, duly corrected up to the latest possible date" in section 49(1) shall be deemed to be replaced by the words "persons who, according to the population register kept in terms of the Population Registration Act, 1950, and on a date not more than 30 days before the delimitation commission begins to perform its functions, would be entitled to be included in any lists of the voters contemplated in section 52 of the House in electoral divisions thereof in the province had the province been divided into electoral divisions of the House on the date in question".

(10) *(a)* A person holding office as State President or Vice State President immediately before the commencement of this Act shall vacate his office at such commencement.

(b) The salary and allowances payable to the State President immediately before such commencement shall be deemed to have been determined in terms of section 12 as the salary and allowances payable to the State President, until they are altered under that section.

(11) At the commencement of this Act the President's Council established in terms of the previous Constitution shall cease to exist and every person who immediately before such commencement is a member of that Coucnil shall cease to be such a member.

(12) The first meeting of the first President's Council established under this Act shall be convened by the State President in such manner and at such time and place as he thinks fit.

Short title and commencement

103. (1) This Act shall be called the Republic of South Africa Constitution Act, 1983, and shall, save in so far as may be otherwise required in order that effect may be given to any provision thereof, come into operation on a date fixed by the State President by proclamation in the *Gazette*.

(2) Different dates may be so fixed in respect of different provisions of this Act or in respect of section 101 in so far as it relates to different laws mentioned in Schedule 2 or to different provisions of any law so mentioned.

(3) A reference in this Act to its commencement shall be construed as a reference to the applicable date so fixed.

(4) The State President referred to in subsection (1) may exercise any power vesting in the State President in terms of any provision of this Act, in so far as it is necessary in order to give effect to such provision or any other provision of this Act as contemplated in subsection (1) or, as the case may be, if the relevant provision has been put into operation as contemplated in subsection (2).

Schedule 1

Subjects referred to in section 14

1. Social welfare, but subject to any general law in relation to—
(a) norms and standards for the provision or financing of welfare services;
(b) the control of the collection of money and other contributions from members of the public for welfare services or charity; and
(c) the registration of social workers, and control over their profession.

2. Education at all levels, including—
(1) instruction by way of correspondence, and institutions providing such instruction;
(2) the training of adults in the trades at centres established by the State President acting as provided in section 19(1)(a); and
(3) training of cadets at schools in terms of section 3(1)(a) of, and subject to, the Defence Act, 1957, and official school sport,
but subject to any general law in relation to—
(a) norms and standards for the financing of running and capital costs of education;
(b) salaries and conditions of employment of staff and professional registration of teachers; and
(c) norms and standards for syllabuses and examination and for certification of qualifications.

3. Art, culture and recreation (with the exception of competitive sport) which affect mainly the population group in question.

4. Health matters, comprising the following, namely—
(1) hospitals, clinics and similar or related institutions;
(2) medical services at schools and for indigent persons;
(3) health and nutritional guidance; and
(4) the registration of and control over private hospitals,
but subject to any general law in relation to such matters.

5. Community development, comprising the following, namely—
(1) housing;
(2) development of the community in any area declared by or under any general law as an area for the use of the population group in question, including the establishment, development and renovation of towns and the control over and disposal of land (whether by alienation or otherwise) acquired or made available for that purpose; and
(3) rent control and control over and clearance of squatting, in such an area in terms of any general law,
but subject to—
(a) any general law in relation to norms, standards and income groups for the financing of housing; and
(b) the provisions of the general law referred to in paragraph (2).

6. Local government within any area declared by or under any general law as a local government area for the population group in question, but subject to any general law in relation to matters to be administered on local government level on a joint basis, and excluding—
(a) any matter assigned to local authorities by or under any general law; and
(b) the exercise by any local authority, otherwise than in accordance with general policy determined by the State President acting as provided in section 19(1)(b), of any power to raise loans.

7. Agriculture, comprising the following, namely—
(1) agricultural development services, which include research, advisory services and extension;
(2) training at agricultural colleges; and
(3) financial and other assistance to farmers or prospective farmers, or for the promotion of agriculture.

8. Water supply, comprising the following, namely—
(1) irrigation schemes;
(2) drilling for water for agricultural and local government purposes;

(3) subsidizing of drilling work and water works for agricultural or local government purposes; and

(4) financial assistance in relation to water works damaged by flood.

9. Appointment of marriage officers under any general law.

10. Elections of members of the House of Parliament in question, excluding matters prescribed or to be prescribed by or under any general law.

11. Finance in relation to own affairs of the population group in question, including—

(1) estimates of revenue and expenditure, but excluding the form in which such estimates shall be prepared;

(2) the appropriation of moneys for the purposes of such estimates, but excluding such appropriation of moneys for any purpose other than that for which they are by or under any general law made available for appropriation;

(3) levies authorized by or under any general law, on services rendered over and above payments for such services;

(4) the receipt of donations;

(5) the making of donations not amounting to a supplementation of appropriations contemplated in paragraph (2); and

(6) the control over the collection and utilization of revenue, subject to the provisions of the Exchequer and Audit Act, 1975,

but excluding the levying of taxes and the raising of loans.

12. Staff administration in terms of the provisions of any general law in relation to staff in the employment of the State.

13. Auxiliary services necessary for the administration of own affairs of the population group in question, including the planning of and control over the work connected with the exercise or performance of powers, duties and functions in a department of State for such affairs, and the services provided by or in such a department, and the acquisition, alienation, provision and maintenance of and the control over land, supplies, services, buildings, works and accommodation, transport and other facilities for the purposes of the performance or rendering of such work and services, but subject to any general law in relation to such matters.

14. The rendering of services, either with the approval of the State President acting as provided in section 19(1)(b) or in terms of arrangements made between Ministers with such approval, to persons who are not members of the population group in question.

Schedule 2

PART 1

A. Repeal or amendment of provisions of the Republic of South Africa Constitution Act, 1961 (Act No. 32 of 1961), as follows:

1. Repeal of the Preamble, Part I, Part II, Part III, Part IV and Part V.

2. Amendment of Part VI—

(a) by the substitution for the words "House of Assembly", where they occur in subsection (3) of section 66, of the words "Houses of Parliament";

(b) by the substitution in subsection (1) of section 68 for the words "this Act" of the words "the Republic of South Africa Constitution Act, 1983,";

(c) by the substitution in subsection (1) of section 69 for the words "this Act", where they occur for the second time, of the words "the Republic of South Africa Constitution Act, 1983,", and for the expression "43(3)" of the expression "49(3) of that Act";

(d) by the insertion in subsection (2) of section 69, after the word "shall" of the words ", in respect of the election of members of the provincial council,";

(e) by the substitution for section 70 of the following section:

"*Membership of provincial councils.*

70. (1) The provisions of section 54, section 55(1) and (2)(a) and section 56 of the Republic of South Africa Constitution Act, 1983, shall apply *mutatis mutandis* to members of provincial councils as they are applicable to members of the House of Assembly.

(2) Any member of a provincial council who becomes a member of the House of Assembly shall cease to be a member of such provincial council.";

(f) by the substitution in subsection (2) of section 71 for the expression "section 53 relating to" of the expression "section 40 of the Republic of South Africa Constitution Act, 1983, in so far as it relates to", and for the words "the House of Assembly", where they occur for the second time, of the word "Parliament";

(g) by the addition of the following words to section 80:
"except in so far as such powers are assigned to a Minister by the State President under the Republic of South Africa Constitution Act, 1983"; and

(h) by the substitution in subsection (1) of section 84 for the words preceding paragraph *(a)* of the following words:
"Subject to the provisions of this Act, the Financial Relations Act, 1976 (Act No. 65 of 1976), and the assent of the State President as hereinafter provided, and except in so far as the provisions of Part IV of the Republic of South Africa Constitution Act, 1983, have under section 98(3)*(a)* of the last-mentioned Act been declared to apply to any ordinance or other law of the province, a provincial council may make ordinances in relation to matters coming within the following classes of subjects, namely—";
and the substitution in paragraphs *(b)* and *(g)* of that subsection for the words "the House of Assembly" of the word "Parliament".

3. Repeal of Part VII, Part VIII and Part VIIIA.

4. Repeal of sections 107 and 108.

5. Repeal of section 109.

6. Amendment of section 110 by the deletion of the words "at the instance of the State or", the words "of any body referred to in paragraph *(f)* of subsection (1) of section *eighty-four* or", the words "circulating in the area of jurisdiction of the authority concerned" and the words "in the area in question".

7. Repeal of sections 111, 112 and 113.

8. Amendment of section 114 by the deletion in paragraph *(b)* of the words "or abridge the powers conferred on provincial councils under section *eighty-four*".

9. Repeal of sections 115, 116, 117 and 118.

10. Amendment of section 119 by the deletion of the words " 'Afrikaans' includes Dutch".

11. Substitution for section 121 of the following section:

"*Short title.*
121. This Act shall be called the Provincial Government Act, 1961.".

12. Substitution for the long title of the following long title:
"To provide for provincial councils and their powers and the administration of provincial matters, and for matters connected therewith.".

B. Amendment of section 10 of the Interpretation Act, 1957 (Act No. 33 of 1957)—

(a) by the substitution in subsection (5) for the expression "20A(1)" of the expression "26", and for the expression "1961 (Act No. 32 of 1961)" of the expression "1983".

(b) by the substitution for subsection (5A) of the following subsection:
"(5A) The provisions of subsection (5) shall apply in so far as the State President does not determine otherwise in the assignment concerned and, if the administration of a provision of any law has been assigned to any other Minister as contemplated in that subsection, but in relation to a category of persons or some other matter specified in the assignment, the provisions of that subsection shall apply accordingly."; and

(c) by the insertion after subsection (5A) of the following subsection:
"(5B) Whenever the administration of a law referred to in subsection (2) of section 98 of the Republic of South Africa Constitution Act, 1983, has been assigned to a Minister of State under subsections (3)*(b)* and (4) of that section, the provisions of subsections (5) and (5A) of this section shall apply *mutatis mutandis* as if the relevant executive committee or other executive authority referred to in the said subsection (2), the department or division of the relevant

provincial administration in which the law was administered, and an officer of that administration, were a Minister of State, the department of State controlled by him, and an officer in the public service, respectively.".

C. Amendment of the Laws of the Coloured Persons Representative Council Application Act, 1982 (Act No. 36 of 1982)—

(a) by the substitution for the words "Until such date as may be fixed in terms of section 4(2) of the South African Coloured Persons Council Act, 1980 (Act No. 24 of 1980)", wherever they occur, of the words "Until other provision is made by or under any law"; and

(b) by the insertion after section 4 of the following section:

"*Effect of repeal of certain laws.*

4A. The repeal of section 17 of the Coloured Persons Representative Council Act, 1964 (Act No. 49 of 1964), and section 5 of the South African Coloured Persons Council Act, 1980 (Act No. 24 of 1980), in terms of section 101 of the Republic of South Africa Constitution Act, 1983, shall not affect the provisions of sections 1*(g)*(ii), 2*(l)*(ii) and 3*(h)* of this Act as amended by the said section 101, or the validity of any proclamation or notice published in the *Gazette* under the said section 17 which was in force immediately before the date of such repeal.".

PART 2

Number and year of law	Title	Extent of repeal
Act No. 65 of 1962	Constitution Amendment Act, 1962	The whole.
Act No. 9 of 1963	Constitution Amendment Act, 1963	The whole.
Act No. 49 of 1964	Coloured Persons Representative Council Act, 1964	The whole.
Act No. 83 of 1965	Constitution Amendment Act, 1965	The whole.
Act No. 29 of 1966	Electoral Laws Amendment Act, 1966 ..	The whole.
Act No. 37 of 1966	Constitution Amendment Act, 1966	The whole.
Act No. 9 of 1967	Constitution Amendment Act, 1967	The whole.
Act No. 31 of 1968	South African Indian Council Act, 1968	The whole.
Act No. 50 of 1968	Separate Representation of Voters Amendment Act, 1968	The whole.
Act No. 52 of 1968	Coloured Persons Representative Council Amendment Act, 1968	The whole.
Act No. 101 of 1969	General Law Amendment Act, 1969 ...	Sections 20, 23 and 24.
Act No. 87 of 1970	Coloured Persons Representative Council Amendment Act, 1970	The whole.
Act No. 91 of 1970	Powers and Privileges of the Coloured Persons Representative Council Act, 1970	The whole.
Act No. 1 of 1971	Constitution Amendment Act, 1971	The whole.
Act No. 67 of 1972	South African Indian Council Amendment Act, 1972	The whole.
Act No. 99 of 1972	Coloured Persons Representative Council Amendment Act, 1972	The whole.
Act No. 102 of 1972	General Law Amendment Act, 1972 ...	Section 20.
Act No. 62 of 1973	General Law Amendment Act, 1973 ...	Sections 22 and 30.
Act No. 79 of 1973	Constitution and Elections Amendment Act, 1973	The whole.
Act No. 33 of 1974	Parliamentary Service Act, 1974	Sections 8, 9 and 10.
Act No. 48 of 1974	Constitution Amendment Act, 1974	The whole.
Act No. 94 of 1974	Second General Law Amendment Act, 1974	Section 47.
Act No. 32 of 1975	Coloured Persons Representative Council Amendment Act, 1975	The whole.

Number and year of law	Title	Extent of repeal
Act No. 66 of 1975	Exchequer and Audit Act, 1975........	So much of the Schedule as relates to the Republic of South Africa Constitution Act, 1961, and the Coloured Persons Representative Council Act, 1964.
Act No. 60 of 1976	Constitution Amendment Act, 1976	The whole.
Act No. 65 of 1976	Financial Relations Act, 1976	So much of Schedule 3 as relates to the Republic of South Africa Constitution Act, 1961.
Act No. 94 of 1976	Coloured Persons Representative Council Amendment Act, 1976	The whole.
Act No. 123 of 1977	South African Indian Council Amendment Act, 1977	The whole.
Proclamation No. R.249 of 1977	Amendment of (1) the South-West Africa Affairs Amendment Act, 1949, (2) the Republic of South Africa Constitution Act, 1961, and (3) the South-West Africa Constitution Act, 1968	So much as relates to the Republic of South Africa Constitution Act, 1961.
Act No. 83 of 1978	South African Indian Council Amendment Act, 1978	The whole.
Act No. 84 of 1978	Coloured Persons Representative Council Amendment Act, 1978	The whole.
Act No. 57 of 1979	Coloured Persons Representative Council Amendment Act, 1979	The whole.
Act No. 99 of 1979	Constitution Amendment Act, 1979	The whole.
Act No. 100 of 1979	Pension Laws Amendment Act, 1979 ...	Section 1.
Act No. 13 of 1980	Period of Office of Members of the South African Indian Council Extension Act, 1980.......................	The whole.
Act No. 24 of 1980	South African Coloured Persons Council Act, 1980	The whole.
Act No. 28 of 1980	Republic of South Africa Constitution Third Amendment Act, 1980	The whole.
Act No. 67 of 1980	Railways and Harbours Acts Amendment Act, 1980	Section 13.
Act No. 70 of 1980	Republic of South Africa Constitution Amendment Act, 1980	Sections 1 and 2.
Act No. 74 of 1980	Republic of South Africa Constitution Fourth Amendment Act, 1980	The whole.
Act No. 101 of 1980	Republic of South Africa Constitution Fifth Amendment Act, 1980.........	The whole, except sections 29, 30, 31, 32 and 33.
Act No. 40 of 1981	Republic of South Africa Constitution Amendment Act, 1981	The whole.
Act No. 70 of 1981	South African Indian Council Amendment Act, 1981 ....,.....	The whole.
Act No. 101 of 1981	Republic of South Africa Constitution Second Amendment Act, 1981	The whole, except sections 7, 8 and 9.
Act No. 99 of 1982	Constitution Amendment Act, 1982	The whole, except section 4.
Act No. 104 of 1982	Elections Amendment Act, 1982.......	Sections 1 and 2.

Index

Adam, H, 43n79; & Giliomee, H, vi, 43n60, 225n33
Amendments, constitutional, 3, 52, 53; 111–12, 182; South Africa 14, 74–5, 202–3;
     United Kingdom 7; United States 13, 48; Zimbabwe 118–22
Apartheid, vi, 82, 106n200, 197, 198, 211, 218, 219, 223; *see also* Separate develop-
     ment, Group areas, Race classification
Austria, 45, 47, 49, 50, 52, 54, 56, 57, 62

Barry, B, 62, 67n13, 69n69
Bekker, S, 32, 36–7, 105n168
Belgium, 45, 49, 50, 51, 53, 54, 68nn31 and 34
Bicameralism, 4, 12, 24, 52, 78, 110, 112, 119, 159
Bills of Rights, 3, 14, 39, 96, 110, 114, 117, 120–3, 126–7, 182, 194, 208
Blacks, 36, 40, 65, 79, 80–2, 86, 127–9; 1977 constitution 156; 1983 constitution
     193–5, 218–20; citizenship 92–4, 218–19; local authorities 87–9, 132, 222; parti-
     tion 89–94; President's Council 163, 173, 175, 185; separate development 86–9
Bloemfontein guidelines, 178–9, 180, 192
Bophuthatswana, 124, 125, 126–7, 224n25
Britain, constitution 4–6; majoritarianism 6–8; limits on majoritarianism 8–11, 48;
     see also Westminster system
Bureaucracy, 4, 11, 39, 50, 63, 77, 122, 173, 187, 208
Buthelezi commission, 115, 137–9, 224n20

Cabinet—*see* Executive
Canada, 54, 62, 69nn54 and 64, 111, 127
Chiefs, 90, 119, 120, 125–6
Ciskei, 90, 92, 124, 125, 126, 224n20; Quail Commission 134–6, 224n20
Citizenship, 92–4, 114, 132, 136, 150, 152, 218–19
Coalition, 9–10, 48, 96, 122, 123; *see also* Grand coalition
Coloureds, 36–8, 80, 81, 82–5, 112–14, 129–31, 216, 218, 222; *see also* New constitu-
     tion, Separate development
Communal representation, 80–9, 119, 120
Conservative Party, 141n4, 188n6, 194, 212nn22 and 26, 215n159
Consociationalism, approaches 45–6; characteristics 46–51; and commissions 129,
     132–3; and control 220–2; and corporatism 54; critiques 62–4; disadvantages
     61–2; favourable conditions 56–9; and federalism 51–3, 110–11; and liberal
     constitutionalism 18, 45–6, 62; optimal framework 59–61; 178; and pluralism 25,
     31, 32, 34–5, 38, 45, 46, 47, 56; in practice 54–6; President's Council 164, 184–6;
     PFP 110–11; and South Africa 57–8, 61, 64–6, 73, 77–82, 96–8, 113, 135–6;
     subnationally 135–6, 138–9, 184; Zimbabwe 120–3; 1977 constitution, 150–1;
     1979 bill 156–7; 1983 constitution 195, 216–20
Constellation of States, 94, 129, 135, 219, 223, 224n24
Constitutionalism, v–vi, 1–3, 50, 110, 117, 126–7, 194, 204–5
Control, vi, 220–2
Conventions, 76–7, 78, 102n65, 152, 195, 204, 217
Corporatism, 11, 21n70, 54, 64, 77
Council of cabinets, 153–5, 156, 200
CPRC, 81, 83–5, 86, 112, 114, 130, 151, 152, 158, 192
Cyprus, 52, 54, 55, 56, 70n78
Daalder, H, 57, 66n5, 70n87
Dahl, R, 2, 41n30, 71n116, 157, 191n104
Dean, W H B, 101n48, 145n120, 188n14, 224n7
Degenaar, J, 33–4, 37, 39
De Lange Commission, 140, 180, 212n41